Women and English Piracy
1540–1720

Women and English Piracy
1540–1720
Partners and Victims of Crime

John C. Appleby

THE BOYDELL PRESS

First published 2013
The Boydell Press, Woodbridge
Reprinted in paperback 2015

ISBN 978 1 84383 869 2 hardback
ISBN 978 1 78327 018 7 paperback

The Boydell Press is an imprint of Boydell & Brewer Ltd
PO Box 9, Woodbridge, Suffolk IP12 3DF, UK
and of Boydell & Brewer Inc.
668 Mount Hope Avenue, Rochester, NY 14620–2731, USA
website: www.boydellandbrewer.com

The publisher has no responsibility for the continued existence or accuracy of
URLs for external or third-party internet websites referred to in this book,
and does not guarantee that any content on such websites is,
or will remain, accurate or appropriate

A CIP record for this title is available
from the British Library

CONTENTS

MAPS AND ILLUSTRATIONS

ACKNOWLEDGEMENTS

Although the idea for this book is rather recent, I have been working on the subject for a long time. My initial interest grew out of my experience as a research fellow in the Institute of Irish Studies at the Queen's University of Belfast, and I am indebted to Professor Mary O'Dowd for her interest and encouragement many years ago. I have talked about aspects of the subject to students and other audiences over the years, and I am grateful for their curiosity and occasional disagreements which have all helped to formulate my approach to the subject. More recently I was honoured with an invitation to participate in a seminar on the wider subject of piracy at the University of Hull to commemorate the work of Professor Kenneth R. Andrews FBA. Ken was an outstanding scholar who guided my early research, as a postgraduate student, in the records of the High Court of Admiralty; he became a good friend and a source of wise guidance and counsel thereafter. I am particularly grateful to Professor David J. Starkey for arranging the seminar and for the invitation, as well as for the conversations on piracy and other matters. The reports of the two readers on the original proposal were invaluable in sharpening the structure and focus of this study, though any remaining limitations are my own. I am also very grateful to Mrs Sandra Mather for preparing the maps with such skill. Finally I thank Dr Michael Middeke and his colleagues at Boydell and Brewer for their encouragement, support and forbearance.

A NOTE ON CONVENTIONS

This study follows the common convention of using Old Style English dates which were slightly out of step with the New Style adopted by most European countries after 1582. The start of the year, however, is taken as 1 January. English currency is in old pounds, shillings and pence (£ s d). Pieces of eight, or Spanish silver dollars, a phrase widely used by pirates and rovers, were worth about four shillings and two to four pence during this period, though values could vary slightly. Quotations are given in the original spelling, but abbreviations and contractions have been expanded.

ABBREVIATIONS

APC	*Acts of the Privy Council*
Baer (ed.), *British Piracy*	J. H. Baer (ed.), *British Piracy in the Golden Age: History and Interpretation, 1660–1730*, 4 vols (London, 2007)
BL	British Library
CSPC	*Calendar of State Papers Colonial*
CSPD	*Calendar of State Papers Domestic*
CSPF	*Calendar of State Papers Foreign*
CSPI	*Calendar of State Papers Ireland*
CSPV	*Calendar of State Papers Venetian*
DRO	Devon Record Office
HMC	*Historical Manuscripts Commission*
Johnson, *General History of the Pyrates*	D. Defoe, *A General History of the Pyrates*, ed. M. Schonhorn (London, 1972)
TNA, CO	The National Archives, Colonial Office Papers
TNA, HCA	The National Archives, High Court of Admiralty
TNA, SP	The National Archives, State Papers

Map 1 England, Wales and Ireland

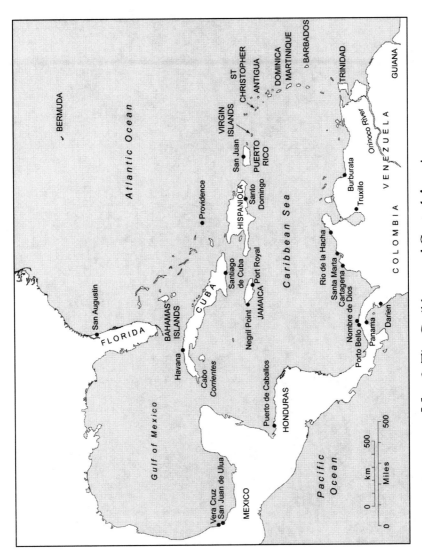

Map 2 The Caribbean and Central America

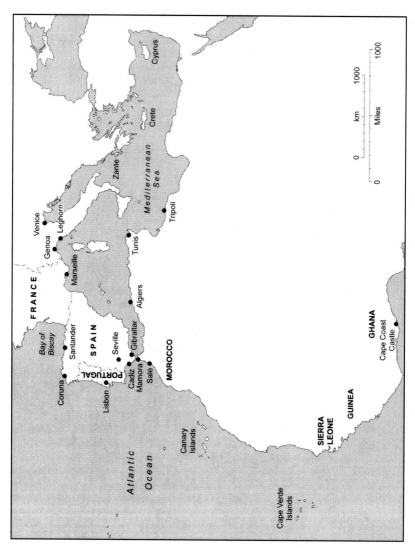

Map 3 The Mediterranean Sea and West Africa

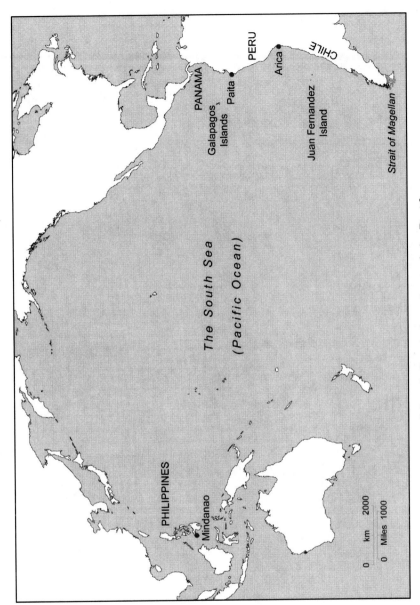

Map 4 South America and the Pacific

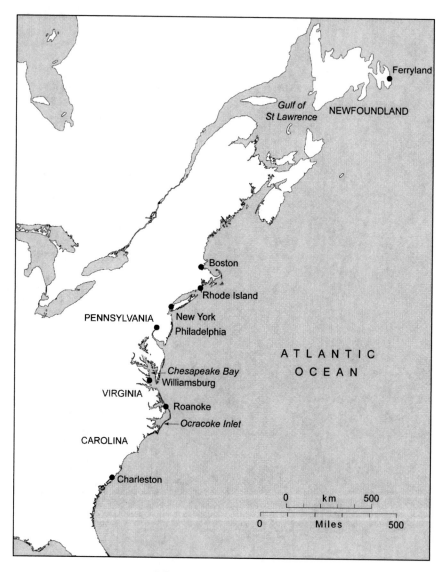

Map 5 North America

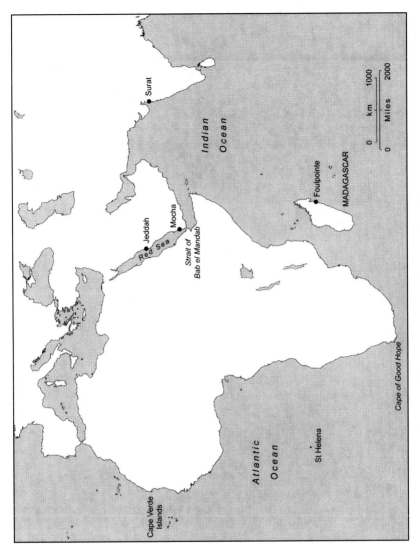

Map 6 Africa and the Indian Ocean

Introduction

Staging an execution was a tricky business. Combining real and symbolic meanings, the spectacle of punishment and penitence depended on the key actors playing their parts according to the demands of the state and the expectations of the audience. Such scenes were memorialized for a wider public in the illustrations which appeared in criminal biographies of pirates and highwaymen with growing frequency during the early eighteenth century. One striking example shows the execution of the pirate captain, Stede Bonnet, in November 1718. It is from *A General History of the Robberies and Murders of the Most Notorious Pyrates* by captain Charles Johnson, which was published in London during 1724. Bonnet was an unusual recruit to piracy. Described by Johnson as a 'Gentleman of good Reputation' of Barbados, his acquaintances believed that he was tempted into the business because of a 'Disorder in his Mind' brought on by 'some Discomforts he found in a married State'.[1] As a pirate, he met with little success. For a brief period he consorted with Edward Teach, commonly known as Blackbeard, who was killed during a violent encounter off the coast of Carolina. Bonnet and his men were subsequently captured further along the coast during September 1718. The pirates were tried and found guilty at a court held in Charleston. On 8 November twenty-two of the company were executed at White Point. Bonnet was hanged several days later. According to Johnson, he struggled to live up to the role expected of him. His 'piteous Behaviour under Sentence, very much affected the People of the Province, particularly the Women, and great Application was made to the Governor for saving his Life, but in vain'.[2] Bonnet was so fearful and overwrought, that he was almost insensible at the time of his execution.

As illustrated in Johnson's *History*, the scene of execution is crowded. Against a background of ships, identified as a forest of masts, Bonnet's body swings, stripped of wig and other marks of identity or dignity. Officials on horseback are in attendance to maintain order, while the presence of a man-of-war, its jack unfurled and blowing in the wind, signals the growing

---

[1] Johnson, *General History of the Pyrates*, p. 95.
[2] Ibid., p. 111. There is little evidence to support Johnson in *The Tryals of Major Stede Bonnet and Other Pirates* (London, 1719), pp. 37–43, where a shameful Bonnet changed his not guilty plea to guilty.

1

success of the royal navy in its war against the pirates. With a large crowd in attendance, viewers have clambered aboard the upper structure and rigging of vessels in the harbour for a better vantage point. Those closest to the swaying body of the pirate include several women. Framing the scene with unexplained dynamism, one woman on a cart beckons towards Bonnet while another, with her back half-turned, seems about to engage an onlooker in conversation.[3]

The presence of women at Bonnet's execution, though not unusual, illuminates the way in which their lives intersected with those of pirates and sea rovers during the early modern period. Despite their dangerous and disordered careers, including irregular and unpredictable absences at sea, pirates maintained relationships with wives, mothers and other kin, as well as casual female acquaintances ashore. Bonnet's associate, Teach, was married with a wife and family in London. One of his predecessors, the equally notorious John Ward, married a renegade Christian woman in Tunis during the early seventeenth century, abandoning his wife in England. Henry Avery, whose infamy and celebrity were the subject of histories, ballads and plays, seems to have retired from the sea during the later 1690s, fashioning a new life with another woman, conveniently ignoring his spouse in London.[4] These unusual careers should not be taken as representative of pirate lives. But they provoke questions regarding the wider relationships between pirates and women, as yet unexplored, which this study seeks to address for England and its American colonies, during a period of sustained activity when seaborne predation acquired a global dimension.

Narrowly defined piracy was one of the most gendered forms of criminal activity. Thousands of men, including a significant number of boys, were recruited as pirates during the period from the 1540s to the 1720s, but the number of women who accompanied them was tiny. Their direct participation in maritime robbery, at sea or along rivers, was also marked by ambiguity and confusion. Pirates, indeed, were perceived to be among the toughest and most disorderly members of a heavily masculinized seafaring culture. Their conduct varied considerably, but the cruelty and violence they inflicted on victims suggested a pathological, at times unforgiving, pattern

[3] M. Rediker, *Villains of All Nations: Atlantic Pirates in the Golden Age* (London, 2004), p. 3. For women attending executions and scaffold rituals, see V. A. C. Gatrell, *The Hanging Tree: Execution and the English People 1770–1868* (Oxford, 1990), pp. 65, 68, 80–9, 260, 599.
[4] *CSPC, 1717–18*, pp. 146–3; *CSPC, 1719–20*, pp. 332–4; C. M. Senior, *A Nation of Pirates: English Piracy in its Heyday* (Newton Abbot, 1976), p. 94; J. F. Jameson (ed.), *Privateering and Piracy: Illustrative Documents* (New York, 1923), pp. 159, 171–2.

of behaviour which was shared by few women. Captain Tomkins, sentenced to death for piracy in 1610, 'only regretted that he had not killed everyone he found on board'.[5] Such aggressive predators acquired unenviable reputations. Often described as the 'common enemies of society', who nevertheless might be of use to the state, attitudes hardened as the threat to commerce and civil society grew worse.[6] By the early eighteenth century they were labelled as inhuman, barbaric monsters who needed to be removed from the seas by any means possible. The shift in tone and perception, from the image of outlaw in society to outcast of it, indicated a deeper unease over the need for inclusion or exclusion, which had far-reaching implications for the maintenance and definition of piracy as a crime.

Wherever organized plunder developed during this period, it rested on secure bases and markets.[7] In some regions seafaring communities and their hinterlands were heavily involved in supporting piratical activity. Under such conditions the structure of piracy provided opportunities for the indirect participation of women which varied according to context and chronology. Female support was encouraged or facilitated by the confusion between different forms of maritime depredation. As the law proclaimed, piracy was a felony punishable by death. By contrast a close, at times overlapping relation, privateering, was a legitimate enterprise. Growing out of the law and custom of reprisals, though going far beyond it during time of war, it was encouraged by the state as a means of weakening enemy commerce. Privateering ventures were licensed by letters of reprisal or marque which, as yet, lacked clear distinction. Buccaneering, though originally a description for the lifestyle of hunters on Hispaniola and Tortuga in the Caribbean, appeared to fall between these extremes, especially as it developed in Jamaica during the 1650s and 1660s. Adventurers such as Sir Henry Morgan claimed to sail with lawful commissions or authority, but this was under dubious jurisdiction which was challenged by the Spanish. The issue of commissions by the governor of New York during the 1690s was dismissed as licensing piracy by some, including his successor.[8] In practice, therefore, these distinctions between different

---

[5] *CSPV, 1610–13*, p. 57.

[6] *CSPI, 1608–10*, p. 29; C. Harding, '"Hostis Humani Generis" – the Pirate as Outlaw in the Early Modern Law of the Sea', in C. Jowitt (ed.), *Pirates? The Politics of Plunder, 1550–1650* (Basingstoke, 2007), pp. 20–38; R. G. Marsden (ed.), *Documents Relating to the Law and Custom of the Sea*, 2 vols (Navy Records Society, 49 & 50, 1915–16), II, p. 250.

[7] D. J. Starkey, 'Pirates and Markets', in C. R. Pennell (ed.), *Bandits at Sea: A Pirates Reader* (New York, 2001), pp. 107–24.

[8] *The Present State of Jamaica* (London, 1683), pp. 60–3; *CSPC, 1697–98*, pp. 221–9,

forms of plunder repeatedly broke down, usually to the advantage of shore-based dealers.

*

Chapter 1 provides a context for women's involvement in piratical activity, with a survey of the rise and fall of English piracy from the 1540s to the 1720s. Drawing together a wide body of work, it reveals the changing character of piracy, marked by instability and fragmentation. The peculiar, protean characteristics of such enterprise enabled it to flourish in many regions of the British Isles. Much of it was small-scale, haphazard and opportunistic in appearance. It was usually undertaken by mariners for whom piracy was part-time employment. Highly localized in context, it was heavily focused on the plunder of overseas vessels, especially of French origin. It was maintained by close links with landed communities. During the 1570s this petty plunder and scavenging led to the development of more professionalized enterprise, manifest in the emergence of a loose pirate fraternity or fellowship. More ambitious in the scale and scope of their ventures, these rovers ranged into the Atlantic, to the coasts of Portugal and Spain. Such voyaging was accompanied and sustained by the establishment of a wide-ranging network of bases and harbours across south-west England, Wales and Ireland. Against a background of deteriorating Anglo-Spanish relations, it was increasingly targeted on Iberian trade and shipping.

This rising tide of plunder was justified and inflamed by shifting rivalries and grievances. It confused the permeable boundary between piracy and more lawful enterprise at sea, while laying the foundation for the growth of long-distance plunder. At the same time localized and indiscriminate piracy persisted around the British Isles, though it was overshadowed by the activities of overseas raiders, including the Barbary corsairs. Such a prolonged period of maritime predation, from the 1540s to the 1620s, had significant consequences for the character and structure of piracy. By the early seventeenth century its development pointed in two directions, with large groups of rovers operating from overseas bases for plunder in the Atlantic or the Mediterranean.

The socio-economic characteristics of piracy during this period included

279–89; R. C. Ritchie, *Captain Kidd and the War Against the Pirates* (Cambridge, Mass., 1986), pp. 7–10, and D. J. Starkey, 'Voluntaries and Sea Robbers: A Review of the Academic Literature on Privateering, Corsairing, Buccaneering and Piracy', *Mariner's Mirror*, 97 (2011), pp. 128–47, for varieties of plunder. K. E. Lane, *Pillaging the Empire: Piracy in the Americas 1500–1750* (Armonk, 1998), pp. 164–5, and C. H. Haring, *The Buccaneers in the West Indies in the XVII Century* (London, 1910), pp. 66–8, for buccaneering.

a dense structure of support on land. As well as operating as an unusual form of organized criminality, piracy was a maritime enterprise which was run as a business. At times of intense activity at sea it involved an extensive range of transactions, based on shadowy networks of support that formed a partly concealed economy driven by the circulation of booty, channelled through irregular pirate marts. The offer of gifts and competitive rates of exchange attracted large numbers of dealers to well-known pirate haunts, such as Studland Bay in Dorset or Mede Hole on the Isle of Wight. As Chapter 2 demonstrates, the supporting mechanisms for piracy included a varied pattern of interdependency between pirates and women. As receivers and maintainers, they were involved in close relations with sea rovers. Acting on their own, or through male agents, they purchased plunder from pirates, providing lodging, entertainment or provisions in exchange. Working as alehouse-keepers, often in partnership with spouses, they ran safe houses where pirates could meet to dispose of booty. In London such disorderly establishments were convenient places for pirates to assemble and plan raids along the Thames. The growth of river piracy, which was localized in its development, enabled women to play a distinctive part in the disposal and distribution of stolen goods, exploiting their position in the second-hand and pawnbroking trades.[9] In many cases these contacts were based on previous relations, though receivers, either male or female, often tried to portray themselves as unwitting participants in irregular, but essentially lawful exchanges. As wives, mothers or other kin, and as friends or neighbours, women were entangled in discrete networks which allowed piracy to flourish. At some risk to themselves, they protected and defended spouses or sons. For their part, many pirates retained close contact with wives and family, arranging clandestine meetings ashore while providing women with a variety of gifts, such as small items of jewellery, clothing and parrots.

The expansion of English piracy, including the use of overseas bases, had contradictory consequences for the development of female agency. The emergence of long-distance plunder, preceding or following in the wake of colonial enterprise in the west and commercial reconnoitring in the east, continued to allow women to retain links with pirates, but they were stretched to breaking point. As Chapter 3 argues, the scope for agency narrowed in accordance with the widening range and changing structure of piratical enterprise. In the Caribbean the organization of buccaneering, as

[9] G. Walker, 'Women, Theft and the World of Stolen Goods', in J. Kermode and G. Walker (eds.), *Women, Crime and the Courts in Early Modern England* (London, 1994), pp. 88–93; P. Linebaugh, *The London Hanged: Crime and Civil Society in the Eighteenth Century* (London, 1991), pp. 145–6.

a predatory business and a form of private war, marginalized the role of women as receivers. At Port Royal on Jamaica they provided entertainment and sexual services for the buccaneers, underlining the symbiotic relationship between piracy and prostitution. Elsewhere in the ports and havens dotted along the eastern seaboard of colonial North America, pirates and other rovers benefited from close relations with women, who were part of a wider web of coastal contacts which provided support and assistance often with the connivance of local officials. But there is little evidence of women playing an economic role either as the receivers or distributors of pirate booty. Moreover, long-distance piracy enabled men to escape from unhappy domestic circumstances or responsibilities. The remarkable survival of a cache of letters from pirates' wives in New York to their partners, may demonstrate the long-suffering loyalty of women, but it also suggests that Stede Bonnet was not the only recruit escaping from a broken relationship ashore.

The widening, globalized range of piratical activity, spreading from the Caribbean to the South Sea and beyond, brought pirate companies into contact with native women at remote locations, irregularly visited or neglected by Europeans. While the evidence for these relations is circumstantial and one-sided, it suggests that such women were often exploited and abused, sometimes as servants or slaves aboard pirate and privateering ships. Occasionally women served as cross-cultural intermediaries, in return for gifts that may have enhanced their status in native societies. But the short-term partnerships that visiting rovers established with women on islands in the Indian Ocean and elsewhere seem to be part of a libertine lifestyle adopted by pirates which was careless and confusing in effect.

The tension between agency and victimhood running through many of these contacts and relations is explored in Chapter 4. Adopting a different perspective, it examines the consequences for women of the raiding of the Barbary corsairs in northern European waters. Raids on vulnerable ports and havens in south-west England and Ireland were the dramatic projection of a longer period of seaborne plunder, during which thousands of seamen were captured and carried off into captivity in North Africa. Although a small number of women were taken and held as captives, a much larger number were left as single spouses, parents or widows, struggling to make ends meet in difficult and challenging circumstances. Yet women also managed to assert agency, petitioning institutions, officials and the monarchy for support in the release of imprisoned husbands, sons or relatives. At a time when indiscriminate charity was in decline, these women presented themselves as innocent victims who were entitled to assistance. Their appeals for support, sometimes in the form of a licence to beg, drew on an established pattern of petitioning, while deploying a range of imagery to emphasize the un-Christian cruelty inflicted on English slaves in Barbary.

Women were also the targets of pirate abuse and aggression. Chapter 4 suggests that the violence intensified during the seventeenth and early eighteenth centuries, particularly with the emergence of long-distance plunder. Such enterprise weakened the links between sea and shore-based communities, while widening the contacts between pirate groups and women of different backgrounds. Although the scale and extent of pirate violence are difficult to gauge accurately, at times its employment was gratuitous and contradictory in purpose. In regions such as the Caribbean it was inflamed by ethnic and religious differences, and justified as retaliation or revenge for former wrongs.

Despite the impressive evidence for female agency in supporting piracy, throughout the period covered by this study it remained a male enterprise. As some observers noted, it was an outlet for aggressive masculinity which found release in the conduct and behaviour of groups of men at sea. As demonstrated in Chapter 5, the number of women pirates was exiguous, and their presence aboard pirate ships was unusual and remains open to interpretation. Within a maritime world characterized by heavy drinking, blasphemous language and petty violence, the activities of Anne Bonny and Mary Read may affirm female independence and autonomy. But their short-lived and unsuccessful piratical careers were unprecedented. The absence of a tradition of female seafaring, more generally the result of a combination of custom and culture, was reinforced by limited opportunity and ambition. Very few women were attracted by sea life or the prospect of sailing with disorderly and potentially dangerous gangs of rovers. Nevertheless, as this study shows, indirectly many women were closely involved in the business of piracy. As agents and victims, the record of their relations with sea rovers provides an unusual but illuminating perspective on the wider ramifications of English and Anglo-American piracy as it developed from the 1540s to the 1720s.

– 1 –

The Rise and Fall of English Piracy
from the 1540s to the 1720s

The development of English piracy from the 1540s to the 1720s drew on a well-established tradition of seaborne plunder. A pattern of enterprise emerged during the Anglo-French conflicts of the early sixteenth century which laid the basis for future expansion and elaboration. It included an extensive infrastructure of support, enabling piracy to take on the appearance of a business and commercial operation. Thereafter its growth was sustained by war and international rivalry, particularly with Spain, often in association with lawful forms of sea-roving. The link between piracy and reprisal venturing or privateering was an enduring characteristic of the period. According to captain Charles Johnson, whose *General History of the Pyrates* published in 1724 provided testimony of public interest in the subject, pirate leaders such as Edward Teach, the infamous Blackbeard of legend, and the women pirates, Anne Bonny and Mary Read, served on both kinds of ventures.[1] Careers that criss-crossed the boundary between the lawful and unlawful indicate the contested nature of piracy as a crime, which provoked varied responses. It flourished within the uncertain, negotiated space between war, policy and maritime plunder.

Piracy developed as a dynamic, but unstable enterprise, thriving on ambiguity or adversity. It was encouraged by international conflict and rivalries, and fuelled by socio-economic dislocation and distress within a world of widening horizons and changing opportunities. While it fed off commerce, following in the path of its expansion within and beyond Europe, piracy exploited weakness. Limitations in state power and international law were prerequisites for the growth of robbery at sea. Labouring under severe financial constraints, and faced with recurrent domestic turmoil, the

---

[1] Johnson, *General History of the Pyrates*, pp. 71, 156, 165. Claims that Johnson was Daniel Defoe have been contested by P. N. Furbank and W. R. Owens, *The Canonisation of Daniel Defoe* (New Haven, 1988), pp. 39–40, 100–14; A. Bialuschewski, 'Daniel Defoe, Nathaniel Mist, and the *General History of the Pyrates*', *The Papers of the Bibliographical Society of America*, 98 (2004), pp. 21–38, argues that the author was Mist.

English monarchy was ill-equipped to deal with the problem. As a result the monarchy and its officials were occasionally lured into ambivalent alliances or partnerships with sea rovers of dubious provenance. Queen Elizabeth's support for Francis Drake, knighted after a spectacular voyage of plunder against the Spanish in 1580, or the tolerant attitude of Charles II towards the buccaneers, whose leader, Sir Henry Morgan, inflicted terror on the Spanish Caribbean during the 1660s and 1670s, only represent the more visible aspects of a deeper, corrosive relationship between the state and private enterprise. In its debased form it was manifest in the disorderly and controversial voyage of captain William Kidd. Sent out during the later 1690s by a syndicate of high-ranking politicians, with the approval of William III, on an expedition to take pirates, the voyage ended disastrously with Kidd's execution for piracy and murder.[2]

The versatility of organized piracy compounded the difficulties facing the state. Piracy was a felony, often violent and murderous in intent. It ranged from small-scale opportunistic theft, which involved less than a handful of men operating on their own, to more ambitious plunder undertaken by packs of marauders, mimicking the structure of naval forces. At the same time, it was a form of maritime enterprise and sea power, representing the disorderly culture of seafaring communities at sea and on land. Although pirates were dismissed as barbaric and uncivil, their fighting qualities were widely recognized. Identified as traitors by some, nonetheless they were also deemed to be bold, and capable of redemption.[3] Their role in the peculiar pattern of trade, plunder and settlement, so characteristic of English expansion during the late sixteenth and early seventeenth centuries, persisted in attenuated form with the activities of the buccaneers in the Caribbean. The spread of piracy and plunder into the Indian Ocean, followed by the establishment of a pirate settlement on Madagascar, appeared to presage the emergence of an informal, alternative empire of outlaws and renegades. Motive and mobility allowed piracy to re-appear in various guises, taxing the resources of a newly-unified British state while threatening its commercial and colonial ambitions.

---

[2] K. R. Andrews, *Drake's Voyages: A Re-Assessment of Their Place in Elizabethan Maritime Expansion* (London, 1967), pp. 81–2; R. C. Ritchie, *Captain Kidd and the War Against the Pirates* (Cambridge, Mass., 1986), pp. 43–55; D. Loades, *England's Maritime Empire: Seapower, Commerce and Policy, 1490–1690* (Harlow, 2000), pp. 123–31, 200–1.

[3] G. E. Manwaring (ed.), *The Life and Works of Sir Henry Mainwaring*, 2 vols (Navy Records Society, 54, 1920), II, p. 42. Ordinary seamen were often included under such descriptions. On the possibility of redemption see the character of a pirate in W. J. Paylor (ed.), *The Overburian Characters* (The Percy Reprints, 13, Oxford, 1936), pp. 50–1.

For its success, piracy rested on safe bases and access to markets. The existence of both, though partially concealed, indicated that organized piratical enterprise was woven into the economic and social fabric of many maritime communities. Such conditions supported the spread of seaborne robbery, as it ranged from the British Isles to North America and the Caribbean. At various times along this sea frontier piracy flourished as a business. Those who profited, with some notable exceptions, were well-placed brokers and receivers ashore, who operated with the connivance or support of local officials. From this perspective, however, the emergence of a pirate base on Madagascar during the 1690s, beyond the reach of English jurisdiction, was a startling development, suggesting a novel departure in the structure and organization of piracy.

The development of English seaborne predation during this period, its expansion and decline, was driven by the interplay between opportunity and necessity. Its persistence over time encouraged the formation of a pirate culture and a rival form of sea power, which was increasingly expressed in an indiscriminate attack on trade and shipping. By the early eighteenth century the problem was so serious that it galvanized the British state into a determined campaign to eradicate the problem.[4] Despite volatile fluctuations in its scale and scope, one of the underlying, unifying themes of the period was the way in which piratical activity was shaped by context and geography. Yet if the ever-widening range of pirates and sea rovers was an alarming prospect, it also hinted at fragmentation, as well as diffusion, which the state was able to exploit with increasing effect after 1714.

*

Around the British Isles: sea, coast and river

From the 1540s to the 1620s piracy was a serious problem within the waters around the British Isles. Coastal plunder, closely linked with shore-based communities of supporters, flourished at various locations in England and Wales, especially in the south west. Such activity spilled over into Scotland and Ireland, as pirates searched for new bases and markets. With the inclusion of Ireland, a loose but widespread network was established which supported the outward thrust onto the high seas. Initially concentrated in the Channel and western approaches, piracy soon spread into the Bay of Biscay and along the coasts of Spain and Portugal, as sea rovers sought out richer hunting grounds. At the same time, river piracy along the Thames, a busy, crowded commercial highway, acquired fresh momentum, exposing

[4] P. Earle, *The Pirate Wars* (London, 2003), pp. 183–208.

the vulnerability of the trade of London to organized gangs of thieves and robbers.

There were few years during this period when pirates and sea rovers were inactive. Although subject to fluctuation from year to year, and characterized by regional variation, the volume of piratical venturing grew in intensity and extent. Its rapid development during the 1540s was followed by sporadic, occasionally intense activity, which paved the way for a sustained increase from the late 1560s to the 1580s. At times the endemic nature of the problem was reflected in anarchic conditions at sea. To some extent the outbreak of war with Spain in 1585 inadvertently helped to contain the threat, but only by channelling piratical enterprise into the legalized plunder of enemy shipping. The subsequent confusion between unregulated privateering and piracy, aggravated by the English attack on neutral trade and shipping, provoked outrage among the victims of a semi-public conflict that lay beyond effective state control. Although the end of the war brought a brief lull, it was soon shattered by the resurgence of piracy which persisted at least until 1615. As Anglo-Spanish relations deteriorated, small-scale activity during the early 1620s was overtaken by the revival of lawful plunder following the outbreak of wars with Spain and France.[5]

No reliable estimates survive for the scale of piratical activity, either in terms of recruits or shipping. Scattered and fragmentary evidence suggests that during peak periods, such as the 1570s, the number of pirates operating at sea may have reached 2,000 or more. Bolstered by unemployed seamen from privateering vessels, who were thrown out of work at the end of the Spanish war in 1603, more than 1,000 pirates were active during the period from 1604 to 1614. While most of these recruits were drawn from maritime communities, especially in London and south-west England, a small proportion were of more diverse backgrounds, including a number of gentlemen and yeomen.[6] Many were part-time practitioners, drifting in and out of piracy, partly in response to changing opportunities in the labour market. An increasing number, such as John Callice, one of the leading pirate captains of the 1570s, who was in the forefront of the expanding

---

[5] K. R. Andrews, *Elizabethan Privateering: English Privateering During the Spanish War 1585–1603* (Cambridge, 1964), pp. 24–5, 234–8; J. C. Appleby, *Under the Bloody Flag: Pirates of the Tudor Age* (Stroud, 2009), pp. 41–54, 114–27, 211–14; C. M. Senior, *A Nation of Pirates: English Piracy in its Heyday* (Newton Abbot, 1976), pp. 13–42.

[6] Senior, *A Nation of Pirates*, pp. 30, 48, 68, 96; C. A. Fury, *Tides in the Affairs of Men: The Social History of the Elizabethan Seamen, 1580–1603* (Westport, 2002), pp. 22–6. On the activities of a gentleman-pirate see A. Hassell Smith *et al.* (eds), *The Papers of Nathaniel Bacon of Stiffkey* (Norwich, 1979), pp. 213–18; *CSPD, 1595–97*, p. 205.

range of piratical enterprise, were effectively career pirates.[7] Disregarding the offer of pardons and despite their occasional protestations of patriotism and loyalty to the monarchy, some men almost seemed to be in rebellion against authority. The successors of Callice, active during the early seventeenth century, included captain Thomas Salkeld, described as a 'divellish rebell', who established himself as the self-styled king of Lundy Island in 1610.[8] According to one report, his prisoners were held as slaves, and forced to renounce their allegiance to king and country under threat of execution. Such disavowals of loyalty were taken a step further in the Mediterranean, where some pirates assumed new identities in a cultural re-fashioning widely known as 'turning Turk'.[9] Their leading representative was John Ward, who used Tunis as a base for his piratical career. Ward's reputation as a pirate-renegade was sealed when he adopted local dress and custom, which included re-marriage and a change of name.

Despite a common goal, the character of piracy varied. The variety betrayed its deep-rooted ambiguity, as a criminal activity and commercial enterprise. It was acutely exposed by the tension and overlap between piracy and irregular privateering. While there was a fundamental and acknowledged difference between these potentially competing ventures, buttressed by law and reinforced by custom and regulation, the distinction repeatedly broke down. Not only did the state lack the resources and power to enforce a firm borderline between piracy and lawful seaborne plunder but also, all too often, it lacked the will to do so. From the 1540s onwards, during times of war successive regimes deliberately encouraged privateering as a means of weakening enemy trade and shipping. In effect private enterprise, under the guise of large-scale reprisals, was exploited to compensate for poor naval resources, and in circumstances that ignored law and regulation in favour of tactical and financial gains. The ambiguity, moreover, was not limited to England. Those adventurers, pirate outcasts or renegades, who established themselves in bases, such as Algiers and Tunis in North Africa, during the early seventeenth century, entered a maritime world with a different tradition. Piratical enterprise from northern Europe was thus grafted onto well-established corsair enterprise within the Mediterranean, with confusing

---

[7] C. L'Estrange Ewen, *The Golden Chalice: A Documented Narrative of an Elizabethan Pirate* (Paignton, 1939); D. Mathew, 'The Cornish and Welsh Pirates in the Reign of Elizabeth', *English Historical Review*, 39 (1924), pp. 345–6.

[8] TNA, SP 14/53/100. Salkeld was thrown overboard by Peter Easton in 1610. *CSPI, 1608–10*, pp. 480, 495. On the vulnerability of Lundy Island see *APC, 1596–97*, p. 237.

[9] Senior, *A Nation of Pirates*, pp. 78–97; G. Bak, *Barbary Pirate: The Life and Crimes of John Ward* (Stroud, 2006), pp. 171–89.

results. Ward, for example, was reviled as an infamous renegade and pirate in England, but he enjoyed the lifestyle of a successful and reputable convert and corsair captain in Tunis.[10] Operating in a shadowland of cross-cultural compromise and coercion, the careers of men like Ward exposed the inherent fluidity of pirate culture, particularly when it developed overseas.

The ambiguous nature of piracy had far-reaching consequences for its organization, structure and recruitment. It ranged from opportunistic and haphazard spoil or theft to more carefully prepared and planned plunder. At the same time, it was undertaken by groups of men, sometimes assisted by boys, who were informally, almost accidentally assembled, as well as professionalized gangs collected for a particular purpose or even a specific target. The size of pirate companies varied, partly as a result of the mobility, death or capture of recruits. Small groups of men, acting in pairs or up to about six in number, including occasional lone operators, were able to work along the Thames. Larger companies of about twenty and above haunted coastal waters. They included heavily manned vessels with complements of between sixty and seventy recruits, which became more common as pirates sailed on longer voyages to the coasts of Spain and Portugal.[11]

Pirate ships were usually trading vessels which were put to another use. Some may have undergone slight modification, including the use of netting and a canvas screen to prevent boarding and to conceal the company. Captains appear to have claimed property rights to such vessels, unlike later practice during the early eighteenth century, when ownership was more commonly vested in the crew. Most vessels were of modest or small size, of between 30 and 90 tons burden. They were commonly well manned, but poorly armed with ordnance. If they had to use force to take prizes, pirates relied on light cannon and a variety of hand weapons, including pistols, muskets and swords. Inventories of two pirate ships, of 1584, describe small, well-furnished vessels, one of 60 tons, which carried light and mobile pieces of ordnance. One was armed with five falcons or falconets; the other carried only two falcons.[12]

Organization and structure influenced the choice of pirate hunting

---

[10] Bak, *Barbary Pirate*, pp. 87–114; Sir G. Fisher, *Barbary Legend: War, Trade and Piracy in North Africa 1415–1830* (Oxford, 1957), pp. 159–60.

[11] Senior, *A Nation of Pirates*, pp. 110–23, includes one of the few studies of piracy along the Thames; K. R. Andrews, 'The Expansion of English Privateering and Piracy in the Atlantic, c.1540–1625', in M. Mollat (ed.), *Course et Piraterie*, 2 vols (Paris, 1975), I, pp. 201–5.

[12] TNA, SP 12/172/91–2. Hand weapons included stones and swords; see R. G. Marsden (ed.), *Select Pleas in the Court of Admiralty*, 2 vols (Selden Society, 6 & 11, 1894–7), I, pp. 73–4. Falcons and falconets were light ordnance capable of firing shot of between one and three pounds.

grounds, their mode of operation and the booty they acquired. Most pirates employed subterfuge and trickery, relying on surprise and speed or intimidation and weight of numbers. Haunting loosely defined, disparate regions, including the North Sea fishery, they seized or scavenged an impressive, but varied amount of booty. At its most basic the plunder included ship's provisions and victuals, including items of clothing and ready money, some of which, including the ship itself, might be returned to the victims. More typical of the booty from short-distance piracy around the British Isles was the array of commodities laden aboard a ship which was taken during 1584 by a pirate group led by captain Charles Jones. The lengthy inventory of the cargo listed an indefinable range of goods, varying in volume or number. It included ninety tanned hides, forty coarse coverlets, three barrels of tar, 110 pairs of knives, sixteen white and green blankets, as well as one barrel of mower's scythes, four dozen small shears, six horse combs and one bag of bayberries.[13]

The maintenance of localized piracy around the British Isles, including the disposal of booty, depended on widespread community support and the connivance of local officials. For much of the period, pirates relied on a network of bases scattered around the coast, though concentrated in southwest England and Wales. At the same time they resorted to well-established prize marts, such as Mede Hole on the Isle of Wight, which served as an open market for pirates and other sea rovers of various backgrounds. These centres generated a considerable business, attracting buyers from a wide hinterland, including London, eager to acquire pirate booty at cheap prices. The networks of commerce and barter which developed during the 1570s supported a hidden economy based on the disposal and dispersal of stolen cargoes. From coastal contact points goods were sold or exchanged, channelled through established fairs and rapidly transported along commercial routes to widely scattered purchasers often unaware of their provenance. By its very nature much of this network, a mix of trade, exchange and gift-giving, was concealed. But it represented an extensive, commercialized and profitable system. While it provided the means for pirates to dispose of miscellaneous commodities, those who made the most profit were probably those who took the least risk, the land-based brokers and officials who colluded with them.[14] Within this infrastructure of support there were opportunities for the assertion of female agency in varied guises. Their role

---

[13] TNA, SP 12/172/93.

[14] Mathew, 'The Cornish and Welsh Pirates', pp. 337–45; C. L'Estrange Ewen, 'Organized Piracy round Britain in the Sixteenth Century', *Mariner's Mirror*, 35 (1949), pp. 29–42; *APC, 1577–78*, pp. 180–1, on Mede Hole; Marsden (ed.), *Select Pleas*, I, pp. 153–5, for south Wales.

as receivers, and participants in a criminal economy of small-scale transactions, had implications for the implementation and perception of the law.

In some regions piracy was a community crime, involving a cross-section of the populace. In the small ports and havens of Dorset, local landowners, tradesmen and innkeepers were heavily involved in the pirate business. The support and connivance of social leaders, such as the Howards around Studland Bay, effectively validated wider community assistance for pirates, allowing them to operate unhindered in some regions. During the 1570s Commissions of Inquiry uncovered a mass of evidence demonstrating widespread support for pirates, against which the regime seemed powerless to act.[15]

The pirate culture which began to coalesce during these years, though part of a broader seafaring society, was heavily influenced by the association between communities at sea and on land. It was based on the emergence of a pirate fraternity during the 1570s, in which pirate leaders such as Callice or Robert Hicks drew on the powerful imagery of brotherhood to demonstrate their loyalty to each other. Its wider application was reinforced by self-definition, sometimes boldly expressed, and the shared experience of seaborne robbery, including the resort to regular haunts which served as sites for the performance of reciprocity and recreation. But the importance of the pirate ship, as a social institution, was qualified by the links many pirates retained with family and friends on land. The tension between these overlapping, but competing, sets of relations gave pirate life its peculiar texture. While retaining irregular contact ashore with wives, partners and others, at sea pirates maintained close relations with shipboard associates and companions.[16]

This culture was demonstrably aggressive in nature. Pirates asserted their masculinity at sea partly through their conduct and behaviour. While the use of violence was often functional, it was easily exaggerated by religious hostility. French or Spanish victims were often subject to ill-treatment and torture, and occasionally cast overboard. If clergy were present, they could be the targets of degrading and humiliating abuse. Patriotism and Protestantism, combined with a self-serving belief that such behaviour was a legitimate reprisal for the mistreatment of English mariners and merchants,

---

[15] P. Williams, *The Tudor Regime* (Oxford, 1979), pp. 246–8, 416–17, 460–1; J. C. Appleby, 'Pirates and Communities: Scenes from Elizabethan England and Wales', in J. C. Appleby and P. Dalton (eds), *Outlaws in Medieval and Early Modern England: Crime, Government and Society, c.1066–1600* (Farnham, 2009), pp. 156–67. For pirates in Lulworth see also M. J. Prichard and D. E. C. Yale (eds), *Hale and Fleetwood on Admiralty Jurisdiction* (Selden Society, 108, 1992), pp. 346–9.

[16] TNA, SP 12/103/61, for correspondence between Hicks and Callice.

provided pirates with a thin veneer of justification which was occasionally used in their defence.[17] As a loosely defined brotherhood, pirates proclaimed their loyalty to each other by hospitality and mutuality. By means of an informal web of communication from ship-to-ship, it was commonly expressed in heavy drinking bouts, music and other forms of entertainment. It was rooted in an almost unwritten rule that prohibited pirate ships from attacking each other. But this emergent culture was based on a hierarchical model. Although there was a system in place for the distribution of booty, shares were weighted according to rank. Roles were also assigned by captains and their officers. There is little evidence that the latter were appointed through election by their companies, or that they were voted out of office. Recruitment to pirate ships, though sometimes deliberately confused, was a structured process which reinforced the link between sea and shore-based communities.[18]

Yet pirate culture was transient and unformed. The product of shared life cycles and experiences among predominantly young men, it reflected the changing circumstances of such recruits, as well as the wider vulnerability of pirate companies to high rates of loss through death, desertion, capture or alternative employment. Undoubtedly these aspects of pirate life played a part in the decline of coastal and localized piracy after 1615, with the notable exception of robbery along the Thames. The loss of safe bases and markets in England and Wales, as well as a slow, irregular improvement in naval patrolling, played on the vulnerability of pirate culture. By the 1620s the threat of large-scale organized piracy in local waters appeared to have been overcome. But English pirates and sea rovers found new bases overseas, initiating a dramatic expansion in piratical enterprise within the Mediterranean and eastern Atlantic.

The emergence of long-distance piracy and plunder

The use of bases beyond the British Isles during the early seventeenth century represented a geographical and structural shift in the development of English piracy. Ranging from North Africa to south-west Ireland, pirate groups demonstrated an ability to adapt to new and challenging circum-

---

[17] For examples of violence see *CSPD, 1547–80*, p. 512; *CSPD, 1581–90*, p. 481; *APC, 1547–50*, p. 489.

[18] Earle, *Pirate Wars*, pp. 18–26; Senior, *A Nation of Pirates*, pp. 19–23. While Anglo-American pirates operating from c.1716 to 1726 exhibited similar characteristics in not preying on each other, most were not so tied to the land; see M. Rediker, "'Under the Banner of King Death': The Social World of Anglo-American Pirates, 1716 to 1726', *William and Mary Quarterly*, Third Series, 38 (1981), pp. 208, 219.

stances by organizational change, as reflected in the emergence of a 'confederation' of deep-sea predators.[19] More systematic and ambitious patterns of predation grew out of piratical reconnoitring and improvised experimentation. As such, long-distance piracy and plunder can be traced back to early English enterprise in the Atlantic. Building on a faltering start, Drake revealed the oceanic capability of predatory venturing in his circumnavigation of 1577 to 1580. Although these widening horizons exploited weaknesses in the Spanish and Portuguese empires, the emergence of oceanic, globalized plunder was weakened by the problems posed by organizing long voyages of prolonged duration into dangerous and hostile environments.

The predatory tendency within commercial expansion was characteristic of English expeditions to Guinea during the 1550s and 1560s. Designed to break into the lucrative gold trade, and promoted by prominent London traders and shipowners, they attracted a rough breed of captains, such as Thomas Wyndham or Martin Frobisher, whose behaviour was often piratical in purpose. The slave-trading ventures of Sir John Hawkins during the later 1560s directed this aggressive commerce towards the Caribbean. In both regions the Iberian monarchies, insisting on prior rights of discovery, identified the English as interlopers and pirates. The failure of Hawkins' last slaving voyage, culminating in a violent confrontation with a Spanish fleet at San Juan de Ulua along the coast of Mexico, combined with escalating Anglo-Spanish tension within Europe, strengthened the piratical tendency within overseas expansion, while lending it greater ambition.[20]

The attack on Spanish shipping, inflamed by anti-Catholic hostility, against a background of religious war and rebellion in northern Europe, profoundly damaged relations with Spain. From the 1540s until the outbreak of war in 1585, Iberian trade became the focus for a disorderly group of predators, sometimes acting in association with Dutch and French sea rovers, whose activities deliberately subverted the meaning of piracy. Robert Reneger's seizure of a rich Spanish prize in 1545, laden with silver and gold, provoked outrage. A Southampton trader and shipowner, Reneger was feted as a hero in England, but accused of piracy by his victims. Thereafter English adventurers increasingly sailed direct to the coasts of Spain and Portugal in search of richer booty. At times of diplo-

---

[19] Senior, *A Nation of Pirates*, pp. 48–77; C. M. Senior, 'The Confederation of Deep-Sea Pirates: English Pirates in the Atlantic 1603–25', in Mollat (ed.), *Course et Piraterie*, I, pp. 331–58. The description was used during the 1580s, and also to describe gangs of land criminals such as coiners. *APC, 1588*, p. 117; *APC, 1590*, pp. 13–14.

[20] K. R. Andrews, *Trade, Plunder and Settlement: Maritime Enterprise and the Genesis of the British Empire, 1480–1630* (Cambridge, 1984), pp. 122–8.

matic crisis, such as the later 1560s, parts of the Spanish coast were almost under siege from English men-of-war or pirates.[21]

Under these conditions Drake embarked on a private, piratical war against Spain in the Caribbean. It was justified as a reprisal for the losses sustained by Hawkins during his final slaving expedition, on which he had sailed. Taking the Spanish unaware, he focused on the vital but vulnerable isthmus region, across which mule trains laden with silver from Peru were exposed to capture. Early in 1572, with the assistance of French rovers and support from the *cimaroons*, drawn from communities of runaway slaves, he accomplished this task, returning to England with a rich haul of plunder. It was a critical moment in the development of long-distance piracy, not least because Drake retained the spoil, despite bitter complaint from the Spanish monarchy. But there was more at issue in this episode than the apparent connivance of the Elizabethan regime, though its inaction appeared to sanction further expeditions to the Caribbean. For the English, Drake's voyages drew attention to the vulnerability of Spain's empire to assault by small but resolute bands of marauders. They also boosted confidence, demonstrating an ability to plan and organize an audacious strike at the heart of that empire in America. To achieve this, Drake built an impermanent settlement close to the isthmus which enabled him to spend the winter in the region, acclimatizing his company while forging close relations with the *cimaroons*.[22] As a form of plunder, it was of a different order compared to that conducted around the British Isles. It demanded leadership, independence and adaptability, group cohesion and morale. Moreover, Drake's successful return, though potentially embarrassing for the regime, helped to link piracy, as legitimate reprisal, with patriotism and Protestantism within popular culture.

The success of the raid on the isthmus inspired others. During the 1570s Drake was followed by a small stream of successors, though they were much less successful. Spanish retaliation which ended the prospect of an alliance between English pirates and the *cimaroons*, as well as poor or incompetent leadership, disrupted the growth of English piracy and plunder within the Caribbean. Nonetheless these ventures were formative. They raised the prospect of bringing together distinct, but overlapping forms of plunder in a pattern of enterprise that served wider interests, projecting ambitious schemes for transatlantic settlement.

The oceanic potential of this pioneering phase of predatory enterprise was illuminated by Drake's voyage around the world. With covert support

[21] G. E. Connell-Smith, *Forerunners of Drake: A Study of English Trade with Spain in the Early Tudor Period* (London, 1954), pp. 141–52.

[22] Andrews, *Trade, Plunder and Settlement*, pp. 129–32.

from the queen and high-ranking courtiers, Drake departed on a speculative voyage of plunder. He returned three years later, after a voyage of high drama, with a huge haul of booty which has been estimated to be the equivalent of the annual income of the monarchy. His entry into the South Sea took the Spanish completely by surprise. Sailing along exposed and undefended coasts, he was able to select his targets, taking profitable prizes, and prisoners who provided him with valuable information regarding local navigation.[23] Despite angry protest from the Spanish monarchy, the queen held on to the plunder. The voyage thus underlined the way in which English depredation was internationally contested. Inadvertently it may have strengthened a perception among Drake's followers that the sea was common, open to rovers of varying legitimacy and description. In the short term it confirmed Drake's transformation as a folk hero and his absorption into pirate legend. In the longer term it helped to inspire the buccaneering invasion of the South Sea during the later seventeenth century.[24]

The development of long-distance piracy was sustained, though partly concealed, by the long Anglo-Spanish conflict from 1585 to 1603. Justified as a war of reprisals, the seaborne assault on Spain drew on private enterprise including piracy, which the regime mobilized as a means of weakening Iberian trade and shipping. But the inability of the state to regulate the war encouraged a mounting wave of disorder at sea. With at least 100 vessels sailing on lawful voyages of reprisal each year, and a smaller, but unknown number of unlicensed ships also active, the volume of enterprise was on an unprecedented scale. Not all sea raiders operated in a disorderly or piratical manner; a significant proportion acted lawfully, sometimes combining trade with plunder. However the conduct of an uncontrolled, wild element provoked mounting overseas complaints of piracy, including violence and torture at sea.[25]

From an English perspective, the sea war provided an outlet for unruly, aggressive and piratical behaviour. It produced a cohort of seafarers with the experience of sailing on long voyages of plunder, particularly to the Caribbean. It also led a small number of adventurers to follow Drake into the South Sea, but with mixed results. According to a report of 1600, captain Benjamin Wood amassed booty worth nearly £2 million from such

---

[23] Andrews, *Drake's Voyages*, pp. 58–80.

[24] Ibid., pp. 81–2; B. Wathen, *Sir Francis Drake: The Construction of a Hero* (Woodbridge, 2009), pp. 12–17; and N. Gerassi-Navarro, *Pirate Novels: Fictions of Nation Building in Spanish America* (Durham, NC, 1999), pp. 40–54, for Spanish views of Drake.

[25] Andrews, *Elizabethan Privateering*, pp. 32–7, 225–6; idem, *Trade, Plunder and Settlement*, pp. 245–55.

a voyage. Running out of provisions, however, the voyage ended with members of the company resorting to cannibalism in the Caribbean to stay alive.[26] Attracted by the prospect of rich Spanish booty, there was no shortage of recruits to serve aboard such men-of-war; many of them were the casualties of maritime unemployment, which emerged as a serious problem during the closing stages of the conflict.

The war at sea confirmed the capability and confidence of English predatory activity, but it also revealed potential weaknesses. The lack of overseas bases constrained the development of long-distance plunder in the Caribbean, despite the ambitions of a small group of colonial promoters interested in the settlement of North America partly as a means of establishing an outpost for the plunder of Spanish shipping. Sir Walter Raleigh's abortive attempt to establish a settlement on Roanoke, along the eastern seaboard, was abandoned in 1590, leaving the colonial movement in crisis. As the regulation of the war weakened, however, an increasing number of adventurers began to resort to overseas ports and markets, ranging from Ireland to North Africa, in search of provisions and outlets for the illicit disposal of plunder. The emergence of this extensive network during the closing stages of the war laid the basis, in terms of commercial infrastructure, for the resurgence of organized piracy after 1604.

The outbreak of maritime disorder and violence that prevailed during the ensuing decade witnessed the sustained growth of long-distance piracy within the Atlantic and the Mediterranean. It was accompanied by the persistence of small-scale spoil within the coastal waters of the British Isles, and by an upsurge in river piracy by well-organized gangs operating along the Thames. The rapid revival of piracy was the product of peace with Spain. Within months thousands of men who had served aboard lawful men-of-war were out of work, congregating in London and large provincial ports, such as Plymouth. Fuelled by resentment and motivated by greed and ambition, including an undercurrent of hostility towards Spain, unemployed seafarers provided a large pool of ready recruits for piracy. The problem was exacerbated by the deterioration in the navy under James I, which left it poorly equipped to deal with such a widespread threat to trade and shipping. Moreover a former pirate, captain Henry Mainwaring, who was pardoned and knighted by the king, claimed in his unpublished 'Discourse on Piracy' that many of the 'common sort of seamen', whom he dismissed as 'most uncivil and barbarous', were

---

[26] N. E. McClure (ed.), *The Letters of John Chamberlain*, 2 vols (Philadelphia, 1939), I, p. 106; K. R. Andrews (ed.), *English Privateering Voyages to the West Indies 1588–1595* (Hakluyt Society, Second Series, 111, 1959), for examples.

emboldened by a belief that only their leaders would face execution if caught.[27]

Two distinct, but overlapping strands of piracy emerged after 1604. They pointed towards different forms of enterprise. Within the Atlantic a large, fluctuating group of pirates rapidly appeared after the peace of 1604. Playing on persistent animosity towards Spain, leading members of this group portrayed themselves as patriotic rovers who shunned the prospect of preying on English shipping. Mainwaring claimed that he recaptured English ships and goods taken by the Turks, which he then restored to their original owners. In these extenuating circumstances piracy might even be seen as an 'honourable crime'.[28] By contrast the pirates who operated within the Mediterranean plundered Christian shipping indiscriminately. As a result of the provocative behaviour of the more notorious leaders, such as Ward, this group were increasingly identified as renegade outcasts or traitors.

At its height the Atlantic community of pirates included between thirty and forty vessels, manned with a total complement of at least 1,000 recruits. In terms of their organization and independence, they have been described as a 'pirate confederation' which was shaped by capable and respected leaders, including captain Richard Bishop as well as Mainwaring.[29] At times such men were loosely acknowledged to occupy the position of admiral. In practice the description may be misleading, at least for pirate tactics and strategy. While pirate ships assembled in larger groups within safe havens, at sea they still tended to operate in much smaller packs. Despite their common purpose and bonds of association, the pirate community was weakened by rivalries between captains and disputes over the division and distribution of booty.[30]

The degree of organization that underpinned the Atlantic brotherhood was linked with a regular pattern of venturing. As described by Mainwaring this was based on voyages between the Atlantic coasts of North Africa and south-west Ireland. Leaving their base in Mamora early in the year, they cruised along the coasts of Spain and Portugal during the spring, using Irish harbours as places to clean and trim their vessels, while taking on fresh provisions and recruits. For Mainwaring, indeed, Ireland was both the

[27] Manwaring (ed.), *Life and Works*, II, pp. 18, 42; at least ten manuscript copies survive. Senior, *A Nation of Pirates*, pp. 9–10, discusses general conditions.
[28] Manwaring (ed.), *Life and Works*, II, pp. 10–11; Senior, *A Nation of Pirates*, pp. 42, 49–50.
[29] Ibid., pp. 30–1, 35, 68–9; *CSPI, 1608–10*, pp. 277–8.
[30] Senior, *A Nation of Pirates*, pp. 30, 43, 59. Bishop reportedly detested Ward for associating with the Turks and capturing Christians; *CSPI, 1608–10*, pp. 279–80.

'Nursery and Storehouse of Pirates'.[31] Although the regular hunting grounds lay in the eastern Atlantic, a few of the more enterprising pirate captains crossed the Atlantic in search of prey. During a lengthy voyage from 1608 to 1609, captain Tibault Saxbridge led his company to Guinea and thence the Caribbean. Three years later captain Peter Easton crossed the Atlantic for a raid on the fishery at Newfoundland.[32]

Longer voyaging had wide-ranging consequences for the social and physical structure of pirate ships and the lives of their companies. In general, compared with the activities of the pirate brotherhood during the 1570s, vessels were larger, commonly ranging from 90 to 150 tons burden. They were manned with larger companies, of between forty and eighty men. At the same time pirate vessels were often better armed, carrying between twenty and thirty pieces of ordnance. There was still room for smaller operators: Saxbridge's vessel, the *Phoenix*, was only 35 tons. But such ships and their companies were more vulnerable to counter-attack by determined defenders. During a raid at Newfoundland, Saxbridge and his men were driven off by French resistance. The pirate captain subsequently died from his wounds.[33]

Longer voyages increased the importance of the pirate ship as a social institution. The experience of cruising with few or no breaks ashore changed the social dynamic aboard some vessels, strengthening the self-identification of crews as little communities. Mainwaring described his own company as a commonwealth, though an unruly and uncivil one, whose members were kept in order by strong leadership and severe punishment.[34] Independence and autonomy were qualified by companionship and cama-raderie. Pirate culture continued to be characterized by heavy drinking and violence, but prolonged voyages at sea created challenges for the provision of recreation, entertainment and health care. Gambling and gaming seem to have been commonplace, but also potentially divisive. Music, dancing and singing, staple features of shipboard life, did more to promote group harmony and morale. At the same time, despite the length of some voyages, the Atlantic pirates did not sever ties with family or friends at home. Some retained links, by messages and gifts, with wives and partners. Others devel-

[31] Manwaring (ed.), *Life and Works*, II, pp. 15–16; R. Dudley Edwards, 'Letter-Book of Sir Arthur Chichester 1612–1614 in the Library of Trinity College, Dublin', *Analecta Hibernica*, 8 (1938), pp. 62, 102, 120; M. MacCarthy-Morrogh, *The Munster Plantation: English Migration to Southern Ireland 1583–1641* (Oxford, 1986), pp. 214–22; A. F. Williams, *John Guy of Bristol and Newfoundland* (St John's, 2010), pp. 101–2.
[32] Senior, *A Nation of Pirates*, pp. 29–30, 62, 68–9.
[33] Ibid., pp. 29, 64–5.
[34] Manwaring (ed.), *Life and Works*, II, pp. 42–3.

oped brief, informal relations with women, including prostitutes. According to Mainwaring, groups of English, Scottish and Irish women resorted to visiting pirates along the coast of south-west Munster.[35] Haunting the unlicensed alehouses that sprang up in the region, they seemed to form part of a wider sub-culture of disorder and criminality which alarmed colonial officials concerned to promote civility and reform.

But the Atlantic pirate brotherhood was a vulnerable and fragile community. The presentation of pirates as patriotic, anti-Spanish adventurers, rather than hostile outlaws, may have been self-serving, but it provided the early Stuart regime with a powerful tactical weapon, in the use of pardons, which played on weaknesses within pirate culture and recruitment. Following negotiations for an amnesty, during 1611 and 1612 at least twelve pirate companies surrendered. They included Bishop, who retired ashore in south-west Ireland.[36] The disorganization of the pirate community was aggravated by the Spanish seizure of Mamora during 1614, which robbed the pirates of a secure and heavily used base along the shore of North Africa.

As Atlantic piracy declined, small groups of survivors drifted into the Mediterranean to join the ranks of English rovers operating from ports and harbours along the Barbary coast. This piratical incursion occurred against a background of armed commerce and disorderly privateering which grew in intensity during the closing stages of the war with Spain. In the face of angry complaints from neutral victims, particularly the Venetian Republic, the regime prohibited reprisal ships from entering the Mediterranean, but with little effect. The disorder encouraged the growth of English piracy after 1604. Based at Tunis and Algiers, the pirates adapted to local practice, taking on many of the characteristics of the corsairs. Operating under the protection of Islamic regencies, they conducted a profitable campaign of plunder against Christian shipping, especially of Venetian origin. They sailed in traditional corsair hunting grounds within the eastern and central Mediterranean, while indiscriminately plundering English vessels. Some of their prizes were spectacularly rich. The *Reniera e Soderina*, an argosy of 600 tons of Venice, was taken by Ward, off Cyprus in 1607, with a lading of spices, silk and cloth, worth as much as £100,000.[37]

Based in Tunis, Ward was the most successful and notorious of the

---

[35] Ibid., pp. 39–40; Senior, *A Nation of Pirates*, pp. 37–9; Dudley Edwards, 'Letter-Book', pp. 29, 62.

[36] Senior, *A Nation of Pirates*, pp. 68, 72–4.

[37] Bak, *Barbary Pirate*, pp. 119–23; N. Matar, *Turks, Moors, and Englishmen in the Age of Discovery* (New York, 1999), pp. 61–2; *CSPV, 1607–10*, pp. 17, 49–50, 72–3, 136–7, 167.

English pirates in the Mediterranean. By 1607 there were about 300 others in the port. A smaller number were located in Algiers. But their success was short-lived. As their semi-independent status was eroded, they were absorbed into locally organized corsair enterprise. Some, like Ward, went further in adapting to Moslem society. Deeply engrained ethnic and cultural hostility may have deterred others from following Ward's example. By 1609 there were only thirty English followers among his company. By this stage, moreover, the number of fresh recruits from England was falling. Volunteers were to be replaced by captives, in a dramatic reversal that saw the corsairs sweep out of the Mediterranean on far-ranging raids to northern Europe.[38]

These two distinct forms of seaborne plunder continued to depend on local support and collusion. This was less of a problem in the Mediterranean, where English pirates were assimilated into longstanding local enterprises, than in the Atlantic, where they were beginning to run out of safe havens. A declining number of rovers were increasingly forced into more remote and distant locations across the Irish Sea. Mainwaring linked this with wider social and legal improvement, claiming that the willingness of the Irish to trade with pirates was due to their lack of 'civil jurisdiction', though in reality it was English settlers, including local officials, who controlled the business.[39] Gradual improvements in administration and policing may have played a part in this migration. But the re-location of piracy to Ireland only delayed its decline, evident by 1615, which was the result of a combination of unfavourable conditions and narrowing opportunities. While the Atlantic brotherhood was weakened from within, it was subject to mounting external pressure. By the 1620s and 1630s English piracy more generally was overshadowed by the alarming threat from the Barbary corsairs, whose raids and abduction of men, women and children also began to influence social attitudes and responses.[40] Yet the legacy of this period, particularly the organization of long-distance plunder, influenced subsequent developments across the Atlantic.

---

[38] Senior, *A Nation of Pirates*, pp. 94–102; A. G. Jamieson, *Lords of the Sea: A History of the Barbary Corsairs* (London, 2012), pp. 90–1. For the Turkish presence aboard English ships see Manwaring (ed.), *Life and Works*, II, pp. 25–6.

[39] Ibid., pp. 15–16. As the Lord Deputy noted in 1612, the pirates were supported by the English as much as the Irish; Dudley Edwards, 'Letter-Book', p. 62.

[40] K. R. Andrews, *Ships, Money and Politics: Seafaring and Naval Enterprise in the Reign of Charles I* (Cambridge, 1991), pp. 160–4; M. M. Oppenheim, *The Maritime History of Devon* (Exeter, 1968), pp. 53–7; Jamieson, *Lords of the Sea*, pp. 103–21.

Buccaneering in the Caribbean and the South Sea

The transfer of English piracy to America was part of a broader process of trade, plunder and colonization, which enabled sea rovers of varied legitimacy to use ports and havens as safe bases, while disposing of booty in colonial markets. From the outset, the character of English colonization created conditions under which piracy could flourish. Sustained by anti-Spanish hostility and animated by the prospect of gain, the reliance of the state on private enterprise provided motive and means for an undeclared, predatory war against Spain. In these circumstances piratical enterprise went through successive phases of development. A preliminary period of diffuse, sometimes small-scale activity came to an end with the conquest of Jamaica in 1655. Inaugurating a new phase in the growth of English predation in America, the colony rapidly emerged as a buccaneering base, attracting recruits from across the Caribbean. It was a short-lived experiment. During the 1670s and 1680s the buccaneering community fragmented. As potentially rival groups focused their attention on the South Sea, others relocated to the Bahamas ranging further north along the eastern seaboard of North America.[41]

The emergence of American-based piracy during the first half of the seventeenth century grew out of a context of alarmingly disorganized, disorderly and divisive colonial settlement. The reliance on a bound labour force in Chesapeake Bay and the Caribbean raised the prospect of resentful and alienated servants providing a reservoir of recruits for piratical activity. Soon after the establishment of Jamestown in Virginia during 1607, complaints were voiced against a group of 'unhallowed creatures' who abandoned the colony in a small trading vessel, and 'made a league amongst themselves to be professed pirates, with dream of mountains of gold and happy robberies'.[42] The subsequent expansion of piracy and buccaneering exploited the social casualties of colonization among European populations, including a growing number of poor and vagrant, runaway servants and transported criminals, as well as African slaves and seafarers.

Much of this activity took the form of confused cruising within the Caribbean. It was reliant on the availability of Bermuda, settled after

---

[41] B. Little, *The Buccaneer's Realm: Pirate Life on the Spanish Main, 1674–1688* (Washington, DC, 2007). Defoe was very interested in the commercial potential of the South Sea; see D. Defoe, *A New Voyage Round the World (1725)*, ed. W. R. Owens and P. N. Furbank (London, 2009), pp. 37–42.

[42] *A True Declaration of Virginia* (London, 1610), reprinted in D. B. Quinn, A. M. Quinn and S. Hillier (eds), *New American World: A Documentary History of North America to 1612*, 5 vols (London, 1979), V, pp. 255–6.

Virginia, as a safe haven and market for booty. At times piracy appeared as unofficial privateering, particularly as both forms of enterprise targeted the Spanish. Greater coherence was provided by the settlement of Providence Island in 1630 by a group of ambitious and influential puritan promoters. The new colony combined plunder with planting, where slaves and servants cultivated cotton and tobacco. It acted as a magnet in the region for colonial outcasts and predators, though the settled population of the island, free and unfree, was rarely more than 1,000 in total. As the anti-Spanish purpose of Providence was clarified, in 1639 the governor, Nathaniel Butler, raided Truxillo, in the Gulf of Honduras, which was ransomed for 16,000 pieces of eight. While previously serving on Bermuda, Butler had been repeatedly accused of supporting pirates.[43] Although the expedition of 1639 built on a firmly established piratical tradition, it also foreshadowed the emergence of buccaneering with its primary focus on raiding settlements rather than shipping.

The development of organized buccaneering was delayed by the outbreak of civil war and rebellion within the British Isles. The domestic conflict led to a revival of widespread plunder in coastal waters, as both the monarchy and parliament authorized privateering on an extensive scale, with some sharp operators sailing with commissions from both sides. Under royalist auspices this was extended to the use of Irish bases, including Wexford, as outposts for a mixed force of men-of-war which included privateers from Dunkirk.[44] The disorder at sea was contained during the 1650s by the expansion and effective use of the parliamentary navy. Following the outbreak of war with Spain during the protectorate of Oliver Cromwell, the navy was employed in an ambitious assault on the Spanish Caribbean. It was inspired by the legacy of Drake, and justified by long-standing commercial grievances. Although the Western Design failed to take Hispaniola, its intended target, the seizure of Jamaica, a sparsely settled and neglected neighbour, provided the republican regime with a strategically located base for pursuing the war against Spain.

The early years of the new settlement were a frightening ordeal. Faced with rising mortality, irregular supplies from England, and fearful of Spanish reprisals, colonial leaders authorized a disorderly campaign of maritime plunder. It provided an outlet for aggressive and resentful soldiers and settlers, while attracting an ill-assorted group of anti-Spanish pirates

---

[43] A. P. Newton, *The European Nations in the West Indies 1493–1688* (London, 1933), pp. 172–82; K. O. Kupperman, *Providence Island, 1630–1641: The Other Puritan Colony* (Cambridge, 1993), pp. 25–8, 267–94.

[44] E. Murphy, *Ireland and the War at Sea 1641–1653* (Woodbridge, 2012), pp. 107–23.

and rovers which laid the basis for the growth of buccaneering at the end of the war with Spain, after 1660. With the tacit support of the restored monarchy, colonial officials employed the buccaneers in an unofficial conflict against the Spanish. During the 1660s between ten and twenty vessels were reported to be based at Port Royal. Most were small or modest-sized ships, heavily manned, but often carrying a limited number of ordnance. They conducted damaging raids across Central America and the isthmus region. Under cover of large-scale amphibious raiding, opportunistic adventurers, often acting alone, also engaged in predatory strikes against local and coastal shipping. Taking advantage of changing conditions in the Caribbean, improvisation gave way to organized enterprise. With little effective rival at sea, at times the buccaneering force took on the appearance and characteristics of a private fleet, with elected captains and an appointed admiral. In association with the French, and including men of diverse backgrounds within their ranks, they brought chaos and terror to parts of the region.[45]

While the buccaneers drew their recruits from the floating seafaring community, a proportion was composed of poor, discontented servants. Characterized by their youth, lack of control and social isolation, with few or no family ties, they were sustained by the prospect of rich Spanish booty and wild nights of drink and debauchery ashore at Port Royal. Disorderly and dissolute, flaunting their short-lived wealth, the buccaneers drew on pirate custom and tradition to establish a distinctive way of life which attracted a stream of recruits. One of their recruits, Alexander Exquemelin, left France for Tortuga in 1666 as a servant for the West India Company. Suffering harsh treatment at the hands of the governor, whom he described as a cruel tyrant, he was sold to a surgeon. His new and more humane master apparently offered Exquemelin his freedom on condition that he paid him 100 pieces of eight when he had the means to do so. In these circumstances he joined the buccaneers. According to his later report, he was received into 'this Society ... with common consent both of the superior and vulgar sort'.[46] He remained with them until 1672 when he returned to his native land in Europe.

[45] BL, Additional MS 11410, f. 7v; Additional MS 12430, f. 27; A. P. Thornton, *West-India Policy Under the Restoration* (Oxford, 1956), pp. 56–66, 78–87, 97–8; J. Marx, *Pirates and Privateers of the Caribbean* (Malabar, 1992), pp. 139–41. On the wider economic significance see N. Zahedieh, '"A Frugal, Prudential and Hopeful Trade": Privateering in Jamaica, 1655–89', *Journal of Imperial and Commonwealth History*, 18 (1990), pp. 145–68.

[46] J. Esquemeling, *The Buccaneers of America*, ed. W. S. Stallybrass (London, 1924), pp. 21–2.

Exquemelin wrote a vivid, entertaining and sensationalized account of the buccaneers which was originally published in Amsterdam in 1678 as *De Americaensche Zeerovers*. Such was its appeal that translations soon followed. A second English edition, of 1684, included additional reports by buccaneering authors of their exploits in the South Sea. Exquemelin provided a racy and raw description of these men which he insisted was based on first-hand experience. He effectively immortalized several leaders in a series of shocking portraits of cruel and violent individuals who seemed to lack compassion and empathy. Although most of his subjects were no longer alive by the time of publication, one notable survivor, Sir Henry Morgan, sued the publisher for libel, denouncing his portrayal as a pirate.[47]

During the time that Exquemelin sailed with the buccaneers, they were at the height of their success. Benefiting from the erosion of Spanish naval power, they conducted a marauding campaign directed against Spain, accompanied by increasing violence and extreme cruelty. According to modern estimates, from 1655 to 1671 they raided and ravaged more than twenty cities and towns as well as thirty-five villages, several of which were repeatedly assaulted.[48] Under the leadership of Morgan, a large, but unwieldy force, composed of English and French recruits, exposed the inability of Spain to defend its Caribbean heartland of empire. This pattern of raiding became more systematic and structured during the later 1660s and early 1670s. As the brutality and torture, including the rape of women, grew worse, the violence was accompanied by striking developments in the organization of buccaneering. Expeditions began with an assembly of shipping at a designated rendezvous. Cow Island off the south coast of Hispaniola was a favoured resort for such gatherings. At the same time plans for the voyage were discussed at a council representing the company. Thereafter, under the command of a leader such as Morgan, expeditions proceeded with a degree of military discipline. At the end of the voyage the booty was shared out among the company. Partly in response to pressure from below, the buccaneers adopted an innovative, rudimentary form of social insurance, according to which recruits were awarded compensation for injuries sustained during an expedition.[49] The scheme affirmed a

[47] Esquemeling, *Buccaneers of America*, pp. 81–100, for a portrait of L'Ollonais; J. Baer, *Pirates of the British Isles* (Stroud, 2005), pp. 50–1. Morgan had a commission for the raid on Panama; *The Present State of Jamaica* (London, 1683), pp. 60–76.
[48] A. P. Thornton, 'Agents of Empire: The Buccaneers', in idem, *For the File on Empire: Essays and Reviews* (London, 1968), p. 84; Earle, *Pirate Wars*, p. 94.
[49] Some of the reports of cruelty may have been sensationalized, as noted by Earle, *Pirate Wars*, pp. 101–8; Gerassi-Navarro, *Pirate Novels*, pp. 33–4. The attraction of buccaneering, according to the sailor Uring, was the reduced work and risk. See A.

contract among the company in a public demonstration of responsibility and reciprocity.

Morgan's raids on Porto Bello, as well as Maracaibo and Gibraltar along the Spanish Main, culminated in an assault on Panama in 1671. With a fleet of more than thirty vessels and nearly 2,000 men, the buccaneers crossed the isthmus with the help of 'banditti' guides, seizing the city after a battle that lasted for three hours.[50] During the violent and disorderly aftermath, Panama was destroyed by fire which some, including Exquemelin, blamed on Morgan. Squabbling among themselves, the buccaneers were deeply disappointed with the booty. As rumours circulated that they had been cheated, Morgan reportedly stole away to sea 'not bidding anybody adieu'.[51]

The attack on Panama represented the zenith of buccaneering enterprise. But it occurred at an inopportune moment in Anglo-Spanish relations; consequently it was a step too far even for Morgan's supporters in London. Following decades of benign neglect, the late Stuart regime adopted a more assertive policy in an attempt to curtail their activities. Policy was reinforced by wider economic and commercial change within the Caribbean. The growth of a profitable plantation economy, based on sugar and slavery, was at risk from disorderly groups of rovers who were in danger of being identified as outcasts of the sea. Under this new climate even Morgan, briefly recalled to London, turned against the buccaneers on Jamaica.[52]

The decline and fragmentation of the buccaneering community, intensified by Anglo-French rivalries, paved the way for the expansion of English plunder into new hunting grounds. While groups of buccaneers crossed the isthmus in an attempt to open up the South Sea, others sailed north to join the ranks of pirates and privateers operating from bases in the Bahamas and the North American colonies. The invasion of the South Sea appeared

Dewar (ed.), *The Voyages and Travels of Captain Nathaniel Uring* (London, 1928), pp. 66–7, 165.

[50] Esquemeling, *Buccaneers of America*, p. 184; O. H. K. Spate, *The Pacific Since Magellan, Volume II: Monopolists and Freebooters* (London, 1983), p. 134; J. Latimer, *Buccaneers of the Caribbean* (London, 2009), pp. 209–22.

[51] Esquemeling, *Buccaneers of America*, p. 223; P. Earle, *The Sack of Panama: Captain Morgan and the Battle for the Caribbean* (London, 1981), pp. 209–22; Thornton, *West-India Policy*, pp. 102–3, 119–20; B. Little, 'Eyewitness Images of Buccaneers and Their Vessels', *Mariner's Mirror*, 98 (2012), pp. 312–15, 318, for descriptions of *piraguas*.

[52] Earle, *Pirate Wars*, pp. 95–6; C. H. Haring, *The Buccaneers in the West Indies in the XVII Century* (London, 1910), pp. 14–15. R. Blome, *The Present State of His Majesties Isles and Territories in America* (London, 1687), p. 13, reported 4,000 'Privateers, Sloop and Boat-men' on Jamaica, as well as about 100 sugar works which were increasing every year.

as a wave-like movement, uncontrolled in character.[53] It was weakened by tension between different groups and internal division within companies, leading to further fragmentation and a chaotic pattern of venturing, which affected their ability to exploit Spanish vulnerability in the region. Characterized by profound ambiguity, its wayward and wanton features, reflected in disunity and separation, led to a loss of momentum, carrying within it the seeds of its own decline.

The spread of English plunder in this fashion was inaugurated by an expedition led by John Coxon with about 330 men. Following an attack on Porto Bello in April 1680, the buccaneers crossed the isthmus with the assistance of the Moskito Indians. Their aim was to plunder gold mines near Santa Maria. On discovering that the gold had been moved, they seized several vessels off Panama, cruising in a strange fleet of canoes and *piraguas*. Following a dispute, Coxon departed for Darien across the isthmus, leaving Richard Sawkins in command. When he was killed during a raid on Pueblo Nuevo, the company elected Bartholomew Sharp as his successor. Sharp's proposal to hunt for prey in the South Sea, returning to the Caribbean through the Straits at the southern tip of South America, provoked another division, leaving him in command of two vessels and a company of about 150 men.[54]

For the remainder of the year the buccaneers cruised along the coast of Peru, but they met with little success. Adapting to the environment, they spent Christmas at Juan Fernandez Island, which was to become a favoured buccaneering haunt thereafter. In an example of shipboard democracy, Sharp was de-selected as commander and replaced by John Watling. The stay at Juan Fernandez was cut short by the arrival of three Spanish warships. In their haste to depart, a Moskito Indian was inadvertently marooned on the island. During a subsequent raid on Arica, in January 1681, Watling and other members of the company were killed. Sharp reassumed command, restored flagging morale, and led the expedition north. At La Plata more than forty buccaneers, including William Dampier and Lionel Wafer who wrote accounts of their experiences, left in favour of returning to Darien.[55] Later in the year Sharp and the remaining company

[53] Spate, *The Pacific Since Magellan*, pp. 140–59.

[54] Esquemeling, *Buccaneers of America*, pp. 257–83, 297–475; J. F. Jameson (ed.), *Privateering and Piracy in the Colonial Period: Illustrative Documents* (New York, 1923), pp. 84–133, for narratives; Spate, *The Pacific Since Magellan*, pp. 140–4; G. Williams, *The Great South Sea: English Voyages and Encounters 1570–1750* (New York, 1997), pp. 84–90.

[55] W. Dampier, *A New Voyage Round the World*, ed. N. M. Penzer (London, 1937); L. E. Elliott Joyce (ed.), *A New Voyage and Description of the Isthmus of America by Lionel Wafer* (Hakluyt Society, Third Series, 73, 1934).

seized a Spanish vessel off La Plata. The booty included a large atlas, containing invaluable information of the South Sea, which was subsequently presented to Charles II. Thereafter the buccaneers returned to the Caribbean, in a sea voyage that lasted nearly six months before land was sighted. They reached Barbados early in 1682.[56]

Despite its disorganization, this was a pioneering voyage. It helped to open up the South Sea to bands of sea raiders, exposing Spanish weakness, providing a pathway for others to follow. But it was also piracy, no matter how the English tried to dress it up. Facing angry protest from Spain, Sharp was put on trial in London, but acquitted. In these circumstances, his expedition was followed by a larger, second wave of buccaneering composed of English and French companies.[57] At its height it involved between 800 and 1,000 men, driven by the prospect of plunder from sea and coastal raiding, and buoyed up by dreams of gold and silver mines along the South American coastline. While they were occasionally able to assemble as a large, concentrated force, sailing in smaller groups was more commonplace, though potentially less productive. Tactically they relied on the availability of island bases, usually uninhabited, including Juan Fernandez and the Galapagos Islands, where they were able to provision themselves with supplies of turtles.[58]

Much of this sea roving was uncoordinated and highly individualistic. It met with mixed success and occasionally disaster. By the end of 1686 the buccaneers had taken more than seventy Spanish vessels, about two-thirds of the merchant shipping in the region.[59] Most of these were small, coasting vessels, laden with cargoes of provisions and local commodities. Coastal raids likewise produced uneven results. An assault on an inland settlement, Santa Pecaque, by captain Swan's company in February 1686 led to the loss of more than fifty men, killed in an ambush. The plunder from such actions was often small, while officials delayed ransom negotiations in the expectation of the arrival of reinforcements. Attacks on Arica and Paita by captain Davis' company during 1687 were more profitable. According to one recruit, each man received a share of 400 pieces of eight.[60]

The expansion of buccaneering into the South Sea exposed the strengths and weaknesses of long-distance predatory enterprise. Adaptability and improvisation were qualified by indiscipline and mismanagement. The use

---

[56] Williams, *South Sea*, pp. 87–9; N. J. Thrower (ed.), *A Buccaneer's Atlas: Basil Ringrose's South Sea Waggoner* (Berkeley, 1992).

[57] Spate, *The Pacific Since Magellan*, pp. 145–56; Williams, *South Sea*, pp. 93–102.

[58] Ibid., pp. 116–18.

[59] Spate, *The Pacific Since Magellan*, pp. 145–52.

[60] Ibid., pp. 149–51.

of island bases was of limited compensation for the lack of a more effective structure of support.[61] There was, moreover, a paradox at the heart of buccaneering, in that an essentially cooperative venture, in which recruits were investors, struggled to maintain relations among its members. The division and disunity exposed the buccaneers to the dangers of a Spanish counter-response, as well as to changes in international diplomacy. Buccaneering by French companies continued into the 1690s, but most of their English counterparts left the South Sea. Their legacy included a wide range of publications, notably Exquemelin's work, which exploited and fuelled a craze for travel and pirate literature. Those by Dampier and Wafer, based on careful reportage, contained detailed information on native people and their habitats. Others uneasily yoked together sensationalism and popularization, emphasizing heroism and bravado. All were edited for publication. Collectively they were intended to provide justification for the spread of lawlessness and violence into the South Sea under the guise of buccaneering.[62]

Into the Indian Ocean

As the buccaneering invasion of the South Sea faltered, it was overshadowed by the emergence of long-distance privateering and piracy to the Red Sea from bases in North America. These ambitious, but speculative ventures confirmed the breakdown of an attenuated Elizabethan pattern of enterprise, focused on Spain, which had influenced the activities of the buccaneers from the 1650s to the 1680s. The intrusion of English predators into the Indian Ocean, to spoil non-Christian trade and shipping, was part of a wider re-structuring of privateering and piratical enterprise after 1689. Though justified by the outbreak of war with France, in which England was allied with Spain, it was disorderly, unfocused and increasingly indiscriminate in character. Some of those involved in the expansion of maritime depredation to the Red Sea sought to defend their actions on ethnic and religious grounds. In effect the spoil of Moslem vessels was preferable to the plunder of Spanish shipping. Though sometimes authorized by commissions issued by colonial officials, this was piracy, a product of the globalized spread of English seaborne robbery. It underlined the ability of predators to find and exploit areas of weakness. The growth of eastern piracy was also sustained by the establishment of a pirate settle-

---

[61] On the lack of friendly harbours see Williams, *South* Sea, p. 83.
[62] On the publications see Spate, *The Pacific Since Magellan*, pp. 156–8; Williams, *South Sea*, pp. 82–92; idem, *Buccaneers, Explorers and Settlers: British Enterprise and Encounters in the Pacific, 1670–1800* (Aldershot, 2005), pp. 115–17.

ment on the strategically situated, as yet uncolonized, island of Mada-gascar.[63]

Although the emergence of piratical activity in the Red Sea was encour-aged by local opportunities, it occurred against a broader background of English enterprise in the east. From its origins in the later sixteenth century, such activity was motivated by commercial ambition, part of a European movement to tap eastern wealth. It was led and organized by the East India Company, which established itself as a powerful corporate enterprise with far-reaching political influence. As a result of demanding maritime condi-tions, including rivalry with the Dutch, the company developed a fleet of strong, well-armed vessels which were the rival of many naval ships. They were able to defend themselves against pirate attack, while overawing native shipping in the Indian Ocean. Depending on local political conditions, company ships were not averse to resorting to occasional, opportunistic piratical activity. The challenges facing the company included the irregular threat of interlopers, privateers and pirates. Yet the inherent difficulty of long-distance plunder, compounded by the lack of bases and markets, restricted the growth of English piracy at least until the 1690s. Its devel-opment thereafter, though short-lived, not only threatened local shipping, but also put at risk the authority and jurisdiction of the company.

Partly the result of the pirate dispersal from the Caribbean, the emer-gence of Red Sea piracy was supported by promoters in North American ports, particularly New York. It was encouraged by the opportunities for profitable plunder in the region. The Red Sea was long, deep and in places hazardous for inexperienced navigators. But it was a busy shipping lane, supporting a regular, passenger traffic to Mocha and Jedda for pilgrims bound to Mecca, as well as trade in precious stones, pearls and ivory. It was widely known by the 1690s that ships in the region were also laden with supplies of European money, including Spanish silver. Many of the vessels involved in these trades were large and well manned, but lacking effective ordnance. They were ill-equipped to deal with the small host of European predators who congregated at the Straits of Bab al-Mandab, a narrow exit and entry point, thus avoiding the dangers of coral reefs within the Sea itself.[64]

[63] Earle, *Pirate Wars*, pp. 111–24; N. A. M. Rodger, *The Command of the Ocean: A Naval History of Britain 1649–1815* (London, 2004), pp. 24, 162–3.
[64] C. Matson, *Merchants & Empire: Trading in Colonial New York* (Baltimore, 1998), pp. 62–4. On the Red Sea see K. N. Chaudhuri, *Trade and Civilisation in the Indian Ocean: An Economic History from the Rise of Islam to 1750* (Cambridge, 1985), pp. 129–31, 147–8, 156, 214; and J. Ovington, *A Voyage to Surat in the Year 1689*, ed. H. G. Rawlinson (Oxford, 1929), pp. 267–74.

The arrival of pirate groups during the 1690s represented an audacious expansion in the range of English or Anglo-American plunder. Long voyages across the Atlantic and into the Indian Ocean, even with the use of shipping bases on the island of St Helena and at the Cape of Good Hope, taxed the endurance of seafarers. They also called for organization and investment. The latter were provided by merchant promoters in New York who saw the potential of a curiously amalgamated, speculative business, which linked piracy or privateering with the development of slaving and provisioning trades on Madagascar. With the support of wealthy traders and land speculators, including Frederick Philipse, a small group of captains, such as Thomas Tew, led the way, reaping such profits as to inspire a growing number of followers. These early ventures were often authorized by commissions issued by the governor of New York, though they were of dubious validity and seen by some as little more than licences for piracy. Succeeding voyages, led by men such as Henry Avery, were overtly piratical in intent.[65]

The career of Samuel Burgess illuminates the character of this enterprise, which enabled recruits to weave together piracy, trade and settlement over the course of migratory, unsettled working lives. He was probably typical of a wider group of pirates and sea rovers who were attracted by the lifestyle and rewards of plunder in the Indian Ocean.[66] Of a seafaring background in New York, during 1689 Burgess served aboard a buccaneering vessel with William Kidd in the Caribbean. Kidd was abandoned by his company at Antigua. Under a new captain, the buccaneers sailed to New York. Later in the year Burgess joined the company of a privateer, sent out to attack the French in the Gulf of the St Lawrence. During the course of the voyage seven French prizes were taken, while Burgess was promoted to the post of quarter-master.

In 1690 he sailed on his first expedition to Madagascar. Outward bound the company seized at least one vessel and raided a Portuguese settlement at the Cape Verde Islands. Burgess was left at Madagascar by his shipmates who were suspicious about his behaviour. He was there for about six months, until he was allowed to rejoin the ship on its return under a new captain, Edward Coates. By June 1692 the pirates were in the Red Sea region, where they seized four vessels laden with valuable booty, including gold and other coins. Each man received a share valued at £800. At a time

---

[65] Earle, *Pirate Wars*, pp. 115–31; Matson, *Merchants & Empire*, pp. 27, 63, 65, 99, 373 n28.

[66] On Burgess see R. C. Ritchie, 'Samuel Burgess, Pirate', in W. Pencak and C. E. Wright (eds), *Authority and Resistance in Early New York* (New York, 1988), pp. 114–37.

when the annual pay of a mariner was about £20 to £25, this represented an astonishing amount of disposable wealth. With their plunder, the pirates returned to Madagascar, haunting the island of Saint Mary off the north-east coast. The island served as a pirate base, with the advantage of a fortified stockade ashore. Adam Baldridge, a resident agent in the employ of Philipse, ran a flourishing business dealing with visiting rovers, providing them with provisions and alcohol, and clothing, as well as guns and powder.[67]

Burgess and company sailed back to New York from Saint Mary. After discrete negotiation and the gift of their vessel to the governor, Benjamin Fletcher, who was rapidly earning a notorious reputation for his support for pirates, they were welcomed ashore. Burgess bought a house in the city, and turned to more legitimate employment in Philipse's service. As a trader, land dealer and treasure hunter, with burgeoning interests in the Madagascar trade, Philipse would have been keen to acquire such an experienced hand. Typical of many other sea rovers, Burgess was unwilling to retire with his wealth. He served on two voyages for Philipse to Madagascar in 1695 and 1698. These ventures mixed slaving with the pirate trade, which included the lucrative passenger traffic in returning pirates to New York, on payment of about 100 pieces of eight for each traveller. On the second voyage Burgess also carried correspondence for pirates from wives in New York.[68]

The second voyage ended badly. Returning with more than 100 slaves and nineteen pirate passengers, Burgess' ship and company were arrested by a suspicious commander of an East India Company vessel at the Cape of Good Hope. By August 1701 Burgess and his men were in London. Based partly on evidence provided by a former pirate and associate, Robert Culliford, Burgess was put on trial for piracy. Although he was found guilty, he was later pardoned on the grounds that he had previously received a pardon from Fletcher's successor as governor of New York. On gaining his freedom, Burgess was involved in various maritime enterprises, including a brief spell of service aboard a privateering expedition led by Dampier. Returning to New York, he sold his property and settled briefly in London during 1704. Several years later he served as chief mate on a trading voyage to Madagascar.

When Burgess arrived at his old haunt in 1708 he returned to piracy, joining the company of captain John Halsey. On Halsey's death, the following year, he had acquired at least £1,200, with which he settled on

[67] S. C. Hill, *Notes on Piracy in Eastern Waters* (Bombay, 1923), pp. 96–7.
[68] Ritchie, 'Burgess', pp. 121–2; TNA, HCA 1/98/116–8, 172–3.

Madagascar. He may have returned to piracy on several occasions, while dealing in the slave trade. According to Robert Drury, the author of an account describing his own life on the island over a period of fifteen years, by 1715 he intended to leave Madagascar aboard a slaving ship. Because of his local experience, the captain sent Burgess on a mission to appease a local ruler, who had him poisoned.[69] Like so many of his pirate associates, Burgess seems to have deliberately chosen to follow a rootless life at the edge of, if not beyond, empire. It was a career that interspersed piracy and violence with more peaceful, legitimate ventures. Typically, too, perhaps, it ended violently.

The interweaving between piracy and trade, as represented by Burgess' career, sustained a significant pirate presence within the Indian Ocean, based on Madagascar. At its greatest extent, it may have included between 900 and 1,000 pirates, sailing in ten to twelve vessels. With their transatlantic backgrounds, they developed a culture and social organization which was heavily influenced by previous custom and practice as developed by the buccaneers. There is little evidence, however, that they sailed in organized fleets; most preferred to operate individually or in small flotillas of two or three ships, while assembling in larger groups at safe harbours. They pursued a violent and disorderly way of life, motivated by greed and varied personal circumstances. Unsettled and alienated, a growing number appear to have been seeking new lives beyond the reach of metropolitan regulation, control or civility. They formed part of a larger band of transient European sailors and outcasts who traversed the Indian Ocean, occasionally settling on small islands before moving on to a new destination.[70]

While the pirate incursion into the region was fed by recruits from the Caribbean and North America, it was sustained by the establishment of a base on Madagascar. As a case study in pirate settlement, this was an unprecedented development, demonstrating the adaptability and experimentation of English predatory enterprise, though it provoked widespread concern and curiosity in England. It proceeded by exploiting conditions on the island. When the pirates arrived, it was experiencing political disunity, rivalry and endemic warfare between competing rulers. Visiting pirates and traders, which native people may have found difficult to distinguish, were welcomed as commercial and political partners within a wider relationship of trade, exchange and diplomacy in which women may have

[69] Ritchie, 'Burgess', pp. 129–30. On poisoning among Africans see Ovington, *A Voyage to Surat*, pp. 54–5.

[70] Earle, *Pirate Wars*, pp. 126–30; M. Carter, 'Pirates and Settlers: Economic Interactions on the Margins of Empire', in S. Agha and E. Kolsky (eds), *Fringes of Empire: People, Places, and Spaces in Colonial India* (New Delhi, 2009), pp. 45–68.

been used as pawns. As such the pirate outpost on the small island of Saint Mary was well situated for defence and access to the Red Sea. While lacking the elaborate infrastructure of support that had been available at Port Royal on Jamaica, it served a similar purpose, providing a secure location for pirates to gather and recuperate, while sharing out booty and celebrating their successes in drinking and feasting.[71]

The pirates on Madagascar occupied an uneasily negotiated cultural space that was shore-line in appearance and essentially transient in character. Most were impermanent visitors, using the island for short visits and occasionally longer stays, sometimes lasting for several years. Remarkably a smaller number adapted to native society, inter-marrying with local women, while acting as commercial entrepreneurs and mercenaries. A few set themselves up as local leaders, with some of the trappings of native rule and power, acquiring servants or slaves as followers. Pirates such as John Plantin, originally from Jamaica, showed ingenuity in responding to their new surroundings, but they remained outsiders who always ran the risk of being caught in local conflicts. As the number of pirates declined dramatically after 1708, their position grew increasingly tenuous. By the time Daniel Defoe published his fictional account of *A New Voyage Round the World* in 1725, the 'little Common Wealth of Robbers' was reduced to a 'Gang of desperate Rogues', some of whom were in a 'sorry Condition'.[72]

For a brief period English and Anglo-American piratical activity within the Indian Ocean was a flourishing but fragile business. Reports from the 1690s of the return to North America and the Caribbean of prizes worth £200,000 or £300,000, if accurate, represent a staggering haul of booty. Each member of the pirate company of Henry Avery reportedly received a share of between £600 and £1,000 from their plunder of the *Gang-i Sawai* in 1697.[73] While some of this booty was dissipated on Madagascar, much of the spoil seems to have been taken out of the region and transferred to North America. As a significant proportion was made up of gold, silver and coinage, it was easily dispersed across formal and informal networks of trade and exchange. The circulation of pirate loot, though impossible to gauge, thus represented a significant injection of bullion and ready money into colonial economies. During the 1690s eastern plunder contributed to western plantation, compensating in some regions for commercial depression and disruption.

This far-reaching profitable, but criminal enterprise threatened to spread

71 Ibid., pp. 54–8; Jameson (ed.), *Privateering and Piracy*, pp. 180–7.
72 Defoe, *A New Voyage Round the World*, pp. 64–5, 70, 78.
73 *CSPC, 1689–92*, pp. 674–5; *CSPC, 1693–96*, pp. 114, 135–6, 510–13, 518, 520; *CSPC, 1696–97*, pp. 20, 222, 397; *CSPC, 1697–98*, pp. 370–1.

its corrupt tentacles across English colonies in North America and the Caribbean. On the other side of the Atlantic, in London, the prospect of sharing in the booty of the pirates inflamed the greed and ambition of groups of politicians and projectors, who put forward proposals for their redemption and return to England. This followed complaints from the East India Company to parliament in 1706 about the large numbers who were settled on Madagascar. Daniel Defoe examined the issue in the *Review* he edited during these years. Warning of the danger of the pirates being able to 'form a Nation, a State, at War with all the World', he dismissed claims that dealing with them might be seen as scandalous, but insisted on the need for urgency to root them out.[74] The most effective and cheapest tactic, given the cost and hazard of naval expeditions, was for the regime to issue a pardon. In exchange it would be legitimate for the state to retain their booty, though Defoe was doubtful about the 'long Tales' regarding the reported wealth of the pirates.[75] In the end, such speculative schemes were abortive. For his part, moreover, Defoe was more interested in reviving longstanding ambitions for seizing the Spanish silver fleet. Harking back to the days of Drake, he claimed that this was a time when the realm was amply furnished with treasure plundered from Spain.

Despite the mixed responses it provoked, the aggressive intrusion of pirates into the Indian Ocean was not maintained. They continued to haunt Madagascar until the 1720s, but their number declined after 1706. Faltering pirate expansion was the result of practical problems in sustaining long-distance plunder in a remote region, including the wear on shipping and men. Travelling to Surat in 1689, John Ovington reported an encounter with three pirate vessels returning to New York from the Red Sea which were forced into St Helena. While the ships were so weather-beaten and lacking in canvas that the sails were made from plundered silk, their weary companies stifled their 'Melancholy Reflections' in a drinking binge of wine and liquor.[76] The impact of these practical problems was reinforced by changing international conditions. In particular the outbreak of the War of the Spanish Succession in 1702 provided an alternative outlet in privateering, within more accessible hunting grounds that drew off potential

---

[74] D. Defoe, *A Review of the State of the British Nation, Volume 4: 1707–8*, 2 vols, ed. J. McVeagh (London, 2006), II, p. 551. On the plan see A. Bialuschewski, 'Greed, Fraud, and Popular Culture: John Breholt's Madagascar Schemes of the Early Eighteenth Century', in C. I. McGrath and C. Fauske (eds), *Money, Power, and Print: Interdisciplinary Studies in the Financial Revolution in the British Isles* (Cranbury, 2010), pp. 104–14.

[75] Defoe, *Review*, II, pp. 549, 553–4, 565.

[76] Ovington, *A Voyage to Surat*, p. 64.

recruits. Changes in the law, including legislation of 1699 and 1700, providing for the trial of suspected pirates in colonial vice-admiralty courts, may also have had some effect, though it depended on the cooperation of local officials. But the pirates may have overplayed their hand. The abuse and violence of groups such as Avery's provoked swift reprisals from native rulers, which threatened the trading and political interests of the East India Company.[77] At the same time, their conduct and behaviour challenged the self-image and ambitions of an emergent and expanding British state.

Pirate counterpoint: a 'golden age' of plunder?

Following the renewal of war with France in 1702, predatory enterprise within the Caribbean went through a confused period of privateering and piracy. The inability of the state to draw a line between such activities, partly the result of naval weakness and legal limitations, was compounded by the unprecedented circumstances of the conflict. Even lawful men-of-war struggled to adapt to a war in which England was allied with a broad coalition against France. Under the cover of war and disorderly depredation, piratical enterprise underwent another process of restructuring and reorganization, but with results that were not fully apparent until after the peace of 1713. As colonial officials predicted, the end of the war was followed by a resurgence of piracy. A new generation of captains, including men such as Edward Teach, appeared to threaten the future of the colonial trades of the British state. Set against a longer perspective, however, the misleadingly labelled 'golden age' of piracy looked more like the violent death throes of an anarchic, anachronistic business, as it struggled to sustain itself within a changing and increasingly hostile environment.[78]

By the early eighteenth century the islands of the Bahamas were an established focal point for piratical activity in the Caribbean. Weakly administered by proprietary authority in England and irregularly settled, they served as bases for pirates, treasure hunters and transient seafarers. Providence, in particular, was the hub from which much of this enterprise radiated. Its inhabitants were described in 1702 as outcasts or outlaws who welcomed sea rovers of varied background. Among those who haunted the islands was the black pirate, captain Symms, whose reputation included responsibility for the decapitation of a surgeon. Alarmed at the growing threat from the disorder at sea, officials warned that the Bahamas could

---

[77] Ibid., pp. 239–44, 271, for retaliation.

[78] Rediker, "'Under the Banner of King Death'", pp. 225–6; Earle, *Pirate Wars*, pp. 183–206; D. J. Starkey, *British Privateering Enterprise in the Eighteenth Century* (Exeter, 1990), pp. 85–116.

become another Madagascar, with a loosely scattered population of between 400 and 500, willing to support visiting and resident pirates. About the same time, the larger island of Bermuda was described as the new Algiers by one official from England.[79]

Elsewhere maritime adventurers operated under a more respectable guise. While the governor of Jamaica claimed that strict implementation of the law had forced pirates from the island to seek refuge in other colonies, the outbreak of war revealed a persistent, predatory interest which was manifest in privateering. Responding to demands from the seafaring community, the governor issued commissions authorizing the plunder of the enemy. Initially they were only for six months, and on terms that included bonds for good behaviour at sea. By July 1702 eight small men-of-war were cruising against Spain. In a revival of buccaneering operations and tactics, a force of at least nine vessels landed about 530 men at Darien. Joining with a larger group of 800 natives, they went on to seize and spoil the town of Santa Maria. Between May 1702 and March 1704 the privateers of Jamaica seized forty-one prizes, amounting to a value of nearly £18,000.[80]

Across colonial America, from Barbados to Boston, officials followed suit, but with mixed results. At least three privateering vessels were operating from Boston during the summer of 1702. On Bermuda more than ten commissions were issued for private men-of-war. While governors responded to popular pressure in authorizing predatory enterprise, in some colonies its revival was driven by necessity. In August 1703, for example, a report from Antigua indicated that 'the ruin'd people are all turned privateers'.[81] Commercial conditions were exacerbated by enemy reprisals. As adventurers remained focused on attacking the Spanish, colonial trade in the Caribbean was exposed to plunder by French men-of-war. Based on Martinique, as many as thirty privateers were at sea during 1704. By June they had seized more than 160 vessels of Anglo-American origin.[82] The success of the privateers was thus offset by heavy losses to the French who inflicted widespread damage on inter-colonial trade. The economic damage was made worse by the severe disruption of an illegal, but lucrative smuggling trade, organized on Jamaica, with Spanish America.

These conditions deepened the lawlessness and disorder at sea. Reporting on the decline of commerce and the ruin of the Spanish trade,

[79] *CSPC, 1702*, pp. 449–50, 454–5, 463–5 (on Symms); *CSPC, 1706–8*, pp. 112–15.
[80] *CSPC, 1702*, pp. 489–90, 673; *CSPC, 1702–3*, pp. 843–4 (prizes at Jamaica); *CSPC, 1704–5*, pp. 70–1.
[81] *CSPC, 1702*, pp. 501–5, 537–42, 592–5, 612–13 (report of Antigua).
[82] *CSPC, 1702–3*, pp. 668–9, 710–12, 812, on Martinique.

in 1707 one official warned that 'when Peace shall come' it would 'leave to the world a brood of pyrates to infest it'.[83] The following year, the governor of Jamaica requested advice from the Board of Trade on the procedure to be adopted in dealing with prizes taken by vessels which had no commissions. At the same time he claimed that privateering companies put prisoners ashore and sank captured vessels, in order to conceal prize cargoes. By such means they avoided paying tenths due to the Lord Admiral. The disorder, he warned, grew out of the social organization that prevailed aboard men-of-war. Among the privateers 'their captains have no command, every man is allowed a vote, and so most votes carry the vessel where they please'.[84] They were 'a headstrong, ungovernable people', who employed cruel methods, including the use of torture and violence, against their victims at sea and Indian groups on land.[85]

The confusion between privateering and piracy was apparent in a growing number of mismanaged or misconceived ventures. During 1704 a lawfully commissioned sloop from New England sailed north and piratically raided the settlement of Ferryland on Newfoundland. The inhabitants were plundered of provisions, clothing and money. In a separate incident, the company of a privateering vessel sent out from Boston seized the opportunity to turn to piracy, following the death of their captain. Electing John Quelch in his place, the company sailed to the coast of Brazil where they plundered nine Portuguese ships. Before returning to Boston, the captain and officers changed the ship's journals in an attempt to conceal their actions. The deception failed to work. Shortly after their return, the company were put on trial for piracy and six men, including Quelch, were found guilty and executed.[86]

Despite reports of two English ships sailing in the South Sea during 1709, much of this prolonged outburst of disorderly plunder and piracy was restricted to the Caribbean. Within the region it had serious consequences for commercial activity. According to complaints of 1710 the trade of Jamaica was ruined as a result of privateering. But the disorder seemed to grow worse. Large numbers of sea rovers, privateers and pirates of varied backgrounds regularly congregated at the Sambala Islands off Cartagena, in imitation of the buccaneers. Under the leadership of captain Mitchell, originally from the Canary Islands, they ranged from 500 to 900 recruits. Among them were a large number of experienced men from Jamaica, who

[83] *CSPC, 1709*, pp. 201–2.
[84] *CSPC, 1709*, pp. 270, 282–3.
[85] *CSPC, 1709*, pp. 427–8.
[86] *CSPC, 1704–5*, pp. 130 (attack on Ferryland), 213–18, 449–50, 592–4 (Quelch); Jameson (ed.), *Privateering and Piracy*, pp. 278–84.

deserted the island in protest at the collection of customs duties on prize cargoes.[87]

Although some reports indicated that the exodus from Jamaica may have involved as many as 2,000 or 3,000 seamen, it was difficult to sustain this resurgence of plunder. According to the governor of the island, most of the pirates either perished or dispersed for lack of support. With the decay of Spanish trade and targets, less than 200 remained active along the Main. An increasing number returned to the island, in response to the offer of a pardon. In July 1710 the governor reported the surrender of about 100 rovers, most of whom were 'poor, sorry miserable creatures, in want both for their backs and bellys'.[88] Nonetheless the war seemed to end in a maelstrom of violence and mutual complaint against the disorderly plunder and raids of rival privateers. In April 1713 the recently appointed governor of Jamaica expressed concern that the continuing disruption to commerce would encourage a revival of piracy. Several hundred pirates were reported to have already gathered in the Gulf of Darien. To deal with this potential threat there was only one naval vessel stationed at the island; it was a fifth rate frigate, disabled and unserviceable after a long voyage to Guinea.[89]

The legacy of the war was a prolonged resurgence of piracy which lasted until at least the mid-1720s. Within parts of the Caribbean, maritime lawlessness appeared to be a revival of mixed or hybrid enterprises. In the Darien region piracy was associated with smuggling and logwood cutting. Around the Bahamas it was linked with treasure hunting. In addition, the availability of commissions on Jamaica during the succeeding, short-lived war with Spain continued to confuse legitimate enterprise with piratical activity. The slow recovery of trade combined with limited naval defences thus paved the way for the emergence of violent and indiscriminate banditry at sea which, according to some officials, endangered British trade in America.[90]

It was no surprise that complaint focused on the activities of pirates based on the Bahamas. According to a report of 1714 the islands were a retreat for three groups of rovers, sailing in small vessels with companies of about twenty-five men. Within the space of eight months they reputedly seized booty worth £60,000. Their leaders included Benjamin Hornigold,

---

[87] *CSPC, 1709*, pp. 445, 462–3, 558–9; *CSPC, 1710–11*, pp. 32, 87–9, 102–3.

[88] *CSPC, 1710–11*, pp. 127, 138–9.

[89] *CSPC, 1712–14*, pp. 152–3, 173. S. Willis, *The Admiral Benbow: The Life and Times of a Naval Legend* (London, 2010), pp. 268–9, 347, for a description of a fifth rate of 380 tons and 36 guns.

[90] *CSPC, 1712–14*, pp. 239, 332–4; *CSPC, 1714–15*, pp. 58–60, 222–5, 357–8; Dewar (ed.), *Voyages and Travels of Captain Uring*, pp. 125, 143–50.

one of Johnson's 'famous Pyrates' who was subsequently drowned after being 'cast away upon Rocks, a great Way from Land'.[91] Following reports of Spanish intentions to hunt them down, they dispersed among the islands, ostentatiously disposing of their plunder ashore. Without more effective government, John Graves warned that it was impossible for islanders 'to detect and bring them to justice'.[92] Local officers had taken one pirate who was dispatched to Jamaica in irons, to stand trial, but he escaped after bribing the mate of the vessel on which he was transported. Within two years Hornigold's company, who now numbered about 140, were trying to establish themselves on Providence. The island served as a clearing house for a growing number of seafarers and deserters seeking employment and adventure, with pirates who identified themselves as 'the flying gang'.[93] One of their leaders, Thomas Barrow, while claiming to be the governor of Providence, also threatened to make it a 'second Madagascar'.[94]

The size and armament of many pirate ships, often described as small sloops, and armed with a handful of ordnance, restricted their operations to preying on coastal and other local traffic within the Caribbean. They haunted the coasts of Cuba and Jamaica, while occasionally cruising off islands such as Antigua and Nevis. Unusually one large pirate vessel, reported off Antigua in 1716, carried thirty-six cannon, a match for the small, naval ship based at the island. As in the past, the problem spread, as pirates ranged further in search of potential prizes. In April 1717 the coast of Virginia was infested with pirates sailing between Carolina and New England.[95] By 1720 their raiding extended to Newfoundland and across the Atlantic to Guinea. Local officials seemed to be powerless in the face of the pirate threat. A groundswell of complaint from the colonies exposed widespread connivance and collusion, including overt support for pirate groups. The problem was nurtured by the availability of recruits from seafaring communities. Although many pirates deserted trading ships at sea, a growing number included unemployed mariners, paid off in colonial ports by masters who were under pressure from shipowners to reduce running costs. They also included criminals transported from Britain, alongside a growing number of black recruits, either forced men or volunteers.[96]

[91] *CSPC, 1712–14*, pp. 332–4; Johnson, *General History of the Pyrates*, pp. 42, 71.
[92] *CSPC, 1714–15*, pp. 204–5.
[93] *CSPC, 1714–15*, pp. 204–5, 218; *CSPC, 1716–17*, pp. 139–42 (for the flying gang).
[94] *CSPC, 1716–17*, pp. 140–1.
[95] *CSPC, 1716–17*, pp. 32–4 (pirate off Antigua), 280–1, 285–6 (Virginia); *CSPC, 1720–21*, pp. 11–15 (Guinea), 172–8, 186–7 (Newfoundland).
[96] Rediker, "'Under the Banner of King Death'", p. 205; *CSPC, 1717–18*, pp. 343–7, for 'gaol-birds' gone pirating.

Colonial authorities resorted to various expedients in an attempt to deal with the problem. Small fleets of local ships were sent out from Jamaica to clear the sea during 1715, 'but the remedy was worse than the disease'.[97] The commanders of naval vessels were repeatedly accused of being more interested in carrying cargoes for personal profit than in hunting pirates. Relying on previous practice, the regime in London published a proclamation in 1718 offering a pardon to pirates who surrendered to colonial governors. Reports from the Caribbean and North America indicate that it met with some success. As intended, it had a divisive impact on many pirate groups. Among those who rejected the offer, moreover, it ran the risk, soon fulfilled, of creating a rump community of embittered and alienated rovers who could only be dealt with by more extreme measures. It was accompanied by changes in the behaviour of some pirate groups, as described by colonial officials and others. In May 1718 the governor of Bermuda reported that the captain of a naval vessel was threatened by visiting pirates, whose conduct during a recent voyage appeared to be noticeably more violent. Among the leaders of this surviving community were Teach and Stede Bonnet with a force of 300 men aboard a vessel armed with thirty-six guns. Officials shared a concern that among 'such wretches' the offer of a pardon would have 'small effect'.[98]

In these circumstances the resurgence of piratical activity after 1714 appeared to be highly individualistic and anarchic in character. It lacked the broader, if loose, organization and structure that maintained the Atlantic pirates of the early seventeenth century or the buccaneers who succeeded them. The seaborne banditry and violence may have been driven by common goals, but its key features were the aberrant and contradictory behaviour of men adapting a developing pirate culture to suit their own purpose. It was the product of a fractured and irregular cycle, which included the return of pardoned pirates to the sea, to continue their careers of plunder. Increasingly such men seemed to be beyond redemption. Yet their way of life, based on a pattern that was difficult to break, formed part of a broader, unsettled colonial lifestyle that developed in disorganized and neglected settlements. Exploiting such conditions, pirates continued to haunt the Bahamas, while reconnoitring the prospect of newer outposts on the Virgin Islands. This process of marginalization, among an already marginal group, was a

[97] *CSPC, 1716–17*, pp. 81–2.
[98] *CSPC, 1716–17*, pp. 260–4, 266–7, 326–7, 381–4; *CSPC, 1719–20*, p. 10. In 1612 there were warnings that the 'hard measures' pirates experienced ashore would send them back to sea 'with more eagerness and malice than before'; Dudley Edwards, 'Letter-Book', p. 62.

combination of choice and necessity, though it only served to underline the fragmentation and incoherence of pirate culture.[99]

To some observers this culture was an alarming response to, if not a negation of, the priorities of a commercial and civil society in which the market, profit and politeness were bound together. From such a perspective pirates could be portrayed as groups of self-identified outcasts. As reported in 1719, they 'esteem themselves a community, and have one common interest'.[100] In pursuit of that interest they exploited a well-established repertoire of maritime robbery, while introducing novel features including the use of flags. It included performances of bravado that appeared to be deliberately designed to mock the ambitions of an expanding, imperial state. In January 1719 the governor of Jamaica reported the seizure of the *Kingston* of London, within sight of Port Royal, laden with a cargo of goods valued at £20,000, by captain Thompson. The pirates' success exposed the absence of naval ships, forcing the governor to commission two sloops to pursue them. Sailing along the south-west coast of the island, they encountered two vessels, one of which hoisted a black flag at the top of the masthead.[101] The use of such symbols as warning signs and marks of identification departed from the longstanding employment of subterfuge and surprise by pirate groups. As recently as the 1690s pirates operating in the Red Sea flew a range of flags, English, French and Dutch, to confuse potential prey.

This sustained and threatening wave of plunder represented an irregular and improvised form of sea power which developed a contradictory code of conduct and operations at sea. The pirates' preference for the use of limited force in the seizure of vessels, for cargo and recruits, compelled them to adopt a variety of intimidatory methods and tactics. This could involve a combination of coercion and conciliation. According to the governor of Virginia, Alexander Spotswood, it was common practice among rovers, 'upon the pillaging of a ship to make presents of other commodities to such masters as they take a fancy to in lieu of what they have plundered them of'.[102] In 1720 captain Knott, a recent victim of pirate attack, was relieved of English silver and guineas, but out of caprice it was reported that he was given Portuguese currency above their value in exchange. The following

[99] Rediker, "Under the Banner of King Death", pp. 223–4, emphasizes the 'collectivistic ethos' of the pirates.
[100] *CSPC, 1719–20*, p. 10. The company of Bartholomew Roberts mocked the pardon offered by King George; Jameson (ed.), *Privateering and Piracy*, p. 315.
[101] *CSPC, 1719–20*, pp. 12–21. On the use of flags see Rediker, "Under the Banner of King Death", pp. 222–3.
[102] *CSPC, 1719–20*, pp. 18–19 (for Knott); *CSPC, 1720–21*, p. 41.

Figure 1 This illustration by a nineteenth-century French artist shows a group of pirates posing as women waving at a passing American vessel as a decoy, while their well-armed companions lie hidden on the deck. It was probably inspired by the resurgence of Cuban piracy in the Caribbean. Pirates employed various stratagems and developed a repertoire of behaviour, in order to lure potential victims, including disguise, though there is little evidence that English rovers resorted to cross-dressing. (Pirates dressed in women's clothing attempt to decoy a merchant ship, by Auguste-Francois Biard, copyright National Maritime Museum, Greenwich, London, catalogue number 0436).

year the master and company of the *Calabar Merchant*, taken by captain Edward England along the coast of Guinea, were beaten and abused. After being detained for about nine weeks, however, the ship was returned with twenty-one slaves, as satisfaction for the damage. According to a report of October 1723, captain George Lowther placed lighted matches between the fingers of his victims, to persuade them to reveal the location of hidden gold. Among some captains the torture seems to have grown more extreme and elaborate: captain Low, for example, reportedly cut off the lips of his victims in an unusual display of gratuitous cruelty.[103]

[103] *CSPC, 1720–21*, pp. 272, 278; *CSPC, 1722–23*, pp. 364–5; *CSPC, 1724–25*, pp. 71–3; Johnson, *General History of the Pyrates*, pp. 33–4, for Low.

It was the scale and extent of piracy that seemed to be so alarming during the period from 1714 to 1726. Although the cost is impossible to quantify economically, pirates inflicted serious damage on trade within the Caribbean and with North America, including the fishery at Newfoundland. At least twenty vessels were taken or destroyed during a pirate raid on the latter in 1720. According to one modern estimate, as many as 2,000 vessels were lost to piracy during these years.[104] For a brief period pirates also wrought havoc on the slave trade in West Africa. The disruption to the supply of slave labour had profound implications. In July 1724 the Council for Trade and Plantations advised the king that the future of the sugar colonies depended on the safe arrival of slave ships. During the past two years, however, nearly 100 vessels had been taken by pirates along the coast of Guinea.[105] The wider damage included rising protection costs, as well as rates of insurance, and delays in the return of ships which were forced to await the assembly of larger fleets to undertake the Atlantic crossing.

Piracy exposed and exploited weaknesses, while also provoking reprisals from the Spanish. A bold pirate leader, like Teach, appeared to be capable of holding to ransom a small colonial port such as Charleston. But his brief blockade of the port was a successful attempt to secure medical supplies rather than booty. Spanish trade and settlements were even more exposed to this kind of raiding. In response the Spanish monarchy authorized a force of sea raiders, or *guarda de la costas*, to protect commerce and take pirates. Their success and indiscriminate conduct provoked angry complaints from British merchants who described them as pirates. A petition by a group of nearly 100 London traders of May 1726 claimed that they frequently operated under pirate flags. Since 1713, moreover, their losses to the Spanish amounted to £300,000.[106] In addition to the seizure of shipping, the Spanish raided exposed regions of the Caribbean. Cat Island, one of the Bahamas group, was plundered so often that it was abandoned by settlers.

Under these conditions it became increasingly difficult for pirates to operate with an acceptable level of success that attracted new recruits. Although some observers were convinced that 'nothing but force will subdue them', by the mid-1720s the pirate community was displaying signs

---

[104] *CSPC, 1720–21*, pp. 186–7; Rediker, *Villains of All Nations*, pp. 29–37; M. Ogborn, *Global Lives: Britain and the World* (Cambridge, 2008), pp. 183–94.

[105] *CSPC, 1724–25*, pp. 168–70, 172–85; A. P. Kup, *A History of Sierra Leone 1400–1787* (Cambridge, 1961), pp. 53–7, 106–7, for pirates at Guinea.

[106] *CSPC, 1726–27*, pp. 74–5 (for London's losses); *CSPC, 1722–23*, pp. 222–5 (for Cat Island); R. G. Marsden (ed.), *Documents Relating to Law and Custom of the Sea*, 2 vols (Navy Records Society, 49 & 50, 1915–16), II, p. 261.

of disarray and decline.[107] A combination of external pressure and internal weakness led to a rapid fall in recruitment, at a time when pirates were struggling with a prolonged war of attrition with the British state. Alarmed at the mounting economic cost, and outraged at pirate behaviour, the state employed naval and legal resources in a determined effort to eradicate them from the seas. Under pressure from London, colonial governors were galvanized into action. Identified as monsters, misfits and outcasts, an 'abominable society' which was the 'terror of the trading part of the world', pirate groups felt the full force of a powerful and aggressive state.[108]

Across colonial America the result was demonstrated by an increase in pirate trials and convictions. At the end of 1720 John Rackam and twelve other pirates were tried on Jamaica; all but Anne Bonny and Mary Read were executed. The 'good effect' of the trial was noted several months later, in a report that the 'seas were more free of late from such villains'.[109] In 1723 an associate of Bartholomew Roberts, captain Finn, was tried and found guilty of piracy. He was executed at the high water mark at St John's, on Antigua, and left to hang in chains on nearby Rat Island. Even on Bermuda, despite signs of local opposition, the law began to take effect. A group of four pirates, imprisoned for two months, were discharged despite urgent appeals in the churches for witnesses; nonetheless two were later re-taken, tried and executed. The following year eleven pirates were executed on St Christopher's. Further north sixteen pirates were put on trial in Boston during 1726, four of whom were found guilty. Their leader, captain William Fly, was hanged in chains.[110]

The pressure on the pirate community was sustained by determined colonial officials, such as Woodes Rogers and Spotswood, whose actions on land were reinforced by an energetic campaign of naval patrolling against pirate haunts, including the Virgin Islands. While Rogers forced the pirates of Providence either to submit or re-locate, Spotswood improved the coastal defences of Virginia with a battery of cannon. Much of this activity

---

[107] *CSPC, 1720–21*, pp. 165–70; *CSPC, 1716–17*, pp. 226–7. As an example in pirate behaviour James Turner recalled in 1716 that he was shot in the hand by one pirate who prevailed on him to join his company, with a promise of 500 dollars out of the first prize taken, 'to make him satisfaction for the Injury which he had received'; TNA, HCA 1/54, ff. 36v–7.

[108] Johnson, *General History of the Pyrates*, pp. 26, 114; Earle, *Pirate Wars*, pp. 183–206.

[109] *CSPC, 1720–21*, pp. 193–5, 225–6, 334–5.

[110] *CSPC, 1722–23*, pp. 274–7 (for Finn), 294–5, 302–3 (for Bermuda); *CSPC, 1724–25*, pp. 71–3 (for St Christopher's); *CSPC, 1726–27*, p. 138 (for Fly). Fly refused to repent; see D. E. Williams, 'Puritans and Pirates: A Confrontation between Cotton Mather and William Fly in 1726', *Early American Literature*, 22 (1987), pp. 246–7.

may have been uncoordinated, but so was the pirate response. Faced with heavy losses through death and disease, many withdrew from the trade, abandoning piracy in favour of more secure lives on the smaller, remote islands of the Caribbean. In effect the pirates ran out of recruits and safe bases, reduced to seeking refuge in 'lurking holes about uninhabited islands'.[111] There had been warning signs for several years that recruitment may have been in crisis, with an increase in the number of Africans and forced men aboard pirate ships. The division and rivalry that followed exposed the fragility of the pirate community. The war against the pirates during the 1720s thus ended a long tradition of organized sea-roving, which failed to revive despite the persistence of privateering throughout the eighteenth century.

*

The decline of Anglo-American piracy reflected broader changes to pirate behaviour and the responses to it. The accumulation of decades of improvised activity and experience, the conduct of rovers such as Avery damaged the commercial and political interests of the state. Some of his successors went further in repudiating and challenging those interests, threatening to establish a community of outcasts, cut off from civil society. The rough, shipboard democracy that prevailed aboard many pirate ships, including the growing presence of Africans among such companies, challenged hierarchical and racialized conceptions, at a time when black slavery was perceived to be vital for the economic development of the Caribbean colonies.[112] But it was the violence and disorder which did so much to re-shape attitudes towards piracy. It reinforced a longstanding, but often dormant view that pirates were the enemies of all mankind, who had issued a 'Declaration of War against the whole World'.[113] Faced with a wave of uncontrollable and destructive violence, the British state, with one of the largest naval forces in the world, responded in kind.

The cultural legacy of this prolonged period of piratical enterprise was profoundly ambiguous. It was encapsulated by Johnson's *General History of the Pyrates* of 1724, which presented a rogues' gallery of disordered and dysfunctional men, whose conduct was offset by their occasional bravery and gallantry. They were hellhounds, devils and 'inhumane Monsters',

---

[111] *CSPC, 1720–21*, pp. 257–9, 309–12 (for Rogers); *CSPC, 1722–23*, pp. 85–7 (for Spotswood), 199–201, 274–7 (for the navy), 400–3 (for settling ashore); *CSPC, 1724–25*, pp. 112–20, 143–57; *CSPC, 1728–29*, pp. 175–6; D. Cordingly, *Spanish Gold: Captain Woodes Rogers and the Pirates of the Caribbean* (London, 2011), pp. 132–60.
[112] *CSPC, 1724–25*, pp. 168–70; J. Darwin, *Unfinished Empire: The Global Expansion of Britain* (London, 2012), p. 22, on the perceived value of slaves to the sugar colonies.
[113] Johnson, *General History of the Pyrates*, p. 168.

capable of the most shocking brutality and cruelty; yet one of their leading representatives, the 'devil incarnate' as Blackbeard, was a 'courageous brute who might have been a hero in a good cause'.[114] This conflicted perspective has lived on in popular culture, exemplified in ballads and stories which drew on memory and oral tradition. Benjamin Franklin recalled in his *Autobiography*, that as a young man, at the encouragement of his brother, he wrote a ballad or a 'Sailor Song on the taking of *Teach* or Blackbeard the Pirate', though it was 'wretched Stuff, in the Grubstreet Ballad Style', and did not sell well.[115] The publication of such works suggested the potential interest in pirate legend which would be taken up by others. At the same time it seemed to represent the symbolic containment of a form of maritime enterprise that had spread organized criminality and violence across the globe.

[114] Ibid., p. 82.
[115] J. A. Leo Lemay and P. M. Zell (eds), *Benjamin Franklin's Autobiography* (New York, 1986), p. 10.

– 2 –

Pirates, Female Receivers and Partners
The Discrete Supporters of Maritime
Plunder from the 1540s to the 1640s

In October 1581 the Privy Council in London was informed that John Piers, a notorious pirate, had been captured in Studland Bay by Thomas Walshe. Apparently the arrest of Piers with fifteen of his company was the result of a chance encounter, though the Bay was widely known as a place much frequented by pirates and other sea rovers. Piers stood accused of piracy and murder, but his notoriety was darkened by the partnership he enjoyed with his mother, Anne, who lived at Padstow and was reputedly a witch, 'to whome by reporte … Piers hathe conveyed all suche goodes and spoiles as he hathe wickedlie gotten at the seas'.[1] The Privy Council acted swiftly to punish and make an example of Piers and his accomplices, instructing local officials to execute some of the pirates by hanging them around the Bay. Piers escaped from Dorchester gaol through the connivance of the keeper, but he was soon recaptured. In March 1582 he was executed. Little evidence survives for any action against his mother, other than an instruction that she was to be examined following the arrest of her son. While she had acquired a reputation for disorderly living, leading members of the community provided testimony that refuted the charge of witchcraft. She was arrested at Bodmin, during the week of the assizes, while trying to dispose of some of her son's booty. Among the crowds who flocked into town she was able to sell small items of plate and silver buttons to a silversmith from Plymouth. Arousing suspicion, she was apprehended by one of the under-sheriff's men.[2]

This criminal partnership was an unusual example of the way in which women were involved in piracy and piratical activity during the sixteenth and early seventeenth centuries. Despite its essentially masculine character, the male-dominated world of the pirate was strongly supported by women's

[1] *APC, 1581–82*, pp. 227–9, 232–3, 272–355 *passim*. The case is referred to in J. A. Sharpe, *Instruments of Darkness: Witchcraft in England 1550–1750* (London, 1996), p. 47.
[2] TNA, SP 12/150/94–6.

agency. Pirate culture and custom may have prevented women from directly participating in robbery at sea, unless they were in disguise. The prevailing masculine ethos that flourished among pirate groups, which was articulated in an informal code of conduct that promoted morale and mutuality, as expressed in male companionship aboard ship, might have been severely compromised by the inclusion of women among their ranks. Nonetheless the character of English piracy during the sixteenth and early seventeenth centuries, including the need for shore bases and markets, created opportunities for the widespread, indirect involvement of women in the business. As the receivers of stolen goods, as aiders, abettors and accessories, and as wives or partners, women played diverse roles in maintaining and supporting piracy during this period. Women's lives intersected and overlapped with pirate life cycles, providing revealing evidence for the integration of piracy into the socio-economic structures of maritime communities. Within a wider pattern of connections and contacts, gender and status enabled women to undertake a range of activities which encouraged the spread of piracy around the British Isles and beyond.

While female agency was complementary rather than challenging, and rarely transgressive, at least in terms of culture and identity, it placed some women in a deeply ambiguous position within patriarchal and legal structures.[3] In some communities their willingness to act as the receivers of pirate plunder was part of a discrete economy of commerce in stolen and second-hand goods which was vital to the growth of localized piracy. At the same time, women took determined, occasionally aggressive, action to defend and protect male partners, kin or friends, and to provide them with comfort, companionship and support ashore.

Receivers and dealers

Receiving stolen goods, it has been argued, was one of the few types of female crimes during the sixteenth and seventeenth centuries. To some

[3] Very few of the women in this chapter acted like the notorious Moll Cutpurse (Mary Frith), or at least as she was represented. See J. Todd and E. Spearing (eds), *Counterfeit Ladies: The Life and Death of Mal Cutpurse. The Case of Mary Carleton* (London, 1994), pp. xiv–xvi and *passim*. There was a tradition of female cross-dressing in early modern Europe, but there is little evidence of women serving aboard pirate ships during the sixteenth and early seventeenth centuries. On the tradition see R. M. Dekker and L. C. van de Pol, *The Tradition of Female Transvestism in Early Modern Europe* (London, 1989); and A. Laurence, *Women in England 1500–1760* (London, 1994), pp. 130–1. On patriarchy see R. O'Day, *Women's Agency in Early Modern Britain and the American Colonies: Patriarchy, Partnership and Patronage* (Harlow, 2007), pp. 156–75.

extent it was related to the influence of women in the retail trades, especially in urban centres, which enabled the trade in such commodities to be absorbed within pre-existing networks of commerce and exchange.[4] As a business it involved a large number of small transactions, often of limited value, but it allowed goods of dubious provenance to be widely dispersed, through a succession of deals, providing insurmountable obstacles to their recovery. Despite the modest volume and value of individual transactions, this was an unregulated and usually untaxed enterprise. Profit margins were enhanced by the value of pirate booty, which was sold or exchanged at rates that were well below market prices.

Although men, especially traders and representatives from the provisions industry such as alehouse keepers, played a leading role in the illicit trade in pirate plunder, women were also involved in dealing with pirates. These relations varied considerably, covering a spectrum that ranged from commercialized, market transactions to a form of subsistence exchange. Doing business with pirates and sea rovers demanded flexibility, some degree of knowledge and skill as well as access to goods, provisions or services. At its most basic, it was a small-scale and improvised form of exchange which was often accompanied by hospitality and entertainment. In 1581 John Franke, a gentleman of Hastings in Sussex, admitted that he had been drinking aboard a ship of John Piers. In exchange for allowing Piers to draw fresh water from his land, Franke received two cabbages and half a pound of worsted yarn. About the same time, further west along the coast, Annys Jurde, a widow of Titchfield, had ten or eleven pounds of cochineal from visiting rovers, for providing them with provisions.[5]

As these cases suggest, in a variety of ways, receiving was influenced by local conditions. The organization and structure of the business differed markedly between the seafaring parishes of the East End of London and remote rural settlements along the coast. Despite limitations in the law and its enforcement, moreover, the commerce in pirate goods involved finely balanced personal calculations, in which financial rewards had to be set

---

[4] M. E. Wiesner-Hanks, *Women and Gender in Early Modern Europe* (3rd edition, Cambridge, 2008), pp. 116–17, 123; M. K. McIntosh, *Working Women in English Society 1300–1620* (Cambridge, 2005). It has been argued that courts assumed that women were accessories rather than the initiators of criminal enterprise. This was linked with the view that women were less violent than men; S. Mendelson and P. Crawford, *Women in Early Modern England 1550–1720* (Oxford, 1998), pp. 20–1, 43; G. Walker, *Crime, Gender and Social Order in Early Modern England* (Cambridge, 2003), pp. 165–7, on networks.

[5] TNA, HCA 1/41, ff. 50–1 (for Francke); HCA 1/42, ff. 46–7 (for Jurde).

against the risk of detection and punishment. The evidence, though scattered and incomplete, suggests that the former usually outweighed the latter: women of varied status and backgrounds were deeply implicated in receiving plundered goods. At the same time, it suggests that while women were often associated with men, widows were particularly active in handling pirate plunder.

In longstanding or frequently haunted pirate locations, some women played a dominant or strategic role in establishing commercial relations with visiting rovers. Characteristically these contacts were shrouded with ambiguity, particularly if pirates masqueraded as legitimate men-of-war, or even as traders, in order to dispose of booty as quickly as possible. They involved women with resources and confidence, sometimes acting in partnership with male relatives or friends. During 1547 captain Bartholomew Brewton and his company plundered several Flemish ships in the Channel of cloth, silk, satin and other goods. They sailed into Lulworth, along the coast of Dorset, where they were visited by 'good wyffe Dyvers and her brother, a tall man with a long beard', in the company of another man, seeking to purchase goods.[6] The visitors, identified as Margaret Dyvers, widow, Thomas Edwards and John Rowthe, made two bargains with Brewton. Widow Dyvers subsequently confessed in the High Court of Admiralty to buying one parcel of goods, on 31 August, with her two accomplices, for £60. By her own admission she and Edwards bargained with the pirates for another lading of commodities on the following day, though she denied paying any money for them.[7] Dyvers played a key role in these transactions. At least two of the company, including the captain and master, supped and stayed at her house on their first night ashore. Possibly as repayment for such hospitality, the captain offered the widow and her partners the pick of his plundered cargo.

On going aboard Brewton's vessel, the partners viewed and purchased a variety of cloth. Edwards was responsible for numbering and packing the material, though the master was forced to complete the job when he returned ashore after becoming seasick. The cloth was brought to Dyvers' house, and customs duties were paid on the goods from the first bargain. Thereafter the partners disposed of their wares at Woodbury Hill fair, to which large crowds of people flocked during the third week of September. Mixing with other traders, they sold the cloth to a number of mercers from as far distant as Bristol and other parts of the south west; according to the widow's report, business was so brisk that they disposed of all their wares

[6] TNA, HCA 1/34, ff. 48–62.
[7] Ibid., ff. 56–6v.

within a few days.[8] However the goods from the second bargain were seized by customs officials from Poole, who were suspicious of their legality.

These commercial exchanges were accompanied by small-scale personalized dealings with the rovers. When Dyvers and her partners went aboard the vessel, they were accompanied by several other women, including the wife of Edwards, who purchased three yards of red velvet from one of the company, for which she paid twenty shillings. According to one of the customs officials, the visitors included Lady Howard and her servants. One of the pirates identified her as the lady who came to their pinnace to buy silk, though as it was too coarse, she purchased several pieces of frieze instead. But these dealings came to an end with the arrest of Brewton and his company. The captain's claim that the booty was lawful prize taken from the Scots was contradicted by one of his own men, who admitted to the spoil of the Flemish vessels. While the captain and eleven others were indicted for piracy, Margaret Dyvers and her partners appeared as witnesses and potential accessories before the High Court of Admiralty.[9]

The hospitality and huckstering which occurred during this transaction in Lulworth were characteristic features of localized piracy and plunder. In some cases they were the result of prior contact or relations, though the possibility was not investigated by the court during the indictment of Brewton. The part that Lady Howard played in the business, though apparently limited, underlines the involvement of the gentry in dealing with pirates. Her purchase of cloth may have helped to validate or encourage the participation of others. But it was resourceful and entrepreneurial receivers, such as Dyvers and her partners, who provided markets ashore for booty. Their behaviour, though based on the prospect of profitable exchange, was underpinned by a deep-seated ambivalence towards robbery at sea which was widely shared by men and women.

In these circumstances the Tudor regime struggled ineffectively to contain the spread of piracy after the 1540s. Although receivers and other accessories were warned by proclamation and decree that they faced the same punishment as pirates, the agencies of law and order, which were also occasionally complicit, were unable to deter widespread receiving around the coasts of England, Wales and Ireland. The growth of piracy led to the establishment of Commissions of Inquiry for most of the coastal counties during the 1570s. Despite their limited impact, the piracy commissioners

---

[8] Ibid., ff. 53v–5. On Woodbury Hill see www.bereregis.org/Woodbury.htm (accessed 18 February 2010).

[9] TNA, HCA 1/34, ff. 58–62, 85. Leading members of the Rogers family were involved in dealing with pirates at Lulworth; see M. J. Prichard and D. E. C. Yale (eds), *Hale and Fleetwood on Admiralty Jurisdiction* (Selden Society, 108, 1992), pp. 349–51.

uncovered extensive evidence of receiving within coastal communities.[10] While women played a secondary role to men in much of this business, their dealings with pirates and rovers were varied, reflecting differences ashore as much as at sea.

In some cases women were the unwitting receivers of stolen goods. In April 1578 the bailiffs of Ipswich presented widow Hugget for purchasing coal worth £5 from two men of nearby Chelmondiston, on the grounds that it was unlawfully acquired; however, they admitted that 'she had no cause in our opinions to suspecte any unlawfull mysdemeanor in them therein'.[11] Nonetheless, scattered reports compiled by commissioners and their agents provide detailed evidence for women who were accused of overtly receiving pirate plunder. By its nature this material presents a snap-shot of the activities of receivers, supported by the testimony of various witnesses, which sheds little light on the regularity of such transactions. In most regions it suggests an occasional and opportunistic pattern of activity, involving a number of women, whose dealings with pirates were limited in scale and value, though the interdependency between genders was undoubtedly more extensive than is revealed by the surviving evidence. Some women, who were well placed to take advantage of such opportuni-ties, including the wives of admiralty officials, appear to have been engaged in more substantial and profitable exchanges. In 1574, for example, the wife of George Devereux, a deputy vice admiral in Pembrokeshire, reportedly purchased a vessel and a lading of salt taken by captain John Callice, one of the leading pirates operating during the 1570s. According to local report, she paid between £100 and £400 for the ship and its cargo, much of which was rapidly resold.[12]

Despite their inherent ambiguity, many of these deals were based on trust and credit or family and kin relationships. In December 1577 the piracy commissioners in Suffolk were informed that Margery Lambert of Alde-burgh received eighteen yards of cloth as well as a taffeta hat and cap from her husband, Peter, a pirate. Alice Bevershawe, a neighbour and possibly a relative, received various pieces of cloth, six twists of Venetian gold and silver, and a caliver, from Margery and her husband. According to the evidence collected by the commissioners in Yorkshire, Reynold Farley and his wife went aboard a pirate ship anchored off Filey, under the command of captain Phipson, and purchased soap, pewter ware and other commodi-ties. Another pirate, Robert Scarborough, subsequently went to Farley's

[10] P. Williams, *The Tudor Regime* (Oxford, 1979), pp. 245–8; J. C. Appleby, *Under the Bloody Flag: Pirates of the Tudor Age* (Stroud, 2009), pp. 158–67.
[11] TNA, SP 12/123/23. Both men were fined; SP 12/135/73.
[12] TNA, HCA 13/21, ff. 29v–30.

house with various amounts of lace and silk. In the neighbouring bay, the wife of Robert Mungwaise of Bridlington was accused of providing a quarter of beef for captain Thomson, a visiting rover. In 1578 the commissioners in Dorset reported that the wife of Henry Samways received six barrels of herrings and two bushels of salt from the captain of a pirate ship. Part of the salt was repayment for three shillings which was owed by the captain, possibly from a previous transaction.[13] About the same time, while the High Court of Admiralty was investigating the activities of pirates in Studland Bay, it heard that the wife of one of the company sold a substantial quantity of saffron which her husband brought ashore with some wool and pieces of Spanish gold.[14]

Although the commissioners unearthed evidence of widespread receiving by women, the goods involved were usually of modest value. In Cornwall, the wife of a miller, Margery Nowell, reputedly shared sixteen yards of Scottish cloth with Frances Bodehame, while in Pembrokeshire Agnes Jeffrey received one bushel of wheat from a pirate ship. The largest concentration of female receivers was reported in Northumberland, where ten women were certified to have received wheat and rye from pirates who haunted the coast around Cocket Island. But eight of the women apparently acquired only a small lading of grain from the pirates, valued at 2s 8d. Two others, out of three women identified as widows, received more. How the women paid for these acquisitions was rarely explained, though Isabel Browne supplied the pirates with two sheep and a sack of bread.[15]

This pattern of receiving was a highly localized enterprise which was driven by necessity. In a remote, sparsely populated and poor region, where legal and administrative processes were irregular, subsistence exchange with visiting pirates was part of a strategy for survival. For women whose lives were bounded by poverty, it was characteristic of a broader makeshift economy of the poor, in which the origin of goods was either inapplicable or rarely questioned. But the nature and limited value of these exchanges presented admiralty officials with a problematic issue, particularly as Isabel Browne and the other women who were identified as receivers were reported to be too poor to pay fines. As in comparable cases of petty crim-

[13] TNA, SP 12/123/3, SP 12/135/74v (for Lambert); SP 15/25/54, I (for Farley and Mungwaise); SP 12/135/15v, 114v (for Farley and Samways); BL, Additional MS 12505, ff. 352–3v (for Farley).
[14] TNA, HCA 1/41, ff. 89–9v.
[15] TNA, SP 12/135/28–33, 85, 173v. Reports from the late sixteenth century affirm the poverty of Northumberland, with complaints of the decay of hospitality and shortages of corn and bread; *CSPD, 1595–97*, pp. 420–1.

inality involving women, the activities of such offenders, particularly if they were part of a wider subsistence economy, were often subject to little or no punishment.[16]

On occasion men acted on behalf of women, serving as brokers or middlemen for transactions that ranged widely across neighbouring communities. In January 1581 John Baker, a husbandman of Beer in Dorset, during the course of his examination before the High Court of Admiralty, acknowledged receiving forty shillings from John Ryes of Wareham, for the purchase of hops for Mrs Bradstocke of Witchampton, from pirates in Studland Bay.[17] The following month, William Munday, a mariner of Studland, denied buying any goods from the pirates, though he confessed that he was aboard their ship drinking a can of beer. At the same time he admitted that Robert Declam of Corfe purchased a parcel of four pounds of saffron from the pirates, at the request of his wife, which she subsequently sold to Robert Dye of Christchurch. Munday also deposed that while he was away, she kept a bag of saffron for John Mourton, as 'he hath understode bye his children since his comeinge from sea'.[18] Despite his denials and confusion, Munday's testimony, inadvertently confirmed by one of the pirates, revealed that he and his wife kept a disorderly household. Admitting that he entertained the pirates ashore with food and drink, in his defence Munday insisted that he was unable to apprehend them. The pirate, Clinton Atkinson, a recipient of Munday's hospitality, later claimed that his 'house is the hell of the worlde, and he the divell'.[19]

The High Court of Admiralty heard other evidence concerning the pirates in Studland Bay, which illuminated the structure and character of an extensive, but small and sometimes *ad hoc* business. John Traves, a fisherman of Christchurch, deposed that he transported George Dorsett out to their ship. A merchant, Dorsett was acting for Mrs Dunston of Sopley. He purchased three bags of Spanish wool, at £3 each, which were carried to Christchurch. He then arranged for the wool to be taken to Dunston's house, laden on her cart and accompanied by two of her servants with the assistance of Traves. About a week later when the fisherman sought recompense from Dorsett for his labour, at the command of Dunston and her daughter he was given the empty bags which contained the wool.[20] As his examination proceeded, Traves recalled a similar, though more disorderly

[16] TNA, SP 12/135/28–33; SP 12/123/3, I. Mendelson and Crawford, *Women*, pp. 47, 172, but they add the important qualification, unless women began to behave like men.
[17] TNA, HCA 1/41, ff. 1–3.
[18] Ibid., ff. 16v–8v.
[19] Ibid., f. 18v; HCA 1/42, ff. 32v, 42.
[20] TNA, HCA 1/41, ff. 23–3v, 86–7v.

case, which occurred two years previously. He was involved in the carriage of two bags of wool to Christchurch for William Newman, a local gentleman. The wool came from a pirate ship at Purbeck. Before its delivery, at the suggestion of James Cooper, a miller of Poole, the carriers, four men in all, agreed to divide it among themselves. At the entreaty of Cooper, they included a share for his wife, 'otherwise she would tell the said Newman'.[21] Each of the five shares amounted to about forty-five pounds in weight, though Cooper's wife helped herself to more before the share-out was completed. However Newman, who was also Cooper's land-lord, found some of the wool which she had taken, and threatened to turn her out of his house and hang her husband for illicitly disposing of it.[22] Before he could recover the stolen booty, the miller had already given his share to one of his accomplices, a tailor of Christchurch, to pay off a debt.

Although local conditions and responses are difficult to gauge, at times women played a prominent part in local networks of support for pirates, despite the risk of provoking disapproval. The activities of Anne Piers of Padstow, who served as a receiver of stolen goods for her pirate son, John, provide a striking example of the resourcefulness of such women, but also of their ambiguity and vulnerability to local rumour and gossip. By 1581, when she came to the attention of the Privy Council in London, John Piers had acquired notoriety as a pirate who operated in local waters around south-west England and Wales, within a region that ranged from the Bristol Channel to the Isle of Wight. Piers' arrest in 1581 was followed by an investigation of his mother's activities in Padstow, which was linked to, if not provoked by, rumours and allegations of witchcraft. The inquiry found no evidence to substantiate the latter, but it exposed longstanding local concern about the disorderly behaviour of Anne Piers, which was connected with her support for her son.[23]

The examination of Piers and others focused on the recent return of the pirate to Padstow, and his disposal of varied items of booty. Several members of the family were implicated, though, with the exception of Anne, they denied receiving anything from him. Honor Piers admitted going aboard the pirates' ship; however, she denied receiving anything from her brother or any of his company.[24] William Piers, the father, also admitted that he was aboard the vessel, but he claimed it was only on one occasion, and in order to help another man recover a debt of £7. Moreover, he insisted it was 'well known that he had renounced his ... sonne for

---

[21] Ibid., f. 23v.
[22] Ibid., ff. 24, 31v–2, 41v.
[23] TNA, SP 12/150/94–6.
[24] TNA, SP 12/150/94.

his lewednes'.[25] While Anne confessed that she was often aboard her son's ship, initially she denied receiving anything from him. In the face of contradictory evidence from others, she was forced to admit that she had various goods from her son. They included a large rug which was brought ashore by two of the pirate company at midnight, and delivered to Piers who was waiting at the waterside with Margery Morgan and Edith Davye. With the assistance of a local man, the women carried the rug, which was intended for a gentlewoman, into Padstow and left it in a barn. When Morgan and Davye were questioned 'whie they went thither so late, they said because Piers promised them some clothe & that he told them they shold come by night, for if they came by daie the officers wold take it from them'.[26] According to John Thomas, a water bailiff, and Robert Orcher, the vicar, Anne Piers also received from her son a collection of smaller, more valuable items, including plate, a silver salt cellar and silver buttons. She took these goods to Bodmin, where their sale aroused the suspicion of a local officer who arrested her for dealing in stolen goods.

The more serious allegation of witchcraft was investigated by Sir Richard Grenville and two other commissioners, the same men who handled the case of receiving. In the opinion of twelve local men, described as being of the better sort and of most credit, who included the vicar, customs officials and constables, she was not a witch; neither had they heard of any previous suspicion of witchcraft. Nevertheless they agreed that she was a disreputable woman of loose life.[27] Such a description could refer to a pattern of disorderly conduct; almost certainly it included her late nocturnal visits to the waterside to collect booty from her son's ship. Even in the company of two other women, unsupervised night-walking would have been enough to provoke gossip and scandal in which the issue of gender was crucial.

This irregular pattern of petty commerce, subsistence exchange and gift-giving persisted into the late sixteenth century, though it was often concealed by uncertainty as a result of the increasing confusion between disorderly privateering and piracy. During the return of captain William Fenner from a piratical voyage to the coast of Spain in 1584, which he claimed was justified by a commission from Don Antonio, the pretender to the throne of Portugal, he was forced into south-west Ireland in search of victuals. In Bearhaven he sold a small chain of gold to the wife of Sir Owen O'Sullivan, in exchange for three beeves, wine, sack and beer. In 1597

---

[25] Ibid.

[26] TNA, SP 12/150/95.

[27] TNA, SP 12/150/96. On the unofficial curfew which operated for women at night see Mendelson and Crawford, *Women*, p. 212; and A. Roger Ekirch, *At Day's Close: A History of Nighttime* (London, 2005), pp. 65–6.

Richard Elton, a brewer of Portsmouth, admitted that he purchased a lading of wheat out of a prize brought in by a man-of-war of dubious legitimacy, out of which his wife also acquired ten pounds of cloves. He was unable to identify the sellers, and he refused to answer further questions put to him regarding the transaction in the High Court of Admiralty.[28]

The disappearance of organized piratical enterprise from around the British Isles during the early seventeenth century effectively curtailed the trade in pirate booty and the business of receiving. Occasional and opportunistic venturing continued, but it was increasingly restricted to remote regions of Ireland. In the aftermath of the wars with Spain and France during the 1620s there was a small, short-lived resurgence of piracy, especially within the Irish Sea. Although the risk of detection may have increased, in some regions pirates and rovers were supported or maintained by the members of coastal communities. In 1633 captain John Norman, generally reputed to be a pirate, spent about three weeks in the small haven of Bolthelly, near Caernarvon.[29] During this period he sold a variety of goods to local inhabitants with the alleged connivance of the deputy vice admiral and other officials. Among the receivers of his booty was Mary Bodvel, the mother of the sheriff and the aunt of the vice admiral. According to Thomas Clarke of Bolthelly, one of the leading witnesses heard by the High Court of Admiralty, the goods were privately conveyed to Bodvel's house by her kinsmen and servants. The pirate captain evidently informed Clarke that 'hee had received more curtesie from ... Mrs Bodvill then from any other there', including the gift of several pies.[30] The pirates also received pastries and pies from the wife of Griffin ap Hugh, in exchange for a cloth gown. In addition John Madrin, the deputy sheriff, was accused of spending several days drinking aboard Norman's ship, while his mother provided two horses to carry the captain to her house for dinner.

The persistence of these varied forms of receiving and exchange was accompanied by a different pattern of activity in London, where the trade in stolen cargoes was the result of the growth of piracy and theft along the

[28] TNA, SP 12/177/46 (for Fenner); TNA, HCA 1/45, f. 3v (for Elton). According to a report of 1589 Munster was 'made a receptacle of Pirats', partly under the sponsorship of Sir Edward and Lady Denny. The latter was allegedly receiving plundered goods in exchange for victuals; SP 63/144/56.

[29] Possibly Bethel. TNA, HCA 13/50, ff. 347–7v.

[30] Ibid., f. 347v. She was probably the sister of Elizabeth Bodvel, daughter of Sir John Wynn; C. Peters, *Women in Early Modern Britain 1450–1640* (Basingstoke, 2004), p. 40. The 'entrepreneurial attitude towards the law' of such widows might be comparable with their dealings with pirates. K. W. Swett, 'Widowhood, Custom and Property in Early Modern North Wales', *Welsh History Review*, 18 (1996), p. 215.

river Thames. While this was undoubtedly a well-established enterprise, it seems to have grown rapidly during the sixteenth and early seventeenth centuries. The expansion of London's overseas trade, and the development of unregulated, loosely supervised docking facilities at St Katharine's and other locations, created opportunities for robbery, petty theft and piracy. From the 1540s onwards, evidence survives for the existence of pirate gangs operating along the Thames, and occasionally raiding further along the coasts of Essex and Kent. So vulnerable was shipping on the river that opportunistic robbers working alone, but sometimes in tandem with receivers, boarded unsupervised vessels during daylight and rifled them of part of their cargoes or stores.[31]

Organized piracy and theft of this nature merged with a wider problem of petty criminality and disorder that flourished in recently established marginal communities, beyond the jurisdiction of the city, where traditional authority and control were weak. While it may not have amounted to a professionalized criminal underworld, as luridly described by publicists and moralists, it was organized and elaborate. It fed off the growing wealth of the city, though it rested on suburban networks of receivers and dealers, who were used to handle and dispose of a diverse range of stolen commodities. Within the rapidly growing and teeming seafaring parishes of the East End, such as Stepney, Rotherhithe and Southwark, women were heavily involved in these illicit trades, occasionally participating in the raids of river-based gangs.[32]

The activities of these groups, opportunistic or organized, confused river piracy with theft. It was usually undertaken not by professional criminals, but by a semi-criminalized class of men and women whose life cycles blended irregular employment with illegality. As might be expected, watermen and others who worked on the river were heavily involved in it. But it demanded the cooperation and connivance of local residents. Due to their involvement in the retail and second-hand goods trades, women were of particular value to river pirates and thieves. Such women were able to

---

[31] Appleby, *Under the Bloody Flag*, pp. 35–6, 97–8; C. M. Senior, *A Nation of Pirates: English Piracy in its Heyday* (Newton Abbot, 1976), pp. 110–22. According to the opinion of the common lawyers in 1615 a man could not be hanged for piracy or robbery on the river Thames; Prichard and Yale (eds), *Hale and Fleetwood*, pp. ccxi–iv.

[32] On the 'underworld' see J. A. Sharpe, *Crime in Early Modern England 1550–1750* (2nd edition, London, 1984), pp. 114–17; P. Griffiths, *Lost Londons: Change, Crime, and Control in the Capital City, 1550–1660* (Cambridge, 2008), pp. 204ff. For a selection of the pamphlet literature see A. V. Judges (ed.), *The Elizabethan Underworld* (London, 1930); and A. F. Kinney (ed.), *Rogues, Vagabonds, and Sturdy Beggars: A New Gallery of Tudor and Early Stuart Rogue Literature* (Amherst, 1990).

assimilate stolen goods into existing networks of exchange, retailing or pawnbroking without arousing as much suspicion as men. The operations of Richard Cocks and several other wherrymen during 1546 may provide a characteristic case of the confusion between petty theft and ship robbery, and of women's participation in the dispersal of stolen commodities, as well as of their potential to be the victims of river piracy. Cocks and his associates stole a large block of tin from a river wharf. In an effort to conceal its provenance, the thieves melted down the original block and divided it into separate pieces, three of which were purchased by Elizabeth Golde, a widow of Southwark. When the High Court of Admiralty heard the case, it emerged that Cocks was also involved in the robbery of a small vessel at Limehouse. He and the other robbers took 19s 6d from a Flemish woman who was aboard the ship, but before departing they gave 8d to a poor man with sore legs.[33]

The character of this business, and of women's role in it, is demonstrated by a variety of cases heard by the High Court of Admiralty. In 1577 the court was engaged in proceedings against Esdras Eardley, a sailor of London, who was accused of robbing a vessel moored off Ratcliffe at ten o'clock in the morning. Finding nobody aboard, Eardley carried off twelve yards of cloth, a frieze jerkin, three pairs of mariners' breeches and one pair of socks. He sold the cloth to one Clarke's wife of Ratcliffe for twelve shillings. Early in 1598 the court heard a similar case, involving the robbery of a small vessel of Leigh by Thomas Billinge and other watermen of Ratcliffe. The plunder included a woman's gown, a pair of breeches and a taffeta hat, which Billinge left with a woman who lived on Fleet Street, intending to collect them later. A quantity of bacon and butter out of the ship was subsequently sold by Billinge to a married couple as they were drinking in an alehouse in Whitefriars.[34]

The growth of river piracy and receiving during the later sixteenth and early seventeenth centuries was reflected in an increasing number of women who were examined before the admiralty court. While the evidence needs careful handling, given the self-evident possibility of misleading or self-interested testimony, it strikingly demonstrates the persistence of a flourishing, but deeply ambivalent business. Much of it was small-scale, partly to allay suspicion, and in terms of organization it ranged from casual and opportunistic activity to well-established and carefully planned arrangements. In some cases wives worked in partnership with husbands, on occasion, no doubt, as unwitting or possibly unwilling accomplices. In June

---

[33] TNA, HCA 1/34, ff. 11–15.
[34] TNA, HCA 1/40, f. 53v; HCA 1/45, ff. 26v–7.

1605 Ellenor Rawlins of Wapping was examined before the court regarding the theft of bed ticks and other goods from a Guernsey vessel at anchor on the river. According to her responses, several weeks earlier her husband, William, a sailor, instructed her to sell such bedding which he had received from several mariners. Along with the bedding, Rawlins was given various items of clothing, including two old sea cloaks and three coarse shirts. Although the clothing could probably be sold locally without arousing suspicion, at her husband's command, Rawlins went to Cornhill and sold three pieces of the bedding to an upholsterer for twenty shillings. Emboldened by this success, she took another three pieces to a shop in Leadenhall, but on this occasion she was arrested by a constable.[35] As in many similar cases, however, little is known of Ellenor Rawlins' fate at the hands of the court: depending on circumstances, she could have been fined or reprimanded.

The difficulties facing legal authorities in tracking the dispersal of pirate booty by dealers and receivers are illustrated by the plunder of the *Elephant*, a Flemish vessel, by a group of pirates in January 1615. The robbers made off with an impressive haul of jewels, silks and other rich fabrics. It was rapidly divided, concealed or disposed at various locations along the river. During a subsequent investigation, the High Court of Admiralty examined a large number of witnesses and suspects, though much of the booty seems to have long since disappeared. Rose Bolton, a resident of Barmesey Street in Southwark, admitted that her husband, Steven, had recently returned home with assorted fragments of jewellery, including a ring, a piece of gold chain and another piece of a gold bracelet. She passed these items on to a neighbour, 'goodwife Gregorie, who ... delivered them over to some Officers'.[36] Another neighbour, Elizabeth Leech, also admitted that she received various goods from her husband, Michael, a sailor, including a pair of old silk stockings, lace and an old shirt. When both women appeared before the court they claimed that their spouses were no longer at home; nor were they able or willing to disclose where they had gone.

Among the other women who were examined by the court in this case, Ellen Rippingham of Blackwall, who seems to have run a lodging house with her husband, admitted receiving a bundle of silk, concealed in a pair of breeches, from John Silly, a mariner. She also acknowledged acquiring three silver spoons, a gold chain, a ring and other small items of jewellery

---

[35] TNA, HCA 1/46, f. 193.
[36] TNA, HCA 1/48, ff. 26–6v. Barmesey or Bermondsey Street was a well-known location for the disposal of illicitly acquired goods; Kinney (ed.), *Rogues*, p. 297.

and silk from Silly and an associate. Although Rippingham was holding these goods for Silly, when she heard of a warrant for his arrest, she handed them over to others for safe keeping. Other pieces of the booty were carried further down the river and beyond. Some of it ended up in Ipswich, where Steven Fisher, a sailor of Plymouth, admitted receiving several items wrapped in linen cloth, while he was in an alehouse, the sign of the Bull, drinking with a company of sailors.[37] Fisher claimed not to know the sailor who handed him the package, but it was intended for Margaret Woodes of Blackwall. When Woodes was examined by the court she acknowledged receiving the package, but denied all knowledge of its contents. During the course of her examination it became clear that she had known Fisher for at least six months. Her admission that shortly before Christmas she had informed William Edwards, 'with weeping teares ... that her brother had drawen Steven Fisher to goe with him and others ... to robbe a pincke', did little to strengthen her defence, even though 'she saieth they brake off and did not goe'.[38]

The growth of alehouses and lodging houses facilitated the disposal of stolen cargoes. Many of these establishments were run by single women or the wives of sailors, who provided safe houses for storing booty and commodities of dubious origin. In March 1619 the court heard evidence from Joan Tolladay, who ran a lodging house in Wapping, concerning two men who had recently brought about six pieces of cloth to her, at daybreak, 'which they intreated ... [her] to laye up for them'.[39] Although she agreed to keep the cloth in a chest in the cellar, it was discovered by a suspicious constable. One of the men identified by Tolladay was John Pickle, who described himself to the court as a gentleman of London, whose parents lived in Ireland. Pickle was a wandering adventurer who became a member of a pirate gang led by captain James Haggerston which was very active along the Thames. Between voyages he lodged at various alehouses, including the Saracen's Head, in Limehouse and Ratcliffe. The cloth which he left with Joan Tolladay evidently came out of a French vessel which the pirates had recently taken in the lower reaches of the river. In giving evidence to the court, Pickle also admitted that he left three bundles of cloth 'with the woeman of the house at the signe of the Fortune in Ratcliffe'.[40] Indirectly, the importance of the alehouse to the maintenance

[37] TNA, HCA 1/48, ff. 27, 29–9v.
[38] Ibid., f. 29v.
[39] Ibid., f. 223. For a case study of female receivers operating in alehouses see A. Clark, *Working Life of Women in the Seventeenth Century* (London, 1919, reprinted 1982), p. 233; and the data in Griffiths, *Lost Londons*, pp. 458–9.
[40] TNA, HCA 1/7, f. 4; HCA 1/48, ff. 221v–3.

of these petty criminal networks is underlined by the comment of Henry Sherman, who denied being at sea with Haggerston and his men, but claimed that the tapster of the Saracen's Head knew where they were.

A number of the women who appeared before the High Court of Admiralty were engaged in small-scale, but complex transactions, which merged with the trade in second-hand commodities and pawnbroking. In 1619 Dorothy Cooper, a resident of Long Lane, purchased two pieces of cloth from Richard Brooke in the house of a neighbour, Mrs Lichpoole. The two women appear to have been partners and dealers in the second-hand trade. Cooper later asserted that William Marriott, a leather seller, vouched for Brooke's honesty. While acting as a middleman in the transaction, Marriott effectively provided a warranty for the goods which originated from a seafarer. When the female partners agreed to purchase the cloth for £4, his role was rewarded with a gift of twelve pence from Cooper and two shillings from Brooke. During proceedings in the admiralty court, it emerged that Lichpoole's husband had warned his wife not to meddle with the goods.[41] But if she or her partner harboured any suspicion of their legality they kept it to themselves, for there were further dealings between them and Brooke. The day after the sale of the cloth, Cooper accompanied Brooke to a pawnshop in Chick Lane, where she paid sixteen shillings to redeem a cloak and a carpet. After giving four shillings to Brooke, she took possession of both commodities. She subsequently sold the cloak for 13s 6d to a buyer from Westminster, whose name was registered in her book.[42] Of the cloth which she and Lichpoole had previously bought, one piece was sold for £2 10s, while another was pawned with a neighbour for £1 10s. Additional evidence presented to the court appeared to show that these commodities were part of the cargo of a French vessel, which was plundered by a pirate gang off Gravesend.

Where the provenance of stolen goods could be concealed through multiple transactions, some women were unintentionally involved in receiving pirate booty. In March 1619, for example, Francis Crosfield, a tailor from Ratcliffe, sold two pieces of cloth out of the French vessel to a servant of Mrs Evans, a shopkeeper in Fenchurch Street, for £2 19s. On the following day, Crosfield returned, in the company of a sailor, and sold another piece of cloth to the servant. Crosfield later admitted that he received the cloth from Richard Catro, a pirate commonly known as Dick of Dover, who claimed that he had 'them … of a friend in London to make

---

[41] Ibid., ff. 240–1. On pawnbroking and the 'alternative economy' of riverside communities, see J. Boulton, *Neighbourhood and Society: A London Suburb in the Seventeenth Century* (Cambridge, 1987), pp. 81–92.
[42] TNA, HCA 1/7, ff. 240–40v.

money ... to helpe a brother of thieves who was in prison'.[43]

Opportunistic and organized robbery along the Thames continued to be a problem, despite the decline in English piracy around the British Isles during the early seventeenth century. At the admiralty sessions held at Southwark in 1623 a group of ten men, including John Twirle, alias Toodle, and his wife Elizabeth, were indicted for stealing goods laden aboard two ships. More evidence for the direct involvement of women in river raiding seems to have been presented to the sessions of 1634. Among the prisoners were William Patrickson and his wife Elizabeth, Edmund Harris and his wife Joanna, Jane Francis, Mary Percevall, a spinster, and Anna Carey, who were indicted for spoiling a vessel. In addition, Mary Percevall was accused of receiving small amounts of sheets, clothing and other goods. Frances Stoddard, who was not listed with the prisoners, appeared before the court for allegedly receiving a pair of green curtains and other commodities. While little information was provided about the background of these women, they resided in parishes in Southwark and Smithfield, and with the exception of Patrickson, their spouses were employed in positions – as a porter, coachman or victualler – where the acquisition or movement of such goods may not have aroused suspicion.[44] Further allegations of women participating in the robbery of vessels on the river, in association with their husbands or other male accomplices, were heard by the court in 1638. But in at least one case the evidence appeared to indicate an overlap between robbery and receiving, while revealing the dispersal of stolen goods along existing networks of exchange and debt relations.[45]

Collectively this evidence illustrates the varied role played by women in receiving pirate booty. Directly or indirectly, they were engaged in commercial relations, barter and exchange, acting on their own or with husbands and partners. Many of these transactions may have been small-scale, and limited in value and volume, but they were profitable to the participants. They were part of looser networks of the trade in stolen goods, which provided outlets for the disposal of pirate booty among a large and scattered range of receivers and dealers. Inherently, much of this activity was opportunistic, intermittent and barely recorded. Nonetheless, it is evident that female participation in the business was shaped by local opportunities and

---

[43] Ibid., ff. 241v–2.

[44] TNA, HCA 1/60, ff. 118–19v, 122 (for Twirle); HCA 1/50, ff. 1–1v and HCA 1/7, ff. 102, 111 (for Patrickson). And see below, pp. 204–5.

[45] TNA, HCA 1/101, ff. 85, 88. The participation has parallels with the role of women in burglary, on which see G. Walker, 'Women, Theft and the World of Stolen Goods', in J. Kermode and G. Walker (eds), *Women, Crime and the Courts in Early Modern England* (London, 1994), pp. 85–6.

constraints, which were in turn qualified by gender and status. In London poorer women from the rapidly growing parishes of the East End seem to have been particularly involved in handling stolen goods from the river, specializing in selected types of commodities, such as cloth, fabrics and clothing, which could be readily assimilated into pre-existing business and commercial activities.

Female receivers and dealers, like many of their male counterparts, operated in a resourceful and business-like manner, even when dealing with potentially intimidating legal institutions. While some women might justifiably have claimed ignorance of the origins of the goods they handled, those who appeared before the High Court of Admiralty sometimes tried to conceal and protect the identities of suppliers and customers. Receiving was a complicated crime for the court to deal with at the best of times. But it could be confounded by the difficulties of investigating the activities of poor, sometimes recalcitrant women, who were unwilling witnesses or uncooperative suspects. In exceptional cases some women seem to have been able to undermine legal process in the admiralty court. In 1618 Elizabeth Rogers, alias Fisher, of Tenby, was accused of receiving stolen goods belonging to a merchant of Dublin. Although she was ordered to appear before the court, a local officer was unable to guarantee her presence 'for that shee was soe great with childe as shee coulde not bee committed without imminente danger of her life, and shee was so bigge that noe bodie wulde bee bounde for her'.[46]

Wives, partners, aiders and accessories

To some extent the role of women as receivers grew out of their relationships with pirates as wives, partners or friends. It was usually through such relations that women acted as accessories and aiders. Spouses provided comfort, support and companionship when pirates came ashore. Family members shielded suspected pirates from the law, showing loyalty and determination in providing safe sanctuary for relatives, or in assisting their escape from gaol. Despite the practical difficulties of communication, and regardless of the risks, pirates maintained relations with their wives. In 1620 the Venetian ambassador in London reported that many pirates were tired of their lives at sea, consequently they 'frequently venture into the nets, landing in the kingdom and going to see their wives or other relations,

---

[46] TNA, HCA 1/48, ff. 167v–8. And see Walker, 'Women, Theft and the World of Stolen Goods', pp. 81–105, for an interesting discussion and re-evaluation of women, crime and receiving. Pregnancy could result in a sentence not being enforced; in legal terms, of course, it was delayed, not cancelled; Mendelson and Crawford, *Women*, p. 46.

believing that they will not be recognized'.[47] The interdependency between the lives of women and of pirates created a discrete maintenance and support system, which was usually beyond the detection of legal authorities. As in the case of receiving, however, this placed some women in a deeply ambiguous position. If the masculinized world of the pirate threatened to rob them of agency, it also exposed them to dangers.

While piracy was organized criminal activity, calling for extended or irregular absences at sea, those engaged in it had plenty of opportunity to return ashore to see wives, lovers or prostitutes. For some pirates, in addition to the provision of companionship and comfort which was different from the fellowship that prevailed at sea, these relationships may have been of considerable tactical value. During the later 1540s, for example, Richard Coole, a pirate captain who operated off south-west England and Ireland, married an aunt of Barry Oge in Munster. The relationship enabled Coole to use Oge's castle at Kinsale as a safe haven and refuge for his piratical ventures. In July 1548, the local authorities of Kinsale complained that Coole was exploiting the castle to spoil shipping entering the port. Although Coole suffered a brief period of imprisonment in the Tower of London, he resumed his piratical activities in the Irish Sea during the early 1550s, though without the use of the castle at Kinsale.[48]

Pirates and their female partners demonstrated ingenuity or boldness in maintaining relations between sea and shore. In April 1567 a group of rovers including their captain, John Frobisher, landed at Dawlish in Devon, with the purpose of seeing their wives. Frobisher's spouse was the daughter of Thomas Stukeley of Coldridge, where he was seized by a local constable. He escaped using an alias, but the rest of his company were taken and imprisoned in Exeter gaol. About a decade later, in the neighbouring county of Cornwall, John Tregose was accused of receiving goods from Robert Hicks, the pirate captain, as well as providing lodging for his wife, and the wives of two of his company. Hicks' wife, in the company of another woman, was taken out to the pirates' ship in a boat borrowed from Tregose.[49]

The determination of spouses to maintain such uncertain relations is demonstrated by the experience of several pirates and their partners during the 1570s and 1580s. According to evidence presented to the High Court

[47] *CSPV, 1619–21*, p. 358.
[48] TNA, SP 61/1/29.
[49] DRO, Exeter, ECA Book 57, f. 171v (for Frobisher); TNA, SP 12/123/28 and SP 12/135/83 (for Hicks). John was the brother of Martin Frobisher. Both were involved in irregular, piratical venturing during the 1560s; J. McDermott, *Martin Frobisher: Elizabethan Privateer* (New Haven, 2001), pp. 56–69.

of Admiralty, in 1583 Clinton Atkinson, a notorious pirate, was able to meet his wife at a lodging house at Erith, along the Thames. Their meeting was cut short by the arrival of a constable, who was later forced to deny suspicions of allowing the pirate to escape. When the constable arrived, he found the table prepared for supper, but Atkinson had fled, only half an hour earlier.[50] The landlord, John Fludd, who was ill in bed when the constable arrived, subsequently insisted that he thought Atkinson was an honest man, such as a trader, though his unwillingness to allow the constable to search his property did little to stifle suspicions of his connivance in this short-lived tryst. Atkinson spent the night in a nearby field, before getting a boat to Brainford and thence to the Isle of Purbeck in Dorset.

Several years later, in January 1586, Gillian Aston was questioned by magistrates about her former husband's piracies. Described as 'sometymes wyffe of Thomas Clarke', she acknowledged regular visits by her husband to their home at Hoddesdon in Hertfordshire.[51] But she denied any knowledge of his robberies at sea. In response to further questioning, she admitted that at least on one occasion Clarke had returned with money and plate, some of which was sold by a servant, Henry Topcliffe. Claiming that he 'played the thief', and stole money from her, she had the servant arrested.[52] During the course of her testimony, she also deposed that there were various dealings, involving loans and bonds, between Clarke and his mother, Thomasine. After meeting her husband at different locations, on his instructions she travelled to Gravelines in the Netherlands, to be with him, accompanied by her brother-in-law. Soon after their arrival Clarke was killed; his widow returned to England and remarried.

Gifts were an important aspect to these contacts. They were employed in a variety of ways, as tokens of love and affection, as a return for hospitality, as an overt bribe and even possibly as compensation for the loss of a spouse at sea. Officials and their wives seem to have been the regular recipients of presents from pirates and rovers. In September 1565 John Hooper and his company, who had spoiled several ships in the Channel, including a rich Spanish vessel laden with tapestry, cloth, plate, carpets and satin, provided the wife of a vice admiral on the Isle of Wight with a gift of cloth. She also received forty pieces of silver from William Hooper, while her husband acquired two silver whistles. According to a servant of Henry

[50] TNA, HCA 1/40, ff. 149–55. In the later 1530s William Scarlett was arrested on suspicion of piracy after 'he repayred home to see his wyffe and his children'; HCA 1/33, ff. 68v–70v.
[51] TNA, SP 12/186/15, I; *APC, 1586–87*, pp. 82, 285.
[52] TNA, SP 12/186/15, I.

Wotton, during 1577 he returned from a trip and informed his wife that George Phipson, a well-known pirate, had commended her, 'and having but smale quantitye of money sent her a bolt of black threede for a token'.[53]

Pirates employed a diverse, sometimes unusual range of presents to serve their purposes. Stephen Haynes, a pirate captain, gave three parrots to one of his suppliers who sold him three hogheads of beer, one of which was for Mrs Joan Fielde, a widow of Poole. William Kinge of Corfe also received a parrot from one of Haynes' company, whom he then arrested on suspicion of piracy. The bird was passed on to others, ending up with the wife of one Josephe of Christchurch. Kinge also claimed that Lord Howard's cook, who was aboard the pirate ship, received two parrots and a monkey; the latter he gave to the dowager Lady Howard.[54] According to the testimony of the wife of Henry Hornes, given in 1581, he was presented with a parrot, a small barrel of soap and two calivers, during a meeting with John Piers off Lundy Island. The parrot ended up in the hands of a vice admiral; the calivers were still in Hornes' house at the time of her examination. In an attempt to find favour with the Lord Admiral, in 1615 the pirate captain Lording Barry handed over a variety of presents to an admiralty officer at Bearhaven in south-west Ireland. They included pieces of silver cloth and lace, other commodities, and a negro girl or woman, all of which were valued at £100.[55] This was a very unusual gift. There is no evidence of white female captives being used in this way, at least by English pirates operating around the British Isles, though the Barbary corsairs were raiding in northern waters for slaves by the early seventeenth century. The pirate's present foreshadows deeper issues regarding gifts, gender and ethnicity which were to become more problematic with the occasional capture of slaving vessels. Their seizure left some pirate groups facing both a practical and moral dilemma.[56]

Some pirates showed deep concern to provide for wives and children. According to Richard Lane, during the early 1580s captain Philip Boyt, who was condemned for piracy, 'at his going to execucion wylled ... [him] to tell his wife that such goods as were saved of this voyage, they shold be parted betwixt her and his sonne'.[57] Occasionally the distribution of gifts

[53] TNA, HCA 1/38, ff. 30–44v (for Hooper); HCA 1/40, f. 50 (for Phipson). For other gifts see HCA 1/45. f. 5.

[54] TNA, HCA 1/41, ff. 78–81 (for Fielde); ff. 189–91 (for Kinge).

[55] TNA, SP 12/150/95 (for Piers); HCA 1/48, ff. 104–4v (for Barry).

[56] See below, pp. 180–8. On the Barbary corsairs see J. B. Wolf, *The Barbary Coast: Algiers Under the Turks 1500 to 1830* (New York, 1979), pp. 184–8; and R. C. Davis, *Christian Slaves, Muslim Masters: White Slavery in the Mediterranean, the Barbary Coast and Italy, 1500–1800* (Basingstoke, 2003), pp. 27–65.

[57] TNA, SP 12/123/37.

was more widely scattered. In 1584, following his return from a piratical voyage to the coast of Spain, William Fenner presented a gift of sugar to his uncle's wife, while various pieces of white cloth were bestowed among the maids of the house. Part of the cloth was also given to John Sawyer's spouse of Chichester and others.[58] Sawyer served as a corporal with Fenner, and may have lost his life during the voyage. In another example of the pirate gift, which was possibly widely used, in 1586 Edward Roche, one of Callice's company, sent eight packs of linen cloth to his betrothed on the Isle of Wight; one week later they were married.[59]

Even when pirates were unable to return ashore, they managed to send gifts and tokens to their partners, using customary seafaring networks. In June 1608 Thomas Mitten, a sailor from Southampton, who was one of the company of John Ward, a prominent pirate who operated in the Mediterranean, informed the High Court of Admiralty that 'hee sente tenne poundes into Engelande by one Fletcher, one of the *Husband's* companie, to bee delivered to [his] wiefe'.[60] Ward and one of his officers also sent gold coins to their wives by John Pountis, the master of the ship. When the *Husband* reached England, however, the coins were confiscated by Sir Richard Hawkins, the vice admiral of Devon. According to the author of *Newes from Sea*, an account of Ward's career published in 1609, the pirate enriched his wife and friends by sending gifts to them. In the case of his wife, however, little of this seems to have arrived, for she reportedly remained in very poor circumstances. Ward had recently given booty worth £100 to the master of a merchant vessel, which was intended for his spouse. Others of his company had done the same. Unfortunately the master neglected his errand. During a subsequent encounter with the pirates he was roughly handled, ducked at the yard arm and killed.[61]

The case of Ward suggests that when pirates abandoned wives in England, they retained some sense of responsibility or obligation towards them. In some cases the desertion of spouses and families, where it was not deliberate, was the result of the irregular life cycles of men who were at sea, in hiding or on the run. Pressing personal circumstances drove some men into disjointed and disorderly lives. The gunner of a pirate ship, active during the early 1580s, was reported to be an occasional resident of Rother-

---

[58] TNA, SP 12/177/46.
[59] TNA, HCA 13/26, ff. 51–1v and 122 for a gift to the wife of Carew Raleigh.
[60] TNA, HCA 13/39, ff. 225–7. The dispatch of gifts to spouses by mariners at sea may have been customary; see for example TNA, HCA 13/41, ff. 45v–6.
[61] TNA, HCA 13/39, ff. 64–7, 227v, 229; *Newes from Sea* (London, 1609), reprinted in Baer (ed.), *British Piracy*, I, pp. 21–2.

hithe, where he had three children maintained by the parish.[62] Nicholas
Gower, one of a group of rovers taken by a royal vessel in 1584, temporarily
deserted his wife in a bid to repair his financial estate. According to a family
servant, after his marriage to the daughter of a landowner of Surrey, he
'consumed greate wealthe which he had with his wiffe'.[63] When he went to
sea with his son, sailing for a time under the dubious authority of a foreign
commission, his wife returned to her father's house. Until his ship was sunk
off Gore End, he maintained correspondence with his spouse, occasionally
returning with gifts of plunder, including on one occasion a barrel of fish
and a bag, which his son described as being full of stuff. More commonly,
perhaps, men ran away from home to evade arrest. Benjamin Bolden, the
leader of a gang of pirates who seized a vessel on the Thames in 1643,
allegedly laden with money and provisions for the king, fled to Dunkirk
after officials began to investigate the case. He managed to inform his wife,
Sara, before leaving. Later in the year he sent her a parcel of gifts and
tokens. Although he returned home to Ratcliffe in December, as officers for
the High Court of Admiralty were seeking him, the visit was brief.[64]

Irregular relationships between pirates and female partners accompanied
the spread of organized piracy across the Irish Sea during the early seventeenth century. One prominent pirate, Tibault Saxbridge, who was killed
during an attack on a French vessel at Newfoundland in 1609, left a widow
and two daughters who ran an alehouse near Dublin. In some parts of
Ireland, women formed part of a small colonial sub-culture which developed within a disorderly, lawless environment. Under the protection of local
officials, a growing number of pirates used the harbours of the south west
as safe bases, to take in provisions and dispose of plunder. The expansion
of piracy into the Atlantic led to the formation of varied relations between
native inhabitants, English settlers and visiting pirates. As in regions previously frequented by pirates in England and Wales, women were involved
in these contacts as dealers, as the recipients of gifts or as the providers of
sexual services. In 1610, for example, John Bedlake, one of the company of
captain William Baugh, sent a gift of striped canvas and starch to the wife
of John Worth of Donderry in county Cork. Baugh, who was negotiating
his surrender to the crown, also presented a gift of plate to the wife of
Henry Skipwith, the keeper of Kinsale castle.[65]

In many parts of Munster these contacts were maintained with the

---

[62] TNA, HCA 1/41, f. 115v.

[63] Ibid., 1/42, ff. 43v–5.

[64] TNA, HCA 1/50, ff. 133–7; HCA 13/39, ff. 64–7.

[65] Lambeth Palace Library, Carew MS 619, f. 119 (for Bedlake); Senior, *A Nation of Pirates*, pp. 64–8.

connivance of local officials who were implicated in receiving pirate booty. In October 1618 Sir William Hull, the deputy vice admiral of the province who was widely suspected of dealing with pirates, reported the arrival at Leamcon of captain Ellis and his company, with beaver skins plundered from a French vessel. According to Hull's report the pirates were entertained in a house at Schull, drinking all night, without fear of arrest. He admitted that at least one of the pirates' wives dwelt on his land. Hull appeared to make no effort to stop the night-time revelry, but the pirates departed following the arrival of a naval vessel under the command of Sir Thomas Button. Three weeks later Hull reported that the pirate's wife had also escaped, possibly accompanying her spouse aboard Ellis' vessel.[66]

The support for piracy in south-west Ireland aroused serious concern, especially as it was seen to be part of a wider problem of crime and disorder that stood in the way of metropolitan ambitions for reform through the spread of English civility. The scale of piratical activity in Ireland threatened to subvert these pretensions. Among some leaders of the colonial community, single women or those living alone were targeted as scapegoats for the frequency with which pirates haunted the coast. According to one report, most of the victuallers of pirate vessels in Baltimore were women who were either friends or wives of the pirates. During 1610, as the Council of Munster struggled to deal with the growing number of pirates visiting the south west, it singled out for particular condemnation 'such shameless and adulterous women, as daylie repaired unto them, and especially by the meanes of divers Taverns, Alehouses, and victualling houses' where they were entertained.[67] According to a published report of the trial of nineteen pirates in 1609, at least one Irish woman went to sea with her pirate consort, captain Jennings, but with disturbing consequences for the rest of his company.[68] The council tried to deal with the problem by suppressing all superfluous taverns, except for those used by fishermen and travellers. Furthermore the owners of such establishments were to provide security that they would neither receive nor relieve pirates and their consorts.

[66] Chatsworth House, Lismore Papers, 9, no. 115.

[67] BL, Cotton MS, Otho E VIII, f. 368. Complaints against uncontrolled drinking establishments attracting 'all sorts of rebellious, idle, and disorderly vagrants' continued; *CSPI, 1647–60 & Addenda*, pp. 169–70. Mainwaring's comments suggest that prostitution was a commercialized business which some may have viewed as a profession. For different conditions during the medieval period see P. J. P. Goldberg, *Women, Work, and Life Cycle in a Medieval Economy: Women in York and Yorkshire, c.1300–1520* (Oxford, 1992), pp. 149–56.

[68] *The Lives, Apprehensions Arraignments, and Executions of the 19 Late Pyrates* (London, [1609]), reprinted in Baer (ed.), *British Piracy*, II, p. 25. See below pp. 195–6.

It was but a short step from this view to link the problem of piracy with prostitution. Although the association deserves detailed examination, pirates and prostitutes were linked in relationships which operated within the broader context of seafaring culture and community. John Broke, a mariner of St Katharine's parish in London, who was one of the company of a disorderly, piratical man-of-war, was forced to leave the ship at Portsmouth, in 1538, to get 'helpe of surgery, because ... [he] was hurte with a woman, before his goyng from London'.[69] The transient, irregular life cycles of many seafarers may have created both need and opportunity for the use of prostitutes. Their careers, to some extent, were mirrored by those of women who engaged in prostitution as a temporary or occasional activity. In the case of pirates, sudden wealth provided the means for heavy drinking and the purchase of sex. In these circumstances, sexuality and exchange may have reinforced the reputation of prostitutes as the receivers of stolen goods. As such, it hardened perceptions of them as unruly women who threatened social and cultural values.[70]

Prostitution was not yet fully criminalized. Unofficial brothels continued to exist in urban centres, though changing attitudes exposed prostitutes to moral disapproval and prosecution. Their resort to unlicensed and irregular alehouses, often run by single women, which were frequented by pirates, reinforced the link with petty criminality and disorder. The situation in Cardiff, a favourite haunt of pirates during the 1570s and 1580s, suggests an interesting pattern of activity which spread across the Irish Sea in the early seventeenth century. In 1583 Elenor Williams, a widow, was prosecuted for being a bawd. The following year, when eleven strangers were tried for piracy, two women, including another widow, were tried for running bawdy houses.[71]

The relationship between piracy and prostitution was acknowledged by Sir Henry Mainwaring, a former pirate captain who was pardoned by James I. In his 'Discourse on Piracy', Mainwaring claimed that pirates visited

---

[69] TNA, HCA 1/33, ff. 61–1v, 69.

[70] R. M. Karras, *Common Women: Prostitution and Sexuality in Medieval England* (Oxford, 1996), pp. 35–6, 50–4, 100, 130, 137–41; Goldberg, *Women, Work, and Life Cycle*, pp. 150–6; Mendelson and Crawford, *Women*, pp. 292–5; O. Hufton, *The Prospect Before Her: A History of Women in Western Europe. Volume I, 1500–1800* (London, 1995), pp. 247–9. And on changing attitudes in a wider perspective see J. Rossiaud, *Medieval Prostitution*, translated by L. G. Cochrane (Oxford, 1988), pp. 128–59.

[71] J. H. Matthews (ed.), *Cardiff Records*, 6 vols (Cardiff, 1898–1911), II, pp. 158–9; Laurence, *Women in England*, pp. 72–3. On prostitution and crime in London see Griffiths, *Lost Londons*, pp. 72–3, 153–4. And on alehouses see Peters, *Women in Early Modern England*, pp. 59, 79–80.

Munster because of the 'good store of English, Scottish and Irish wenches which resort unto them, and these are strong attractors to draw the common sort of them thither'.[72] When the naval captain William Monson entered Broadhaven along the west coast, pretending to be Mainwaring, the local lord 'spared not his own daughters to bid them welcome'.[73] Further north, in 1627 captain Claes Campaine, one of the most successful Dutch pirates operating during the 1620s, who reputedly captured more than 130 vessels, arrived at Killybegs, where his men 'glutted themselves with drinkeing and whoering'.[74] According to the report of Sir Basil Brooke, the Dutch pirates possessed plenty of Spanish silver and ducats. Brooke complained of their dissolute behaviour, but added that, 'by reason of the numbers of his men on shoare drinckinge with all Comers … it was a most easye matter for twenty good men to have Cutt all their throats that weare then on board, and to have possest the shipp'.[75] The opportunity was lost, apparently because of the connivance of the high constable, James Hamilton, and the minister, his brother, William.

In some cases reports of prostitutes in Ireland providing services for pirates were from the hostile perspective of outsiders, who may have misunderstood or misinterpreted the insecure and intermittent relationships which existed more generally within many maritime communities. Contact between pirates and female partners led to fleeting and short-lived unions which were characteristic of seafaring culture. Baptist Ingle, a young man of nineteen, who originally came from King's Lynn in Norfolk, arrived at Whiddy Island in 1612 aboard a pirate ship, and 'often went ashore to make merry with a young woman that lay at Ballygubbin'.[76] The pirates had returned on the promise of a pardon, but before it was finalized, Ingle, who was talking about marrying a local woman, had fled ashore with £100 stolen

---

[72] G. E. Manwaring and W. E. Perrin (eds), *The Life and Works of Sir Henry Mainwaring*, 2 vols (Navy Records Society, 54 & 56, 1920–2), II, pp. 39–40; J. C. Appleby, 'Women and Piracy in Ireland: From Grainne O'Malley to Anne Bonny', in M. MacCurtain and M. O'Dowd (eds), *Women in Early Modern Ireland* (Edinburgh, 1991), pp. 59–61, reprinted in C. R. Pennell (ed.), *Bandits at Sea: A Pirates Reader* (New York, 2001).
[73] M. Oppenheim (ed.), *The Naval Tracts of Sir William Monson*, 4 vols (Navy Records Society, 22–23, 43, 45 & 47, 1902–14), III, pp. 58–69. Some of these comments should be seen against an English perspective which identified Irish women as lewd; see Wiesner-Hanks, *Women and Gender*, p. 288.
[74] BL, Harleian MS 390, f. 101v; TNA, SP 63/244/659 and 678; J. C. Appleby (ed.), *A Calendar of Material Relating to Ireland from the High Court of Admiralty Examinations 1536–1641* (Dublin, 1992), pp. 154–6.
[75] TNA, SP 63/244/659 and 678.
[76] Appleby (ed.), *Calendar*, pp. 130, 132. On marital arrangements see also J. R. Gillis, *For Better, for Worse: British Marriages, 1600 to the Present* (Oxford, 1985), pp. 210, 234.

from the company's chests. He was arrested and briefly imprisoned in Cork, but freed by captain Skipwith.

Some women may have been able to benefit financially from their encounters with pirates; however they were also potential victims of dissolute, unruly men, whose lifestyles provided opportunities for bigamous or parallel relationships. John Waters, a pirate who served with captain Haggerston during 1617 and 1618, was reported to lodge at an alehouse in the East End of London known as the 'Checquer, & his whore called Alice useth to lye there, & his owne wife dwelleth in the Minories'.[77] Of greater notoriety, John Ward may have sent booty to his wife in London, but this did not prevent him from remarrying and settling down in his Mediterranean base at Tunis.

If women provided comfort and sustenance for pirates, they were also prepared to assist partners or kinsmen in more practical and direct ways, at risk to themselves and their reputations. From this perspective female agency was manifest in the way in which women helped pirates to evade arrest or escape from gaol, and in their willingness to conceal pirate booty. Diverse cases from the later sixteenth and early seventeenth centuries illuminate the nature of this support, ranging from ambivalent, possibly unintentional aid to defiant, occasionally provocative assistance.

Pirates used family connections and friendships to store chests of personal possessions and plunder with trustworthy and careful women. In September 1565 Rose Brexton of Winchester unwillingly admitted before the High Court of Admiralty that she had stored a chest of wares in a loft for a young man, whom she claimed not to know, while her husband, a butcher, was away. One of her maid servants identified the man as John Cooke. She also informed a tapster and his wife about the chest, reporting that it contained pewter, basins, pots and other goods. Acting on the servant's gossip, the bailiff searched Brexton's dwelling and seized the hidden chest. When the case was heard by the admiralty court, it became clear that the chest belonged to Edward Cooke, a pirate of Southampton; it had been carried to Brexton's house by his brother John, under cover of night. During the course of her examination Rose Brexton was compelled to admit that she knew Edward Cooke very well. Moreover they had met about three months before the arrival of the chest, when Brexton expressed relief that he was out of trouble. The court did not explore the relationship between Brexton and the pirate. However she refused to compromise her husband with his booty, claiming that he was unaware of the chest in the loft, until it was taken by the bailiff.[78]

[77] TNA, HCA 1/48, ff. 221v–3, 225v–6.
[78] TNA, HCA 1/38, ff. 46–53, 80–8.

Trust and mutuality also enabled pirates to lodge ashore despite the dangers of detection or arrest. In May 1577 the deputies for the Commissioners for Piracy in Weymouth reported the arrival of a pirate ship with three prizes. The pirates regularly came ashore at Lulworth, with little fear of being apprehended, and 'were lodged and supported in dyvers howses'.[79] Among those who were reported for being their chief lodgers was Mistress Rowes. Within the East End parishes of London, women – many of whom were widowed or married to mariners – played a specialized role in providing lodging and accommodation for seafarers, which imperceptibly merged with harbouring pirates and receiving stolen booty.

Other women, especially wives or close family relations, were more daring in their support for pirates. During the later 1570s the piracy commissioners in Suffolk were informed of the arrest of the pirate Peter Lambert of Aldeburgh, and of his subsequent escape from prison using a file smuggled in by his wife, Margery, and a neighbour, Alice Bevershawe.[80] Such was the condition of prisons that women, in particular, were able to convey tools and clothing to prisoners, with little fear of detection. With the assistance of a female accomplice, during the 1590s Adam Warner, who was committed on suspicion of piracy, escaped from the Marshalsea prison in London, disguised as a woman. According to an account of the escape, which came into the hands of Lord Burghley, Elizabeth's chief minister, Warner was regularly visited by a woman, allegedly of lewd life.[81] As 'notable theves never lacke such instrumentes', the woman bribed the prison porter, with a pair of new stockings, to loosen the iron shackles around the legs of the prisoner.[82] But they were left so loose that 'he might at pleasure putt them over his heade & soe did & left them in the hall & escaped' with his accomplice, who 'brought womens apparel & conveyed him out by that meanes'.[83] In October 1599 Edey Haggarde, described as a spinster aged twenty-eight, was examined by the High Court of Admiralty about Warner's escape. Although she denied knowing how he got out of gaol, she admitted to visiting him several times in the Marshalsea. A similar escape from prison was made by Peter Philip, who was also committed for piracy; teasingly, he left his irons in the porter's lodge before getting away.[84]

---

[79] TNA, SP 12/113/9 and 24.
[80] TNA, SP 12/135/75.
[81] BL, Lansdowne MS 142, f. 101.
[82] Ibid.; TNA, HCA 1/45, ff. 100v–1.
[83] BL, Lansdowne MS 142, f. 101.
[84] TNA, HCA 1/45, ff. 100v–3 (for Haggarde). There were risks: in 1588 Margaret Ward was executed for helping a priest to escape from prison, by providing him with a rope; P. Crawford, *Women and Religion in England 1500–1720* (London, 1993), p. 62.

Some women were willing to go to great lengths to shield suspected pirates from arrest, sometimes with the connivance of local officials or the passive support of the community. Such action may have grown out of the customary responsibility of women to take care of sons, enabling them to act as a gatekeeper of the household. When family loyalties were involved, moreover, it could involve disruptive and provocative behaviour which spilled over into aggression and violence.[85]

A particularly protracted case from the early seventeenth century exposed the limitations of legal authorities when faced with local hostility and obduracy. It concerned the efforts of John Pecksall, an officer of the High Court of Admiralty, to arrest Edward Edmondes for piracy during 1604. In July, Pecksall travelled to Henbury in Gloucestershire, where Edmondes reputedly lived, with a warrant for his arrest from the court. He also carried letters of assistance from the Privy Council, requiring the support of local officials. When Pecksall arrived at Henbury, he was informed that the nearest constable lived two miles away and that the bailiff was sick. He acquired the assistance of Large, the steward of the manor, who seems to have been an enemy of Edmondes. Large agreed to help in the arrest of the latter, on the following day, while he was attending church; until then, he advised Pecksall not to go abroad. On Sunday, as the court officer related, 'Edmondes came not to churche eyther in the forenoone or afternoon, but in the evening ... [he] espied the said Edmondes come out of his mothers house & goe into an alehouse with two others that were in his companye'.[86] They were followed by Pecksall and the steward, who had apparently got the assistance of another local man, the tithing officer. After a confused struggle, during which the latter refused to help, Edmondes escaped to the house of his mother.

The following morning, accompanied by the high constable, Pecksall went to search the house for his quarry. Edmondes' mother claimed that her son had left for King's Weston the previous night. She advised Pecksall to stay while she sent for him, insisting that he would provide bond for his appearance in London, 'for that she would not have him pursued aboute the Cuntrey'.[87] But Edmondes could not be found. Frustrated by these delays, Pecksall unsuccessfully attempted to arrest the tithing-man, on the grounds

[85] Wiesner-Hanks, *Women and Gender*, pp. 282–4; Walker, *Crime, Gender and Social Order*, pp. 80, 95, for women protecting the household.

[86] TNA, HCA 13/37, ff. 95v–7. Matriarchal support for wayward sons may have been widespread. The official legal response varied: in 1631 the Attorney-General was prepared to pardon a mother who harboured her sons, because 'one should "favour a mother in such a case"'; Mendelson and Crawford, *Women*, p. 44.

[87] TNA, HCA 13/37, ff. 95v–7.

that he had allowed the suspected pirate to escape. When Pecksall was informed that the local man was hay-making in a meadow, two miles away, he warned his wife of the danger her husband was courting. Boldly 'she answered that her husband could not feare the matter, for that mistris Edmondes would save him harmless, & not see him dampnified'.[88] A subsequent attempt to arrest the tithing-man at day-break, while he was still in bed, proved fruitless. Like the main suspect, he seemed to have disappeared; as a result, Pecksall left with his mission unaccomplished.[89]

Later in the year Pecksall travelled to King's Weston in search of Edmondes. He was accompanied by Pierre Gohary, a Frenchman who was acting on behalf of the victims of the pirates. On this occasion when Pecksall went to Edmondes' house he was supported by the tithing-man, six or seven of his neighbours, a farmer and another group of men. The party was informed by Edmondes' wife, who 'answered out of a Windowe, that he was not at home'; furthermore, she refused to let any of the group in to search the house.[90] Calling upon three or four other men, the party surrounded the house for more than one hour until she opened the door, and allowed the tithing-man and three others in to undertake a search. Pointedly, she refused access to Pecksall, warning him 'to looke to himselfe'.[91] The search was fruitless. Nonetheless the admiralty officer insisted on his right to investigate. After several hours of further delay, during which Edmondes' brother emerged from the house to warn off the local official, Gohary broke open a door, allowing several of the party to enter. Pecksall was prevented from following by Edmondes' wife, who 'stood at the doore with a pott of water in her hand sayenge he should not come in'.[92] His angry request that she be placed in the stocks, so that he could search the house unhindered, was ignored by the local men. However their investigation was perfunctory at best. The Frenchman later complained that they all remained in one room, making no attempt to find the suspect.[93]

Gohary persisted, offering ten shillings to John Leonard, a local man, to help him search the house. They found Edmondes hiding in the loft. When Gohary went to call for support from the rest of the party, he 'found the stayres doore shut & Edmondes' wife and her sister, the one with a rapier & the other with a dagger cumminge upp upon him, & the said

[88] Ibid.
[89] Ibid.
[90] Ibid., ff. 121–2v.
[91] Ibid.
[92] Ibid.
[93] Ibid.

Edmundes came downe with a rapier'.[94] In fear for his life, he fled down-stairs with the help of Leonard. At no stage during this commotion did the rest of the party go to the Frenchman's assistance. Indeed they had left the house, effectively abandoning any attempt to take Edmondes. Complaining of their partial behaviour, Pecksall left some of the local men to guard the building. They failed to stop two servants of Edmondes' mother, one of whom was reportedly another member of the pirate company, from carrying more weapons into the house. When Pecksall returned with Gohary, they were informed that they would need to hire 'sixe tall fellowes to enter the house & fetch Edmondes out, otherwise no man would venture' to follow.[95]

With evening approaching, Pecksall and Gohary were compelled to seek lodging in Bristol, leaving strict instructions with the local officer to keep watch over Edmondes. The following morning, after complaining to a local magistrate, they returned to King's Weston to find that Edmondes had escaped. According to the report of a local man, 'his mother had byn there in the evening & had willed her sonne & his wife to heate scalding water & cast [it] upon them & heate spits hot & to run at them therewith'.[96] Soon after this display of aggression Edmondes was rescued by a small party of four horsemen.

This was an unusually detailed report of an unsuccessful attempt to arrest a suspected pirate. It revealed widespread collusion and disobedience among the local community, many of whom may have participated as spectators and onlookers, which thwarted the efforts of the admiralty court in London to take action against one of its members. The response may not have been uncommon, especially when outside agencies were trying to deal with a contested criminal activity such as piracy. Yet the most striking feature of the case was the leading role played by women in protecting Edmondes. His mother and wife put up a resolute and determined defence, ultimately enabling him to escape.

Legal and political authorities struggled to deal with such resistance or collusion. Indeed, the inability of the state to prevent the spread of piracy provoked draconian proposals for dealing with the problem. Faced with an almost overwhelming situation in parts of Ireland, in 1609 the Lord Admiral, the Earl of Nottingham, proposed that the shore-based supporters of piracy should face the death penalty.[97] Little came of the suggestion, possibly because of its far-reaching social implications. More-

[94] Ibid., ff. 125v–7v.
[95] Ibid.
[96] Edmondes was later captured but pardoned; TNA, HCA 1/5, ff. 44, 212.
[97] TNA, SP 14/48/103.

over the rapid decline of organized piracy around the British Isles after 1615 reduced the need for such drastic action.

Nonetheless the persistence of robbery and piracy along the Thames, which remained a serious, if occasional and opportunistic criminal enterprise, continued to be widely supported. Even as witnesses or accessories women were involved in a web of illegal activity, part of a broader disorderly way of life, which was sustained by alehouses and other irregular drinking establishments. It was common practice for small gangs of river pirates to assemble at such locations, awaiting the fall of darkness, when they were able to operate more freely. In November 1588 John Talbot, a young sailor of St Katherine's, admitted to the High Court of Admiralty that with a group of mariners he was drinking in the house of Joan Longe, at Greenwich, until about ten o'clock at night. Thereafter they used a rowing boat to board and rob a small vessel of clothing and other goods.[98]

In a more ambivalent case heard by the court the previous year, Kathryn Wechell, a widow aged thirty, of Lambeth, appeared as a witness and potential accessory in proceedings against Henry Primer, who was involved in the robbery of a vessel of Faversham. Wechell worked at the Golden Hind in Lambeth, where she served beer and ale.[99] Primer, whom she described as a gentleman, stayed as a guest for one month, which ended with a visit from a constable. Apparently Wechell informed the constable of his presence among the guests. Although she admitted to the court that she warned Primer of the constable's visit, she denied urging him to leave. Nonetheless, immediately after his departure, Primer fled, with the assistance of Wechell who instructed a 'little wenche of the house to open the [back] gate & to lette him goe'.[100] During his absence she took some cloth from under the bedstead in his room. Later that night, about eleven o'clock, Primer returned with four others, but he left before the arrival of the constable the following day.

Family and friends provided river pirates with sanctuary against the threat of detection and arrest. According to a report of Henry Sherman, during 1618 and 1619 captain Haggerston and other members of his company, who were wanted on suspicion of piracy, had scattered to the safety of the homes of their mothers. Haggerston was in hiding at Tilbury; Richard Catro and two others were reported to be with his mother at Birchington; and John Smith was at his mother's home at Hadley, near Ipswich. About the same time, Joan Parks was ordered to appear before the admiralty court for 'abet-

---

[98] TNA, HCA 1/42, ff. 160–0v and ff. 170–1, 173v–4, for other examples of the use of alehouses.

[99] Ibid., f. 134.

[100] Ibid., f. 135.

tinge Simon Willamett one of the pirates & makeinge sale of a cloake for him'.[101] Catherine Sheppard, alias Sutton, was also accused of harbouring Catro and one of his associates, as well as receiving a piece of cloth from them. The petty thieves and pirates, who lived off the river, with the support of women, and through informal networks of ale- and lodging houses, seemed to be part of a nascent criminal underclass which was beyond the reach of effective supervision and regulation. In 1620 the judges at the assizes held in Chelmsford were informed that many alehouses had been suppressed by the magistracy, but they reappeared with licences as inns, and continued to harbour thieves and pirates.[102]

The underlying ambiguity of women's participation in piracy is encapsulated by a case heard by the High Court of Admiralty in 1643. It involved a gang of five or six men, opportunistically seeking to exploit the unusual conditions of the civil war. Assembling at the sign of the Parrot in Greenwich during November 1642, two of the group tried to recruit a young apprentice, William Bell, asking 'whether hee woulde adventure his fleshe with them to get purchase, for now there was noe law'.[103] Although each member of the gang was in possession of a sword, they only had one pistol between them. Giving money to Bell, to purchase shot for them, he seized the opportunity to run off. Undeterred the gang proceeded down the Thames in a rowing boat until they reached Shell Haven. According to a local husbandman, Benjamin Sticklorum, who denied accompanying the gang on the river, they stayed three or four nights. Despite the time of year, 'they had noe other lodging but Cribbs of straw'.[104]

During their stay, at night time, they boarded a small vessel, the *Seaflower* of Colchester, and carried off various amounts of pepper, cloth and other goods, as well as forty-six or forty-eight shillings. Benjamin Bolden, the leader of the gang, with the assistance of an alehouse-keeper, described as a Fleming, who provided a cart and two horses, carried the stolen goods to a barn in an isolated marsh, claiming that 'he would soe hide them that the divell should not finde them'.[105] A parcel of the booty was also left with the wife of Sticklorum, Joan. She admitted to the court that members of the gang left a sack of goods in her possession, with instructions to 'lay them up for them'.[106] The goods included six or seven pieces of linen, one piece

---

[101] TNA, HCA 1/7, f. 2.
[102] J. S. Cockburn (ed.), *Calendar of Assize Records: Essex Indictments, James I* (London, 1982), p. 241.
[103] TNA, HCA 1/50, f. 115v.
[104] Ibid., f. 131.
[105] Ibid., f. 134.
[106] Ibid., f. 131v.

of say cloth, two women's coats, a horseman's coat and a pillowbear. The thieves, whom she denied any previous knowledge of, said they would return within three or four days, but they failed to appear. After informing her husband, and possibly alarmed at the inquiry of a local official, she carried the goods to the alehouse. Meanwhile two members of the gang recovered the booty from the barn. Returning to London, they sold some of the goods at Grays to a female shopkeeper.[107]

One of the last witnesses to appear before the court in this case was Sara Bolden. She deposed that about three months earlier her husband, a mariner, departed for Dunkirk. A fortnight before her appearance, 'hee sent her by a strange woman, which shee never saw before, for a token, ten shillings in money, a peece of green say, a little bundle of lockram & some pepper, about halfe a pecke in a pillowbear'.[108] Bolden returned home shortly after, with a bundle containing an old shirt and a sheet, but within a week he left, apparently bound for the sea.

*

Despite a gender distinction which characterized piracy as a male crime, during the sixteenth and early seventeenth centuries many women played an active part in its maintenance. In effect female agency formed part of the hidden undergrowth of organized criminality and disorder at sea. At times it was of particular utility, especially as women were able to operate in a discrete manner without attracting too much suspicion. Their role underlines the wider social dimension to the prevalence of piracy during these years, and the interdependency between land and sea, as well as between genders, which was essential to its growth. The ramifications of these links repeatedly undermined efforts of the regime to deal with it.

The discrete role of women, as partners, receivers and accessories, illuminates the profound ambiguity of piracy during the period. The inability of the state to maintain a clear distinction between legal and illegal forms of plunder at sea, which was confused with popular social attitudes, enabled piratical enterprise, or sea-roving in the eyes of its defenders, to flourish as a commercialized enterprise with widespread community support. Under these conditions it was difficult to represent pirates as a fraternity of dangerous criminals or outlaws. All too often they were husbands, brothers, sons, relatives or lovers, whose lifestyles were supported by female associates operating in various guises. While the motives for these relationships varied, their inadvertent consequence was the partial empowerment of women, such as Margaret Dyvers, Anne Piers

[107] Ibid., f. 134v.
[108] Ibid., ff. 136v–7.

or Margery Lambert. Operating in an entrepreneurial or resourceful way, they shared in the illicit returns from piracy, benefiting from the acquisition of a range of commodities, which in some regions were in short supply or unobtainable.

No typical profile emerges for the female partners of piracy from the evidence assembled in this chapter, though many shared a link with the sea through husbands, sons, other relatives and friends. A significant number were widowed or single, and living under modest or poor conditions. Perhaps the most revealing aspect of their role was its varied and opportunistic nature. Acting in association with other family members and neighbours, or alone, the behaviour of women helped to validate piracy as a commercial or semi-legitimate business, reinforcing wider perceptions regarding its uncertain and contested criminal status. Yet piracy was a dangerous and violent crime. For women especially, the potential rewards or benefits of dealing with pirates had to be set against a range of risks. It is a measure of the character of English piracy during this period that few women appear as the victims of pirate violence. In one shocking incident, John Piers, whose relationship with his mother introduced this chapter, raped the daughter of an inhabitant of the Isle of Wight in 1581.[109] But this seems to have been an unusual case; moreover, Piers had acquired a reputation at sea as a callous murderer. As the character and structure of piracy began to change during the seventeenth century, however, so the dangers to women also began to increase.

---

[109] BL, Lansdowne MS 33, f. 183v.

– 3 –

Wives, Partners and Prostitutes
Women and Long-Distance Piracy
from the 1640s to the 1720s

The development of English plunder during the seventeenth and early eighteenth centuries, culminating in a so-called 'golden age of piracy', had far-reaching and contradictory consequences for women. Published works from the period described the emergence of groups of professionalized, hard-bitten career pirates, the product of an aggressive and alienated outlaw culture, which exposed women to unrestrained predatory behaviour that seemed to flout customary and moral obligations. The anonymous author of *The Grand Pyrate* of 1676 reported that captain George Cusack, 'the great Sea-robber', was captured in bed with a woman, 'who was brought along with him, forthwith to the *Old-Baily*'.[1] The story was enlivened by the claim that the woman was Cusack's sister. Alexander Exquemelin's *The Buccaneers of America*, which first appeared in a Dutch edition of 1678, provided a vivid and entertaining collection of anecdotes concerning the debauchery of the rovers who haunted Jamaica. It included an unusual case, which Exquemelin claimed to have witnessed, of a pirate who gave a 'common strumpet five hundred pieces-of-eight only that he might see her naked'.[2] Furthermore, one of his masters disposed of 3,000 pieces of eight during a brief bout of drinking and womanizing which left him in so much debt that he was sold into servitude. Such behaviour appeared to plumb new depths in the account of the career of Edward Teach by captain Charles Johnson. In his popular and influential *History of the Pyrates*, Johnson claimed that Teach married fourteen wives, the last of whom, a young woman of sixteen, was forced 'to prostitute herself' to his companions, 'one after another, before his Face'.[3]

[1] *The Grand Pyrate: Or, the Life and Death of Capt. George Cusack the Great Sea-Robber* (London, 1676), reprinted in Baer (ed.), *British Piracy*, II, p. 96.
[2] J. Esquemeling, *The Buccaneers of America*, ed. W. S. Stallybrass (London, 1924), p. 75. Such stories were based on the circulation of gossip, the social function of which, within a colonial context, is examined by M. B. Norton, *Founding Mothers and Fathers: Gendered Power and the Forming of American Society* (New York, 1996), pp. 253–61.
[3] Johnson, *General History of the Pyrates*, p. 76.

These stories, which their authors insisted were based on unimpeachable evidence, including eye-witness testimony, were intended to provoke and entertain readers. They confused fact with fiction, retailing gossip and rumour, while imaginatively re-creating pirate lives as part of a growing discourse on crime and society. Contrary to the author of *The Grand Pyrate*, for example, evidence from the High Court of Admiralty indicates that Cusack was taken on a Sunday morning in August 1674 aboard his ship, after a visit to a tavern along the coast of Essex.[4] While it is revealing that women were used in such cultural representations of piracy, to reinforce the immoral profligacy of the actors, the deeper ideological purpose of published works, as exemplified by Johnson, was to portray pirates as the 'enemies of all mankind', as men who stood outside of society, preying on the commercial arteries of an expanding imperial state and economy.[5] The threat to commerce was fundamental to the creation of the image of the pirate desperado as a 'terror to the trading part of the world'.[6] But it was reinforced by the portrayal of an 'abominable Society' of predators or hell-hounds, which challenged the self-image and pretensions of civil and commercial society.[7] In particular, the reported behaviour of pirates towards women, at a time when female roles, responsibilities and rights were under widespread discussion, threw into relief middle-class ideals of companionate, romantic partnerships.[8] Accounts of pirate debauchery and violence, while serving to shock and titillate, also suggested a pattern of extreme conduct that was unforgiving, unrepentant and beyond the bounds of civility.

While acknowledging the violence and terror that pirates were capable of inflicting on their victims of either sex, the growth of long-distance piracy during this period had a more mixed impact on female agency and intervention. Partly as a result of the confusion between piracy, buccaneering and privateering, women's lives intersected with those of sea rovers in varied ways. The transfer of English depredation across the Atlantic and beyond served to narrow the economic opportunity for women to participate in piracy as a business, while widening the settings and sites for social interactions. The maintenance of complementary gender relationships,

---

[4] TNA, HCA 13/142, ff. 143–62.

[5] Johnson, *General History of the Pyrates*, p. 26.

[6] Ibid., pp. 26–7.

[7] Ibid., p. 114.

[8] K. O'Brien, *Women and Enlightenment in Eighteenth-Century Britain* (Cambridge, 2009), pp. 35–67. See also the contributions in S. Knott and B. Taylor (eds), *Women, Gender and Enlightenment* (Basingstoke, 2005), especially pp. 357–88 (essays by R. Perry and S. Stuurman).

which characterized piratical activity around the British Isles during the sixteenth century, was difficult to sustain in such diverse and scattered locations. The movement of pirate groups within the Caribbean, along the coasts of North and South America, to West Africa and into the Indian Ocean and the Red Sea, weakened bonds of affection and obligation between pirates and their spouses and families. Under these conditions there was an apparent decline in the number of pirates who were married, which was linked with an emerging preference for single recruits. At the same time the role of wives as receivers or partners began to change, partly as a result of the lack of opportunity. Women who were at times effectively abandoned by migratory pirate spouses were compelled to resort to other expedients and strategies to survive.

The narrowing of female agency was an inescapable consequence of the structure and organization of long-distance piracy, and a re-fashioned but increasingly fragmented pirate culture. It was expressed in the lives and life cycles of a growing number of pirates who developed their own social codes, customs and regulations. While drawing on a longstanding pirate tradition, it was shaped by the communitarian and egalitarian instincts of seafaring life that were influenced by deeper changes to the merchant marine. Pirate culture was varied, short-lived and in a state of almost permanent flux. In form it was essentially ephemeral, lacking deep roots or structure. Its chief characteristic, as reflected in the increasing importance of the pirate ship and company, had wide-ranging consequences. As a result of the nature of pirate voyaging and enterprise, the ship acquired the appearance of an alternative home or habitation for many of its members. In effect the company became a self-contained community, if not a surrogate family, which was concerned for the health and welfare of its members, as well as the overriding quest for booty.[9]

In these circumstances the social world of the pirates was marked by an intensified masculinization which grew more pronounced during the early eighteenth century. Although pirate companies were diverse, mixing volunteers with forced recruits, and young males of varied ethnicity, they were composed of men from mainly maritime backgrounds. The dangers of long-distance piracy strengthened the camaraderie of the sea, building on a tradition of seafaring fellowship and mutuality. Paradoxically the pirate ship might have been a haven for male security.[10] A growing number of

[9] P. Earle, *The Pirate Wars* (London, 2004), pp. 101–6. For a globalized perspective see M. Ogborn, *Global Lives: Britain and the World* (Cambridge, 2008), pp. 169–94.
[10] For the idea of the sea as an area of 'masculine security' see C. P. Kindleberger, *Mariners and Markets* (Hemel Hempstead, 1992), pp. 61–2.

recruits also demonstrated an alienation from, if not hostility towards, commercial and civil society. The self-serving patriotism which justified the plunder of Spanish commerce and colonies during the 1660s and 1670s grew weaker, leading to indiscriminate attacks on shipping. The bravery and courage of pirates, though acknowledged by many, tipped over into violence and casual brutality which were channelled into the punishment or torture of victims. Johnson portrayed Teach as a devil incarnate, but noted that his bravery and courage would have made him a hero if it had been employed in a good cause.[11] Such men operated at the same level as wild beasts.[12] The use of torture was intended to force unwilling ship masters into revealing concealed valuables; at times, however, it was explicitly judgemental and designed to punish officers who were known to have mistreated their companies. William Snelgrave, a captain of a slaving vessel who was taken by pirates off Sierra Leone in 1718, noted that they wanted 'to revenge themselves on base Merchants, and cruel Commanders of Ships'.[13] Among some pirate groups this aggression was turned inwards, provoking rivalries and disputes which were difficult to contain.

The extent to which these conditions affected the sexuality or sexual behaviour of pirates is unclear. Some recruits to piracy may have been driven by an underlying hostility towards women and family responsibilities; others demonstrated a deep attachment to wives and girlfriends, though this appears to have grown more instrumental over time. Pirates engaged on long voyages, and absences from shore, may have resorted occasionally to same-sex relationships, as others did aboard sailing vessels, but there is no evidence to indicate the prevalence of homosexuality among pirate groups. Indeed the internal organization and overcrowding of most pirate ships would have limited the opportunities for sexual relations, particularly by comparison with trading vessels where officers were able to abuse boys in private quarters. The accounts of Exquemelin and Johnson tend to present an image of sex-starved men who threw away their booty in short-lived drunken debauches with prostitutes in ports such as Port Royal on Jamaica, or who resorted to short-term and opportunistic relationships with women.[14] On lengthy voyages, moreover, the companies of

[11] Johnson, *General History of the Pyrates*, pp. 82, 85.

[12] Ibid., p. 114.

[13] W. Snelgrave, *A New Account of Some Parts of Guinea, and the Slave Trade* (London, 1734), p. 225; M. Rediker, *Villains of All Nations: Atlantic Pirates in the Golden Age* (London, 2004), pp. 87–93.

[14] Esquemeling, *Buccaneers of America*, pp. 44–5, 74–5, 140–1; Johnson, *General History of the Pyrates*, pp. 59–62, 117, 192, 226, 485–6, 494. For interesting comment on practice in the Pacific see L. Wallace, *Sexual Encounters: Pacific Texts, Modern Sexualities*

pirate and privateering vessels adopted customary seafaring practice, soliciting for sex at various landfalls.

The structural features of long-distance piracy had profound implications for female agency. Women's responses to changes in the sites and geographical scope of piratical enterprise varied, as they adapted to, or were forced to operate within, a changing and increasingly hostile environment. The growth of transatlantic piracy led to the transfer of pre-existing patterns of activity and behaviour, but within the context of new or emerging colonial societies women faced different challenges and opportunities which reinforced the fragility of pirate partnerships. Thereafter the global spread of piracy was accompanied by promiscuous behaviour, mainly by men, whose impact on native societies, their inadvertent or willing hosts, may have been disproportionate to its scale and extent. Within remote, far-flung locations, ranging from the Caribbean to the Indian Ocean, the lives of women were thus entangled with those of transient pirates. While these contacts or relationships reflected the peculiar influence of local conditions, they also exposed an increasingly common experience that betrayed a tension between female agency and passivity.

Wives, prostitutes and concubines: England and the Caribbean from the 1640s to the 1680s

Conditions at sea around the British Isles during the 1640s and 1650s provided an environment in which older patterns of agency persisted. But the resurgence of disorderly depredation in local waters was rapidly superseded by the growth of organized plunder within the Caribbean. The growth of such piratical enterprise proceeded in tandem with the support of women of varied backgrounds, whose lives were loosely linked with sea rovers through the exchange of services, gifts and booty. Wherever they sailed, pirates and buccaneers bartered for sex, companionship and affection, establishing contacts or relations with prostitutes and native women,

(Ithaca, 2003), pp. 41, 56. On same-sex relations see R. C. Ritchie, *Captain Kidd and the War Against the Pirates* (Cambridge, Mass., 1986), pp. 123–4. It has been argued that there was an 'almost universal homosexual involvement among pirates' of the Caribbean by B. R. Burg, *Sodomy and the Perception of Evil: English Sea Rovers in the Seventeenth-Century Caribbean* (New York, 1983), p. 173. But the evidence is scant, and if same-sex relations were determined by power, this would make such relationships aboard pirate ships potentially problematic. On the issue of power see A. Bray, *Homosexuality in Renaissance England* (London, 1982, revised edition, New York, 1995), p. 56. For a recent discussion distinguishing homosexual behaviour from identity see K. M. Phillips and B. Reay, *Sex Before Sexuality: A Premodern History* (Cambridge, 2011), pp. 60–87.

alongside marital unions. While the underlying trend pointed towards the economic marginalization of women, their responses called for flexibility and resourcefulness, as they adapted to distant, occasionally abusive and fleeting relationships.

The revival and expansion of English piracy occurred against the background of civil war and disorderly privateering, in which women participated as accessories. Fuelled by ideological differences, seaborne plunder was portrayed as piracy by both sides. Royalist activity presented an acute problem for parliament, particularly as in a number of prominent cases it was supported by wives and kin. In November 1649 the Council of State sought the advice of the navy committee and Trinity House on how to deal with the families of royalist pirates, who benefited from raids on English shipping. Captain Alleyne, one of these so-called pirates, was taken and imprisoned for 'levying war against the commonwealth', but he escaped with the aid of his wife, Rebecca.[15] Another royalist adventurer who acquired a reputation as an infamous pirate, captain Richard Beach, was captured during 1654, but later claimed that he 'walked out of prison undiscovered, by putting on a suit of black and a periwig that his wife brought him'.[16] The spouses of other royalist captains at sea assisted their husbands in different ways. The wife of William Balthazar, reputedly the 'grand pirate' who sailed out of the French port of Brest, petitioned the commonwealth regime in June 1653 for his release from the Tower of London.[17]

The republic struggled to deal with the wider social ramifications of royalist privateering or piracy. In some cases it placed the partners of royalist captains in custody, as a surety for the behaviour of their husbands. The wife of one such captain, Mrs Pennell, was imprisoned in Peterhouse during 1650, but was subsequently freed upon bond.[18] Faced with the alarming prospect of having to execute royalist adventurers for piracy, the regime resorted to expediency, including the transportation of groups of pirates to colonies in the West Indies. Partly by these means the problem was displaced, but in such a way as to reinforce the transatlantic transfer of piracy and privateering, building on and elaborating pre-existing enterprise.

[15] *CSPD, 1649–50*, pp. 405, 536, 544.
[16] *CSPD, 1655–56*, pp. 260, 266, 285, 357. Plymouth council gave a tankard to the captor of Beach the pirate; R. N. Worth (ed.), *Calendar of the Plymouth Municipal Records* (Plymouth, 1893), p. 164.
[17] *CSPD, 1652–53*, pp. 423, 440; *CSPD, 1653–54*, pp. 254, 283, 358, 448, 567. And B. Capp, *Cromwell's Navy: The Fleet and the English Revolution, 1648–1660* (Oxford, 1989), pp. 60–72, for royalist privateering.
[18] *CSPD, 1650*, p. 249.

The consequences of the transatlantic spread of plunder were first felt on Jamaica. Following its conquest by the English in 1655, the island became a hub for trade, including contraband commerce with Spanish America, privateering, buccaneering and piracy. But the development of a hybrid maritime economy contained weaknesses and contradictions, particularly between the strategic priorities of plantation and plunder. Benjamin Worsley, the colonial projector, encapsulated the problem in his unpublished 'Discourse of the Privateers of Jamaica'. As he noted, the buccaneers were neither versed in planting nor 'accustomed to any such regular course of life, but do rather abhorre it'.[19] At the same time Worsley observed that they lacked cultivable land or a stock of servants or slaves to work it, in addition to 'any capacitie in themselves to procure these'.[20] The buccaneers were nothing more than a 'crew of wild, dissolute and *tattered* fellows ... who hath hitherto been acquainted with nothing but Prey'.[21] He canvassed various remedies for the problem, designed to promote Jamaica as the commercial centre of the West Indies, including the possibility of providing compensation for those who retired from the sea. In the short term he appeared to envisage that some of the wild crew of buccaneers could be encouraged into settled lives ashore, presumably by marrying local women, though in the longer term he was aware of the need to ensure that the island was populated with people of industry and sobriety.

Buccaneering accentuated the underlying masculinity and fragility of colonial society on Jamaica, while enabling women to share in the irregular but profitable influx of booty usually as the providers of sexual and other services. The rapid growth of Port Royal as one of the largest commercial centres in English America witnessed the development of a boisterous and bawdy seafaring culture, characterised by heavy drinking, gambling and prostitution, underpinned by petty violence and hostility towards Spain. To some extent this was a legacy of the lifestyles of the original buccaneers, the cattle hunters of Hispaniola, who, according to Exquemelin, visited neighbouring Tortuga to 'celebrate the festivals of Bacchus', and the 'goddess Venus, for whose beastly delights they find more women than they can make use' of.[22] But it also reflected in an extreme way a longer tradi-

---

[19] BL, Additional MS 11410, f. 309; T. Leng, *Benjamin Worsley (1618–1677): Trade, Interest and the Spirit in Revolutionary England* (Woodbridge, 2008), pp. 148–50, 160–2.

[20] BL, Additional MS 11410, f. 309v.

[21] Ibid., f. 303v. On the origins of the buccaneers see the recent discussion in M. Parker, *The Sugar Barons: Family, Corruption, Empire and War* (London, 2011), pp. 108–10, 133, 140–1.

[22] Esquemeling, *Buccaneers of America*, pp. 44–5. On the growth of Port Royal see M. Pawson and D. Buisseret, *Port Royal, Jamaica* (Oxford, 1975), pp. 80ff.; A. Taylor, *Amer-*

tion of maritime life and custom, especially among seafarers engaged in long-distance voyaging: thus the tavern keepers and strumpets of Tortuga awaited the buccaneers 'after the same manner that they do at Amsterdam for the arrival of the East India fleet'.[23]

Within the favourable environment of the Caribbean buccaneering acquired a local texture which left a deep imprint on Port Royal. By 1670 it was identified by godly observers as a latter-day Sodom, sustained by pirate booty, with an unruly culture of taverns, punch-houses and brothels. According to one report the number of tippling houses had more than doubled in recent years.[24] The buccaneers and other sea rovers flocked to such establishments in search of entertainment and comfort. In these settings, as Exquemelin reported, some men were willing to pay exorbitant sums of money merely to see a woman naked. In consequence, some buccaneers, including Sir Henry Morgan's following, became trapped in a cycle of plunder and debauchery. According to Exquemelin, Morgan's men 'ceased not to importune him for new invasions and exploits, thereby to get something to expend anew in wine and strumpets, as they had already wasted what was purchased so little before'.[25] Within a community renowned for its liberality and generosity, plunder was soon dissipated on women and wine. Captain Bartholomew Sharp, one of the leaders of the buccaneer invasion of the South Sea, 'wasted all his money ... in good fellowship'.[26] It was such generosity which led to Sharp's arrest in London during 1682, after he aroused the suspicions of his landlord and landlady with the gift of £50 to a female acquaintance.

Although buccaneering encouraged the growth of organized and open prostitution in Port Royal, it also fed off the voluntary and forced migration of female servants and criminals, including whores. Within twenty years of the English arrival, unusually there were nearly as many women as men living in the port, while many of the latter were migratory seafarers. As an institutionalized manifestation of a disorderly and insecure colonial community, it was maintained by an improvised culture in which respect for reputation and sexual conduct was weak, or at least the subject of negotia-

ican Colonies: The Settlement of North America to 1800 (London, 2001), pp. 218–20; D. L. Hamilton, 'Pirates and Merchants: Port Royal, Jamaica', in R. K. Skowronek and C. R. Ewen (eds), *X Marks the Spot: The Archaeology of Piracy* (Gainesville, 2006), pp. 13–26.
[23] Esquemeling, *Buccaneers of America*, p. 45.
[24] Pawson and Buisseret, *Port Royal*, pp. 84–5, 107–8, 119; *The Present State of Jamaica* (London, 1683), p. 12.
[25] Esquemeling, *Buccaneers of America*, p. 173.
[26] Ibid., pp. 75, 282; TNA, HCA 1/51, ff. 183–4v (for the arrest of Sharp).

tion between local elites and a rapidly growing, but divided population, living with high mortality. At the same time the toleration of prostitution reflected the growth of a transient colonial community facing multiple problems. It was accompanied and qualified by the introduction of a rudimentary disciplinary apparatus that emphasized gender distinctions and power. Alongside the ale- and punch-houses, Port Royal acquired a prison and a cage to punish prostitutes and to 'allay the furie of those hot Amazons'.[27]

Little is known of the scale and organization of prostitution at Port Royal. The census of 1680, after the heyday of the buccaneers, identified only one brothel, run by John Starr, though it was a large enterprise with twenty-three women, two of whom were black. There were others, unidentified and smaller in size, among the taverns and punch-houses. Large entrepreneurs, such as Starr, operated in loose association and competition with organizations run by the 'rum-punch women' who distilled and sold the infamous 'kill-rum' on their own premises, sometimes as family businesses in partnership with their daughters.[28] Under these conditions prostitution occupied an ill-defined, semi-public space, where women were expected to advertise themselves to potential customers. Indeed, Exquemelin's account of the buccaneers' behaviour in Port Royal suggests that voyeurism may have been a distinctive feature of their conduct towards prostitutes. While the identities and lives of such women are difficult to recover, most were probably young, poor and vulnerable servants or former servants, whose status placed them in an ambiguous or uncertain legal position. If some may have benefited from the prodigality of men who dissipated their new-found wealth in bouts of drink and debauchery, many probably handed most of their earnings over to a master or mistress. Moreover, they were exposed to misuse and cruel treatment by hardened rovers

---

[27] D. Buisseret (ed.), *Jamaica in 1687: The Taylor Manuscript at the National Library of Jamaica* (Kingston, 2008), p. 240; Pawson and Buisseret, *Port Royal*, pp. 86, 114. On sexuality more generally see Norton, *Founding Mothers*, pp. 232–4; and L. Stone, *Road to Divorce: England 1530–1987* (Oxford, 1995), pp. 67–70. Demographic failure had far-reaching consequences; see T. Burnard, *Mastery, Tyranny, and Desire: Thomas Thistlewood and His Slaves in the Anglo-American World* (Chapel Hill, 2004), pp. 17–20.
[28] Pawson and Buisseret, *Port Royal*, p. 119; R. S. Dunn, *Sugar and Slaves: The Rise of the Planter Class in the English West Indies, 1624–1713* (2nd edition, Chapel Hill, 1999), pp. 181, 185; Burg, *Sodomy and the Perception of Evil*, p. 95, argues that the shortage of women encouraged same-sex relations among men in the Caribbean. On space and prostitution see E. Kowaleski-Wallace, *Consuming Subjects: Women, Shopping, and Business in the Eighteenth Century* (New York, 1997), pp. 129–36. Many of these women may have been recruited from transported prostitutes; R. Thompson, *Women in Stuart England and America: A Comparative Study* (London, 1974), p. 231

who were capable of extreme violence and savagery at sea, while labouring under a regime heavily influenced by disease and high mortality.[29]

The symbiotic relationship between buccaneering and prostitution encouraged the formation of irregular and indeterminate unions. In some cases this could lead to marital relations, even at the risk of provoking scorn and ridicule in some quarters. At the same time some buccaneers and pirates retained links with wives in England. Under such conditions women could find themselves in distant, difficult and occasionally dangerous partnerships. Yet the prospect of abandonment and the risk of ill-treatment were qualified by mutuality, affection and even signs of love. Among seafarers in general, lengthy absences from home were often allayed by gifts and presents, 'as is usuall for seamen to send their wives', noted the widow of one mariner in 1690.[30] Despite their transient and chaotic lives, it was a practice that some members of the buccaneering community adhered to.

Although the surviving evidence is fragmentary, it sheds light on the episodic, precarious and unusual nature of these relations, while also suggesting their occasional strength and durability. In May 1684 the governor of Jamaica offered a pardon to captain Laurent, a French buccaneer, which included a promise of a safe conduct for his wife, living on the Canary Islands, on condition that he purchased a plantation and settled in the colony. The following year, while lying in wait for a Spanish fleet off Panama, captain Charles Swan wrote to his father, urging him to 'presente my faithfull love to my Deare wife, and assure her shee is never out of my mind'.[31] Swan's voyage had so far been unsuccessful. Nonetheless he hoped to return to England with riches for his spouse, though he was evidently unsure as to his welcome. Although he had some money for his wife, Swan hoped 'with God's Assistance [to] doe things (that were it with my Prince's leave) would doubtless make her a Lady, but now I cannot tell but it may bring mee to a halter'.[32]

During the 1680s members of the buccaneering fraternity were able to

---

[29] Esquemeling, *Buccaneers of America*, pp. 45, 74–5, 142; S. D. Amussen, *Caribbean Exchanges: Slavery and the Transformation of English Society, 1640–1700* (Chapel Hill, 2007), pp. 156–7; S. Stark, *Female Tars: Women Aboard Ship in the Age of Sail* (London, 1996), pp. 29, 32–7, for lifestyles. See also B. Little, *The Buccaneers' Realm: Pirate Life on the Spanish Main, 1674–1688* (Washington, DC, 2007), pp. 45–60, 165–70. Mary Carleton, executed at Tyburn in 1673, may represent an extreme example; Pawson and Buisseret, *Port Royal*, p. 119.

[30] TNA, HCA 13/133, Response of Elizabeth Chinnery, 17 May 1690.

[31] TNA, CO 1/54/ 114 (for Laurent); CO 1/57/69 (for Swan).

[32] TNA, CO 1/57/69.

retire from the sea, marry and settle down in the colonies, but with mixed consequences for their spouses. According to a later account by the governor of Bermuda, in about 1686 a pirate ship arrived at the island after a voyage to the South Sea. Because of a lack of evidence and witnesses, the case against the company was dismissed. The mate, one Leak, 'married here, and about 3 or 4 years afterwards died, leaveing with his wife some papers which he told her might be of use to some body'.[33] Evidently they were the 'Journals of all their Transactions & Navigation with a particular account of all that Coast & a description of its Harbours & strengths'.[34] Unknown to the widow, who 'suffer'd these papers to lye up & down loose', it was an invaluable collection of material.[35] More than a decade later she had a lodger, described as a mercurial fellow with some learning, who stole the manuscript and published it as a journal of a voyage he had undertaken.

In an unusual and revealing example of the close relations that could bind sea rovers and their female partners together, one buccaneer, captain Bear, cruised the Caribbean during the later 1680s accompanied by his mistress who was disguised in male dress. Bear had originally sailed from Jamaica with a commission to take pirates. By August 1687 he was reported to have turned pirate, robbing several English vessels of money and other valuables. According to a Spanish report he married his partner, who he claimed was of aristocratic background, at Havana, 'where hee desired hee might bee entertained as a faithful subject of the King of Spain's ... being both of the same Religion with them'.[36] The ceremony was attended by the governor and other prominent figures, and the guns of the castle were fired to celebrate the occasion. The governor of Jamaica sent an agent to Havana, demanding that Bear be returned as a pirate and English subject. The agent was also instructed to inform the Spanish of Bear's background, and 'how hee has imposed upon them about the Nobleman's daughter, who is a strumpet hee used to carry with him in Mans Apparel, & is the daughter of a Rum-Punch woman upon Port Royal'.[37] To the governor's anger, the mission failed. Not only did the Spanish take Bear into their service, but also they continued to protect him against English hostility. Little is known about Bear's wife, and there is no record that she continued sailing with him after their marriage. To some extent their association looks like a care-

---

[33] TNA, CO 37/26/27.
[34] Ibid.
[35] Ibid.
[36] TNA, CO 138/6/41–2. Bear was described as a 'man of good repute and an ancient trader to Jamaica'; Buisseret (ed.), *Jamaica in 1687*, pp. 108–9; Little, *The Buccaneer's Realm*, p. 62.
[37] TNA, CO 138/6/43.

fully orchestrated elopement, including a transfer of loyalty, which led to a new life on Cuba.

The lifestyles and feckless conduct of the buccaneers left some women in difficult circumstances, trapped in abusive relationships, and the victims of repeated cruelty and violence. The wife of captain Grubbin, one of a growing number of rovers who served with the French during the 1690s, fled from Hispaniola to Jamaica as a refugee from such ill-treatment. Her means of escape was fortuitous, and provoked a violent response from her husband. Apparently by chance, during 1694 she encountered the company of a man-of-war from Jamaica who were reconnoitring the coast of the neighbouring island. According to one report, the English 'would have left her there, where they found her, but she earnestly desired to go with them and be quit of her husband because (as she said) he used her very ill'.[38] Although she was taken to Jamaica, the governor, Sir William Beeston, intended to send her back because she was French. However, by the terms of a local agreement with the governor of Hispaniola, he could not force her to return, particularly as 'she earnestly desired to stay and to have protection'.[39] In revenge, Grubbin, who had acquired a notorious reputation for raiding remote and vulnerable plantations on Jamaica, threatened to abduct women from the island until his wife was returned. Shortly after, during a night-time raid on an isolated plantation belonging to the widow of a clergyman, he 'plundered all her Negroes, household Goods and all she had, tortured her to confess if she had money, and then took away with him her Mayden Daughter ... of about 14 years and carried her to Petit Guavas'.[40]

Alongside marital relationships and the resort to prostitutes, during the 1670s and 1680s members of the buccaneering community established cross-cultural contacts and relations with native women, within and beyond the Caribbean. For the buccaneers such relationships served several purposes. While assisting their adaptation to, and exploitation of, new environments, they also asserted the subservience of native women. On occasion they appeared to be part of a cultural re-fashioning, hinting at shifts in identity and allegiance, which developed under unusual conditions. Whether they were intended to challenge or subvert the coded denial of cross-cultural intimacy among English colonists is less clear. In practice many of the liaisons and marriages between buccaneers and native women were temporary and often predatory in nature. They were informed, more-

---

[38] TNA, CO 137/44/41, I. It has been suggested that in traditional societies men's response to marital breakdown was often violent; R. Phillips, *Untying the Knot: A Short History of Divorce* (Cambridge, 1991), p. 232.

[39] TNA, CO 137/44/41, I.

[40] Ibid.; Amussen, *Caribbean Exchanges*, p. 101.

over, by the wider context of Caribbean slavery, especially as it was developing on Jamaica.[41]

According to Exquemelin, these relationships were confused and possibly self-defeating in purpose. His description of a buccaneering voyage along the coast of Costa Rica indicated that the company had 'women-slaves' who served in 'their ordinary employments of washing dishes, sewing, drawing water out of wells … and the like things'.[42] Two of the women were killed in an ambush ashore by hostile Indians. They appear to have been the victims of symbolic or ritualistic violence, possibly as a result of their association with the English. Thus Exquemelin recorded that in their bodies 'we saw so many arrows sticking as might seem they had been fixed there with particular care and leisure, for otherwise we knew that one of them alone was sufficient to bereave any human body of life'.[43] Depending on local conditions, such women were acquired either by raiding or trading. Off Costa Rica, Exquemelin noted that friendly relations with the natives had been destroyed by an abuse of trust, including the 'barbarous inhumanities' of the buccaneers in 'taking away their women to serve their disordinate lust'.[44] At the pirate haven near the Cape of Gracias á Dios, where good relations still prevailed, native women could be acquired through trade and exchange. According to local custom,

> when any Pirates arrive there, every one has the liberty to buy for himself an Indian woman, at the price of a knife or any old axe, wood-bill, or hatchet. By this contract the woman is obliged to remain in the custody of the Pirate all the time he stays there. She serves him in the meanwhile, and brings him victuals of all sorts that the country affords.[45]

The Indians of the region enjoyed close and cordial relations with the buccaneers. Men and boys served at sea as fishermen and hunters for tortoise, while women were prepared to act as temporary partners. Exquemelin's report of these unions was abbreviated and discrete, perhaps deliberately so, though he claimed that 'if any Pirate marries an Indian woman, she is bound to do with him in all things as if he were an Indian man born'.[46] As marriage required the consent of parents, if 'anyone desires to take a wife, he is first examined by the damsel's father concerning several

[41] This was subject to contradictory currents. The Indian community at the Cape of Gracios á Dios, where the buccaneers acquired women, also had negro slaves according to Esquemeling, *Buccaneers of America*, p. 234.
[42] Ibid., p. 231.
[43] Ibid.
[44] Ibid., p. 225.
[45] Ibid., p. 233; Little, *The Buccaneer's Realm*, pp. 60, 141, 158.
[46] Esquemeling, *Buccaneers of America*, p. 238.

points relating to good husbandry'.[47] Although Exquemelin provided few details of such marital arrangements, he presented a detailed and diverting portrait of Indian society. He observed with some indelicacy relations between native men and women. As a sign of great affection for their partners, evidently males pierced their genital parts with small darts, a practice which was undertaken 'when they make love unto any woman'.[48] Though he claimed to have witnessed such actions, coyly he avoided any suggestion that his fellow buccaneers resorted to local custom.

The voyages of captain Bartholomew Sharp and his successors during the early 1680s illuminated the opportunistic contacts and relationships which buccaneers established with native women, and their spread beyond the Caribbean. They were recounted in published reports by some of the leading participants, including the journals of William Dampier. It was partly through these works that Dampier successfully transformed himself from a pirate-buccaneer into a scientific traveller and observer. The publication of such narratives, with their tales of robbery and violence mixed with detailed descriptions of native flora and fauna, contributed more widely to the recovery and representation of the buccaneers' image.[49] Early on in the voyage the buccaneers seized a Spanish prize along the west coast of the region around the isthmus. Among the passengers was a Moskito Indian woman, who was detained aboard the buccaneers' ship for at least two nights. During this time she 'was very familiar' with one of the company, a Dutchman, Jacobus Marques, who was known as Copas.[50] He was enamoured with her, presenting her with several valuable gifts. Subsequently Copas deserted ashore with 200 pieces of eight. It is not clear if he was accompanied by his female associate, but he reportedly fled into the woods, and was never seen again. Shortly afterwards the rest of the company divided at the isthmus, with one group, including Dampier and Lionel Wafer, deciding to return overland to the Caribbean. It was a dangerous and difficult journey. Although Dampier later drew a clear distinction between Europeans and Indians, he recognized the dependence of the pirates on native groups for guidance and aid. The buccaneers sought the help of the Indians through the use of gift exchange, initially with toys and baubles. Native women played a key role in some of these transactions.

[47] Ibid., p. 236.

[48] Ibid.

[49] This was possibly part of the 'domestication' of the buccaneers, on which see A. Neill, *British Discovery Literature and the Rise of Global Commerce* (Basingstoke, 2002), pp. 23–4, 31, 41–5.

[50] J. F. Jameson (ed.), *Privateering and Piracy in the Colonial Period: Illustrative Documents* (New York, 1923), pp. 120–1.

During the course of an uneasy encounter with one group, it was clear that the offer of presents was not working. When the wife of the leader was given a sky-coloured petticoat, however, he was persuaded to provide the buccaneers with a guide. During Dampier's second voyage in the South Sea he recorded that the company had the benefit of a female guide, a mulatto, whose child, a boy aged seven or eight, was kept by them.[51]

The potentially destabilizing consequences of such contact for rootless, increasingly nomadic bands of predators were strikingly revealed by the experiences of Wafer, who was one of Dampier's companions during the isthmus crossing. Following an accident, when he was scorched by gunpowder, he and several others were left behind by the main party. He survived with the assistance of a friendly Indian group, and by adapting to their way of life. As a surgeon apparently he cured the wife of the leader by bleeding her. Thereafter, according to his subsequent account, the Indians adored him as some sort of god. Adopting their lifestyle, Wafer intended marrying the daughter of the chief when she reached a suitable age. He discarded his European clothes, going as 'naked as the Salvages', and allowed a group of women to paint his body, though he refused to let them prick his skin, 'to rub the Paint in'.[52] It was in this condition, adorned with body paint, naked to the waist and with a nose piece hanging over his mouth, that he was recovered by his former company. It took more than an hour for him to be recognized, as he squatted on his haunches aboard their vessel.

Under captain Swan a group of Sharp's men, including Dampier, entered the South Sea on a second voyage. Sailing to the East Indies, they stopped over at various locations. During a lengthy stay at Mindanao, part of the Philippines, nearly one-third of the company went ashore, hiring or buying houses, to live with female concubines, described by Dampier as their comrades or pagallies. His account of the buccaneers' stay at Mindanao indicates that they were able to take advantage of the different code of sexuality and sexual behaviour within Pacific island communities, which had shocked earlier groups of Spanish adventurers. These cross-cultural liaisons were unusual. The more common buccaneering experience in the South Sea was based on visits to remote and uninhabited islands such as Juan Fernandez. The sexual encounters of the buccaneers preceded the widely reported traffic in sex that became common after the 1760s, during the European exploration and settlement of the Pacific. Although the irreg-

[51] W. Dampier, *A New Voyage Round the World*, ed. N. M. Penzer (London, 1937), pp. 174–5.

[52] L. E. Elliott Joyce (ed.), *A New Voyage and Description of the Isthmus of America by Lionel Wafer* (Hakluyt Society, Third Series, 73, 1934), pp. 21–2, 27.

ular and infrequent landfalls by buccaneering groups such as Dampier's provided opportunity for brief relationships, they were arbitrary and random in nature, and apparently of limited impact.

Nonetheless the relationships which Dampier's companions established on Mindanao revealed the disturbing role of the buccaneers as predators who now seemed to be capable of sailing the globe in search of plunder and sex. Implicitly they also challenged the ethnic and cultural boundaries of an expanding imperial state. Such behaviour undermined the primacy and values of family life, threatening the image and interests of civil society. However, not all of Swan's company took partners ashore. Dampier remained aloof from such contact, later reporting that the wages of sin inexorably pointed in one direction. Within months of their arrival, sixteen of the company were dead, the result of unrestrained behaviour ashore, especially 'dallying too familiarly with their Women'.[53] At various stages during the rest of the voyage the buccaneers had the chance to take advantage of similar opportunities. As Dampier recounted, at Pulo Condere the company were offered women according to local custom, as well as 'black misses' or 'Dalilahs' along the coast of Guinea.[54] At the island of St Helena, the location for a small English town and fort, the company sought refreshment in the punch-houses, striking up liaisons with women, several of whom returned to the Caribbean to marry their partners. Dampier tended to see such sexual commerce, through the disapproving gaze of an outsider, as controlled by men who hired women out for economic gain. Subsequent encounters in the Pacific suggest that female participants may have acted on their own initiative either for the material or for the cultural rewards of consorting with powerful strangers.[55]

---

[53] Dampier, *A New Voyage*, pp. 244–9, 254. For earlier Spanish contact see A. de Morga, *Sucesos de las Islas Filipinas*, ed. J. S. Cummins (Hakluyt Society, Second Series, 140, 1971), pp. 250–1, 274–8.

[54] Dampier, *A New Voyage*, pp. 268–9, 363–6.

[55] W. Dampier, *Voyages and Discoveries*, ed. C. Wilkinson (London, 1931), pp. 16, 34. For subsequent practices see Wallace, *Sexual Encounters*, pp. 13–16, 40–3 (for women in search of *mana* or status); J. Linnekin, *Sacred Queens and Women of Consequence: Rank, Gender and Colonialism in the Hawaiian Islands* (Ann Arbor, 1990), pp. 55–7, 61–9 (for women 'marrying up' and making alliances); N. Thomas, *Islanders: The Pacific in the Age of Empire* (New Haven, 2010), pp. 13, 23–4, 55, 60–3, 88 (for the perception that sailors might have been seen as divine on some islands); Phillips and Reay, *Sex Before Sexuality*, pp. 136–8. On the role of St Helena see P. J. Stern, 'Politics and Ideology in the Early East India Company-State: The Case of St Helena, 1673–1709', *Journal of Imperial and Commonwealth History*, 35 (2007), pp. 1–23.

Partners and abandoned women: North America and Madagascar during the 1690s

The experience of piracy and buccaneering within the Caribbean indicated that the emergence of long-distance depredation narrowed the opportunities for female agency, particularly as the receivers and distributors of pirate booty. The contact between women and pirates was often limited, and at times indirect and inadvertent. Increasingly it was the product of brief encounters and short-term liaisons. This pattern was qualified by the spread of maritime plunder beyond the Caribbean to the eastern seaboard of North America. The confused surge of predatory enterprise during the 1690s, and the subtle shift from buccaneering to disorderly privateering and piracy, allowed some women to play a more active part in the business. To some extent the expansion of seaborne plunder during these years continued to be assisted by ambiguous, occasionally accidental relationships with women. Ranging from the wild, anarchic island communities of the Bahamas to Boston in godly New England, these links were varied in character and purpose. Many were probably unstable, short-lived and self-serving. While providing pirates and other rovers with female companionship, security as well as lodging and entertainment ashore, they also provided a convenient cover for intermittent visits ashore. Wives and partners were also actively involved in the defence of men arrested for, or accused of, wrongdoing at sea. But the interaction between pirates and women was uneasy and vulnerable to local pressures. Some women maintained stable contacts with men who were recruited into piracy, voluntarily or by force, and benefited from the return of plunder and gifts from the sea. Others were the victims of semi-detached, abandoned relations which left them in straitened circumstances, struggling to survive by expediency or dependency on others.

Such partnerships occurred in most of the English colonies in North America, in addition to the contact which pirates maintained with women in England. Jeremiah Basse, the agent acting for colonial proprietors in America, drew attention to the problem, and its wider social ramifications, in July 1697. While warning the secretary to the Council of Trade and Plantations, William Popple, of the dishonour and damage caused by the growth of piracy, he advised that the colonies 'have not a little contributed to this increase'.[56] In an effort to limit its spread, Basse indicated that on occasion, 'several vessels, suspected to be bound on this design, sailed from one province or another of the continent, leaving some of their wives and

[56] *CSPC, 1696–97*, p. 557; H. F. Rankin, *The Golden Age of Piracy* (Williamsburg, 1969), pp. 54–6.

families as pledges of their return'.[57] But the impact of these measures was undermined by a widespread desire to share in the growing volume and circulation of booty, particularly hard currency, silver and gold. The people, he continued, 'make so much advantage from their money, that they will not be very forward to suppress them, unless it be enjoined on them by a power that they dare not disobey'.[58]

The prospect of reaping rich rewards from pirates returning with booty from the east encouraged widespread connivance and collusion among colonial officials and communities. The proprietary colonies, especially, were singled out as 'a sort of a Recepticle or refuge for Pyrates and unlawfull Traders'.[59] According to George Larkin, who conducted an inquiry across the colonies for the Council of Trade and Plantations, there was 'scarce a family in three in the Government of Rhode Island but some of them have been concerned in Privateering, as they term it, and a great many in Pennsylvania and the Jerseys'.[60] Larkin reported on the activities of two of captain William Kidd's company who returned to Pennsylvania, following their trial in England, to recover £1,500 and £800 'which they had buryed in the woods when they first landed. These fellowes', he continued,

> have been hugg'd and caressed after a very strange manner by the Religious people of those parts, no money to be seen amongst them now but Arabian Gold, and to demonstrate to your Lordships that Pyrates are esteemed very honest men, the President of the Councill of New Hampshire, Secretary of the Province and Clerk of the Inferiour Court, is going to marry his daughter to one of these villains.[61]

Larkin's report suggested that there was little shame or stigma attached to marriages which proceeded through a combination of greed and gullibility. In 1698, for example, the daughter of colonel William Markham, deputy governor of Pennsylvania, married James Brown, one of the company of the pirate captain Henry Avery. Brown's pirate background was widely known in Philadelphia, though he tried to conceal it by claiming that he was engaged on a trading or privateering voyage to Madagascar, where he joined Avery's ship for passage to Europe, 'not knowing what

[57] *CSPC, 1696–97*, p. 557.
[58] Ibid.
[59] TNA, CO 5/715/47; *CSPC, 1701*, p. 659.
[60] TNA, CO 5/715/47.
[61] Ibid. Kidd's men claimed to have each been paid 300 guineas for their freedom. Larkin's activities provoked widespread anger and complaint. In Bermuda he was accused of seducing a mulatto woman. *CSPC, 1701*, p. 658; *CSPC, 1702–3*, pp. 618–33.

design they had been upon, till he was on board for some time'.[62] In response to allegations that pirates paid for his 'favour and protection', Markham admitted that 'they had been very civil to him, but that they brought in money, which was an advantage to the country'.[63] In a more brazen and unusual case of 1700, a chaplain in New York married the wife of Edward Buckmaster, one of Kidd's company, to Adam Baldridge, another pirate. The recently appointed governor of New York, Richard Coote, Earl of Bellomont, was enraged by such behaviour, particularly as he was involved in a sustained campaign against piracy. As Bellomont informed officials in London, it was 'an arch peice of villanie'.[64] Smith, the chaplain, requested the lieutenant governor to sign a blank marriage licence, while the governor was away, claiming that the couple desired to conceal their names. Suspicious, the lieutenant governor refused the request. Nonetheless Smith returned with a

> licence filled up with the names of Adam Ball and the maiden Name of a married Woman; he afterwards adds a sillable to the Man's Name in the licence (after the Lieutenant Governor had signed it) and then it was Baldridge the Pirate ... And the woman was the Wife of Buckmaster, a Pirate who escaped out of the Gaol of this Town.[65]

In his defence Smith claimed that the bride insisted on oath that she had never been married to Buckmaster. On further investigation, as Bellomont reported, she had been wed by a justice in 'one of the Jersys, which is their way of marrying there'.[66] To compound his villainy, Smith had the impudence to question the governor's authority in dismissing him.

Bellomont's campaign against piracy and disorderly privateering met with varied success, provoking passive resistance from some colonists including women. In May 1699 he reported the capture of fifteen or sixteen pirates in Boston, but complained of his inability to take any of the company of captain Tew in New York. Aware that 'two or three of 'em have wives' in the port, he reported how he 'laid out for 'em ... but they are too

[62] *CSPC, 1699*, pp. 382–3.
[63] *CSPC, 1697–98*, pp. 211–12.
[64] TNA, CO 5/1045/7, I.
[65] Ibid.; *CSPC, 1700*, p. 609. Surrogates and blank licences were used in England; Stone, *Road to Divorce*, pp. 102–3.
[66] TNA, CO 5/1045/7, 1; E. R. Snow, *Pirates and Buccaneers of the Atlantic Coast* (Boston, 1944), pp. 45, 70, 183, includes examples of other marriages. On bigamy and such 'self-defined' marriages see Norton, *Founding Mothers*, pp. 70–1; and R. H. Bloch, 'Women and Morality in Anglo-American Culture, 1650–1800', in idem, *Gender and Morality in Anglo-American Culture, 1650–1800* (Berkeley, 2003), pp. 81–93.

well befriended in this town to be given up to Justice'.[67] Tew sailed with a commission from Bellomont's predecessor, colonel Benjamin Fletcher. Doubts about the legal status of such commissions, and the conduct of Tew and his men at sea, exposed them to charges of piracy. Indeed, for Bellomont they were Fletcher's pirates. Among them was captain Hyne, 'a bloody villain, [who] has murther'd severall men, and will give no quarter, they say, to Spaniards that he takes'.[68] Like others, his wife and family lived in New York.

The experiences of Avery and his company during the later 1690s revealed the varied and unstable relations between women and pirates. While fluctuating in length and intimacy, such contacts could be of considerable value either to pirates or their pursuers. Following the capture of the *Gang i-Sawai*, at the mouth of the Red Sea, the pirates sailed for Providence in the Bahamas, where they shared out the booty and scattered. Under the protection of the governor some stayed at Providence, others sought refuge in Pennsylvania, Carolina and Virginia, while Avery and another group returned to England. In 1697 Robert Sneed, a justice, informed the deputy governor, Markham, that some of Avery's men were living in Philadelphia. Markham refused to provide Sneed with any assistance; moreover, his wife and daughter, now married to James Brown, warned the pirates of the justice's intentions. The latter reported that the women were 'so impudent as to call me informer as I passed in the streets'.[69] They repeated the accusation when he complained to Markham of their behaviour, 'his wife & daughter then being in the Room, said they did hear it, & that I was no better than an Informer & deserved to be so called'.[70] Thereafter Sneed sought the support of two fellow justices. One of them, whose kinswoman was married to a Danish member of Avery's company, refused to act until he threatened to complain to the authorities in London. When three of the pirates were arrested, however, they were either released without bail or escaped from prison. Sneed, moreover, was disarmed until they had left town.

Sneed's report was supported by information from Thomas Robinson, who arrived in Philadelphia with a commission to apprehend the pirates. On hearing that two of the principal prisoners, Clinton and Lassel, had escaped from jail, he complained to Markham that it was a 'very ill

[67] TNA, CO 5/1042/26; *CSPC, 1699*, p. 191. In 1697 Benjamin Bullivant of East Jersey complained that he was unable to sleep because of sea rovers 'making merry' with women; Ritchie, *Captain Kidd*, pp. 36–8.
[68] TNA, CO 5/1042/26; Ogborn, *Global Lives*, pp. 177–8.
[69] TNA, CO 323/2/114, I.
[70] Ibid.; *CSPC, 1697–98*, pp. 184, 212–15.

managed business'.[71] After a visit to the prison, from which the pirates allegedly escaped by ripping off the bottom of a door, Robinson expressed his disbelief that 'men of that Bulk could get through at such a place, especially Clinton who is said to be a very fatt gross man'.[72] Markham was compelled to take action to pursue them, promising a reward of £5 to anyone who was responsible for their capture. Shortly after, Hannah Witt reported seeing the two men hiding in bushes near the centre of the town. Clinton apparently was well armed with a sword, two pistols and a musket. However the sheriff, John Claypoole, 'told the woman that he was sure she was mistaken, for they were not there'.[73] Both men escaped aboard a sloop from Carolina. Another member of the company, Charles Goss, was killed in a quarrel with a French man, after he 'came to one Widdow Hutton's house to take his leave of her'.[74] Two days later a riot occurred at his funeral during which Sneed was violently assaulted.

Although Avery and a group of others returned to England, it was unclear if they were planning to renew contacts with their wives and families. Given the dangers and the wealth they had acquired, some seem to have been intent on establishing new lives for themselves. In a determined effort to catch the culprits, officials in London and elsewhere collected and collated information from various sources about their families and places of residence. According to a report of August 1696 Avery's wife lived along Ratcliffe highway, where she sold periwigs, though the neighbourhood had a longstanding reputation as a thoroughfare for prostitution and petty criminality. His mother lived near Plymouth. But Avery, who was known to travel under the name of captain Henry Bridgman, appears to have made no effort to contact either, successfully carving out a new identity and life for himself. He returned across the Atlantic accompanied by the wife of Henry Adams, his quarter master. Both went ashore at Donaghadee in Ireland. Thereafter Avery effectively disappeared. Another member of his company, John Dann, who was caught in Rochester 'by meanes of a Maid, who found his Gold Quilted up in his Jackett', reported an encounter with Mrs Adams in St Albans as she was getting into a stage-coach, on her way to meet captain Bridgman, but she 'would not tell him where he was'.[75]

William Philips, one of Avery's crew, provided further information on

[71] TNA, CO 323/2/114, I.

[72] Ibid.

[73] *CSPC, 1697–98*, pp. 213–14.

[74] TNA, CO 323/2/114, I.

[75] *CSPD, 1696*, pp. 331–2 (for Avery's wife); Jameson (ed.), *Privateering and Piracy*, p. 171; E. T. Fox, *King of the Pirates: The Swashbuckling Life of Henry Every* (Stroud, 2008), pp. 136–8.

the marital circumstances of some of his companions. Richard Chope, though previously married in Dublin, travelled to England, where he had another wife in Wapping. Thomas Johnson, the cook, whose wife lived in East Smithfield, London, was reportedly still in Ireland. Nathaniel Pyke was in Dublin, although his wife lived at Chatham, while James Murry, whose father lived near Armagh, was married to a woman at Derry. John King, 'if in England, is near Oxford, his wife lives near Windsor'.[76] In addition, James Craggett, who was lodging in Dublin, was married to a woman who lived near Avery's wife. Craggett was caught several years later. He denied being a member of Avery's company, but according to one account his denial was contradicted by a letter to him from his wife.[77] Another member of the pirate crew, William May, returned to Bristol from Virginia, but was captured near Bath as he was travelling to London. During his trial one of the witnesses for the prosecution, John Gravet, a mariner who had refused to join Avery's company, recollected that May 'took me by the hand and wished me well home, and bid me Remember him to his Wife'.[78] In his defence May claimed that he was forced to join the pirates. Thus he had requested Gravet to pass on his remembrance to his wife because he was 'not like to see her; for none could go, but who they pleased'.[79] Unfortunately May's only witness was in Virginia. His story was also contradicted by Gravet, who recalled that far from being compelled, he was 'very merry and jocund'.[80] It did not take the court long to return a guilty verdict on May and the others who were tried with him.

It is not clear how women coped with such wayward or failed relationships. Either by design or death it is unlikely that many of Avery's company returned to their wives. For many of these men, as indeed for a growing number of recruits, turning to piracy was increasingly something of a rite of passage. It left wives abandoned and deserted, living under conditions that amounted to informal separation or divorce. Seafaring custom provided some obligation for widows and abandoned women to be supported, but it was variable and often dependent on the reliability of third parties. On balance it seems unlikely that many spouses shared in the booty of their husbands.

The difficulties facing women were strikingly revealed by the experience of Sarah Birch of Bermuda, whose husband went roving to sea with William

[76] *CSPD, 1696*, p. 331.
[77] *CSPD, 1698*, pp. 404, 430.
[78] *The Tryals of Joseph Dawson [et al.]* (London, 1696), reprinted in Baer (ed.), *British Piracy*, II, p. 127.
[79] Ibid., p. 136.
[80] Ibid., pp. 137, 140.

Griffin and Daniel Smith in 1695. She never saw him again. According to subsequent report, the group sailed to Carolina and thence Madagascar. Here they split up, as Smith and Griffin joined the company of another ship. Nine or ten months later, by which time Birch had acquired booty worth £800, they met up at the island. It was a violent encounter. Griffin and Smith admitted that 'their Company Robbed all the Shipp's Company that Birch was in'.[81] The latter, moreover, seems to have been among the casualties. By way of expiation, both men apparently promised that the widow 'should not want for Five pounds, and afterwards told her that if [she] would come to either of [them] that shee should have Tenn or a Dozen pounds'.[82]

Some women demonstrated considerable determination in defending claims to the property of spouses. In 1701, more than five years after the deaths of their husbands aboard Kidd's vessel near Madagascar, Elizabeth Mead and Gertrude Beck resorted to various tactics to recover their possessions. According to custom at sea, the clothes, books, instruments and other goods, including brandy, tobacco and sugar, of Mead and Beck were sold at the mast to the highest bidder. Those of the former, the master of the vessel, raised 900 pieces of eight, while the effects of the latter fetched half that amount. The money was held by Kidd, but it was impounded on his return and arrest for piracy. Imprisoned in Newgate, he conveyed a message to the two widows, by a relative, that it had been seized by the governor of New York, and 'proceeded against in ... Court as the Goods of Pirates'.[83] Insisting that their husbands died before any act of piracy was committed, in November 1700 the women petitioned the Lords of the Admiralty, seeking permission to visit Kidd in jail. They were informed that 'there was time enough for them to lay Claim to what was due to them and were referred to the Keeper of Newgate as to their gaining admittance to speake with ... Captaine Kidd'.[84] Despite the keeper's attempt to deny them access, he was compelled to admit the widows following an appeal to the king. Emboldened by Kidd's information, they presented another petition to the crown for the recovery of their late husbands' estates. On being advised that 'they must Claim the same in proper Course of Law', they brought an action in the High Court of Admiralty, although no evidence survives as to the outcome of the suit.[85]

[81] *CSPC, 1699*, p. 129.

[82] *CSPC, 1699*, p. 129.

[83] TNA, HCA 24/127/57; *CSPD, 1700–2*, p. 348; R. Zacks, *The Pirate Hunter: The True Story of Captain Kidd* (New York, 2002), p. 340.

[84] TNA, HCA 24/127/57.

[85] Ibid. For cases of women petitioning for the wages of husbands who died at sea see TNA, HCA 24/128/210 and 365.

As these cases suggest, female agency in piracy was increasingly coincidental or contingent, although evidence uncovered in New York indicated that some women continued to play a more active, if almost hidden, role in assisting pirates or disorderly privateers. Based on their relationships with such men, they were involved in a wider web of contacts which formed part of a network of support and maintenance. While this network was dominated by pirate brokers, as one official described them, whose interests were essentially economic, it included wives and other female associates who were motivated by bonds of loyalty and personal feeling as much as financial gain.

The character of these contacts, which provided for the widespread circulation of stolen cargoes, was revealed by various reports and investigations. Undoubtedly, some occurred in ambiguous circumstances, as indicated by a case concerning Daniel Latham, a shipwright, which came to the attention of the council of New York in 1700. It was alleged that Latham, a Quaker, had acted as an agent in carrying plundered commodities between colonies, some of which were part of Kidd's booty. Thus he was employed by several people as 'a Carrier Clandestinely and in the night time to carry and Convey East India goods from Connecticutt to New York'.[86] Latham denied the charge, but admitted that he had served as such for Mrs Smith, the wife of English Smith who was one of Kidd's company. As a reward, he received money and four or five yards of muslin.

Latham may have been an unwitting accessory, but officials such as Bellomont were well aware of the support for piracy among many colonists. The latter included old or former pirates who had retired from the trade, and their wives. For example, Thomas Pain, who lived on Conanicut Island in Rhode Island, and Andrew Knott and his wife, who were resident in Boston, provided refuge for pirates and safe houses for their booty, while also acting as messengers and carriers. The significance and scope of such support were exposed by Bellomont's search for James Gillam, a notorious pirate captain who had taken plunder reputedly worth two million pounds. In November 1699 the governor provided the Council of Trade and Plantations in London with a detailed narrative of Gillam's capture. It was 'so very accidentall that ... one would believe there was a strange fatality in that man's starrs'.[87]

Earlier in the month Bellomont was informed by the judge of the admiralty in Rhode Island that Gillam had recently departed thence for Boston,

[86] TNA, CO 5/1184/295.
[87] TNA, CO 5/ 861/4; *CSPC, 1699*, pp. 551–2; Jameson (ed.), *Privateering and Piracy*, p. 238.

intending to find a ship for Jamaica or Barbados. Unfortunately two weeks had elapsed since his departure, and Bellomont was pessimistic at the prospect of finding him. The messenger, however, was able to identify the horse on which the pirate travelled. Consequently the governor sent him, in the company of a constable, to search the local inns for the mare. At the 'first Inn they went to, they found her tied up in the yard'.[88] According to the innkeeper and others, the rider had left about a quarter of an hour earlier without speaking to anybody. No one returned to look after or secure the mare. The following day Bellomont summoned the council and published a proclamation offering a reward of £200 for the capture of Gillam. After an extensive and fruitless search, he later admitted that he would have escaped but for information that captain Knott, a former pirate, was 'likely to know where [he] ... was Conceal'd'.[89] Bellomont's initial examination of Knott yielded no evidence, despite a promise that he would not be prosecuted or molested. Thereupon the governor questioned Knott's wife on oath and separated from her husband. She 'Confess'd that one who went by the name of James Kelly had lodg'd severall nights in her house', and that he was currently lodging across the river in Charlestown.[90] Armed with this information, and aware that Gillam used the name of Kelly, Bellomont re-examined Knott, 'telling him his wife had been more free and Ingenious [than] him, which made him believe she had told all'.[91] As a result he informed the governor that Gillam was staying with Francis Dole, another ex-pirate, in Charlestown.

Bellomont sent a party of six men, accompanied by Knott, across the river. But a search of Dole's house proved fruitless; moreover, Dole denied all knowledge of Gillam or Kelly. By this stage it was ten o'clock at night and most of the search party must have considered that they had lost their elusive quarry. Yet two of their number 'went through a field behind Dole's house, and passing through a second field they met a man in the dark' whom they arrested, and 'it happen'd as oddly as luckily to be Gillam; he had been treating [two] young women some few miles off, in the Country, and was returning at night to his landlord'.[92] In custody, the prisoner resolutely denied the charges against him, though he was contradicted by members of Kidd's company. Bellomont described him as the 'most Impudent hardn'd villain' he had ever seen.[93] The evidence against him appeared

---

[88] Ibid., pp. 238–9.
[89] Ibid., pp. 237–8; *CSPC, 1699*, pp. 551–2.
[90] Ibid., p. 552.
[91] Ibid.
[92] Ibid.; Snow, *Pirates and Buccaneers*, p. 240.
[93] *CSPC, 1699*, pp. 470–9, 516–17, 551–2.

to hinge on information that in the east Gillam had 'served the Mogul, turn'd Mahometan and was Circumcis'd'.[94] The governor had him physically examined by a surgeon and a Jew of Boston. Both confirmed the circumcision which, according to the latter, was 'not after the manner practised by the Jewes according to the Leviticall Law'.[95]

More evidence concerning Gillam's movements ashore emerged during an investigation in Rhode Island. According to Mary Sands, a resident of New Shoreham, who was examined with others by the judge of the local admiralty court, in 1699 Gillam returned from Madagascar aboard Kidd's vessel. Shortly after their appearance off the coast, Kidd's wife arrived off Block Island and requested Sands to accompany her aboard the ship. Her husband, Edward, carried the women out to sea in his sloop. On board she met and spoke with Gillam. He 'seemed to be very urgent to go to Rhode Island', to see Robert Gardiner, an 'old acquaintance at Jamaica ... [who] had sent him word he would secure him', if he caused no trouble.[96] About two weeks later Gillam came to New Shoreham accompanied by John Carr. Mary's sister, Sarah, was informed by the latter that 'he was not under any trouble', though he added that 'no man durst to meddle with the said Gillam, he walking freely about Newport streets'.[97] During a visit to Newport that lasted several weeks, the pirate seems to have swaggered about the community, feeding off his reputation and notoriety, while seeking to contact old friends and companions. Apparently he appeared at the door of Sarah Little's house, on horseback, in search of one Peter Lawrence, thereafter riding through the town in daylight. At least one member of the community was 'much troubled that people would be so base as to Council him'.[98] On another occasion he was entertained by Thomas Mallet and his wife, in the company of Mary Carr and her brother, Sion Arnold. Another local man, Richard Cornish, later admitted that he identified Gillam, though he refused to confirm his identity to the inquisitive Mrs Mallet, despite her persistent questioning. Cornish was uncomfortable in Gillam's presence, claiming that he had little conversation with him, and that was unfriendly: 'I saying, I see you are not drowned yet, he answered, nor you hanged yett'.[99]

Gillam departed in a small boat accompanied by Edward Sands. He was bound for New York, but on the way he visited Gardiner's Island or the

---

[94] Ibid., p. 552; Jameson (ed.), *Privateering and Piracy*, p. 240.
[95] *CSPC, 1699*, p. 556.
[96] TNA, CO 5/861/4, IX.
[97] Ibid.
[98] TNA, CO 5/861/4, XII.
[99] TNA, CO 5/861/4, XIII.

Isle of Wight, to collect some jewels, gold and money which he had left with his old acquaintance, Gardiner. He was away from home when Gillam called, and his wife 'told him that she did not care to meddle with anything' until his return.[100] In reality, according to her husband's account, she was afraid to tell the pirate that Gardiner had handed the booty over to Bellomont. A few days later, while Gardiner and his wife were away, Gillam returned, only to discover from one of his men that his booty was missing. The pirate swore he would be revenged, warning that he 'would not spare man, woman nor Child', and promised to return and burn down the house and barns and destroy the livestock.[101] Anxiously Gardiner informed an associate that he and his wife lived in fear until Gillam was taken and executed.

From Gardiner's Island, Gillam, now using his alias Kelly, travelled to Boston, where he lodged with Andrew Knott and his wife. Knott later admitted that he knew the pirate about sixteen years ago, when they had sailed in the South Sea with captain Cooke. During a voyage lasting nearly four years they took about sixteen Spanish prizes, but 'put no persons to the sword'.[102] Gillam paid twenty pieces of Arabian gold to Knott for lodging and entertainment at his house. Knott's wife exchanged it with a goldsmith, and the money was used to buy clothes for the family and to pay off debts.[103] Although the pirate had more plunder to collect in New York and the Whorekill, time was running out for this violent, but versatile fugitive. Following his arrest, he was returned to England, tried and executed.

The ease with which Gillam travelled around the colonies depended on widespread popular collusion and support, of a kind which prevailed in parts of the British Isles during the sixteenth century. Pirates and rovers were assisted by an extensive web of support and mutuality linking pirate or privateering haunts along the eastern seaboard. These links, and the communication and trust that bound them together, left little evidence. But they involved women, often acting in partnership with husbands, in associations with pirates. Some wives played more active and visible roles following the arrest and imprisonment of spouses, while relying on a network of former pirates and accessories for support. In July 1699, writing from Boston gaol, where her husband was a prisoner, Sarah Kidd asked captain Pain to send twenty-four ounces of gold, part of a larger amount he

---

[100] Gardiner, an old associate of Kidd, owned the island; Jameson (ed.), *Privateering and Piracy*, pp. 220–3.

[101] TNA, CO 5/861/4, VIII and XIX.

[102] Jameson (ed.), *Privateering and Piracy*, p. 244; TNA, CO 5/861/4, XVII.

[103] Ibid.; Ritchie, *Captain Kidd*, p. 162.

was holding, 'for it is all we have to support us in time of want'.[104] The messenger was Knott, in whose house the incriminating letter was found. He admitted receiving seven bars of gold from Pain, for which he gave a receipt, but one apparently was lost during his return to Boston through a hole in his pocket. He handed the rest over to Rebecca, Kidd's servant maid, and later received twenty-four pieces of eight for undertaking the journey. Bellomont was convinced, after uncovering this evidence, that Pain had a lot more of Kidd's booty, but as he was beyond his jurisdiction, he was unable to pursue it.[105]

Women's collusion with piratical enterprise was acutely vulnerable to the changing structure of pirate lives. During the 1690s the expansion of seaborne plunder into the Indian Ocean and the development of distant, overseas bases, which came to serve as temporary habitations, revealed the fragility and flexibility of pirate relations with women. Visiting pirates were able to take advantage of conditions on Madagascar to establish a fluctuating and transient community of between 400 and 900 men on the island of Saint Mary's, off the north-east coast. Endemic rivalries and conflict enabled a number to enter the service of local rulers either as advisers or mercenaries, creating opportunities for some to inter-marry, in one case possibly into a ruling dynasty. Practice varied and was qualified by mutual suspicion which limited such liaisons. Nonetheless, remote regions, especially those not yet subject to the force of European colonialism, provided favourable conditions for the expression of the sexual freedom of pirates. In some native societies such contacts or unions may have had a deep, far-reaching localized impact, entering folklore, oral tradition and memory. Although the evidence is circumstantial, according to later report, the descendants of pirates were to be found among the inhabitants of Foulpoint in the north of Madagascar. They included Tom Similo or Similaho, and his sisters, whose father was reputedly an English pirate, known as Tom, who married the daughter of a local ruler.[106] Scant written evidence survives of the native women involved in these partnerships. If not victims, they were the silent accessories and witnesses to the pirate incursion into the region. In some cases they were probably pawns in wider political and diplomatic negotiations, as local leaders sought to

[104] *CSPC, 1699*, pp. 553, 557; TNA, CO 5/1184/340; Jameson (ed.), *Privateering and Piracy*, pp. 223–4.

[105] *CSPC, 1699*, p. 553; Jameson (ed.), *Privateering and Piracy*, p. 243; Zacks, *Pirate Hunter*, pp. 262–4.

[106] S. Randrianja and S. Ellis, *Madagascar: A Short History* (London, 2009), pp. 99–102, 105–6, 118; P. Oliver (ed.), *Madagascar: Or, Robert Drury's Journal, During Fifteen Years' Captivity on That Island* (London, 1890), pp. 44, 367.

contain or control the arrival of groups of unruly and potentially violent, well-armed rovers.

By contrast the survival of a handful of letters to and from Madagascar, among the records of the High Court of Admiralty, sheds light on the consequences of long-distance plunder for women who were left behind in the American colonies or England. The correspondence was carried by captain Samuel Burgess, who was employed by Frederick Philipse, a wealthy New York merchant and shipowner. Philipse developed a significant interest in Madagascar during these years, ranging from slaving and trading to supplying pirates with provisions and a passage to America. His vessels provided a means by which wives and partners were able to maintain links with pirates and seamen sailing in the Indian Ocean, though with varying degree of success. Such evidence demonstrated the determination of spouses to maintain contact with each other, as testimony of personal feelings and responsibilities, though it also underlined the resilience and resourcefulness of widows seeking to lay claim to the property of deceased partners.

The correspondence included details of bequests left by pirates to their wives and families, despite their lengthy absences from home. In a letter of March 1698 from Bristol, addressed to Adam Baldridge, who for several years ran a trading post on the island, Ann Cantrell explained that she had been informed of the death of her husband, John Read, at Madagascar, and that he 'left a Considerable sume of mony in your hands for myselfe and his Children'.[107] Advising Baldridge that she had authorized John Powell, a friend, to receive the money and other possessions, she concluded with the hope that he would be 'soe kind as to pay it, for myselfe and family are in very poor Condition, and in great want thereof'.[108] Unable to sign her name, Ann Cantrell left a mark, indicating that a neighbour or a clerk helped in its compilation. The correspondence was accompanied by a letter of attorney for Powell and a certificate of marriage to Read. The former authorized Powell, a mariner who was bound to New York and thence Madagascar, serving as second mate to Burgess, to recover Read's effects, with an allowance of one-eighth for himself. The certificate, drawn up by the vicar of St Austin's parish in Bristol, provided proof that Ann was the wife of Read, a mariner; furthermore, they had lived together for four years, during which time she gave birth to a son and a daughter. Thereafter Read went to sea, never to return. At the time of his death, he had been absent

---

[107] TNA, HCA 1/98/92, ff. 94–6; Jameson (ed.), *Privateering and Piracy*, pp. 176–7, 180–7; S. C. Hill, *Notes on Piracy in Eastern Waters* (Bombay, 1923), pp. 96–7.
[108] TNA, HCA 1/98/92, ff. 94–6.

from Ann and their children for nine years. In May 1693 she married John Cantrell, a cordwainer, presumably on the grounds of her abandonment by Read. Another correspondent, Mrs Whaley, received a letter from St Mary's, dated 6 April 1699, in a hand which is not easy to decipher, with information of her 'hosbondes will which is left wholey to you and your Children'.[109] Although the letter writer did not know the exact sum, it amounted to at least 3,000 pieces of eight which were reportedly in the hands of captain Shelly.

Some of the problems facing abandoned wives, including the stark sense of loss felt by family members, were revealed in a letter of June 1698 from Henry Crossley, in New York, to his brother, Robert, at Saint Mary's. While providing news of his wife and family, Crossley reported that they had been forced to stay with friends on Long Island, 'for she could nott Live any longer whear you left her', following the death of her father, and 'nott heareinge from you hath beene a great truble to her, she haveinge two small Children to mentaine'.[110] Indeed family and friends believed that he was dead, until Henry met a man who knew of his brother, and was able to give an account of where he was. Sending the letter by a neighbour, he hoped that Robert would return out of consideration for his wife, 'for I am shuer that your life cannott be soe Comfortable theare, as it would be with your owne flesh and bloud'.[111]

Such correspondence may have been neither unusual nor isolated. Some women seem to have sent letter after letter to Madagascar in the hope of receiving a reply. Although abbreviated, they contained family news, occasionally including local gossip and information. Above all, they testify to the loyalty and love of women who were forced to wait with patience for reports of their spouses. Two surviving letters by wives to partners of Kidd's company illustrate the nature of this correspondence. Neatly written in a clear hand, carefully folded and sealed, as well as bearing the signatures of both women, and dated 5 June 1698, they were addressed to their husbands at Madagascar or elsewhere. Both showed an urgent desire to hear news from them, while conveying strong feelings of love and separation. 'My Deare Deare Jacob Horne', began his wife Sarah, who hoped 'to God that these few lines will find you in Good Bodely helth as they Leave mee at this present time'.[112] She included news of their children. In accordance with the wishes of her husband, however, their son had been put out to a cousin, until Horne returned home. Sarah had written two previous letters, and

109 TNA, HCA 1/98/171.
110 TNA, HCA 1/98/153–5.
111 Ibid.
112 TNA, HCA 1/98/118. On correspondence see Ritchie, *Captain Kidd*, pp. 121–3.

received one reply, but she was concerned to hear from her husband, 'for wee here abundance of flying News concerning you'; as she prayed for his 'Helth and hapiness', she remained a 'true and faithfull wife tell Death'.[113] Sarah Horne's letter was accompanied by another from Flushing in New York to Richard Wilday from his wife, Edie, who hoped it would reach him in those remote parts of the world. Addressed to her dear and loving husband, Wilday's main concern was to inform him that she and their two children were in good health, despite suffering some sickness since his departure. Her other news included the death of their uncle and his son, and complaints against the high price of corn which left her in straitened circumstances. While hoping to see her husband 'if it weare the will of god', she was resigned to waiting for the return of his ship: 'I have not more to Inlarge', she concluded her brief letter, 'but only true Love to you with Dayly wishes for your Company is the Continuall Longing Desire of your true and loveing wife'.[114]

Wives received letters or replies, but in some cases it is not clear whether they were from pirates or seafarers. In April 1699 Abraham Samwaye sent his love to his wife and child in Bristol, insisting that he remained of 'an honeste mind to her still'.[115] Thomas Pringle of New York wrote to his wife of his love for her, while blessing their children, and hoping that she had saved the 200 pieces of eight which he sent her. Evan Jones, originally of Cardiff, informed his spouse that he intended to return home within the next five years, presumably after his success improved.[116]

The survival of this correspondence furnishes an unusual perspective on the relations between women and their pirate partners, although it provides little indication of their scale or extent. At its height about 1,000 men were engaged in piratical enterprise within the Indian Ocean. It is impossible, however, to determine the number of those who were married, single or associated with local women. A proposal for dealing with the pirates at Madagascar, presented to parliament in 1707, warned of the consequences of peace, 'and the Pyrates generating with the Women of the Country, their Numbers should be increased, they may form themselves into a Settlement of Robbers, as Prejudicial to Trade as any on the Coast of *Affrica*'.[117] Such

---

[113] TNA, HCA 1/98/118.

[114] TNA, HCA 1/98/116.

[115] TNA, HCA 1/98/172–3.

[116] TNA, HCA 1/98/187; R. C. Ritchie, 'Samuel Burgess, Pirate', in W. Pencak and C. E. Wright (eds), *Authority and Resistance in Early New York* (New York, 1988), pp. 121–2.

[117] [P. Osborne], *Reasons for Reducing the Pyrates at Madagascar* (London, 1707), reprinted in Baer (ed.), *British Piracy*, III, p. 419; TNA, CO 323/6/80–1.

language suggested that the pirates had abandoned wives and family in England and colonial America. But the following year forty women presented a petition to Queen Anne requesting that they be allowed to return home voluntarily with their personal possessions and plunder. The proposal was put forward as an effective, but cheap way of dealing with the problem, and of preventing the development of a permanent pirate settlement on the island. While demonstrating organization and cooperation among the female petitioners, they were manipulated by more powerful and predatory interests who were keen to share in the reported wealth of the pirates at Madagascar. There is little evidence that any of the women benefited from it. Unlike the fictional future wife of Daniel Defoe's repentant pirate captain, Bob Singleton, who sent substantial sums of money to the sister of his friend and companion in robbery, William the Quaker, few wives shared in their partner's plunder.[118]

Native companions and spouses: Madagascar, the Caribbean and Guinea during the 1720s

Defoe's portrait of captain Singleton suggested that alienated criminal entrepreneurs were capable of reform and rehabilitation particularly through a reaffirmation of family life. Reflecting values and morality at odds with the experiences of many rovers, the pirate captain expressed his yearning for a refuge: 'for really a Man that has a Subsistence, and no Residence, no Place that has a Magnetic Influence upon his Affections, is in one of the most odd uneasy Conditions in the World; nor is it in the Power of all his Money to make it up to him'.[119] Accompanied by William, he returned to England, both disguised as Persian merchants, finding undeserved happiness in marriage with his companion's sister. It is a striking example of the possibility of finding redemption in the love of a good woman, though it flew in the face of reality. The resurgence of piracy after 1714 stretched family bonds and loyalties to the limit. An increasing number of estranged recruits seemed to sever ties with family and friends ashore in favour of the autonomy and companionship aboard pirate ships. Although the lives of women and pirates continued to intersect, female agency was attenuated, and increasingly paradoxical and problematic in character.

Despite the decline and eventual break-up of the pirate settlement on

[118] D. Defoe, *The Life, Adventures, and Pyracies, of the Famous Captain Singleton (1720)*, ed. P. N. Furbank (London, 2008), pp. 221–3.
[119] Ibid., p. 224. But he was not a very convincing repentant figure according to P. Earle, *The World of Defoe* (London, 1976), pp. 229–30.

Madagascar, groups of rovers continued to haunt the island. A few joined the ranks of a growing number of scattered, solitary Europeans, marginal men who lived between cultures, cohabiting with native women, while retaining space between themselves and their hosts. Not much is known of these relationships, though they were colourfully portrayed by Charles Johnson as part of a pirate utopia where men lived a carefree life of sexual indulgence. Johnson's fictionalized account of the pirate commonwealth of Libertalia claimed that pirates consorted with local women, whose descendants formed a 'large motly Generation of Children and Grand-Children descended from them'.[120] According to his colourful report, which seemed designed to exploit the interest of a growing reading public in sex and scandal, 'they married the most beautiful of the Negroe Women, not one or two, but as many as they liked, so that every one of them had as great a Seraglio as the Grand Seignior at *Constantinople*'.[121] Robert Drury's journal of his fifteen years of captivity on the island may have drawn on Johnson's work to elaborate anecdotal evidence of liaisons between native women and pirates. But Drury also reported that at St Mary's they 'lived most dissolute and wicked lives, stealing away and ravishing the wives and daughters of the natives, living by this means in a state of continual war'.[122]

Inter-ethnic liaisons on Madagascar occurred within a wider context of private plantation by competitive, and occasionally cooperative, groups of French and English adventurers. The relationships pirates formed on the island were thus part of a pattern of irregular commerce and contact, which included slaving and plunder. But the intrusion of newcomers, voluntary or forced migrants who included occasional castaways, had the potential to disrupt and destabilize native communities. In these circumstances relations between pirates and local women were probably limited by mutual suspicion and ethnic antipathy. Drury, for example, almost apologized for the relationship he formed with one such woman, expressing concern that readers would doubt his passionate love for her.[123]

Nonetheless evidence presented to the High Court of Admiralty demonstrated that a number of pirates settled on Madagascar and other islands in the Indian Ocean, living like native lords, while forming relations with local women. According to a report of 1722, the pirate captain Edward Conden and some of his men inhabited the Mascarene Islands. They were reported

[120] Johnson, *General History of the Pyrates*, pp. 61, 426.
[121] Ibid., p. 59.
[122] Oliver (ed.), *Drury's Journal*, pp. 229, 232, 298, 309.
[123] Ibid., pp. 172–3. Drury's work has sometimes been dismissed as fabrication, but for a modern defence see M. Parker Pearson and K. Godden, *In Search of the Red Slave: Shipwreck and Captivity in Madagascar* (Stroud, 2002).

to be wealthy enough to 'live handsomely for the rest of their lives'.[124] Several of Conden's company, including John Plantin, were established on Madagascar. Plantin was a creole from Jamaica. Like Conden he seems to have retired from a life of piracy as a rich man. He lived with his wife and family on an offshore island in a fortified stockade, at a place he called Ranter Bay. One of the members of a naval expedition, sent out to track down pirates, met him on the beach, and later recalled that 'the Natives inhabiting the said Island sung songs in praise of Plantin the King of Ranter Bay'.[125] Although nothing is known of Plantin's native partner, she was an essential part of his presentation as an island chief. When Plantin met other members of the naval force, he was accompanied by a large group of between thirty and forty black men, carrying firearms, lances and a flag of St George, and two other Europeans, identified as James Deering, a Scot or Dutchman, and a Danish or Swedish companion. Despite this impressive display of Plantin's local power, its uncertainty and ambiguity were exposed by his reported lament that 'he would give half of what he was worth to be in a Christian Countrey'.[126] A day of convivial entertainment, feasting and trading was cut short when Plantin and his companions were abruptly forced to leave, following reports that his stockade was under attack.

Plantin's experience on Madagascar was complemented, and to some extent countervailed, by that of another white planter and trader, Cockburn. Although Cockburn informed members of the naval expedition that he had lived on the island for some time, little evidence survives of his background. It is possible that he was a former pirate. He was with another white man, and possibly accompanied by several black women, when he met some of the sailors near Charrock Point, known as the pirate rendezvous on the island. Evidently Cockburn was married; he also owned a large plantation on which he cultivated sugar and distilled rum. In addition he dealt in cattle and slaves which he received from a local ruler, identified as the king of Marthalea. Cockburn reported a recent visit by a company of pirates who forcibly recruited natives and all the white men

[124] TNA, HCA 1/55, f. 97v.
[125] Ibid., f. 79v; Plantin is named John and William in admiralty court records (TNA, HCA 1/54, ff. 138–8v and 1/55, ff. 81–91); Hill, *Notes on Piracy*, pp. 152–3; C. Downing, *A Compendious History of the Indian Wars: With an Account of the Rise, Progress, Strength, and Forces of Angria the Pyrate* (London, 1737), pp. 63–4, 105–16. There is no mention of Plantin in Johnson. The only person identified as marrying and having children on Madagascar was captain White; Johnson, *General History of the Pyrates*, pp. 485–6.
[126] TNA, HCA 1/55, f. 94.

they could find on the island, though he evaded their search parties. As a result he indicated that the natives would refuse to supply pirates in the future, though he advised the sailors that as long as they were civil, and took no slaves, they would receive as much provisions as they wanted.[127]

The pirate settlement of Madagascar was part of a broader, unpredictable, unsettling and often violent pattern of cross-cultural contact that swept across the Atlantic world during the early modern period. Its spread into the Indian Ocean, partly in the guise of anarchic predatory enterprise, produced confusing, if not contradictory responses, particularly in regions not yet fully exposed to European colonization. Native people, including women, may have been the occasional beneficiaries of the spread of piracy, but they were also its victims. Even in those unusual cases where pirates seem to have established stable relationships with native women, they were self-serving in purpose. More commonly, perhaps, such women were the short-term partners of visiting groups of pirates seeking entertainment and sexual gratification ashore for gifts of provisions and clothing. As such they exploited expectations among some of the inhabitants who lived in regions regularly visited by European seafarers. At the Cape of Good Hope, used as a harbour by pirates as well as traders, native men reportedly danced naked, shaking their genitals at visiting seamen, while 'offering their Wives for a bit of rolled Tobacco'.[128]

The behaviour of the pirates who haunted Madagascar was symptomatic of broader changes to the character of piratical enterprise which had profound implications for women's agency, including their relations with pirates. Faced with unfavourable and increasingly hostile conditions, pirate bands appeared to be running out of safe havens, while at the same time the number of voluntary recruits showed signs of decline. According to Johnson, no land would receive such a dangerous collection of outlaws.[129] The dramatic resurgence of piracy after 1714 was thus both short-lived and unusually violent in nature. A new generation of pirate leaders, such as Edward Teach or Charles Vane, were increasingly restricted to unsafe outposts among smaller, less regulated and more recent settlements in the Caribbean. These bases included the Bahamas where officials continued to warn of inhabitants 'who live without any Face or Form of Government, every Man doing onely what's right in his own Eyes'.[130] At such locations

---

[127] Ibid., ff. 98–100v.

[128] W. Hacke, *A Collection of Original Voyages* (London, 1699), pp. 33, 35. At Cape Verde loose women were 'easily led away by the Sailors' according to J. Ovington, *A Voyage to Surat in the Year 1689*, ed. H. G. Rawlinson (Oxford, 1929), p. 30.

[129] Johnson, *General History of the Pyrates*, pp. 6–7, 41–2.

[130] TNA, CO 37/10/4.

piracy became an expression of an alienated sub-culture of petty criminality and disorder. As the governor of Bermuda complained in 1723, 'Piracy & Accessarys to Piracy are Crimes here just as Epidemick as whoreing & drinking; nor is it lookt upon by us to be more enormous than smuggling is in Brittain'.[131] Pirates used the islands as temporary stopping-off points, adapting to a 'maroon life', a wandering, seaborne, vagrant lifestyle marked by erratic relations with women ashore.[132] Although it remained possible for pirates to find wives and partners, their relationships depended on the availability of surplus women on islands such as Bermuda, where significant imbalances in the sex ratio were reported by colonial officials.

Scattered evidence concerning conditions in the Caribbean indicated the persistence of marital relations between women and pirates. According to a report from Antigua of 1712, Tempest Rogers 'formerly a notorious pyrate' married a woman who was of the 'same stamp' as an 'old antiquated whore'.[133] Two years later the governor of Bermuda complained that the islands were a 'Retreat for Three Setts of Pyrates': two of the leaders were 'refug'd among those people', including captain Cockram who 'marry'd the daughter of one Thomson, one of the richest Inhabitants of Harbour Island'.[134] Preying on the Spanish, in small open boats, the pirates had taken booty to the value of £60,000 in eight months, most of which was rapidly and riotously spent ashore. At the same time, a list of rovers operating from the nearby settlement of Ilureathia included James Bourne, John Cary, John Kemp, Matthew Lowe and Daniel Stillwell, who were all married. Stillwell's wife was the daughter of John Darvill, a part-owner of one of the pirate vessels, the company of which included his son, aged seventeen.

Among some of the more recent island communities, officials warned of reformed pirates joining the ranks of debtors and criminals, marrying and settling down in poor conditions that seemed incapable of improvement. In July 1724 the governor of St Christopher's reported that the population of the Virgin Islands was 'increased by pirates, who have come in upon acts of Grace, and are married and settled there, whose posterity not knowing the world, remain there and cultivate the ground for a wretched subsistence'.[135] Lacking any form of justice, he assumed that the settlers retained close relations with pirates who were still at sea.

[131] *CSPC, 1722–23*, pp. 287–8; TNA, CO 37/26/27.
[132] *CSPC, 1724–25*, pp. 67–71. On sex ratios see reports in *CSPC, 1717–18*, p. 151; *CSPC, 1722–23*, pp. 171–4.
[133] *CSPC, 1712–14*, p. 88; TNA, CO 152/42/92.
[134] *CSPC, 1712–14*, p. 334.
[135] *CSPC, 1724–25*, pp. 143–4, 148–9.

Little evidence survives of the women involved in these partnerships. In the growing literature on piracy, including Johnson's popular *History*, they appeared to inhabit a shadowy world of ambivalence and brutal uncertainty. Johnson's work intended to demonstrate the 'otherness' of pirates as outlaws or outcasts, living beyond the pale of civil and commercial society, whose relations with women bordered on lurid fantasy. The image was epitomized by his account of Teach, the infamous and mythic Blackbeard, whose short and violent career as a pirate was cut short by his death in 1718. Yet there is no evidence, beyond Johnson, to support the portrait of a man who prostituted his young wife to other members of his company. The only reference that seems to survive of his relations with women is a report that he had a spouse and children in London. Stede Bonnet, an occasional associate of Teach, was also married, though for Johnson this was enough to explain his abandonment of planting on Barbados in favour of the sea. Thus the decision to become a pirate was the result of a disordered mind brought on by an unhappy marriage.[136]

While rovers deserted wives either through choice or necessity, they continued to benefit from female hospitality and assistance in some parts of the Caribbean, as the activities of Richard Tookerman of Carolina demonstrate. A resident of Charleston, Tookerman was widely suspected of assisting and trading with pirates, including Bonnet. Evidently he employed a sloop which regularly sailed to the Bahamas for that purpose. In 1718 he was arrested on suspicion of helping Bonnet and another pirate to escape from gaol. Although he was discharged, Tookerman was re-arrested for dealing in stolen goods, including pieces of silver, coral and amber. The evidence was found in his own possession, while his wife, Katherine, and several of his slaves were also implicated. He was fined and released. Subsequently he left Charleston clandestinely, travelling overland to Virginia with two or three slaves and several stolen horses. He moved on to Barbados, where a sister, Ann Foster, resided. It was a brief visit, during which he stole a small vessel in order to embark on a career of piracy or reprisals against his enemies in Charleston, 'having threaten'd several Gentlemen and Traders to that Effect'.[137] He was arrested during a visit to Jamaica by Edward Vernon, a naval captain. According to the case against him in the High Court of Admiralty of 1721, this was not for his activities at sea but for celebrating the birthday of the Stuart pretender to the throne, with a gun salute in Port Royal while he was dining ashore at the home of

---

[136] Johnson, *A General History of the Pyrates*, pp. 95ff; *CSPC, 1717–18*, p. 149 (for Teach's wife).

[137] TNA, HCA 1/54, ff. 132–2v; 1/55, ff. 1–4v.

Mrs Pendigrass. Public marks of dishonour towards the Hanoverian monarchy may have been common among pirate groups operating during these years. Johnson claimed that the king was derided by some pirates as the 'turnip man'; his comments were supported by reports that their 'expressions at drinking were Damnacon to King George'.[138] The political ideology behind such behaviour was limited and crude, but the alienation of pirates from the regime may have facilitated the formation of loose links with Jacobite sympathizers, especially among Irish Catholic communities in the Caribbean colonies.

As the conditions that sustained piracy grew less favourable during the 1720s, the relations between women and rovers became increasingly arbitrary and ambivalent. While there remained room, even in inadvertent or contingent circumstances, for female agency, it was overshadowed by the prospect of women becoming the victims of pirate groups. The tension between agency and victimization became overt during the late seventeenth and early eighteenth centuries, reflecting underlying changes to the character of piracy, particularly with the development of global venturing. In one form it was manifest in the situation of wives or mothers whose husbands or sons were forced to serve aboard pirate ships. Forced recruitment was a difficult issue, not only for victims and families but also for courts and legal authorities. Some pirates on trial for their lives insisted that they served under compulsion or the threat of violence and torture. The problem was intensified by the apparent decline in voluntary recruits. Although pirate companies tended to select single men against those who were known to be married, they also showed a marked preference for able and skilled seafarers.[139] By chance or design this included a proportion of married men, some of whom were undoubtedly less unwilling to serve than others. Judges and legal officials were aware of the problem, and tried to handle it in an effective, though expeditious, fashion. Yet claims regarding the use of force were usually insufficient on their own for a case to be dismissed. Courts also took notice of the testimony of other witnesses concerning conduct and behaviour, in addition to marital status. In some circumstances the existence of wives and families may have influenced the outcome of legal proceedings. While providing a context for judges and jurors, concern for women and children helped to shape responses to individual cases.

[138] *CSPC, 1717–18*, pp. 263–4; Johnson, *General History of the Pyrates*, p. 276; Jameson (ed.), *Privateering and Piracy*, p. 315; Rankin, *Golden Age*, pp. 95–6. Highwaymen of the 1690s also expressed Jacobite sentiments; L. B. Faller, *Turned to Account: The Form and Functions of Criminal Biography in Late Seventeenth- and Early Eighteenth-Century England* (Cambridge, 1987), p. 210.
[139] Earle, *Pirate Wars*, pp. 207–8.

Published reports of trial proceedings, though not necessarily representative, shed light on the problem. One of the largest trials, held at Cape Coast Castle in Guinea during March and April 1722, involved more than ninety men who faced charges of piracy. Among the accused at least eight were married men, most with children. Four were acquitted. They included William May who in support of his claim to be a forced recruit 'said he had a Wife and Family that was too near to him, to think of leaving for such a Life as Pyrating', and Roger Pye, a newly-wed, whose wife was pregnant.[140] Henry Glassby's case was supported by the evidence of witnesses that he was a reluctant participant in piracy. Glassby was one of the few defendants who admitted to sending money to his wife. In addition, Richard Scot was acquitted partly on the evidence of Glassby, who overheard him 'talking pathetically of his Wife and Child that must be sufferers by this unhappy Accident'.[141] Those who were found guilty included Robert Harris, married with five children; William Petty, with a wife and three children; and William Taylor and George Wilson, both married with children. Taylor's sentence was changed to a term of servitude in West Africa. The execution of Wilson, a surgeon, was delayed awaiting a pardon from the king.

Yet there were some recruits who volunteered to serve aboard pirate ships despite their marital status. Among a group of ten men who left a slave ship off Sierra Leone in 1718 to join a company of pirates was Simon Jones, who justified his conduct by his domestic circumstances. According to the captain whom he deserted, 'he had a Wife whom he could not love; and for these Reasons he had entred with the Pirates, and signed their Articles'.[142]

Women responded to these challenges in resourceful and sometimes creative ways. In some cases wives demonstrated initiative and considerable resolve in trying to defend and protect the interests of spouses. In a case of 1700, Elizabeth Davis, whose husband, John, was forcibly recruited to serve with pirates, petitioned the Commissioners of the Admiralty, in an attempt to avoid the risk of her husband being put on trial if they were taken. She provided the commissioners with evidence which was supported by two witnesses, including the master of the vessel in which her husband had served. Concerned that both men were soon likely to return to sea, she

---

[140] *A Full and Exact Account, of the Tryal of all the Pyrates Lately Taken by Captain Ogle* (London, 1723), reprinted in Baer (ed.), *British Piracy*, III, pp. 92–3. The manuscript copy is in TNA, HCA 1/99/3.

[141] *A Full and Exact Account*, reprinted in Baer (ed.), *British Piracy*, III, pp. 100, 105, 117–19, 139, 155–6, 163–4.

[142] But he was despised by 'his Brethren in Iniquity … and … died a few Months after'; Snelgrave, *Guinea*, pp. 219–20.

successfully appealed to the commissioners for the judge of the High Court of Admiralty to take their testimony under oath before they departed.[143]

The changing nature of female agency was underlined by the experiences of native women along the coast of Guinea. Despite the dangers of disease or capture, an increasing number of pirate groups haunted the region, seeking men and provisions from slave ships and opportunities for sexual liaisons. In 1683 captain John Cooke and his company acquired a number of African girls at Sierra Leone. They were forced to sail with them aboard a recently captured prize, which had been re-named the *Batchelor's Delight*, on a voyage into the South Atlantic where most of the girls died.[144] Such behaviour became more common during the 1720s. Johnson claimed that in one harbour captain Edward England and his men 'liv'd ... very wantonly for several Weeks, making free with the Negroe Women, and committing such outrageous Acts, that they came to an open Rupture with the Natives, several of whom they kill'd, and one of their Towns they set on Fire'.[145] At the Cape Verde Islands several of captain Howell Davis' men were 'so charm'd with the Luxuries of the Place, and the free Conversation of some Women, that they staid behind'; one, Charles Franklin, reportedly married and settled down, 'and lives there to this Day'.[146] At Sierra Leone sexual relations were apparently facilitated by a small settlement of traders who had spent some of their lives 'privateering, buccaneering, or pyrating, and still retain and love the Riots and Humours, common to that Sort of Life'.[147] Maintaining cordial relations with local people, they employed male and female servants. The latter were 'so obedient, that they are very ready to prostitute themselves to whomsoever their Masters shall command them'.[148]

Although Johnson embroidered his text, his description of pirates seeking entertainment and sex with African women is, to some extent, supported by captain William Snelgrave's account of Guinea which was

[143] TNA, HCA 1/29, ff. 214–15.
[144] O. H. K. Spate, *The Pacific Since Magellan, Volume II: Monopolists and Freebooters* (London, 1983), p. 145.
[145] Johnson, *General History of the Pyrates*, p. 117.
[146] Ibid., p. 170.
[147] Ibid., p. 226. White residents lived there as 'free Merchants' according to Snelgrave, *Guinea*, p. 202.
[148] Johnson, *General History of the Pyrates*, p. 226; *A New Generall Collection of Voyages and Travels*, 4 vols (London, 1745–7), II, pp. 316–17. Residents included John Leadstone, known locally as Crackers, a former buccaneer who reputedly kept the best house in the region as well as a harem, and John England, brother of the pirate Edward England, who lived along the river Gambia. TNA, HCA 1/30, f. 116; A. P. Kup, *A History of Sierra Leone 1400–1787* (Cambridge, 1961), pp. 52–3, 56.

published in 1734. An experienced slaving captain who was captured by pirates near Sierra Leone in 1718, Snelgrave devoted the third part of his book to recounting his experiences as a prisoner of captain Cocklyn. Noting that the rule among the pirates was 'not to allow Women to be on board their Ships, when in Harbour', at Sierra Leone 'they went on Shore to the Negroe-Women, who were very fond of their Company, for the sake of the great presents they gave them. Nay, some white Men that lived there, did not scruple to lend their black Wives to the Pirates, purely on account of the great Rewards they gave.'[149] The use of gifts, as in other contexts, was essential to the maintenance of such contact. Indeed Snelgrave complained that the African servants of white traders grew very insolent as a result of the 'large quantity of Goods given them by the Pirates, [and] that they would do nothing but what they pleased'.[150]

The extent of contact between pirates and African women is difficult to gauge. According to Snelgrave, only Cocklyn and two other pirate captains went ashore, decked out in second-hand coats taken from the slaving vessel. Evidently they had drawn lots for the clothes. To his displeasure, Cocklyn, a short man, got the longest of the coats which reached almost to his ankles. His companions reassured him, explaining that as 'they were going on shore amongst the *Negro-Ladies*, who did not know the white Mens fashions, it was no matter. Moreover, as his Coat was Scarlet embroidered with Silver, they believed he would have preference of them, (whose Coats were not so showy) in the opinion of their Mistresses.'[151] When the three captains returned aboard ship they met with hostility from the rest of the company, who were angered that the coats had been taken without the permission of the quarter master.

The African women who were involved in these encounters appear as anonymous and silent presences. While responding to the appearance of white pirates along the coast, their behaviour may have been the product of customary practice and sociability. Within societies where polygamy was widespread, at least among ruling elites, and within a context of competitive cross-cultural commerce and exchange, women were used as diplomatic and sexual pawns or gifts, in return for pirate booty and other favours. Coincidentally, the spread of piracy to West Africa occurred at a time when the slave trade was growing very rapidly. Snelgrave noted that the number of English slave ships grew from thirty-three in 1712 to more than two hundred in 1726.[152] While there was a distinction between pirates and

[149] Snelgrave, *Guinea*, pp. 256–7.
[150] Ibid., p. 262.
[151] Ibid., pp. 256–7.
[152] Ibid., Introduction (unpaginated), pp. 124–30.

slavers, this may have been of little practical consequence in parts of the region during a period of commercial expansion which fuelled endemic native rivalries and conflict, to the benefit of English and other European adventurers. According to Snelgrave, for example, the ruler of Dahomey 'bestowed ... some of his near Relations for Wives' on one English trader.[153]

Under these conditions, while native women in West Africa may have been unwitting spectators to the disturbing intrusion of pirates, they were also likely to be passive or unwilling sexual partners, if not the victims of gift exchange. During the course of the trial of pirates at Cape Coast Castle in 1722, it emerged that one of the accused, William Davies, had previously consorted with a native group at Sierra Leone, receiving the gift of a woman. Davies subsequently sold the woman to an unidentified buyer, provoking angry complaints from her friends to the local agent of the Royal African Company, in whose service he was currently employed. In response the agent apparently gave Davies to the Africans, telling them 'they might take his Head off if they would'.[154] Instead he was sold to a black Christian, subsequently joining the pirate company of captain Bartholomew Roberts.

*

As the evidence assembled in this chapter demonstrates, the oceanic expansion of English piracy from the 1650s to the 1720s created opportunities and problems for women. To some extent female agency supported the spread of plunder across the Atlantic and beyond. Yet the lives of women intersected with those of buccaneers, pirates and other rovers in shifting and occasionally surprising ways. Their role in such enterprise was varied and vulnerable, reflecting underlying changes to the character of piracy, especially its fragmentation and dispersal to diverse regions, ranging from the Caribbean to the Indian Ocean. Within these different contexts piratical venturing, and the responses it provoked, were qualified by local conditions, which in turn helped to shape or influence female participation. There were, for example, far-reaching differences between conditions on Jamaica during the 1660s and 1670s and on Madagascar twenty or thirty years later.

A common thread which linked these disparate locations was the way in which agency was articulated through the relations between women and pirates. In the Caribbean, colonial North America or elsewhere, women seemed to be much less involved in the business of receiving or dealing in

[153] Ibid., p. 8.
[154] *A Full and Exact Account*, reprinted in Baer (ed.), *British Piracy*, III, pp. 144–5.

plundered booty. Instead they were engaged in contacts or negotiations with pirates that evolved under different conditions. As piracy spread across the Atlantic, moreover, it became confused with a broader culture of irregular relationships and prostitution in emergent colonial societies, which drew on, but was separate from, the customs and behaviour of seafaring communities. At the same time the intrusion of growing numbers of pirates into the South Sea and the Indian Ocean encouraged the formation of inter-ethnic liaisons, although the limited evidence, if not at times silence, regarding these links, has obscured their significance.

The overriding characteristic of many of these relationships, including female agency more generally, was its profound ambiguity. While the nature of piracy and pirate life during these years tended to marginalize women, it also compromised their roles as wives, partners, prostitutes or mothers. In effect there was an inherent, and increasingly overt, tension between the position of women as agent or victim. The ambivalence is curiously captured in a story repeated by Johnson concerning the execution of a group of pirates which was intended to demonstrate 'how stupid and thoughtless they were at their End'.[155] As the pirates 'walk'd to the Gallows without a Tear, in Token of Sorrow for their past Offences', one of them, recognizing a woman in the crowd, exclaimed that 'he had lain with that B___h three Times, and now she was come to see him hanged'.[156] Though meant as an entertaining and moralizing vignette, the vicious language betrayed a thinly veiled prejudice, while laying bare the uncertain and unruly relations between women and pirates.

[155] Johnson, *General History of the Pyrates*, p. 286.
[156] Ibid.

~ 4 ~

Petitioners and Victims
Women's Experiences from the 1620s
to the 1720s

In 1614 Richard Daniel, a ship-master from Youghal, was seized with the rest of his company by pirates and sold into slavery. Four years later his wife, Ellen, received a licence from the Lord Deputy of Ireland, authorizing her to beg for two years, to support herself and five small children, while collecting money for his ransom.[1] How she survived with such a burden is unknown. Like other women in similar situations, she may have received help from kin or neighbours, including support from parish relief which was supplemented by earnings from low-paid casual work as well as unlicensed begging. As in so many other cases involving the poor during this period, her life appears as a fleeting, fragmentary episode whose personal dramas and crises are veiled by a lack of evidence. Whether she was successful in recovering her husband from captivity is also unknown, though as the years passed the prospect of his return receded. Daniel's difficult circumstances formed part of a broader pattern experienced by thousands of women whose spouses, partners or sons were taken prisoner and enslaved by the Barbary corsairs, a hybrid collection of pirates and sea raiders operating from bases in the Mediterranean and North Africa. The scale of the problem provoked various solutions and remedies, some of which were profoundly revealing about wider attitudes towards women. The anonymous author of the 'Seamen's New Year's Gift to the King', of January 1636, glossed over the plight of women such as Ellen Daniel, arguing that prostitutes and others should be exchanged for male captives in Barbary. Claiming that one woman could be used to release six male captives, the proposal may have had some appeal as a means of rescuing honest men from the 'lustfull desires of the heathen Turkes', while removing loose-living, disreputable females, who 'Comitte sinn with gredines'.[2]

---

[1] *CSPI, 1615–25*, p. 209.
[2] TNA, SP 16/311/9; N. Matar, *Turks, Moors, and Englishmen in the Age of Discovery* (New York, 1999), pp. 40–1. The idea of exchanging criminals for Christian captives

Although there is little sign that the proposal was seriously considered, it exposed a wider reluctance to acknowledge the victimization of women by corsairs and pirates, which can still be detected in modern works on the subject.

Yet the upsurge in raiding by the Barbary corsairs, accompanied by the global expansion of English piracy, exposed a growing number of women to opportunistic and predatory violence. In one notorious incident which cast a dark shadow over English interests in India, during 1695 captain Henry Avery and his company seized one of the Surat trading fleet, the *Ganj-i Sawai*, as it was sailing from Mocha richly laden with cargo and passengers returning from a pilgrimage to Mecca.[3] During a frenzied, uncontrolled assault, an elderly high-ranking woman from the Mughal's court was abused, several others were raped, and at least two female passengers were reported to have killed themselves, to avoid the shame and humiliation of returning to their husbands. The incident provoked angry retaliation, including the arrest of English merchants in Surat and elsewhere, and demands that the East India Company provide protection at sea against the danger of attack by pirates. Johnson noted in his *General History of the Pyrates* that 'the great Noise this Thing made in *Europe*, as well as *India*, was the Occasion of all these romantick Stories which were formed of *Avery's* Greatness'.[4] Bizarrely, they included false rumours that Avery married one of the Mughal's daughters who was a passenger aboard the *Ganj-i Sawai*. At the same time, the stories and tales of Avery's exploit denied, elided or ignored the violent assault on the women. The confusion and self-denial were acknowledged by the author of the fictional history of Avery, *The King of Pirates*, which was published in 1720. Under the guise of the narrator, Avery rebutted reports in England that he ravished the granddaughter of the Mughal, insisting that 'like a true Pirate ... [he] had more Mind to the Jewels than to the Lady'.[5] Nor, it seems, were any of her companions assaulted: 'We did, indeed, ravish them of all their Wealth, for that was what we wanted, not the Women.'[6] Yet in a disturbing and revealing addition, the pirate-author

in North Africa lingered on into the 1780s; S. Rees, *The Floating Brothel* (London, 2001), p. 55.

[3] J. F. Jameson (ed.), *Privateering and Piracy in the Colonial Period: Illustrative Documents* (New York, 1923), p. 159; L. Benton, *A Search for Sovereignty: Law and Geography in European Empires, 1400–1900* (Cambridge, 2010), p. 142.

[4] Johnson, *General History of the Pyrates*, pp. 53–4.

[5] *The King of Pirates: Being an Account of the Famous Enterprises of Captain Avery* (London, 1720), p. 58; *The Life and Adventures of Capt. John Avery* (London, 1709), pp. 28–32.

[6] *King of Pirates*, p. 59.

admitted that women of lesser rank were repeatedly violated, but as they 'made no Opposition, so the Men even took those that were next them, without Ceremony, when and where Opportunity offer'd'.[7]

These two episodes, though separated by time, geography and culture, illustrate how women of varied backgrounds were the victims of piracy and piratical violence. As the case of Ellen Daniel suggests, however, there was a close association between victimhood and agency which was modified by context and conditions, and by unwritten assumptions concerning the status of the victim. As the widows, mothers, wives and relatives of men who were killed or kidnapped by pirates, English women were innocent victims, whose circumstances aroused widespread sympathy, providing some compensation for the limited availability of institutional support. They might be perceived as deserving victims who enjoyed a degree of power that in other circumstances would have either been unavailable or denied.[8] By contrast many of the women who were directly subject to pirate assault or rape were almost invisible, literally so in that they were rarely identified and potentially ambiguous victims. As such their status was qualified by wider considerations concerning violence towards women, including ethnicity and religion.

The pattern of female victimization which grew out of organized piracy, though difficult to gauge in terms of intensity, exhibited chronological and regional variations. While closely linked with the changing character and rhythm of piratical enterprise, this pattern also reflected an underlying shift in the character of piracy and attitudes towards it within English society. Despite the limits of a patriarchal society, public concern at the activities of pirates and sea rovers enabled or empowered women, many of humble backgrounds, providing opportunities for them to exert agency as petitioners and victims.

Captives and wives

It was the spread of Barbary raiding beyond the Mediterranean which turned hundreds, possibly thousands, of women into petitioners for assistance to redeem captured husbands, sons, kin or friends. Nor were men and

---

[7] Ibid., pp. 59, 61–3. To some extent this view foreshadows the treatment of rape and the disturbing humour that accompanied it later in the eighteenth century; S. Dickie, *Cruelty and Laughter: Forgotten Comic Literature and the Unsentimental Eighteenth Century* (Chicago, 2011), pp. 190–209. According to one report, Avery bragged about throwing the princess overboard; *CSPC, 1697*, pp. 613–15.

[8] On victims, deserving or otherwise, see S. Walklate, *Imagining the Victim of Crime* (Maidenhead, 2007), pp. 25–7, 44, 106.

boys the only casualties of these raids: a small, but significant number of women were among those carried off into captivity in North Africa. The issue of English enslavement, dramatically publicized by captivity narratives, sermons and other reports, aroused anger and fear which were inflamed by ethnic hostility. A newsletter of 1681, supporting relief for captives in Algiers, complained that there remained under the 'barbarous tyranny of those infidels no less than 14,000 Christians of all nations and of English no less than 2,500'.[9] Among the victims was Seth Sothell, one of the proprietors of the recently established colony of Carolina. Captured while crossing the Atlantic, Sothell was taken to Algiers and detained for two years, reportedly as a slave in chains. He was employed as a labourer, until his captors became aware of his status, after which they demanded a huge ransom for his release. Although the ransom demands for most prisoners were considerably less, even raising smaller sums of twenty to thirty pounds taxed the resources of most families.[10]

The raids of the Barbary corsairs were a legacy of the longstanding conflict in the Mediterranean between Christendom and Islam. As a successor and surrogate to holy war, corsair enterprise developed as a commercialized enterprise, acquiring its own rules and customs, which encompassed plunder at sea and coastal raiding for booty and slaves. Under favourable conditions it expanded rapidly during the sixteenth century, as demonstrated by the striking growth of Algiers and the spread of activity to ports such as Tunis and Tripoli, with the support and protection of local rulers and regents. It was followed by the development of bases along the coast of Morocco, including Mamora and Salé, which coincided with the widening range of the corsairs and their irruption into the competitive and predatory maritime arena of the Atlantic.[11]

Although the dangers of corsair raiding may have been exaggerated, there is no denying its far-reaching social and cultural reverberations. Authors as diverse as Cervantes and Castiglione reflected on the ordeal of capture and imprisonment, as well as on the trauma of captivity. Its impact

---

[9] *CSPD, 1680–81*, p. 598; L. Colley, *Captives: Britain, Empire and the World, 1600–1850* (London, 2002), p. 48, writes of a 'captivity panic'.

[10] *CSPD, 1680–81*, p. 458.

[11] F. Braudel, *The Mediterranean and the Mediterranean World in the Age of Philip II*, 2 vols, translated by S. Reynolds (London, 1972), I. p. 119; II, pp. 971–2, 991–6, 1049–50; R. C. Davis, *Christian Slaves, Muslim Masters: White Slavery in the Mediterranean, the Barbary Coast, and Italy, 1500–1800* (Basingstoke, 2003), pp. 29–33, 75–6; J. Heers, *The Barbary Corsairs: Warfare in the Mediterranean, 1480–1580*, translated by J. North (London, 2003), pp. 21–32, 153–4; P. Earle, *Corsairs of Malta and Barbary* (London, 1970), pp. 40–58.

was a recurring theme for Cervantes, whose profound understanding of the psychology of imprisonment was based partly on his own experience as a captive at Algiers. The indirect consequences, and their potentially ambivalent meanings for women and families, were illuminated by Castiglione's tale of Tommaso in *The Courtier*. Carried off to Barbary, but rescued secretly by one of his sons, Tommaso wrote a letter to his wife announcing his freedom. Overwhelmed with joy at the news, unfortunately she 'fell lifeless to the ground'.[12] Tales and stories, the combination of personal experience, oral tradition and the circulation of narratives, with their subsequent echo in works of fiction, such as Defoe's *Robinson Crusoe*, testify to the deep social and cultural impact of Barbary raiding and captivity.[13]

While English vessels sailing in the Mediterranean were at risk from attack by the corsairs, it was their expansion into the Atlantic during the early seventeenth century which increased the threat of maritime plunder and coastal raiding. The danger was reflected in a rapid increase in the number of English captives held at Algiers. According to the English ambassador in Spain, between 1603 and 1610 at least 466 of his compatriots were taken by corsairs operating from the port.[14] Traditionally the spread of Barbary raiding beyond the Mediterranean has been blamed on renegade pirate captains, notably Ward and Simon Danser. In reality, it was the result of a more complex interplay of expertise, knowledge and shipping, which was driven by local and international competition for prizes at sea. Undoubtedly it was facilitated by renegade and captive mariners from northern Europe, who served as guides and pilots for the corsairs. Prominent renegades earned renown and infamy for their ability to create new lives and identities for themselves in Barbary. The transfer of loyalties and allegiances, part of the process of 'turning Turk', provoked widespread condemnation at the implied threat to Christian culture and religion.[15] But

[12] B. Castiglione, *The Book of the Courtier*, translated by G. Bull (London, 2003), pp. 231–2. On Cervantes see M. A. Garcés, *Cervantes in Algiers: A Captive's Tale* (Nashville, 2002), pp. 134–254; P. E. Russell, *Cervantes* (Oxford, 1985), pp. 10–11.

[13] On the significance of tales and their impact see Colley, *Captives*, pp. 82–98, 113–25; G. Maclean and N. Matar, *Britain and the Islamic World, 1558–1713* (Oxford, 2011), pp. 126–51; M. de Cervantes Saavedra, *The Ingenious Hidalgo Don Quixote de la Mancha*, translated by J. Rutherford (London, 2000), pp. 360–95, for the captive's tale.

[14] J. B. Wolf, *The Barbary Coast: Algiers Under the Turks 1500 to 1830* (New York, 1972), p. 184; and A. G. Jamieson, *Lords of the Sea: A History of the Barbary Corsairs* (London, 2012), pp. 78–103.

[15] A. Tinniswood, *Pirates of Barbary: Corsairs, Conquests and Captivity in the Seventeenth-Century Mediterranean* (London, 2010), pp. 83–5. See also E. Kellet, *A Return From Argier. A Sermon Preached at Minhead in the County of Somerset* (London, 1628), pp. 6, 31–3, 41, 75.

the outrage tended to deflect attention away from those wives and families who were deserted by renegade pirates.

Despite periodic anxiety and alarm, the scale of Barbary raiding in northern waters was often modest and subject to fluctuation. Even so, it exposed the defensive vulnerability and naval weaknesses of the Stuart regime, provoking political controversy about the guardianship of the sea. At times, few places along the Channel seemed to be safe from opportunistic raids. In 1616 a Turkish pirate was taken off Leigh, in the Thames estuary, by captain Mainwaring, who freed the Christian captives aboard.[16] A former pirate who was pardoned and knighted by James I, Mainwaring was the author of a 'Discourse of Piracy' of 1617, which included details of the operation and activities of the corsairs. According to Mainwaring's account, the Algerians usually sailed in fleets of eight or nine vessels, armed with between twenty and thirty pieces of ordnance. Occasionally the number may have been greater. During 1616 seven English fishing vessels, bound for Italy from Newfoundland, were attacked within the Mediterranean by thirty Turkish men-of-war. About the same time a fleet of eighteen corsairs raided the Azores, carrying off men, women and children from Santa Maria Island. Warning that the pirates increased 'like Hidraes', one of James I's courtiers claimed that there were seventy corsair vessels based in Algiers; many were above 200 tons burden, and they were 'for the most part manned with voluntarye renegados of all nations'.[17]

From an English perspective the threat of Barbary raiding was especially acute during the early decades of the seventeenth century. While attacks on shipping within the Mediterranean grew, during the 1620s and 1630s the appearance of corsairs in the Channel was almost an annual event, inspiring fear and alarm in many seafaring communities. The threat, mainly from raiders of Salé, appears to have terrified the inhabitants of fishing ports and harbours in the south west. According to the justices of Cornwall in 1636, local fishermen ran their vessels onto the rocks, preferring to lose their boats rather than their liberty; others were too afraid to put to sea, 'but ... are in greate feare these Turkes will have the boldnes to come on shoare, and take them out of their houses'.[18] The fear was intensified by reports of the ordeal of slavery, reinforced by hostile images of the Turk drawn partly from literary and dramatic representations which played on deeper concerns

[16] J. Maclean (ed.), *Letters From George Lord Carew to Sir Thomas Roe, 1615–1617* (Camden Society, First Series, 76, 1860), p. 51.

[17] Ibid., pp. 50, 61, 139.

[18] TNA, SP 16/328/62; D. D. Hebb, *Piracy and the English Government, 1616–1642* (Aldershot, 1994), pp. 139–45; K. R. Andrews, *Ships, Money and Politics: Seafaring and Naval Enterprise in the Reign of Charles I* (Cambridge, 1991), pp. 161–5.

regarding ethnicity, identity and sexuality. But English responses also betrayed ambiguity, if not confusion, as exemplified in a report of 1617 concerning the presence of Turkish pirates on the coasts of England and Ireland, which claimed that they did no damage, though it was in their power to do so.[19] The corsairs purchased provisions from English fishermen in the Channel, and subsequently seized three Spanish ships, reviving hopes in some quarters of the prospect of an alliance with the Barbary regencies against Spain.

The corsairs seized a large number of vulnerable trading and fishing vessels, including many returning from Newfoundland. During the early seventeenth century they also raided isolated communities in south-west England and Ireland, in random and opportunistic attacks. Following a raid on Baltimore in southern Ireland during 1631, 109 men, women and children were carried off into captivity in North Africa. At the end of the decade, about sixty of the inhabitants of Penzance, including children, were seized by Turkish pirates. Although the level of activity began to fall after the 1640s, a petition from British slaves of 1662 warned that there were still forty corsair vessels based in Algiers, each manned with a company of between 200 and 400 men. They seized merchant ships under cover of Flemish colours, and with Christian captives on deck to avoid detection by naval vessels; and they continued to haunt northern waters. In June 1672 two Turkish men-of-war were reported to be cruising off the Scilly Isles, while another was off the Lizard. Three years later a fleet of seven or eight raiders from Algiers was sailing in the Channel, though it did not attack English ships. Between 1677 and 1680 Algerian corsairs reportedly seized more than 150 vessels from the British Isles, though many were small or modest in size. Although the use of passes may have provided some defence against capture, the plunder of such shipping continued into the eighteenth century.[20]

The impact of Barbary raiding, in human terms, was extensive and enduring, though it varied regionally. From the late sixteenth to the early

---

[19] Maclean (ed.), *Letters*, p. 125; *HMC, Eleventh Report, Part I* (London, 1887), pp. 11, 32, for the alliance. English attitudes towards the Turks were never 'monolithic'; Colley, *Captives*, pp. 102–13. For an invaluable collection of material see D. J. Vitkus (ed.), *Piracy, Slavery, and Redemption: Barbary Captivity Narratives from Early Modern England* (New York, 2001).

[20] Tinniswood, *Pirates of Barbary*, pp. 136–7, 140, 188, 238–9, 256; Davis, *Christian Slaves*, p. 7; D. Ekin, *The Stolen Village: Baltimore and the Barbary Pirates* (Dublin, 2006); M. MacCarthy-Morrogh, *The Munster Plantation: English Migration to Southern Ireland 1583–1641* (Oxford, 1986), pp. 152–5; *CSPD, 1661–62*, p. 285; *CSPD, 1672*, pp. 225, 297; *CSPD, 1675–76*, pp. 134, 136, 172, 186, 320; *Several Voyages to Barbary* (2nd edition, London, 1736), pp. 142–6.

eighteenth centuries, seafaring communities in London and south-west England were more exposed to the seizure of shipping and seamen than those elsewhere. While there were erratic short-term fluctuations in the chronology of raiding, moreover, there was a gradual, but noticeable decline in its intensity across the period. Figures for the number of captives held in Barbary provide crude, but revealing, estimates which shed light on the scale of the problem. According to a report of 1626 there were more than 3,000 captives from the British Isles in Algiers, and between 1,200 and 1,400 in Salé. A petition to the king of October 1640 claimed that there were still about 3,000 of his subjects in captivity at Algiers, who were forced to serve aboard galleys or undertake menial labour and 'divers such unchristianlike works' ashore.[21] The following year, in March 1641, it was reported that Algerian corsairs had taken 131 ships, as well as 2,555 captives, while parliament was informed that between 4,000 and 5,000 prisoners were held in captivity at Tunis and Algiers. According to a modern estimate, based on a careful review of the evidence, between 1616 and 1642 about 400 vessels and 8,000 British subjects were taken by Barbary raiders. During peak periods, especially the 1630s, it is possible that as many as 1,000 inhabitants of the British Isles were taken each year and enslaved by the corsairs.[22]

Although the number of captives declined during the second half of the seventeenth century, even in the Channel shipping and seamen remained at risk. In 1662 at least 300 British captives were held in Algiers. A report of 1670 claimed that the Algerians had recently taken about thirty English vessels and 400 men. The following year it was reported that nearly 100 English captives were at Salé. At least 3,000 captives were taken during the war with Algiers from 1677 to 1682. According to a newsletter of 1680, the total number of English captives in Barbary amounted to about 2,500.[23]

The capture and enslavement of seafarers and others created serious problems, albeit localized and varying in intensity. The experiences of men, women and children contributed to an emerging narrative of victimhood which led to a variety of responses. Lacking well-established and special-

[21] TNA, SP 16/469/23; N. Matar, *Islam in Britain, 1558–1685* (Cambridge, 1998), p. 7; Vitkus (ed.), *Piracy, Slavery, and Redemption*, pp. 14–16.
[22] W. Notestein (ed.), *The Journal of Sir Simonds D'Ewes From the Beginning of the Long Parliament to the Opening of the Trial of the Earl of Strafford* (New Haven, 1923), pp. 418–19, 492; Hebb, *Piracy and the English Government*, pp. 269–70; Davis, *Christian Slaves*, p. 3; C. Lloyd, *English Corsairs on the Barbary Coast* (London, 1981), p. 113.
[23] *CSPD, 1661–62*, p. 285; *CSPD, 1670*, pp. 170, 186; *CSPD, 1671*, p. 389; *CSPD, 1680–81*, p. 598; Colley, *Captives*, pp. 51–2. Corsairs seized 341 captives during the year ending in April 1681; C. R. Pennell (ed.), *Piracy and Diplomacy in Seventeenth-Century North Africa: The Journal of Thomas Baker, English Consul in Tripoli* (London, 1989), p. 128.

ized institutions, such as the religious orders that dealt with redemption in the Catholic countries of southern Europe, the English response was a combination of intermittent government action and irregular private initiatives. Such an approach relied on charity and benevolence, supported or promoted by the church. As a result there was a danger that appeals for aid might be undermined by a discriminating response, qualified by distinctions of gender and class, or tainted by allegations of profiteering and corruption. Consequently captives were redeemed by various means, including the use of armed diplomacy and naval power, as well as ransom and exchange. Collections were authorized, lotteries planned and bequests made, for the benefit of those held in captivity. Merchants and other adventurers were also involved in the recovery of prisoners through the provision of ransom money, in the expectation that it would be refunded in England.[24]

The absence of a central authority or guiding policy in England was a weakness which compounded the inherent difficulties in the way of redeeming captives. The establishment of parliamentary committees and commissions during the later seventeenth century led to some improvement, at least by creating the opportunities for charitable collections throughout the realm. Despite widespread sympathy for the well-publicized plight of captives, however, it was not easy to translate popular sympathy into financial assistance. In January 1671 the Bishop of Lincoln complained of malicious rumours regarding the authenticity of a recent collection which discouraged people from giving. The following year the Privy Council was forced to extend a general collection to Ireland because the amount raised in England was insufficient. In particular, parishes in Gloucestershire were identified as areas that ignored appeals to help captives in Algiers despite royal support and encouragement. As late as 1716 an English captive complained to his wife about the lack of assistance from the government, compared with the support provided by other nations.[25]

In these circumstances the captivity of male seafarers and others had profound consequences for women, not only for wives but also for mothers and kinfolk, including friends and neighbours. While it is impossible to

---

[24] Colley, *Captives*, pp. 50–5, 75–80; Vitkus (ed.), *Piracy, Slavery, and Redemption*, pp. 24–6, 367–8; L. Benton, *Law and Colonial Cultures: Legal Regimes in World History, 1400–1900* (Cambridge, 2002), pp. 73–4; N. Matar, *Britain and Barbary, 1589–1689* (Gainesville, 2005), pp. 45–75.

[25] Colley, *Captives*, pp. 76–81; *CSPD, 1671*, pp. 59–60, 568; *CSPD, 1671–72*, pp. 241, 254, 322; Vitkus (ed.), *Piracy, Slavery, and Redemption*, pp. 27, 29. On 'donor fatigue' see Davis, *Christian Slaves*, pp. 159–60.

estimate the numbers affected, an indication of the potential scale of the problem can be drawn from estimates for the number of captives in Barbary. Assuming that the rate of capture during the years from 1616 to 1642 remained constant, across the period from the 1590s to the 1720s as many as 40,000 inhabitants of the British Isles may have been taken by the corsairs. It is most unlikely that this rate was maintained at such a level. The number of captives taken before 1616 is unknown; though small, it may have amounted to several thousand. In addition there was a progressive decline in the number after the 1650s. By 1694, at the end of a three-year diplomatic residency, Thomas Baker claimed that there were no English captives held in Algiers, Tunis or Tripoli.[26] Given the uncertainties and gaps in the evidence, it might be suggested that the total number of captives taken during the period ranged from about 15,000 to 25,000. Of this total, a proportion, though admittedly small, were female. The number of captives who were married or maintained other family relations is unknown, and must remain a hazardous guess. Many were young, mobile seafarers who lacked domestic ties, though a significant proportion were older, more settled men, with wives, children and wider family responsibilities.

More important, for all those involved, was the duration and meaning of captivity. For a majority of captives redemption was a costly and time-consuming process, with few guarantees of success. Some modern studies suggest that only 3 to 4 per cent of white prisoners were successfully ransomed each year. Such a poor rate of recovery, when combined with mortality rates, meant that most captives had a less than even chance of being released, particularly as the average duration of captivity was about seven years. The situation seems to have been worse for English captives, of whom more than half may never have returned home, although the opportunities for redemption seem to have improved after the 1650s.[27]

The loss of a spouse or a son could have catastrophic consequences for wives or widows. As in parts of the Mediterranean, some women were left in a starkly insecure position, unsure of their status and condition.[28] While

[26] Tinniswood, *Pirates of Barbary*, pp. 275–6. The number of British captives taken from 1660 to the 1730s was at least 6,000 according to Colley, *Captives*, pp. 44, 56. There were 300 British captives at Meknes in 1728; S. Clissold, *The Barbary Slaves* (London, 1977), p. 54.

[27] Davis, *Christian Slaves*, pp. 169–73; Colley, *Captives*, pp. 52–3. Less than one-third may have returned to England; Matar, *Turks, Moors, and Englishmen*, pp. 90–1.

[28] A form of 'social limbo' according to Davis, *Christian Slaves*, pp. 145–6. On 'cruell landlords' threatening to turn two women and their children out of doors, see London Metropolitan Archives, CLC/526/MS 30045/1.

the wives and relatives of mariners may have been hardened to the dangers of sea life, including lengthy absences and casualties at sea, Barbary captivity was a novel and shocking experience; in its own way, it may have been as traumatic for close family members as it was for captives. The psychological impact of the indefinite imprisonment of men in the hands of non-Christian captors is beyond calculation. Nonetheless, captivity and enslavement provoked anger and resentment as much as fear and insecurity, challenging the identity and status of free-born English. To some extent the emotional response played on longstanding hostility and misunderstanding, but it was also fuelled by an underlying concern at the treatment of prisoners, and their vulnerability to forced conversion or sexual abuse and licence. For the wives and families of captives, the response was shaped by the stories and gossip that circulated in seafaring communities, reinforced by letters and captivity narratives, and the less nuanced material found in ballads and broadsides. Personal correspondence to spouses or parents provided spare, but stark details of the condition of enslavement, emphasizing hard labour and brutal treatment, in order to hasten payment of ransom money. Much of this private material reached a wider audience of neighbours and friends. It was reinforced and elaborated by the published reports by, or on behalf of, redeemed captives, whose visible presence as beggars or vagrants was a disturbing reminder of the problem in many parishes.[29]

The accounts which appeared during this period were all written by men, though they varied according to context, as well as in content and character. While providing evidence of English resilience under apparently appalling conditions, inadvertently some of these narratives combined extreme circumstances with the exotic and potentially erotic. Richard Hasleton's account, for example, published in 1595 during the long war between England and Spain, described his capture and enslavement at Algiers, including an unsuccessful escape to Spain and his torture at the hands of a merciless inquisitor. Escaping to sea, he was forced back on the coast of North Africa. Following further mishaps ashore, he was recaptured. In an attempt to persuade him to convert, his captors offered him the choice of a wife and land. To their surprise, Hasleton refused, replying

---

[29] Colley, *Captives*, pp. 46–7, 57–8, 83–5; Vitkus (ed.), *Piracy, Slavery, and Redemption*, pp. 36, 341–4, 347–53; G. G. Harris (ed.), *Trinity House of Deptford Transactions, 1609–35* (London Record Society, 19, 1983), p. 6. For examples of donations to former captives see R. N. Worth (ed.), *Calendar of Plymouth Municipal Records* (Plymouth, 1893), p. 152; DRO, East Budleigh (Register Book) 1180A/PW1(V), ff. 7v, 11v, 15–16, 20, 23, 26v, 28v (for three Irish women and children, 'their husbands being in slavery'), 31, 41.

that he had a wife in England to whom he was tied by a vow 'before God and the world', which could not be broken while they 'both lived'.[30] Thereafter he was forced to labour as a galley slave for three years, until he was redeemed in 1592 by a London merchant.

Subsequent accounts may have been less colourful, but they continued to expose the ordeal of slavery and the broken spirits left by prolonged imprisonment, as well as the disturbing behaviour of English renegades. The account of John Rawlins, 'an unpolished work of a poor sailor' of 1622, reported on forced and voluntary conversions in Algiers.[31] To an English audience the loss of identity was characterized by a change of names which appeared to be part of an alarming surrender of values and culture. Henry Chandler, an 'English Turk', was thus known as Rammathan Rise.[32] Although a later narrative by Joseph Pitts of 1704 described his own forced conversion in Algiers, he noted that Christians were rarely compelled to renounce their religion. Such cultural transfers and personal transitions encompassed marriage and sexuality. Although the number of English captives who entered into liaisons with local women or men was probably small, the sexual dynamics of captivity aroused wide concern and alarm which were reflected in captivity narratives and the recycled and refashioned material in ballads.[33]

Of course many of these narratives freely mixed fact with fiction. The author of one, William Okeley, warned of 'counterfeits of fancy' in the preface to his own account of 1675, in which ethnographic reportage was mingled with prejudice and hostility.[34] Yet this was of little comfort to the wives and families of captives. Within a master narrative of slavery, it seemed that any abuse was possible. Thus it is no surprise that in an appeal to parliament for assistance during the 1670s, spouses and family members complained that slave owners in Algiers sexually abused and tortured captives. This emotionally laden appeal deliberately exploited sexual innuendo in an attempt to galvanize the government into action. At the same

---

[30] Vitkus (ed.), *Piracy, Slavery, and Redemption*, pp. 71–95 (quote at p. 91); L. Colley, *The Ordeal of Elizabeth Marsh* (London, 2007), pp. 41–86, for an interesting case study of a female captive of the 1750s who recorded her experiences.

[31] Vitkus (ed.), *Piracy, Slavery, and Redemption*, p. 98.

[32] Ibid., p. 104.

[33] Ibid., pp. 90–1, 102–4, 305–6; Colley, *Captives*, pp. 83–4. For French parallels see G. Weiss, *Captives and Corsairs: France and Slavery in the Early Modern Mediterranean* (Stanford, 2011), pp. 53, 97–8.

[34] Vitkus (ed.), *Piracy, Slavery, and Redemption*, pp. 124–92 (quote at p. 132). See also M. A. Garcés (ed.), *An Early Modern Dialogue with Islam: Antonio de Sosa's Topography of Algiers (1612)*, translated by D. de Armas Wilson (Notre Dame, 2011), pp. 157, 241.

time it demonstrated that responses to captivity and enslavement were filtered through second- and third-hand reports, popular belief, ignorance and prejudice. The mixture of outrage and helplessness encouraged many to believe the worst, while campaigning on behalf of husbands and other family members. But the emotional content, shared by thousands of women during the period, reflected the intangible and immeasurable costs of captivity.[35]

The loss of men to the corsairs also had serious consequences for the material conditions of women and their families. In some cases they were able to rely on other family members, friends or neighbours for support. Others were reduced to destitution. Re-marriage was a possible, but uncertain response. A survey of the law regarding women of 1632, acknowledging that captivity was a growing problem, claimed that the civil law allowed spouses to remarry if a husband had been absent for five years, and 'nothing knowne whether he lived or no', although the common law decreed that they should 'forbeare Marriage till the death of him or her that is missing be certainly knowne'.[36] Many survived by combining low-paid, occasional work with petty theft, prostitution and begging. Like large numbers of the marginalized or outcast, the lives of most of these women are almost hidden; and when they are revealed, the evidence may exaggerate or distort their resort to crime. As the case of Anne Wrye from the later 1670s demonstrates, however, women who were by no means among the poorest victims were reduced to desperate measures in order to survive. Wrye's husband, George, a surgeon, was captured by corsairs and enslaved in Algiers. In 1680 she was convicted of stealing a piece of silk worth 24s 6d. In her defence, Wrye insisted that this was her first criminal offence. Promising to live honestly in the future, she successfully appealed for a pardon without transportation to the colonies.[37]

A growing number of women responded to their changed circumstances by petitioning for assistance to redeem captured husbands, sons or other family members. These petitions varied, not only from individual to collective action, but also in their intended audience. They demonstrate how women used victimhood to assert agency in a popular cause that prompted charity at all levels of English society. They also brought women into a

---

[35] Colley, *Captives*, p. 57.

[36] [T. Edgar], *The Lawes Resolutions of Womens Rights: Or, the Lawes Provision for Women* (London, 1632), p. 66. According to a legal guide for magistrates, bigamy was a felony, unless the husband or wife had been absent for seven years, and 'the one not knowing the other to be living within that time'. M. Dalton, *The Countrey Justice* (London, 1619), p. 277.

[37] *CSPD, 1680–81*, p. 539.

political or public arena, providing them with access to individuals and institutions that might otherwise have been closed off. Petitions of the 1620s and 1630s, which may have involved large numbers of women, possibly served as a precedent for the better known civil war petitions of women campaigning for peace and other issues, including pensions for dead or maimed partners.[38] At the same time they drew on a longer tradition of female petitioning, especially by well-placed or wealthy women seeking aid from monarchs and lords. Those which were presented to the monarchy and parliament may have broken new ground, at least in terms of their organization among poor women living in London. But there was also a possibility that the primary goals of women were at risk of manipulation by commercial interests in the city. Within the context of a patriarchal society the use of petitions by women provided a means for the public representation of concerns which straddled elite and popular politics, linking personal and public issues. In some circumstances, depending on context and purpose, these petitions may have contained an unintended subversive message, not least by dramatizing female agency in a public sphere.[39] By choice or necessity women sought help from craft or professional associations, while appealing to local and regional agencies as well as petitioning the monarchy and parliament, tailoring their appeals in order to gain sympathy and support.

Appealing to Trinity House of Deptford

Re-established by royal patent in 1514, the Trinity House of Deptford was a mariners' guild designed to maintain and defend the craft of seafarers, primarily with regard to navigation along the river Thames. The revival of a declining brotherhood was linked with the reform of abuses such as the employment of young, unskilled mariners and overseas pilots. With the support of the High Court of Admiralty, it maintained and protected

---

[38] P. Higgins, 'The Reactions of Women, with Special Reference to Women Petitioners', in B. Manning (ed.), *Politics, Religion and the English Civil War* (London, 1973), pp. 179–222; A. Whiting, "'Some Women Can Shift it Well Enough": A Legal Context for Understanding the Women Petitioners of the Seventeenth-Century English Revolution', *Australian Feminist Law Journal*, 21 (2004), pp. 77–100; A. Hughes, *Gender and the English Revolution* (Abingdon, 2012), pp. 42–9, 53–61; G. L. Hudson, 'Negotiating for Blood Money; War Widows and the Courts in Seventeenth-Century England', in J. Kermode and G. Walker (eds), *Women, Crime and the Courts in Early Modern England* (London, 1994), pp. 146–69.

[39] Female petitioning often had a 'political edge' according to Hughes, *Gender and the English Revolution*, pp. 49, 60. In France it led to a 'suspension of gender disabilities' according to Weiss, *Captives and Corsairs*, pp. 32–3.

seafaring skills. Its ruling body was made up of one master, four wardens and eight assistants; collectively, through experience and tradition, it became an important repository of maritime custom and practice. It was regularly consulted for advice on matters such as working conditions at sea, building up a widely respected reputation as a craft and professional institution. As a guild the work of Trinity House included charitable and religious responsibilities. It maintained an almshouse, for elderly and disabled mariners, which was partly funded by a levy from pilots and seafarers. According to its charter and ordinances, women were eligible for membership as sisters within the brethren, though it remained a male-dominated institution. Its success was followed by the re-establishment of similar associations in Kingston upon Hull and Newcastle upon Tyne.[40]

The Trinity House at Deptford was a peculiarly appropriate forum for women to seek support. Although it included prominent figures who were occasionally consulted by the court, as a body it was rooted within the seafaring world of London. During the sixteenth and early seventeenth centuries its role and responsibilities developed with commercial expansion and the growth of the port. For the inhabitants of the parishes of the East End of London, including many of humble backgrounds, it was an accessible and less intimidating institution than the law courts and administrative agencies in Westminster. Although many of its early records were burnt in a fire of 1714, by the early seventeenth century mariners and their wives or widows were growing accustomed to appealing to Trinity House for assistance in the recovery of wages and personal possessions, or for licences to beg.[41]

The capture and enslavement of English mariners in Barbary was an issue that spouses and other family members, as well as redeemed captives, increasingly brought before Trinity House during these years. Such petitioners were not seeking direct financial assistance, which the brethren were usually unable to provide. Instead they were in search of a certificate, confirming their condition or circumstances, which could be used as evidence to authorize collections by them, or on their behalf, to pay ransom money. Trinity House in effect constituted itself as an informal certifying agency providing testimonials for a varied group of victims of sea casualty. Many of these certificates were designed to support petitions to the Lord Chancellor for letters patent to collect alms, though a number were intended to be used to validate such collections in their own right. In the

[40] G. G. Harris, *The Trinity House of Deptford 1514–1660* (London, 1969), pp. 19–30, 63–77, 246.
[41] Harris (ed.), *Trinity House*, p. ix; Sir T. D. Hardy, *Rymer's Foedera*, 2 vols (London, 1873), II, p. 86, for the issue of licences by the Lord Keeper.

former case, successful petitioners were awarded a brief, granted under the privy seal, which recited their losses while authorizing charitable collections on their behalf. The issue of briefs was an established means of assisting those who experienced personal crisis or tragedy, including fire or flood. They were usually addressed to the clergy, in the expectation that they would be read out to congregations. A collection for the cause was taken at the end of the service, and the money handed over to authorized collectors. Some included provision for house-to-house collections by churchwardens, accompanied by clergy and the leading inhabitants of the community.[42] As a result of growing concern over abuses, however, petitioners for briefs often included certificates, issued by quarter sessions and other bodies, confirming the validity of their claims.

Although it may not have been a requirement for Trinity House, to avoid imposters and counterfeit claims, supporting evidence may have been expected where appropriate or available. In recommending the case of Thomas Nichols to the king in August 1610, for example, the brethren included a certificate by the English consul at Algiers confirming his capture by Turkish corsairs during 1608; other evidence was provided to show that Nichols had not been involved in piracy. Disabled and dispossessed during a fight with the corsairs, Nichols was ransomed for £50 at Tunis by the master and company of a London vessel. Lacking the means to repay the money, 'for which his friends stand bond', he requested 'a certificate of his misfortunes' with the support of the brethren.[43] In a slightly different case of June 1613, Trinity House provided a certificate for John Deane, mariner and gunner, who had suffered heavy losses when a ship in which he was interested was taken by the Turks. Deane's long service at sea, certified by the masters with whom he served, had left him lame and unable to maintain himself. Consequently the brethren 'cannot deny him a certificate' which was addressed 'to the good people of Norfolk where he was born'.[44]

Trinity House lent its support to deserving cases in a carefully considered

---

[42] W. E. Tate, *The Parish Chest: A Study of the Records of Parochial Administration in England* (Cambridge, 1969), pp. 120–5; [J. E. Smith], *Bygone Briefs* (London, privately printed, 1896), pp. 15–21, 30, 33, 72–3. For examples of briefs, London Metropolitan Archives, MISC MS/156/9 and P92/SAV/1915, 1918–20, 1922; R. N. Worth (ed.), *Calendar of the Tavistock Parish Records* (Plymouth, 1887), pp. 56–62; P. Laithwaite, 'An Account of Briefs in Bilston Chappell, 1685', in *Collections for a History of Staffordshire* (Staffordshire Record Society, 27, 1938), pp. 206–10, 225. For the varied response of Trinity House see Harris (ed.), *Trinity House*, pp. 15–16.

[43] Ibid., p. 5; the surviving transactions are in London Metropolitan Archives, CLC/526/MS 30045/1 and 2.

[44] Harris (ed.), *Trinity House*, p. 15.

manner that took account of individual responsibilities and circumstances. Its willingness to authorize charitable collections by certificate created an opportunity for women to appropriate institutional authority for well-defined, specific ends. While the number was not large, those women who successfully petitioned the brethren received public acknowledgement of their status as victims as well as official sanction to seek assistance within their communities. This may not have amounted to much in terms of financial support, but as social attitudes towards the poor increasingly discriminated between the deserving and undeserving or fraudulent, certificates issued by Trinity House provided firm evidence for the worthiness of recipients. Within the wider culture of poverty, particularly in London, they helped to distinguish the genuine victim from imposters and counterfeits.[45]

At least seventeen women petitioners can be identified among the surviving transactions of Trinity House from 1609 to 1635. All but three, who were among the earliest cases heard by the brethren, were awarded a certificate. Twelve of these women petitioned as the wives of captive spouses in Barbary, who were unable to raise the money needed for their redemption. They included Ann Dodson, whose husband was held at Tunis where he was reportedly subject to cruel and intolerable treatment, who was struggling to raise a ransom of £160 for him. At the same time the wife of Richard Morris, also held at Tunis, informed the brethren that she was unable to pay a ransom of £240 because of his previous losses at sea. Without support, she and her four small children were 'likely to perish for want of relief'.[46] The other petitioners, five in total, were widows whose husbands were killed in conflict with the corsairs or died in captivity. Henry Cooke died shortly after being taken prisoner, leaving his widow, Mary, in very poor circumstances. Unable to redeem her son, who was taken and enslaved while serving aboard his father's ship, she was awarded a certificate by Trinity House in March 1617. A similar certificate was issued for Elizabeth Young in January 1622 after her husband, the master and part-owner of a London vessel, was killed at sea during a fight with three corsair ships. A respected member of the seafaring community, who was described by the brethren as 'honest and of good estate', Young's death may have aroused widespread sympathy for his widow and two small children.[47] As reported to Trinity House, the master and his company, 'knowing the

---

[45] P. Griffiths, *Lost Londons: Change, Crime and Control in the Capital City, 1550–1660* (Cambridge, 2008), pp. 112–23; J. Marriott, 'The Spatiality of the Poor in Eighteenth-Century London', in T. Hitchcock and H. Shore (eds), *The Streets of London: From the Great Fire to the Great Stink* (London, 2003), pp. 125–33.

[46] Harris (ed.), *Trinity House*, p. 60.

[47] Ibid., pp. 28, 54.

cruelty of those pagans, resolved to die fighting rather than to submit'.[48] During the ensuing conflict the attackers set fire to the ship which sank with Young and seventeen other men clinging to the masts for as long as possible. Evidently the corsairs left them to drown, warning the company of another English ship which they had taken that they would receive similar treatment if they tried to save their countrymen. Young's estate, worth more than £300, was lost with the vessel; as a result his widow and family were left destitute and 'likely to perish without charitable relief'.[49]

Most of these petitions were individual appeals, presented in person by wives or widows. At least two were made with the support or recommendation of neighbours. In 1611 Thomasin Nelme and her neighbours at Poplar appealed to the brethren for a certificate. Nelme's husband, the master of a vessel of Topsham, was taken and imprisoned by corsairs of Algiers, while the rest of the company were enslaved aboard the galleys, until a ransom of £200 was paid. With five small children to support, Nelme was a deserving candidate for community assistance. So too was Mary Temple, a widow of Limehouse, living in poverty with four small children, who solicited neighbours to support an appeal to the brethren and Lord Chancellor in 1614. Her husband had been taken on separate occasions by pirates, suffering heavy losses. In May 1613 he was captured and taken to Salé, where he died within eight days of the bad treatment he received. According to his widow, one of the company was murdered, the rest were tortured, and the ship's boy was forced to 'turn Turk' after being circumcised against his will.[50] Her neighbours, all men, certified the truth of the widow's story, supporting her plea for a commission for a charitable collection in the churches of London and other parishes of the south east.

In addition to these direct appeals by women, in a number of cases petitions and supporting evidence were presented to Trinity House by others on their behalf. At the request of Elizabeth Mason, in August 1616 the rector and parish officials of Whitechapel certified that her husband, a longstanding local resident, had been taken and imprisoned by the corsairs. Because of her poor circumstances, she was unable to provide for her three children or to pay for his ransom. Similarly in January 1626 the parson and others of Rotherhithe provided a certificate for the brethren that the spouse of Thomasin Fletcher had been taken by a Salé corsair. The couple, who they noted lived honestly, were unable to raise his ransom of £300.[51]

The common characteristics and conditions of these women petitioners

[48] Ibid., p. 54.
[49] Ibid.
[50] Ibid., pp. 10, 16.
[51] Ibid., pp. 21–2, 70–1.

were convincing evidence for their inclusion within the ranks of the
deserving poor. But they also suggest either selective access to, or support
by, Trinity House. While their status as lone parents, single wives or widows
undoubtedly was a common experience for hundreds, possibly thousands of
other women, shared misfortune was thrown into relief by the backgrounds
of the petitioners. As a group they displayed an unusual degree of homo-
geneity, representing a smaller sub-group within the wider seafaring
community. Many of these women were established and respected figures
within their neighbourhoods; with their spouses, they enjoyed reputations
for honesty and hard work. Their husbands, moreover, were experienced,
high-ranking members of the maritime world. No fewer than ten were
ship-masters, and in some cases owners or part-owners of the vessels they
were taken in. Another three who served as mates had been masters of
ships in the past. Only three were identified as mariners or seamen, and of
these two were described as 'diligent seamen of good life and estate'.[52]
Many of these men had accumulated years of sea service, acquiring a degree
of experience comparable with the younger brethren of Trinity House. They
were men of some substance and means, whose estates were tied up in their
shipping interests. Their capture by the corsairs therefore was a personal
and financial disaster for their wives and families.

Although no evidence was provided for the ages of these women, most
were neither very young nor very old. Approaching mid-life, they were
forming families and running households with extensive responsibilities.
Only four of the petitioners failed to mention children, who were usually
described as small, in their appeals for support. Among these Sara Short,
Mary Temple and the wife of Richard Morris each had four children, while
Thomasin Nelme and the partner of Thomas Askew, taken and held to
ransom by Flemish privateers, had families of five offspring to look after.[53]

Despite living in straitened circumstances, collectively these women had
the personal resources, capability and community approval to appeal to
Trinity House. Their stories, moving and heartfelt, refashioned the experiences of their husbands to appeal to the sympathy of their audience.
Although the number of such petitions was limited, they were irregularly
scattered across the years from 1611 to 1632, apart from a noticeable clus-
tering during the early 1620s. From 1622 to 1624 the brethren received
ten petitions, a small but revealing indication of a growing problem. With
the exception of 1626, however, there seem to have been none during the

[52] Ibid., pp. 56–7. Richard Daniel, captured in 1614, was noted to be a 'man of good
reputation'; *CSPI, 1615–25*, p. 209.
[53] Harris (ed.), *Trinity House*, pp. 10, 16, 60–1, 71–2.

wars with Spain and France from 1625 to 1630, possibly because of the increased number of heavily armed English men-of-war employed in privateering during these years. There are signs of renewed appeals during the early 1630s, although their form and structure may have been changing. At the same time, geographical access or proximity played a significant part in facilitating the presentation of these petitions. All but one were made by women from parishes in the East End and across the river in Southwark, the centre of London's rapidly growing and diversified seafaring community. Twelve of the petitions were presented by women who were inhabitants of Limehouse, Ratcliffe and Wapping. Elizabeth Haines, whose husband was of Bristol, was the only petitioner who failed to give a local residence in London.[54]

In addition to these individual and usually localized petitions, by the early 1630s Trinity House was beginning to receive appeals from larger groups of women beyond the confines of the capital. In September 1633 the brethren informed the mayor and aldermen of Poole of their receipt of a letter from a group of local women, whose spouses were held in captivity, requesting their intercession with the Lord Keeper. In a striking display of patriarchal protocol and procedure, which threatened to rob the women of agency, they replied to town officials, that 'howsoever the showe seems to bee the womens yet wee conceave the letter to bee yours & written by direction from yow … because [it] is wrote by your Towne Clarke. Therefore to you wee retorne our answere; with them wee deale not.'[55] At the same time, while expressing their willingness to help, the brethren advised the mayor and aldermen against delay, fearing future complaints from the women.

The character of this petitioning strongly suggests that in appealing to Trinity House the scope for female agency was rather limited and selective. Undoubtedly the brethren were prepared to assist and encourage the wives of captives enslaved in Barbary because it was a worthy cause. But it was also an issue that was of growing concern to them. In responding to such appeals for help, it appears that the brethren were looking after the interests of men of their own standing, providing for the spouses of ship-masters and mariners of rank and substance, to the possible neglect of the common mariner. Even in these cases, moreover, Trinity House only provided women with certificates which authenticated or validated their pleas for charity within the neighbourhood and wider community. While this was of value in distinguishing between charitable cases, particularly in a society

[54] Ibid., p. 56.
[55] Ibid., p. 120; London Metropolitan Archives, CLC/526/MS 30045/2, f. 60.

where philanthropy was becoming more calculating and measured, its financial impact is difficult to gauge. It seems unlikely, however, that many of these petitioners, especially those with substantial family responsibilities, were able to raise the money required for the release of husbands. Faced with ransom demands ranging from £30 to £300, and struggling to pay off debts, rent and other bills, wives and widows may have been forced to use their certificates as a means of supplementing family income through charitable collections, while affirming their status as innocent victims of the corsairs.[56]

Petitioning monarchy, council and parliament

The scale of the captive problem during the early seventeenth century encouraged a growing number of women to petition the monarchy and other institutions, including the Privy Council, parliament and royal ministers or favourites. While recognizing differences between the recipients, there was an obvious overlap between these appeals, including similarities in their content, which enables them to be examined collectively. Petitions circulated, passing from the monarchy to the council or other officials. In at least one case of 1629 the council forwarded a petition to the English consul in Algiers with instructions for the ransom of a father and his son.[57] Although designed for a similar purpose, these petitions were of a different order compared to those presented to Trinity House. In providing access to privileged avenues of communication, they enabled women, on their own or in groups, to exert a degree of autonomy in a public cause that was identified as both good and godly.[58] At the same time, despite their common form, petitions helped to memorialize absent or lost husbands and other men, in a way that kept attention focused on the issue.

There was a protocol to petitioning which compelled petitioners to rely on officials for the presentation of their cases, though this was occasionally breached. During 1623 John Chamberlain, the letter-writer, reported that James I was so importuned by the wives and kin of captives at Algiers and Tunis, that he was 'forced sometimes to give them hard usage both in words

---

[56] Harris (ed.), *Trinity House*, pp. 44, 51, 57, 60, 71, for ransoms. Andrews, *Ships, Money and Politics*, pp. 162–3, for Trinity House's interest.

[57] *APC, 1629–30*, p. 97.

[58] On petitioning see D. Zaret, *Origins of Democratic Culture: Printing, Petition, and the Public Sphere in Early-Modern England* (Princeton, 2000). Intriguingly little evidence survives of English husbands petitioning on behalf of wives; Matar, *Britain and Barbary*, p. 109.

and worse'.[59] Moreover, the compilation of written petitions, with their carefully crafted opening and closing sections, and balance between information and intercession, was usually the work of experienced scriveners or clerks. As a result, the production and presentation of women's petitions rested on cooperation or interdependency with men, which occasionally included support from the neighbourhood or wider community. This was the unavoidable consequence of widespread illiteracy among women, but it raised the possibility that their use of petitioning was open to exploitation by other interests who sought to link the captivity issue with commercial and diplomatic ambitions in North Africa.

The petitions presented by women to the early Stuart monarchy drew on a tradition that enabled the representation of grievances in an appropriate manner, which acknowledged rights and responsibilities while reaffirming deference and patriarchy. It was a well-established practice, with a code of conduct and recognized procedure that catered for a range of causes. It served varied purposes, demonstrating hierarchical and gendered relationships and duties. In theory, as an important aspect of monarchy and lordship, it was open to rich and poor, and male and female. In practice, however, it may have been restricted by procedure and protocol, and subject to delay or an informal screening process, which deterred all but the most determined. In 1627 the Privy Council acknowledged that Mary Blundill, whose husband had been a prisoner for at least three years, 'hath been a long suitor to this Board' in seeking a 'generall ransome for the captives in Turkie, and that therby as yet not she but others have received the benefit therof'.[60] The following year it drew up new orders for hearing petitions which emphasized their deferential character, while trying to improve the procedure for their presentation. On a day of ordinary business, 'all peticioners are to be admitted and everie one to deliver his [sic] peticion at the upper end of the table kneeling, and having theire presented theire peticions, they are without talking or troubling the Board to withdrawe themselves and are not to come in afterwards except they be called

---

[59] N. E. McClure (ed.), *The Letters of John Chamberlain*, 2 vols (Philadelphia, 1939), II, p. 507; James was 'inundated with petitioners' according to Zarèt, *Origins of Democratic Culture*, pp. 85–6. A petition to the king by David Crawford of Wapping, c.1619/20, on behalf of himself and his sisters and three other poor widows with 'Sixteene fatherless Children', provides a good example of the interdependency between men and women; London Metropolitan Archives, P92/SAV/1915. A decade later the Privy Council reprimanded the wives of seafarers, whose husbands were held at Algiers, after ignoring a warning to cease importuning the board with their 'clamorous complaints'; TNA, PC 2/43, f. 541.

[60] *APC, 1627*, p. 251.

for'.[61] Although members of the council recognized the problems facing poor petitioners, their remedy was ambiguous and potentially confusing. Thus the clerk of the council was required to note when petitions were exhibited, so that 'the Lords may thereby see how the suitors stand in seniority, and according to that and other necessity of occasion they may be dispatched, wherein respect is to be had to the poorest peticioners, that they be not wearied out with over longe attendance'.[62] For many women, of course, time and resources effectively limited the opportunity for petitioning, regardless of wider concerns over access.

The influence of patriarchy and protocol may well explain the striking absence of direct appeals to the consorts of monarchs. In 1634, at a time when Derbyshire and Nottinghamshire were reported to be experiencing unrest as a result of disturbances among local miners, their wives petitioned the queen, Henrietta Maria, employing their gender in a manner that appeared to acknowledge male perceptions of female weakness. By contrast, however, the petitioners who were seeking Earl support for captives seem to have made no attempt to direct their appeals in this way. While the gendered aspect of petitioning may have reflected wider assumptions and expectations regarding female behaviour, it included the ability of women to exploit what men identified as the privilege of sex, in soliciting support from within a masculine and potentially unsympathetic environment.[63]

In these circumstances it is no surprise that the number of such petitions by women was modest. About two dozen survive for the period from the 1620s to the 1670s. Of these, roughly half date from the 1620s and 1630s. One survives from the early 1640s, followed by a small scattering across the 1650s which continued into the 1660s and early 1670s. Unusually one of the latest, a petition to the House of Commons, was published as a broadside in 1677. About half of the total were intended for the monarch or the Privy Council. A smaller number were presented to the Council of State and Cromwell during the period of republican rule. The remainder were accounted for by petitions to parliament, the Commissioners for the Admiralty and royal ministers or favourites. The latter

---

[61] *APC, 1627–28*, p. 331.

[62] Ibid., p. 332.

[63] *HMC, Twelfth Report, The Manuscripts of the Earl Cowper*, 3 vols (London, 1888–9), II, pp. 61–2; A. Wood, *The Politics of Social Conflict: The Peak Country, 1520–1770* (Cambridge, 1999), p. 257. On assumptions see the advice of Sir Ralph Verney to his wife in 1646 concerning her petition to parliament on his behalf; F. P. Verney, *Memoirs of the Verney Family During the Civil War*, 4 vols (London, 1892–9), II, pp. 239–40; and A. Fraser, *The Weaker Vessel: Women's Lot in Seventeenth-Century England* (London, 1984), pp. 260–8.

usually followed appeals to the monarchy. A petition to the Duke of Buckingham, royal favourite and Lord Admiral, of about 1626, from the 'distressed wives of almost 2000 poore Mariners now remaining most miserable captives in Sally' (Salé), sought his assistance in seeking support from the king, who had failed to respond to many previous appeals, and was accompanied by a separate appeal to parliament.[64] Another petition of 1665 was passed to the Earl of Bath by Charles II, after he was petitioned during a visit to Weymouth by the wives and friends of captives at Algiers.[65]

The early phase of petitioning grew out of the rapid spread of raiding by the Barbary corsairs during the opening decades of the seventeenth century, but its more specific context lay in the commercial politics and diplomacy of the 1620s and 1630s. The earliest petitions by women were preceded by one to the king during 1617, from merchants trading within the Mediterranean. Complaining of the plunder of English and Scottish subjects, including the seizure of more than 300 ships, by corsairs from Algiers and Tunis, to the 'ruine of many of them, theire wives and children', the petitioners called for swift action to combat the threat to trade.[66] As John Chamberlain observed in 1621, the 'loss of so many mariners and ships is no small matter'.[67] Two years later, with between 700 and 800 seamen in captivity, he reported that the king was almost besieged by their wives, kinfolk and friends. Commenting on the impending failure of diplomacy, in the wake of the unsuccessful expedition against Algiers, Chamberlain expressed concern at the prospect of being 'left to the mercie of those miscreants'.[68]

The relationship between petitioning and politics, trade and diplomacy was reflected in appeals to the king and Privy Council during 1624, which claimed to be from a large number of poor women whose husbands, sons or servants were captives in Barbary.[69] According to the council, James wrote to the regent of Algiers on their behalf, and dispatched a consul to negotiate the release of the prisoners. At the women's request, Nicholas Leate, a city merchant with interests in the Barbary trade, offered to

[64] TNA, SP 16/43/46; H. de Castries *et al.* (eds), *Les Sources Inédites de L'Histoire du Maroc: Archives et Bibliotheques d'Angleterre*, 3 vols (Paris, 1918–35), III, pp. 1–3.
[65] TNA, SP 29/138/38.
[66] *APC, 1616–17*, pp. 181–2, 218–19.
[67] McClure (ed.), *Letters*, II, p. 402.
[68] Ibid., p. 507.
[69] *APC, 1623–25*, pp. 318, 335–6, 348–9, 432. In a similar fashion, in France women acted 'politically and juridically' according to G. Weiss, 'Humble Petitioners and Able Contractors: French Women as Intermediaries in the Redemption of Captives', in W. Kaiser (ed.), *Le Commerce des Captifs* (Rome, 2008), pp. 333–44.

advance £1,000 as a contribution towards their ransom. Like other merchants and entrepreneurs who were involved in the redemption business, Leate may have been acting from godly motives, but he also expected to at least cover his costs. Consequently the offer to the women was conditional on his repayment out of money already being collected under charitable briefs granted by the king earlier in the year. The council, 'greatly moved with compassion of the hard estate of the ... captives', readily agreed to the arrangement.[70] In September it instructed the Archbishop of Canterbury, in his capacity as receiver-general of all contributions, to ensure that Leate was repaid out of the first money collected. According to a subsequent order, he received payment of £1,783 18s 9d for his role in the redemption of the captives.

The apparent success of the petitions of 1624 encouraged and influenced others. But an appeal by more than 2,000 wives to Charles I seems to have met with little response. Their petition to Buckingham, as noted above, urged him to intercede with the king on their behalf. In doing so, the women drew on themes and imagery which were to recur in the future. According to the petitioners, their spouses had been held for a long time in captivity, suffering 'such unspeakable misery & tortures that they are almost forced to convert from their Christian religion'; the wives, with a 'multitude of poore Infants' to support, were 'ready to perish heer at home through want of ... meanes'.[71] Despite the king's failure to respond, which may have been as much about protocol as politics, during 1626 diplomatic efforts were made for the release of captives in Barbary. Against objections from the judge of the High Court of Admiralty, however, the attempt to maintain good relations with the Barbary regencies as possible allies against Spain may have created a less favourable environment for pursuing the issue.

In these difficult circumstances women nonetheless continued to seek assistance from the Privy Council. In 1626 Rebecca Daniell successfully petitioned for a share of any money remaining from a recent general collection, in order to pay a debt of 300 crowns to Sir Thomas Roe, the ambassador at Constantinople, for the release of her partner, John. The following year Mary Blundill appealed for aid to redeem her husband, Richard, who like Daniell was held in Turkish captivity. Having 'spent all her meanes in labouring & suing ... for a generall Collection', from which she derived no benefit, Blundill begged the council to instruct Roe to effect the release of

---

[70] Ibid., pp. 335–6; *APC, 1625–26*, pp. 24, 61, 84, 223–4, 243, 257, 260–1, 336.
[71] TNA, SP 16/43/46; Matar, *Britain and Barbary*, pp. 55, 78–92. The petitioning of wives seems to have divided the seafaring community on this issue; see Andrews, *Ships, Money and Politics*, p. 182.

her spouse.[72] She also requested a share in the collection as a contribution towards his ransom. Aware of her protracted suit, the council responded with alacrity to the first part of her petition, ordering Roe, in similar language, to procure Blundill's release. Two years later, following a petition from Dorcas Mot, it sent similar instructions to James Frizell, the consul at Algiers, for the ransom of her husband and son. Out of commiseration for their condition, and 'the calamitie wherein the said Dorcas Mot is fallen by reason thereof', council members urged Frizell to act with as much speed as possible.[73]

The form and structure of women's petitioning which emerged during the 1620s influenced subsequent petitions to the king and council. Not surprisingly their scope and content remained consistent, playing on the miserable servitude or lamentable slavery of captives, at the mercy of unchristian or devilish Turks. But there were differences of emphasis, including reference to specific issues and grievances. Furthermore, several of those presented during the 1630s explicitly reveal the influence of city commercial interests, representing prominent Barbary traders, who were trying to promote closer relations with the ruler of Morocco as a means of encouraging trade.[74] At the same time there was a mix of individual and group petitions, as a growing number of women sought assistance for husbands, sons, fathers and friends.

The range of specific issues, and their relationship to the wider diplomatic context, was demonstrated in an undated petition to the king, which was probably presented shortly after the war with Spain. It was drawn up in the names of Mary and Alice Farr, Elizabeth Saunders, Mabel John, Mary Sly, Jane Rogerson, Margaret Thomas and others, who were seeking royal assistance for the redemption of men held in slavery at Salé. The petitioners were unusually well-informed about recent diplomatic relations with the corsair port, based on information from captain John Harrison, the king's agent to Barbary, who was trying to promote closer contact with the ruler of Morocco. They commended Harrison's success in establishing peace and trade with Salé, but warned that his activities were jeopardized by the recent seizure of a Salé ship by an English man-of-war. Contrary to a recent proclamation, the captors sold the ship, its cargo and company in Spain. As a result, English trading agents and their goods were arrested in

---

[72] *APC, 1626*, p. 335; TNA, SP 16/61/44; *APC, 1627*, p. 251.

[73] *APC, 1629–30*, p. 97.

[74] For Harrison's involvement see TNA, SP 71/12/204. The links between captivity, commerce and diplomacy are illuminated by a petition of captain Edmond Bradshaw, TNA, SP 71/13/50–3. The political dimension is examined by Matar, *Britain and Barbary*, pp. 76–9, 88.

Salé, ships were seized and their crews imprisoned, while prisoners who had been released were re-taken. In seeking assistance from the king, therefore, the petitioners also demanded that those involved in the seizure of the Salé ship should be punished, and ordered to make satisfaction for their conduct, whereby their husbands, sons and friends might be released.[75]

The interplay between public and private interests evident in this petition was manifest in another undated appeal to Charles I, which was probably related to a similar plea received by the Commissioners of the Admiralty in November 1635. In the former, Clare Bowyer, Margaret Hall, Elizabeth Ensam and Elizabeth Newland, with more than 1,000 poor women, appealed on behalf of their husbands who were held at Salé. Claiming to represent about 1,500 captives, the petitioners made use of religious fears as well as more familiar concerns. Although their husbands were held in 'wofull slavery & captivitie, enduring hard & extreame laboure, want of susteynance and greevious Torments through the merciless Crueltie of theire manifold masters', their greatest need was spiritual nourishment.[76] Faced with extraordinary ransom demands, they were informed that the king of Morocco had offered to release all captives, if Charles agreed to send an ambassador or at least royal letters on their behalf. The petition to the Commissioners for the Admiralty, which seems to have followed this appeal, was from a group of poor men, women and children on behalf of male captives at Algiers and Salé. With the help of friends in England, the captives had secured their redemption, but they lacked shipping to bring them home because of the limited trade with those ports. The petitioners thus requested authorization from the commissioners for captain William Bushell, who had lately redeemed thirty captives, to return to both ports for the transportation of others who had gained their freedom.[77]

The cumulative influence of these appeals can be detected in a short-lived upsurge in petitioning during the later 1630s. The appeal of Bennett Wright to the council, for the relief and ransom of her husband, William, a 'most miserable distressed Prisoner under the tyranie of the divelish Turks', employed the by now firmly established language of slavery and captivity, with an unusual religious emphasis.[78] Wright and her friends were unable to raise the money for a ransom demand of £90. If they supported so 'greate a worke of piety', however, the members of the council would

[75] TNA, SP 16/205/30. This petition was presented by Harrison. De Castries *et al.* (eds), *Les Sources*, III, pp. 30–57
[76] TNA, SP 16/306/85. For the influence of earlier petitions see Matar, *Britain and Barbary*, pp. 81–4.
[77] TNA, SP 16/301/66.
[78] TNA, SP 16/408/118.

show themselves as 'Lordes full of religious devotion and lyvely members of Christ crusified in releeveing his distressed bretherin'.[79] About the same time a group of poor women, whose husbands were held at Algiers or Tunis, petitioned the king and council for relief. Claiming that their spouses' captors used torture against body and soul, they appealed for permission to collect alms to supplement a contribution of £100 made by merchants.[80] The council instructed captain Leate to ransom the captives, for which he was to be paid out of money collected in England. According to another petition from distressed wives and children, however, members of the council subsequently issued orders to the contrary, leaving the men with little hope for their release.[81] As the onset of domestic political crisis threatened to overshadow the issue, two years later the captives at Algiers appealed to the king for help. Claiming to represent about 3,000 of his subjects, they warned that many prisoners were forced to convert to Islam as a result of their cruel and insufferable treatment.[82]

Following the outbreak of the civil war and the establishment of republican rule during the 1640s and 1650s, women directed their petitions to parliament, the Council of State or Oliver Cromwell in his capacity as lord protector. Paradoxically, given the campaign of political petitioning by groups of women during these years, the scale of activity, especially during the 1640s, was modest. Yet the issue of Barbary captivity was of serious concern to parliament. During 1642 it passed legislation for a levy of 1 per cent on all goods imported and exported, to support 'so pious a Work of ... releasing ... distressed Captives'.[83] In modified form it was regularly renewed until June 1660. In addition, it was accompanied by an ordinance of 1645 for the collection of £10,000 towards the redemption of prisoners held at Algiers, Tunis and Salé.

The earliest petition to parliament of the period was presented in 1643 by Elizabeth Chickley, Susan Robinson, Mary Savage and four others, on behalf of themselves and others. Tailoring their appeal to a more public and open assembly, the women implored the aid of members in the release of their husbands at Algiers. Although they 'endeavoured (by Sale of their Goods, and Help of their Friends) to raise what Part they can of the ... Fines' or ransoms, they were too poor, with the 'great Charge of Children',

[79] Ibid.
[80] TNA, SP 16/391/95–8.
[81] TNA, SP 16/391/98.
[82] *CSPD, 1640–41*, p. 134.
[83] C. H. Firth and R. S. Rait (eds), *Acts and Ordinances of the Interregnum, 1642–1660*, 3 vols (London, 1911), I, pp. 17, 19, 553–4, 609–11, 731–4; II, pp. 367–8, 824, 1129–30; III, pp. xlvii, xlix, li, xc.

to raise the full amount.[84] In response, parliament authorized charitable collections in the churches of the city of London, Westminster, Southwark and the suburbs. They were to last for two months, and to be held only once in any parish. Churchwardens and other collectors were to return the money to the Commissioners for the Navy, who were responsible for its distribution and use. In July 1648 parliament received another petition from Sara Baugh, Mary Colley, Margaret Howard and other poor women, seeking assistance for the recovery of their husbands, twenty-seven in all, who had been shipwrecked on the coast of Barbary and imprisoned by the king of Morocco.

These appeals were followed by a cluster of petitions during the early and mid-1650s. At this time the use of committees or commissioners became a characteristic response of the Council of State to such appeals. In November 1652 a petition by the wives of captives at Algiers and Tripoli was referred to the admiralty committee. The following year a special committee was appointed to consider an appeal, possibly from the same women, to Cromwell and the council. Presenting themselves as humble supplicants to parliament for more than two years, they claimed that their hopes for the release of husbands and sons had been thwarted when the vessel carrying redemption money was diverted into service against the Dutch. With the money returned ashore and placed in Deal Castle, the petitioners begged Cromwell and the councillors to secure the freedom of the captives through the English agent at Leghorn.[85] Another petition of March 1655 by Elizabeth Hewes, Elizabeth and Susanna Wade, Susanna Pumritt, Elizabeth Mercer and Joanne Parvo, referred by Cromwell to the council, was passed on to the Commissioners of the Customs, with instructions to examine the case and act appropriately.[86] In a separate case, which was not referred to committee, early in 1656 Alice Wheeler appealed for help towards her own ransom. Travelling to New England about six years previously, the ship on which she sailed was taken by corsairs, and her husband and two sons were killed. Wheeler was later redeemed by a German, one Wolfe, but she needed help to pay off the debt she owed him. Her personal circumstances were complicated by surgery, which she was undergoing at the time of her petition.[87]

The restoration of the monarchy in 1660 was followed by a revival of petitioning to Charles II which persisted into the early 1670s. Among those

---

[84] Ibid., I, pp. 134–5; De Castries *et al.* (eds), *Les Sources*, III, pp. 559–60.

[85] TNA, SP 18/36/85–6; Matar, *Britain and Barbary*, pp. 91–2.

[86] TNA, SP 18/75/75; *CSPD, 1652–53*, pp. 44, 387, 402; *CSPD, 1654–55*, pp. 59, 137, 319; *CSPD, 1657–58*, pp. 121, 173, 293.

[87] TNA, SP 25/92/127.

appealing for assistance was the Countess of Inchiquin, whose husband and son were captured at sea and carried off to captivity in Algiers. Responding swiftly to a request from the countess, Charles ratified a recent treaty with Algiers, removing an obstacle to the release of the earl and his son.[88] About the same time a group of 'poor distressed captives' petitioned the king for a share in the sum of £10,000 which parliament had set aside for the relief of all prisoners taken in English vessels since 1642.[89]

The accessibility of the new king enabled a group of wives and friends to petition him during a visit to Weymouth in 1665. Charles passed their appeal to the Earl of Bath. Later in the year the earl was petitioned by the same group, who sought his assistance for the recovery of more than eighty men and boys from Plymouth, Weymouth and the neighbouring region. The petition identified twelve of the Plymouth men, as well as a father and son, who were seized in October 1664 and taken to Algiers, where they languished in a 'very sad and distressed Condition'.[90] The petitioners were supported by the mayor of Weymouth, who provided the earl with the names of another eleven local men who were held at Algiers. Led by Katherine Harris, a widow, the wives, friends and relatives of the men later appealed to the king for help in their release. Describing the captives as 'able Mariners and hopefull young Men', they claimed that on their release they would 'readily and cheerefully' serve in the king's navy, 'untill the Charge of theire respective Ransoms bee satisfied out of theire pay'.[91]

These petitions were followed by others to the monarchy during the early 1670s. Joan Mosley, Hannah Lawson, Edith Smyth and other women of Stepney, whose spouses, sons and kin were prisoners at Algiers, petitioned about 1670 for 'some effectual meanes for the freeing [of] those poore soules from the worst of Bondage and thraldome'.[92] Two years later the parents and other relations of a company of seven mariners, of a vessel of Topsham, appealed for part of a recent voluntary contribution to free them from captivity. The petitioners were very poor inhabitants of Starcross in Devon, who were unable to pay the ransoms required, which in the case of the captain, John Dingle, amounted to £160.[93]

The outbreak of war between England and Algiers during the later

---

[88] TNA, SP 29/10/36; SP 71/1/495–9; R. L. Playfair, *The Scourge of Christendom: Annals of British Relations with Algiers Prior to the French Conquest* (London, 1884), pp. 77–9.

[89] TNA, SP 29/48/96.

[90] TNA, SP 29/138/38, I.

[91] TNA, SP 29/138/38, II; SP 29/441/62.

[92] TNA, SP 29/276/187.

[93] TNA, SP 29/311/160.

1670s provoked further petitions to the king and parliament, at least one of which was overtly addressed to a wider, public audience. In October 1677 the masters and mariners of nearly twenty ships, recently taken by Algerian corsairs, appealed to the king for assistance in releasing them from 'excessive slavery and bondage'.[94] About the same time, the fathers and wives of captive children and husbands presented a petition to the House of Commons which was also published as a broadside. The petitioners complained that English ships continued to be taken by the Algerians, despite carrying royal passes for their safe conduct. Between August and December 1677 about 600 of the king's subjects were captured, although less than half were still alive as a result of the barbarous conditions under which they were held. Following the seizure of more vessels during December, the number of captives rose to 970. In unusually emotive and strong language, designed to shock the public and mobilize support in parliament, the petitioners claimed that the captives were subject to physical and sexual abuse for refusing to forsake their religion. They were repeatedly beaten with a 'Bulls Pisle', assaulted with iron implements, ripped across the stomach with knives, and employed as cart-horses, while forced to carry such burdens on their backs that they were 'Broken-bellied'.[95]

Collectively the petitions presented by women on behalf of captives in Barbary demonstrated the use of female agency in claiming access to privileged, inherently political, forms of communication. But they were the product of an interdependency with men, whose roles as associates, friends or partners were rarely visible. All of the appeals presented during this period seem to have been compiled by male scribes, who may also have acted as advisers on matters concerning procedure and protocol. The cooperation was even more common in informal petitioning or lobbying, especially when parents were seeking help for children or other relatives. In June 1670, for example, James Hickes wrote to Sir Joseph Williamson, one of the king's secretaries, on behalf of an orphaned nephew of his wife, who was a prisoner at Algiers. Hickes' wife delivered the letter in person as a 'humble intercessor'.[96] Her nephew, Samuel Dawkes, had earlier provided his sister with a harrowing account of his capture and imprisonment, urging

---

[94] TNA, SP 29/397/62.
[95] London Metropolitan Archives, Guildhall Library, Broadside 12.12. Similar language and imagery were deployed in some of the literature that appeared during the political crisis that enveloped England as a result of the Popish Plot; J. P. Kenyon, *The Popish Plot* (London, 1972), pp. 4–5, 9, 11. The preacher of the sermon at Minehead in 1628 claimed that the Turks used 'dryed Bull-pizells', whips and knotted ropes against Christian captives; Kellet, *Return From Argier*, p. 39.
[96] TNA, SP 29/276/186.

her to seek assistance from their relatives.[97] A copy of the letter was included in the correspondence to Williamson, with a request that the nephew could be exchanged for a Turkish prisoner who might be taken by the naval fleet then in the Mediterranean. Faced with trying to raise a ransom of £80, the family and friends of Dawkes had little 'hopes of his Redemption except by some extraordinarie act of providence from God'.[98]

Such formal and informal petitioning, particularly when groups were involved, called for organization and leadership; successful presentation, moreover, demanded initiative, information and resourcefulness. While men may have managed several petitions, which consequently camouflaged commercial interests and ambitions, in many cases women, often of humble and uneducated backgrounds, were closely involved, acting independently or in association with others. Although it is unlikely that these campaigns represented the thousands that some petitioners claimed to speak for, in the parishes and seafaring communities of London they were undoubtedly supported by large numbers of women and wider groups of sympathizers. As petitioners women were closely engaged in parish and neighbourhood politics. They used the worthiness of the cause of captives, and their own social capital as victims, to bring concerns or grievances to the attention of the political elite. In effect the process of petitioning facilitated the formation of communities of women, whose shared experiences created the possibility of mutual comfort, sympathy and support.[99] As associates in planning and organizing petitions, women may have benefited from the consolations of companionship while validating or justifying their activism.

Yet the impact of women's petitioning is difficult to determine. It may have had little direct influence on policy, in so far as it existed. Nonetheless the organization and presentation of petitions helped to keep the issue of captivity in the public arena. By their very nature, moreover, they usually compelled monarchs and others to respond in a positive manner. The evidence of responses from the Privy Council suggests that individual petitioners with specific goals stood the best chance of receiving effective assistance.[100] Whether this led to the redemption and return of captives is another matter. On balance it seems unlikely that many of the husbands, sons or other relatives returned to England, though the prospects for

[97] TNA, SP 29/276/186, I.

[98] TNA, SP 29/276/186.

[99] On the significance of petitioning see M. B. Norton, *Separated by Their Sex: Women in Public and Private in the Colonial Atlantic World* (Ithaca, 2011), pp. 60–70.

[100] In 1637 the council responded to specific appeals from Alice Taylor and Bennett Wright for the sale of Turkish prisoners, so that the proceeds could be used to redeem their husbands; TNA, PC 2/47, ff. 256–7.

freedom certainly improved during the later seventeenth and early eighteenth centuries as a result of assertive diplomacy and naval pressure.

The tension between agency and victimhood which characterized this campaign of petitioning was manifest in a rather different petition of 1708. Superficially it concerned the pardon and repatriation of pirates based at Madagascar and elsewhere in the East and West Indies, though it exposed the vulnerability of women's activism to predatory male interests. In a misconceived case of cultural ventriloquism, which barely concealed the financial ambitions of a group of well-connected adventurers and politicians, wives and other relations petitioned Queen Anne allegedly on behalf of the pirates and their accomplices. The petitioners included Mary Read, Elizabeth Woodstock, Olive Lyons, Anne Ashley, Anne Rupert and Elizabeth Waller, who were all identified in the introductory address, as well as another forty-two subscribers including seven men. Unusually, by comparison with previous petitions, they all signed or left their mark underneath the handwritten text. Of the women, eighteen, including Read, left a mark instead of a signature. Claiming to represent husbands or relatives, who acknowledged their crimes as pirates and buccaneers, while expressing a desire 'to returne to their Obedience and Duty', the petitioners requested a general pardon for all 'offences committed either by sea or land to all Degrees of men' amongst them.[101] The pirates, it was argued, should be allowed to return home with their wealth, and 'have their Comfort in a better Course of life in their Owne Country'.[102] The scheme depended on the appointment of trustees who would carry the pardon to the pirates, and safeguard their effects until they returned to England. A group of prospective trustees, evidently nominated by the wives and relatives, who included the Earl of Morton and Charles Egerton, submitted a Memorial in support of the appeal to the Lords Committee of Trade. In exchange for their willingness to act in this capacity, the trustees were to have their charges paid out of the pirates' booty.

The plan was presented as a means of suppressing the pirate settlement on Madagascar, at no cost to the government. Indeed the queen could expect to receive a windfall profit from the customs duty collected on the

---

[101] TNA, CO 323/6/81; A. Bialuschewski, 'Greed, Fraud, and Popular Culture: John Breholt's Madagascar Schemes of the Early Eighteenth Century', in C. I. McGrath and C. Fauske (eds), *Money, Power, and Print: Interdisciplinary Studies in the Financial Revolution in the British Isles* (Cranbury, 2010), pp. 104–14. Although the evidence is lacking, it is not impossible that this Mary Read was the subsequent associate of Anne Bonny; see D. Cordingly, *Life Among the Pirates: The Romance and Reality* (London, 1995), p. 303 n30.

[102] TNA, CO 323/6/81; T. Travers, *Pirates: A History* (Stroud, 2007), pp. 166–7.

plunder. A printed proposal to the House of Commons tried to deal with any ethical unease by claiming that the booty could not be returned to its original owners, the subjects of the Great Moghul of India, because they inhabited such remote parts of the world. Although the scheme attracted the interest of a diverse mixture of politicians and financiers, it was a transparent attempt by the promoters to share in the fabled wealth of the pirates which reputedly lay 'Buried or Useless in or near' Madagascar.[103]

The project of 1708 was initiated and organized by John Breholt and his associates. A ship-master and treasure hunter, whose links with the pirates aroused deep suspicion, Breholt held several large public gatherings at the King's Head Inn along the Strand in London. Among the women who attended, as wives and relatives, were Penelope Aubin, Barbara Ramsey, Anne Rupert and Elizabeth Woodstock. Aubin later claimed that Breholt sought her assistance in identifying 'a person ... who could find out ... the wives or Relations of some of the principall pirates, And in particular the wife of Captain Avery, who he said ... might be very usefull to them'.[104] Although she was offered a share in the venture, in exchange for such information, she turned it down due to her suspicions and poor opinion of Breholt.

The other women were more receptive to the scheme as a result of their personal circumstances. Woodstock and Rupert, who were widows, and Ramsey, all of whom came from St Margaret's parish in Westminster, agreed to sign the petition, as well as a copy of it, and other writings, including a letter of attorney for the nomination of the trustees. Elizabeth Woodstock was willing to support any plan which would hasten the return of her wayward son-in-law who was reported to be with the pirates at Madagascar. According to her testimony, he had gone to sea many years ago, leaving his pregnant young wife in her hands. But the mother seems to have died in childbirth, as Woodstock claimed that she 'kept & maintained the said Child [now aged about ten] at her own charge'.[105]

Despite the interest it aroused in some quarters, the plan for the pardon and return of the pirates from Madagascar failed to proceed. Concern at Breholt's background and motives discouraged potential investors, though the government may never have been seriously interested in the proposal.[106] Despite its failure, it revealed the scope for male manipulation in exploiting the personal circumstances of poor women such as Elizabeth Woodstock, while casting some light on the short-lived business schemes that flourished during the early eighteenth century.

[103] BL, Additional MS 61620, ff. 155v–71.
[104] TNA, CO 323/6/91, V; CO 324/9/200–3v.
[105] TNA, CO 323/6/91, IV.
[106] Bialuschewski, 'Greed, Fraud, and Popular Culture', pp. 111–12.

Seeking help from the magistrate

Regardless of the record of activism outlined above, most women whose husbands were victims of Barbary captivity lacked the resources, time or opportunity for presenting petitions to institutions or individuals in London. Distance was an acute problem for women who lived in remote regions of the south west which were vulnerable to corsair raiding, although it was an issue that affected wives and others from widely scattered parts of the British Isles. During the 1620s and 1630s the scale of corsair raiding had profound implications for the provision of parish charity and poor relief in some communities of the south west. In April 1627 local officials in Weymouth excused their inability to provide shipping for royal service, partly because of the 'Continuall Charge ... in the Relieving of the wyves and Children of many late Inhabitants of this Towne which nowe are Captives and Slaves in Argier and Salley'.[107] In September 1635 the mayor of Dartmouth complained of the intolerable burden of supporting the poor wives and children of nearly sixty local men who had recently been taken prisoner. The following year the magistrates of Cornwall reported the seizure of fishing vessels from Looe, which left 'above an hundred persons ... [to] the pitty of others'; as a result, the inhabitants were 'so surcharged, as they are likely to fall into greate Decay'.[108]

In these circumstances a growing number of women appealed to magistrates, sitting in quarter sessions, for assistance. While their petitions acknowledged the functions of justices in the administration and regulation of the law, they also tried to harness their responsibilities for the poor and poor relief. In the south west, as elsewhere, magistrates were willing to represent the complaints of local officials and communities concerning corsair raiding to the government, while undertaking more direct action to help captives and their spouses and relatives. In 1624 the justices of Devon authorized the repayment of a sum of £137 10s, with interest, used to redeem twenty captives at Algiers, out of money collected for that purpose.[109] By the later seventeenth century county magistrates were willing to provide aid for women petitioners, in the form of a cash payment out of the county stock, which was intended as a contribution to the redemption of husbands and others.

---

[107] TNA, SP 16/61/7 and 16/5/23.
[108] TNA, SP 16/298/50 (for Dartmouth); SP 16/328/62; R. N. Worth (ed.), *Calendar of the Plymouth Municipal Records* (Plymouth, 1893), pp. 154, 204, 219–20.
[109] *CSPD, 1623–25*, p. 350. The responsibilities of magistrates toward the poor were outlined in Dalton, *Countrey Justice*, pp. 19, 81–9. During the 1640s and 1650s women petitioned magistrates for pensions and other aid, not as charity but as part of their rights; Hughes, *Gender and the English Revolution*, pp. 42–3.

Although the local origins of the practice are obscure, the earliest recorded petitions to Sir Thomas Carew and other justices at Exeter were presented in 1673. Among the six women who appealed for assistance was Joan Stephens from the parish of Alphington, whose son, George, was taken in the *Good Success* of Topsham off Cape St Vincent in 1671 by two men-of-war of Salé. He was subsequently sold to a 'most barbarous' owner.[110] As his mother was too poor to pay a ransom of £75, she requested permission to collect charitable benevolences within Exeter and its suburbs. Her petition was supported and signed by parish officers, including the rector, churchwardens and constables. Their statement, promising to 'doe the Like for any of your Inhabitants if they fall into the like misery', was clearly intended for a wider audience than the justices, demonstrating the way in which such appeals were circulated and used within neighbouring parishes.[111] The owner of the ship, Nicholas Brooking of Exeter, added his own confirmation that Stephens was a captive in Barbary.

The other women presenting petitions during the year included Elizabeth Reade of Lympston who was acting on behalf of a neighbour, William Blight. Although he had been in captivity for about eighteen months, Blight had no friends in the parish to organize or provide for his family or ransom, which was set at £50. In bringing the case to the attention of the magistrates, Reade was acting in the interests of the local community as much as Blight. As she pointed out, he had 'Five Motherlesse children' who were dependent on the charity of parishioners.[112] With the support of local officials, including the overseer of the poor, she appealed to the justices either to recommend Blight's case to local gentry and clergy, or to provide a contribution to his ransom out of a recent general collection.

Little evidence survives of the response of the justices to these early petitions, but in at least one case they authorized the use of public funds to support the recovery of a captive. Charitie Tomline, a widow of Topsham, whose son, aged about twenty-two, was held at Salé, was recommended to the bench as a poor woman of virtuous reputation. She was awarded £2 towards the ransom of her son, a 'very hopefull young man', which amounted to £70.[113] Although the amount was modest, it was intended to encourage other donations in the region; moreover, it was followed by many similar awards during the next decade or so.

Between 1673 and 1688 nearly fifty women petitioned the justices for assistance in the redemption of captives in Barbary. Much of this activity

[110] DRO, Devon Q/S 128/1–147. Stephens' petition is Q/S 128/1/1.

[111] DRO, Q/S 128/1/1.

[112] Ibid., 128/77/2.

[113] Ibid., 128/126/3.

was the result of the conflict with Algiers from 1677 to 1682, though not all of the prisoners were taken by corsairs from that port.[114] More than half of the petitions were presented during the brief period from 1682 to 1684. Although ranging across the county, most of the petitioners were residents of parishes along the south coast: nearly half of the total were presented by women from Dartmouth, Topsham and Plymouth. The remainder were spread more widely across neighbouring communities including Churston Ferrers, Kenton, Dawlish, Lympston, Tavistock and Totnes, with one from the northern port of Ilfracombe.

Most of these women petitioners were members of seafaring communities, where lives were shaped by an uncertain and unending relationship with the sea. Many were accustomed to hardship, including the burden of raising young children with the intermittent absence of spouses. Although individual circumstances varied, they were practical, organized and reputable women who possessed the independence and fortitude to plead their cause at the quarter sessions. The majority were wives or mothers, but they included friends, neighbours and kin, as well as one close relation.[115] Among the forty-nine petitions, just over half were from wives seeking support for captive spouses; another third were from mothers on behalf of sons, or in-laws. At least nine of the petitioners had children to raise and maintain at home. Mary Voysie of Dawlish, authorized by the justices in 1681 to collect alms to redeem her husband, was the mother of six small children. Jane Crute, also of Dawlish, who successfully petitioned for assistance in 1682, and Ursula Phippard of Topsham, who appealed for help to redeem her husband and two sons in 1678, both had four children to support. Of the remaining petitioners who identified themselves as mothers, Sarah Bloy of Kingswear, Margaret Cobbold of Newton Poppleford in the parish of Aylesbeare and Elizabeth Knight of Churston Ferrers all had three children to care for.[116] Their husbands had been in captivity for four or five years when they appealed for aid. Margaret Cobbold's plea in 1683 that she had 'three small Children & nothinge now left to mainttaine them but onely her worke', was echoed three years later by Elizabeth

[114] Pennell (ed.), *Piracy and Diplomacy*, pp. 86–7; J. Morgan, *A Complete History of Algiers* (London, 1731), p. v; Wolf, *Barbary Coast*, pp. 238–41.
[115] Mary Robbins' petition on behalf of Pentecost Martaine who had no surviving family; DRO, Q/S 128/78/6. On seafaring wives more generally see C. T. Fury, *Tides in the Affairs of Men: The Social History of Elizabethan Seamen, 1580–1603* (Westport, 2002), pp. 207–21. More broadly, the influence of their position in the labour market is examined by D. Valenze, *The First Industrial Woman* (Oxford, 1995), pp. 14–25.
[116] DRO, Q/S 128/43/2 (Voysie); 43/5 (Crute); 126/4 (Phippard); 73/4 (Bloy); 6/1 and 2 (Cobbold); 32/4 (Knight).

Knight who had 'nothing but her owne industry and labour' to support herself and her children.[117] Three of the remaining petitioners had at least one child to look after. They included Catherine Molle of Kenton, with a 'Sucking Childe & nothing but her poor Labour to … maintain herself & said Childe upon'.[118]

Although the petitions showed some variation, reflecting individual circumstances, they adopted a common form and structure similar to those presented to other individuals or institutions. Like the latter, undoubtedly they were drawn up by scriveners or clerks, based in Exeter, and in some cases with the advice and assistance of friends or parish officials. Presented in the language of poor supplicants, they usually began with a standard introduction, such as the 'humble Request & petition' of Joan Stephens of 1673.[119] The opening appeal was followed by details of the capture and captivity of spouse, son, kinsman or neighbour, and the personal circumstances of the petitioner. Occasionally there was an additional comment testifying to the truth of the petitioner's claims. In nearly all cases parish officials signed at the bottom as evidence of their support and validation. The use of language and the recurrence of certain phrases underlined the degree to which they drew on a common stock or repertoire, especially in the use of the image of cruel and merciless Turks.

In seeking assistance from magistrates, women petitioners emphasized the harsh, intolerable nature of captivity. According to his sister, Oliver Hare was 'subjugated & exposed to a most wretched & remediless Slavery' at Algiers.[120] Elizabeth Matthews likewise claimed that her husband was held in cruel bondage. Similar phrases were used by others, who drew attention to the barbarous and inhuman treatment of prisoners or their sad and miserable condition. Catherine Molle claimed that her husband, John, was held in such cruel conditions that, 'as he sorrowfully writes, [he was] ready to eat his own flesh'.[121] Some deliberately made use of underlying religious hostility and rivalries. In separate petitions to the justices and the Bishop of Exeter, Mary Voysie asserted that her husband was enslaved 'under the tyranny of merciless Infidells & Enemies of our Lord Jesus Christ'.[122]

While recounting the appalling conditions under which captives were held, petitioners also drew attention to their difficult situations. Many were living with varying degrees of hardship and poverty, exacerbated by the possibility

[117] Ibid., 128/6/1 and 32/4.
[118] Ibid., 128/69/9.
[119] Ibid., 128/1/1.
[120] Ibid., 128/57/4.
[121] Ibid., 128/69/9 (Molle); 128/32/2 (Matthews).
[122] Ibid., 128/43/2.

of trauma and loneliness. Mary Sparke of Bridgetown, struggling to raise £100 to ransom her husband, was 'destitute of friends to help her'.[123] Elizabeth Mountstephen and her spouse, Isaac, who was held at Algiers, were 'poore young beginners in the world haveinge no relacions of either side that are able to contribute towards the releife of the poor Captive'.[124] Others, including Jane Clark of Kenton, Mary Oliver of Powderham, Sarah Farrant of Topsham, as well as Rebecca Sulke and Mary Davis of Dartmouth, also lacked friends or relations who could help them. For Rebecca Sulke, a widow for more than twenty years, the capture of her son meant the loss of her mainstay and livelihood. Sarah Bloy of Kingswear was left to care for three small children, the eldest of whom was aged six. She appeared destitute, 'not haveinge anything of moneys worth, nor one penney to help herselfe'.[125] Her only income was twelve pence a week from parish poor relief. In a similar case from Dittisham, local officials petitioned on behalf of the wife of Sampson Caterey, another prisoner at Algiers, and their two small children, 'who would inevitably perrish if not releived by charatable persons'.[126]

Despite being in such difficult circumstances, some women responded energetically to the challenge of raising ransom money, often at great cost to themselves and their children. Priscilla Pearse, a widow of Muker parish, lost her main support when her son was taken by Algerian corsairs. Within three years, however, she had acquired £60 towards his ransom of £80. About two-thirds came from public funds, but the rest she collected from her local community.[127] Yet another widow, Ann Pounce of Paignton, struggling to collect a ransom of £70 for her son, sold her possessions, though she was still £30 short of the total.[128] A few were fortunate to be able to rely on family and kin for assistance. Ursula Phippard of Topsham, whose husband, a ship-master and owner, and two sons were taken by the corsairs, had a 'brother & some relacions of ability', who promised to provide any additional money above £100, 'without making any publique gatherings or colleccions as is usuall in such cases'.[129] Although she was unaware of the ransom price for the captives, Phippard was prepared to sell the house she lived in and her chief possessions, and 'to leave herself bare necessaries', in order to redeem her spouse and sons.[130]

---

[123] Ibid., 128/8/3.
[124] Ibid., 128/126/6.
[125] Ibid., 128/69/3 (Clark); 69/10 (Oliver); 126/2 (Farrant); 42/20 (Sulke); 73/4 (Bloy).
[126] Ibid., 128/44/1.
[127] Ibid., 128/78/7.
[128] Ibid., 128/97/5.
[129] Ibid., 128/126/4.
[130] Ibid., 128/126/4.

These cases of female agency operated within a wider context of support and obligation. In 1682, for example, representatives of St Saviour's parish in Dartmouth petitioned on behalf of James Silby, a captive at Algiers, whose elderly parents, both of whom were above eighty years in age, lacked relations who could help them. For most women, such local support was provided by parish officers who certified the truth of their petitions, often with an explicit statement to that effect, and by signing at the bottom. Elizabeth Reade of Lympston presented a petition to the justices in 1673 which was signed by the rector, churchwardens, constables and the overseer of the poor. The number of such signatories, all male, ranged from one to eighteen, though six or seven seemed to be common practice. Petitions from Dartmouth included the mayor and a public notary among their number. Although rare, parish gentry occasionally served as witnesses. The petition of Priscilla Pearse of Muker was signed by Sir Richard Aycombe and Sir Jonathan Trelawney. Separate certificates might be drawn up by parish officials, in support of appeals to the justices. In 1682 the minister and churchwardens of Lympston certified the bench that George Taylor had been held at Algiers for nearly three years, and that his wife and friends were unable to redeem him.[131]

While representing charitable concern and neighbourliness at a very local level, this process of validation involved informal vetting, unstated calculation and self-interest. At times it also included inquiry into the circumstances of the petitioner. The petition of Charitie Tomline, a widow of Topsham, on behalf of her son, included a note by William Bruen that, though poor, she was of 'a virtuous reputation' while the son was a 'very hopefull young man'.[132] In such circumstances the response to these appeals for financial assistance varied, suggesting that justices were discriminating in the selection of recipients for relief, and in the amount that was awarded. Successful petitions seem to have been endorsed by the clerk of the sessions with a note of the value of the grant. The money was paid out by the treasurer of the county stock, in most cases to local constables, for distribution. Recipients seem to have been under obligation for its proper use. Mary Sparke of Bridgetown received fifty shillings towards the ransom of her husband, set at £100, 'she giving security' for the same.[133] The amount awarded varied, reflecting individual circumstances, community support and sanction, as well as the perceived worthiness of the petitioner. Among the women who petitioned for relief, just over half were awarded £2 10s.

[131] Ibid., 128/42/18 (Silby); 77/2 (Read); 78/7 (Pearse); 77/6 (Taylor).
[132] Ibid., 128/126/3.
[133] Ibid., 128/8/3.

Five petitioners received £3, another three were granted £4. At the extremes one petitioner was awarded £1, and another £5, the largest of its kind.[134] No evidence survives for the award of any relief to the remainder, who accounted for nearly one-third of the total.

The petitions presented to the justices of Devon provide an unusual perspective on female agency, particularly in coping with personal misfortune and crisis. Women such as Ann Pounce or Priscilla Pearse showed resolve, endurance and courage in facing up to the loss of partners to the Barbary corsairs. Within a region where the magistracy had displayed long-standing concern for the social and economic impact of corsair raiding, the justices responded in a sympathetic, charitable, but also discretionary, manner. Yet the effectiveness of these measures may have been limited. Women petitioners were seeking contributions towards ransoms which ranged from £35 to £250. The awards they received out of the county stock were a fraction of such large sums. Assuming that petitioners were as energetic and motivated as Priscilla Pearse, who claimed that she collected £20 from her community in three years, it would have taken a long time, in some cases up to a decade or more, for ransoms to be raised and paid off. In these circumstances, without more effective state action, the capture of husbands or sons consigned wives and widows to burdensome, lonely and abandoned lives. Forced to sell off their possessions, they were pinched even for bare necessities, leading poor and widowed lives in small, poor communities where the provision of charity was the result of uneasy negotiation.

The victims of pirate violence

While women petitioners were part of a larger group who were the indirect victims of piracy, a growing number of women suffered pirate violence more directly, experiencing intimidation and terror as well as physical harm and rape. The physical hurt was accompanied at times by deliberate humiliation and dishonour, and the stain on reputation that followed. Although the scale of the problem is impossible to estimate, the number of women who were the victims of pirate violence increased markedly during the later seventeenth and early eighteenth centuries. In part this was a consequence of the increased presence of women at sea, as passengers or migrants, but it was also the result of the changing character of English piracy and plunder which was linked with the decline of local piratical enterprise around the British Isles and the

---

[134] Jane Crute and four other women all received £3 (ibid., 128/126/7, 43/5, 126/6, 126/8, 126/11); Mary Oliver and two others received £4 (ibid., 69/10, 42/20–1); Margaret Taylor received £5 and Sarah Green £1 (ibid., 77/6, 126/9).

emergence of globalized, long-distance plunder. Under these conditions, although violence at sea and on land by English rovers continued to be inflamed and articulated by deep-seated anti-Spanish hostility, it was overlaid by potential inter-ethnic rivalries within the Caribbean, South America and West Africa, which spread across the Pacific and Indian Oceans. As pirates and other sea predators widened their hunt for booty, a growing number of women became vulnerable to their assault and aggression.

For much of the sixteenth century pirate violence against women was restrained by its community roots, and its projection outwards against overseas targets. Casual aggression towards women undoubtedly occurred, but it was rarely reported or recorded. Nor did it figure prominently in legal proceedings before the High Court of Admiralty, where women appeared more as the supporters of piracy than its victims. Across a broad region stretching from southern England and south-west Wales to the west of Ireland, they provided vital services for pirate groups. Nonetheless some women and girls were exposed to violent assault by disorderly pirates, usually acting alone during visits ashore. This appeared to be random and opportunistic action, which was generally uncharacteristic of many sea rovers. In June 1581 captain Piers, allegedly a murderer who had been previously pardoned for such offences, came ashore at the Isle of Wight, and 'by the hyeway met a very honeste manne's dawghter and forsably Ravyshed her'.[135] Despite the problematic issue of reporting rape and sexual assault, Piers' behaviour seems to have been unusual. At a time when such cases were treated with profound ambiguity, however, following his capture later in the year, he was tried and hanged for piracy. At sea, even within coastal waters, there was also the potential for group violence against women, especially by pirate groups who were using overseas bases. In May 1623, for example, John Nutt and his company seized a small vessel off Dungarvan in Ireland which was carrying twelve or fourteen female passengers, 'all which were ravished by the pyrate's company, but only one, Jones' wife, a sadler of Cork, whom Capt. Nutt took for himself into his cabbin, and there had her a week'.[136] The pirates had spent the last three years on the coast of Barbary. They returned reputedly rich, and in search of a pardon. Nutt, who had a wife and three children at Topsham in Devon, was prepared to pay £2,000 for his.

It was the spread of organized plunder into the West Indies during the

---

[135] BL, Lansdowne MS 33, ff. 183–3v. On the law regarding rape see [Edgar], *Lawes Resolutions of Womens Rights*, pp. 376–402; G. Walker, *Crime, Gender and Social Order in Early Modern England* (Cambridge, 2003), pp. 55–60; M. R. Hunt, *Women in Eighteenth-Century Europe* (Harlow, 2010), pp. 119–23.

[136] R. Caulfield (ed.), *The Council Book of the Corporation of Youghal* (Guildford, 1878), p. xlix.

1650s and 1660s which led to an increase in pirate violence, exposing women of varied backgrounds to assault by pirates and buccaneers. Within the volatile and changing environment of the colonial Caribbean, where servants and slaves were subject to routine maltreatment, the amphibious raids of the buccaneers were characterized by brutality, indiscriminate cruelty and torture, which included the use of women as pawns in the business of ransom and plunder, and their sexual assault or rape. The violence spread across the Panama isthmus and down the coast of South America, with the expanding range of buccaneering activity during the 1670s and 1680s. As the Spanish monarchy struggled to defend its American trade and settlements, the protection of colonial women was scarcely registered, except in the correspondence and complaints of clergy.[137]

Exquemelin provided a shocking portrait of the violent world of the buccaneers. Apparently based on eye-witness testimony, ever since its publication and translation as *The Buccaneers of America* in 1684, his account has been ransacked as evidence for the disordered lives of buccaneering leaders such as Sir Henry Morgan. It was laced with impressionistic and anecdotal evidence, designed to 'pleasure the public' while profiting publishers.[138] The English edition, printed by William Crooke of London, was amended and modified, not least by the inclusion of additional material by Basil Ringrose and others. In the preface the publisher defended the author against accusations that he portrayed English buccaneers 'as the worst of men', insisting that 'he relates ten times greater villainies of his own nation and country people'.[139] Indeed Exquemelin's accounts of Roche Brasiliano or Francois L'Ollonais, of Dutch and French background, shocked readers with their reported use of such barbarous cruelties as roasting alive Spanish prisoners, or beheading them after their surrender. L'Ollonais' attack on Gibraltar, along the coast of the Main, led to the seizure of a large number of women who were sexually assaulted or raped. In an uneasy passage that betrays a wider ambivalence regarding male violence towards women, Exquemelin noted that 'some had been forced, others were volunteers; though almost all had rather taken up that vice through poverty and hunger than any other cause'.[140]

---

[137] For conditions in the Caribbean and beyond see M. Parker, *The Sugar Barons: Family, Corruption, Empire and War* (London, 2011), pp. 108–10; P. T. Bradley, *The Lure of Peru: Maritime Intrusion into the South Sea, 1598–1701* (London, 1989), pp. 151, 166, 195; B. Little, *The Buccaneer's Realm: Pirate Life on the Spanish Main, 1674–1688* (Washington, DC, 2007), pp. 184–5.

[138] J. Esquemeling, *The Buccaneers of America*, ed. W. S. Stallybrass (London, 1924), p. 293.

[139] Ibid., pp. 283–4.

[140] Ibid., pp. 73, 85–6, 98, 103; Dickie, *Cruelty and Laughter*, pp. 193–246.

Figure 2 A romantic portrait of Morgan the buccaneer, toasting his success with a beautiful Spanish woman, as his company celebrate in the background. In reality Morgan was a controversial figure whose conduct towards female prisoners and victims was severely criticized by Exquemelin. (Captain Henry Morgan carouses with wine and women, in true pirate fashion, an illustration from P. Christian, *Histoire des Pirates et Corsaires* (Paris, 1846), copyright National Maritime Museum, Greenwich, London, catalogue number D6170-1).

Controversially, Exquemelin identified Morgan as 'the second L'Ol-lonais', claiming that his attack on Porto Bello in 1668 was accompanied by 'many insolent actions of rape and adultery committed upon very honest women, as well married as virgins, who being threatened with the sword were constrained to submit their bodies to the violence of these lewd and wicked men'.[141] The sexual aggression seemed to follow Morgan and his men around the Caribbean. Shortly after the assault on Porto Bello, the outpost of Chagres was 'turned into a place of prostitution' as the bucca-neers subjected the widows of their Spanish victims to 'all manner of inso-lent actions and threats'.[142] At Panama they allegedly missed the opportunity of taking a rich galleon laden with gold, plate and fleeing nuns, by 'the lascivious exercises wherein they were totally at that present involved with women'.[143] Nor did Morgan set a good example to his followers. With counterfeit civility he tried to debauch one of his prisoners, the young and beautiful wife of a wealthy merchant. When civility failed, he resorted to threats and intimidation, intending to carry her off to Jamaica until a ransom was paid for her release. Yet Morgan had his defenders. According to John Taylor, a visitor to Jamaica during the 1680s and author of a lengthy account of the island, the buccaneering leader demonstrated 'soldierlike conduct' at Panama, to prevent disorderly and irregular behaviour by his men.[144] Thus he ensured that women and children were protected from violence and affront by the imposition of martial law. Contradicting the claims of Exquemelin, Taylor also praised Morgan for the example he set for his men. Written shortly after his death, probably for publication, and based on local report and tradition in Jamaica, Taylor's manuscript reflected the rehabilitation of Morgan's career after his retirement from bucca-neering, while providing justification for his raid on Panama.

If the buccaneers were at war with Spain, however, it was an unregulated

---

[141] Esquemeling, *Buccaneers of America*, pp. 118, 140; N. Zahediah, 'Sir Henry Morgan', *Oxford Dictionary of National Biography* (Oxford, 2004), online edition, www.oxforddnb.com (accessed 12 December 2012), points out that there is no first-hand evidence to support this account of the attack on Porto Bello. See also P. Earle, *The Sack of Panama: Captain Morgan and the Battle for the Caribbean* (London, 1981), pp. 66–7; Little, *The Buccaneer's Realm*, pp. 90, 141.

[142] Esquemeling, *Buccaneers of America*, p. 189.

[143] Ibid., p. 213; Earle, *The Sack of Panama*, pp. 226–7 and 251–2, for a critical assess-ment of Exquemelin. Morgan's instructions apparently contained provision for him to return female slaves to Jamaica, where their sale would help pay for the expedition (male slaves could be put to the sword); *The Present State of Jamaica* (London, 1683), pp. 70–1.

[144] Esquemeling, *Buccaneers of America*, pp. 216–21; D. Buisseret (ed.), *Jamaica in 1687: The Taylor Manuscript at the National Library of Jamaica* (Kingston, 2008), pp. 90–1, 95.

Cap.ᵗ Hen Morgan before Panama wᶜ he took from the Spaniards.

Figure 3 A fanciful illustration of the buccaneering leader Morgan at the sack of Panama. The buccaneers were accused of rape and debauchery during the sack of the city in a later edition of Johnson's history. Although evidence for violence against women seems to be limited, Morgan's men resorted to brutal methods of torture to extract information from Spanish men. According to an Indian prisoner, his company included an old English woman, reputedly a witch, who was taken along to aid the expedition (P. Earle, *The Sack of Panama* (London, 1981), p. 167. Copyright The British Library Board, C. Johnson, *A General History of the Lives and Adventures of the Most Famous Highwaymen, Murderers, Street-Robbers, &c. To which is Added, a Genuine Account of the Voyages and Plunders of the Most Notorious Pyrates* (London, 1734)).

conflict which acquired its own momentum of violence and reprisal. Within an aggressive, sometimes alienated and disorderly masculine culture, where empathy was in short supply, the use of gratuitous punishment and torture may have been widely condoned. At a time when women remained the subject of violent assault by more professionalized military bodies, they could expect little sympathy from a rabble of disordered rogues, despite evidence for a crude code of conduct among the buccaneers. While some raiders may have seen women as prisoners or pawns to be ransomed for booty, they could be the victims of brutal and degrading forms of symbolic abuse. In a report from Jamaica of January 1670, concerning the raid on Porto Bello, John Style, a planter, provided an insight into the nature of this culture. Apparently some members of the expedition later boasted that they roasted a woman who was 'set bare upon a baking stone ... because she did not confess of money which she had only in their conceit'.[145] According to Style only one member of the company, who was sick, expressed regret or sorrow at the deed. On Jamaica, indeed, such reports, including the rape of women, were 'made a jest of even by authority'.[146] But the episode invited retaliation, risking an escalation in the aggressive conduct of male marauders towards women. In September 1705 the Council of Trade and Plantations was informed of a 'horrid and unparall'd cruelty' committed on the wife of the governor of Providence by a group of Spanish raiders.[147] In a shocking incident which mimicked, but went beyond, the earlier raid on Porto Bello, the wife and several other women were raped. Because she refused to confess to the location of her husband and suspected treasure, presumed to be hidden, the assailants of the governor's wife set fire to some rum, 'and put it in her private part, and to make their spleen appear yet greater they cut off a piece of the same'.[148] The council's informant claimed that he had the details from the actors in the tragedy, who later boasted of their exploit in Havana.

The female victims of the buccaneers soon came to include native women within the Caribbean. Exquemelin reported that in the aftermath

[145] *CSPC, 1669–74*, pp. 49–51. P. Leeson, *The Hidden Hook: The Hidden Economics of Piracy* (Princeton, 2009), pp. 114–15, in referring to this incident argues that 'pirates couldn't afford to torture prisoners indiscriminately'. On women and ransoms see R. de Lussan, *A Journal of a Voyage Made Into the South Sea, by the Bucaniers or Freebooters of America; From the Year 1684 to 1689* (London, 1698), p. 65.
[146] *CSPC, 1669–74*, pp. 50–1.
[147] *CSPC, 1704–5*, p. 614.
[148] Ibid.; De Lussan, *Journal of a Voyage*, pp. 77–8, 107, 125, 177–8. The author claimed that Spanish priests warned women that the buccaneers were not human, but cannibals.

of the Panama expedition a group of Morgan's men abducted Indian women at Costa Rica, 'to serve their disordinate lust'.[149] In addition to suffering sexual abuse, the captives were used as slaves, employed in tasks such as washing, sewing and drawing water from wells at temporary bases in the region. These included the Cape of Gracias á Dios, a popular rendezvous, where women could be purchased 'for the price of a knife or any old axe, wood-bill, or hatchet'.[150] Such inter-ethnic relationships were temporary and terminated by the departure of the buccaneers. But they had far-reaching consequences for native women who, even under the most benign circumstances, seem to have been used to facilitate a broader system of exchange that was controlled by men. Although short-lived, these contacts were disruptive and potentially self-destructive. Exquemelin recorded that the behaviour of the buccaneers at Costa Rica eroded friendly relations with the natives despite their shared hostility towards Spain.[151]

The successors of the buccaneers continued to employ violence in a varied fashion. From the 1690s to at least the 1720s, when piracy and privateering flourished during a confused period of war and peace, the threat to women not only spread but also became increasingly indiscriminate. The use of violence varied from uncontrolled individual or group behaviour to more purposeful and planned action. Although firm leadership and organization, as well as self-discipline and peer pressure, could restrain violent conduct towards women, even aboard well-run privateering vessels captains and officers struggled to control unruly and sex-starved mariners. During raids ashore, moreover, women were sometimes specifically targeted by pirates and other raiders. While the behaviour of such predators towards their victims within the Caribbean and South America continued to be driven by anti-Spanish hostility, it was also influenced by wider European rivalries between England and France. Elsewhere, within the Indian Ocean for example, the maritime violence was easily transferred to non-Christians, as demonstrated by Avery's notorious plunder of the *Ganj-i Sawai*. Despites its damaging consequences, the expansion of piracy into the region seems to have been accompanied by a self-serving ethnic hostility, as characterized by the comments of one of the company of a privateering expedition in 1718, who proposed cruising in the Red Sea, 'for, said he, there can be no harm in robbing those Mahometans', while it would be a sin to injure Spanish Christians.[152]

---

[149] Esquemeling, *Buccaneers of America*, p. 225.

[150] Ibid., pp. 233, 238.

[151] Ibid., p. 225; De Lussan, *Journal of a Voyage*, pp. 177–8.

[152] G. Shelvocke, *A Voyage Round the World by the Way of the Great South Sea* (London, 1726), p. 12. The proposal was made by the gunner, who was confined and subsequently

In the violent free-for-all which prevailed in the Caribbean during the late seventeenth and early eighteenth centuries, pirates drew little distinction between the gender, age or rank of victims. Because of their location and vulnerability, including the regular absence of male residents, among landed targets the Bahamas were subject to repeated raids during which women were indiscriminately victimized and violated. In 1701 Read Elding, a popular local leader, was found guilty of piracy and the abduction of the wife of the deputy governor, Major Trott. Elias Haskett, the governor, complained that he was imprisoned in irons for six weeks, while his wife was kept in close confinement for five weeks, during which the pirates would not allow 'her to go to Town, nor to see any of her acquaintance, nor to write to them nor have any communication with them'.[153] In 1708, during a raid by French pirates, led by captain Martel, the wife of captain Edward Holmes was taken aboard their ship where she was stripped naked and threatened with a pistol pointed at her breast, to force her to reveal his hidden wealth. Further indignity followed when one of the pirates searched her hair for small valuables and threatened to throw her overboard. She was then taken ashore and tied to a tree while one of Martel's men beat her with a sword. Despite the pain and humiliation, Holmes' wife seems to have refused to cooperate with the pirates. Indeed it was her husband who finally confessed, but only after they threatened to burn his 'privy members'.[154] During the same raid the pirates killed a local mariner and raped his daughters. A pregnant woman miscarried after being tied up, suspended and beaten with a cutlass. Another woman was burnt alive after being bound and left in a building which was set on fire.[155]

Although the Bahamas were acutely vulnerable to such attack, random raiding occurred across the Caribbean. In June 1709 Daniel Parke, the governor of Antigua, reported a recent visit by the sons of the king of Dominica to complain of a privateering company from Jamaica who had killed some of their men and ravished their women. Parke promised to take action against the miscreants if they entered his jurisdiction. He also gave the Indians a pair of pistols, clothing and a cask of rum and sugar in an attempt to avert the risk of revenge against English traders.[156]

At sea the violence against women was more opportunistic and usually

discharged. On the rape of native women by Kidd's company see R. C. Ritchie, *Captain Kidd and the War Against the Pirates* (Cambridge, Mass., 1986), pp. 104, 110, 119.
[153] *CSPC, 1701*, pp. 696–700.
[154] *CSPC, 1709*, pp. 281–2; M. J. Jarvis, *In the Eye of All Trade: Bermuda, Bermudians, and the Maritime Atlantic World, 1680–1783* (Chapel Hill, 2010), pp. 330–1.
[155] Ibid., p. 331.
[156] *CSPC, 1709*, p. 397.

the work of individuals. Although many pirate groups sailed under a code of conduct, which included sanctions against the assault of female prisoners, the application of informal discipline or peer pressure by older members of the company may have been a more effective restraint. Captain Woodes Rogers, commander of a privateering expedition which circumnavigated the globe from 1708 to 1711, placed a party of prisoners, including a gentlewoman and her daughter, a young newly-wed, in the custody of Lieutenant Glendall, who was above fifty years in age, as 'he appear'd to be the most secure Guardian to Females that had the least Charm'.[157] Elizabeth Trengove, who was taken prisoner by pirates in 1721, later gave evidence before an admiralty court held at Cape Coast Castle that William Mead 'was very rude to her, swearing and cursing, as also forcing her hoop'd Petticoat off'.[158] She was saved from further molestation by the intervention of John Mitchel who advised her to seek sanctuary in the gunner's room. Mitchel made no reference to the incident during his own trial, but after the court found him guilty of piracy, his sentence was subsequently commuted to seven years' servitude in Africa.

The seizure and plunder of the *Ganj-i Sawai* provided an infamous exception to this pattern of individual violence. In October 1695 English officials in Bombay informed the Privy Council of the barbarous behaviour of Avery and his pirate company. Acting as a group, they employed violence and torture against the crew and passengers to elicit information about hidden booty. In addition they raped and humiliated several women. One married woman and her servant killed themselves, 'to prevent the Husbands seeing them, and their being ravished'.[159] The incident provoked outrage and widespread interest, but sympathy for the victims was obscured by concern at the threat to English interests in India as a result of retaliation by the Moghul. The event was soon reshaped by published accounts which disturbingly recreated it as romantic fiction. An inaccurate and confusing biography, *The Life and Adventures of Capt. John Avery* which was published in 1709,

---

[157] W. Rogers, *A Cruising Voyage Round the World* (London, 1712), p. 243. For pirate articles see H. F. Rankin, *The Golden Age of Piracy* (Williamsburg, 1969), p. 31; E. R. Snow, *Pirates and Buccaneers of the Atlantic Coast* (Boston, 1944), pp. 125–6, 307.

[158] *A Full and Exact Account of the Tryal Of all the Pyrates, Lately Taken by Captain Ogle* (London, 1723), reprinted in Baer (ed.), *British Piracy*, III, pp. 112, 142, 164.

[159] TNA, PC 1/46, Part 2, unfoliated. P. Bradley Nutting, 'The Madagascar Connection: Parliament and Piracy, 1690–1701', *American Journal of Legal History*, 22 (1978), pp. 205–6. Avery's exploits became part of seafaring folklore and oral tradition, spreading widely. See, for example, B. Lubbock (ed.), *Barlow's Journal of His Life at Sea in King's Ships, East and West Indiamen & Other Merchantmen from 1659 to 1703*, 2 vols (London, 1934), II, pp. 472–3.

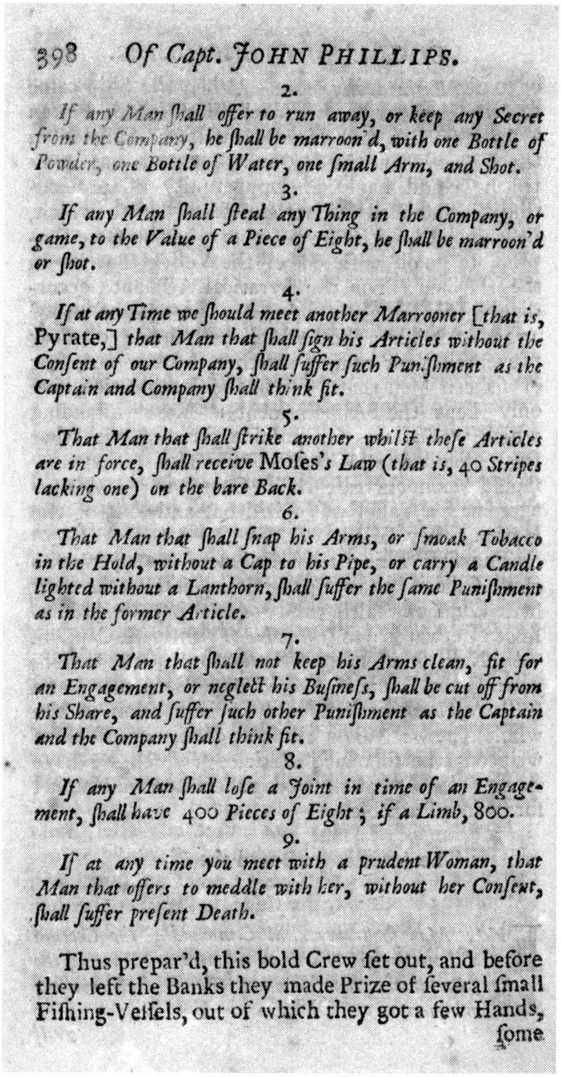

2.

If any Man shall offer to run away, or keep any Secret from the Company, he shall be marroon'd, with one Bottle of Powder, one Bottle of Water, one small Arm, and Shot.

3.

If any Man shall steal any Thing in the Company, or game, to the Value of a Piece of Eight, he shall be marroon'd or shot.

4.

If at any Time we should meet another Marrooner [that is, Pyrate,] that Man that shall sign his Articles without the Consent of our Company, shall suffer such Punishment as the Captain and Company shall think fit.

5.

That Man that shall strike another whilst these Articles are in force, shall receive Moses's Law (that is, 40 Stripes lacking one) on the bare Back.

6.

That Man that shall snap his Arms, or smoak Tobacco in the Hold, without a Cap to his Pipe, or carry a Candle lighted without a Lanthorn, shall suffer the same Punishment as in the former Article.

7.

That Man that shall not keep his Arms clean, fit for an Engagement, or neglect his Business, shall be cut off from his Share, and suffer such other Punishment as the Captain and the Company shall think fit.

8.

If any Man shall lose a Joint in time of an Engagement, shall have 400 Pieces of Eight; if a Limb, 800.

9.

If at any time you meet with a prudent Woman, that Man that offers to meddle with her, without her Consent, shall suffer present Death.

Thus prepar'd, this bold Crew set out, and before they left the Banks they made Prize of several small Fishing-Vessels, out of which they got a few Hands, some

Figure 4 Articles of the pirate ship the *Revenge*. According to Johnson these were written down by one of the company. They were designed to prevent disputes, while settling the pirate commonwealth. Members of the company swore to them upon a hatchet in place of a Bible which was lacking. In addition to regulating the distribution of shares of booty, they covered various aspects of behaviour at sea. According to number nine any man who meddled with a prudent woman faced death, if it was without her consent. By implication this excluded certain categories of women, including prostitutes. The use and effectiveness of such articles remains unclear. In many cases peer pressure from older members of pirate companies may have been more effective in containing unruly, younger companions. (Copyright The British Library Board, C. Johnson, *A General History of the Pyrates* (London, 1725)).

claimed that a beautiful princess, the granddaughter of the Moghul, was among the passengers. According to the author, Adrian van Broeck, a Dutch gentleman who had been a prisoner of the pirates, 'instead of ravishing the Princess, which some Accounts have made Mention of, [Avery] pay'd the Respect that was due to her high Birth'.[160] Thus the pirate married his captive princess, while the 'rest of the Ship's Crew drew Lots for her Servants'.[161] Thereafter, Avery and his men, 'being full of Wealth, when they were almost empty of Love', went on to establish a 'Republick of Pirates' on Madagascar.[162] The author left off his narrative with the pirate leader, now a petty sovereign, unsuccessfully appealing for a pardon: 'To go further than this', he disarmingly wrote, 'would be to impose upon the Veracity of the Relators, as well as the Belief of the Reader.'[163]

The blend of fact and fiction was characteristic of the growing number of works on piracy, as exemplified most fully in captain Charles Johnson's *History*. But these imaginative re-creations, while intended to inform and entertain a mixed audience of readers, effectively effaced the victimization of women by pirates. Moreover, their anonymity and silence were compounded by ethnic and religious differences. While this may have lent an exotic appearance to an appalling episode, it also suggested a broader cultural blindness to acknowledging 'other' women as victims, which was informed by a long-standing ambiguity towards rape and non-consensual sex in general.[164]

The treatment of female victims, including the ambivalent responses it provoked, was strikingly revealed by the experiences of African women. Taken aboard slaving ships, which were increasingly targeted by pirates and others for purposes of recruitment, the status of such prisoners was profoundly uncertain. In 1615, for example, a pirate captain presented an admiralty official in Ireland with the gift of a 'negro wench'.[165] The increase

---

[160] *The Life and Adventures of Capt. John Avery* (London, 1709), p. 30. Subsequent popular accounts insisted that Avery 'ravished the young princess, and used other beastly actions to the ladies of her retinue'. *The Famous Adventures of Captain John Avery, of Plymouth: A Notorious Pirate* (Falkirk, 1809), p. 12, reprinted from *The History and Lives of all the Most Notorious Pirates and Their Crews* (Glasgow, 1788).
[161] *The Life and Adventures of Capt. John Avery*, p. 31.
[162] Ibid., p. 32.
[163] Ibid., p. 59; S. C. Hill, *Notes on Piracy in Eastern Waters* (Bombay, 1923), pp. 99–105.
[164] For modern studies which explore the problem of rape as well as the evidence, see M. Chaytor, 'Husband(ry): Narratives of Rape in the Seventeenth Century', *Gender & History*, 7 (1995), pp. 378–407; G. Walker, 'Rereading Rape and Sexual Violence in Early Modern England', *Gender & History*, 10 (1998), pp. 1–25; Hughes, *Gender and the English Revolution*, pp. 34–5; Dickie, *Cruelty and Laughter*, pp. 209–49.
[165] Captain Lording Barry gave the woman to a servant of Humphrey Jobson, the admiralty official; TNA, HCA 1/48/104v–6v.

in the seizure of slaving vessels during the late seventeenth and early eighteenth centuries, at a time when the slave trade was growing rapidly, occurred within a broader racialized context concerning property and power. In these circumstances women and young girls were subject to appalling maltreatment aboard some slave ships. In 1706 the High Court of Admiralty heard a case concerning the repeated rape of a young African girl at sea. As she subsequently died of a sexually transmitted disease, her owners initiated the suit, claiming loss of property and income.[166]

Against this background there is little evidence that sea rovers were willing to treat captured slaves differently. Some men and boys may have been released and recruited to serve aboard pirate ships, joining the growing number of African seafarers at work in the Atlantic world, but many others were probably sold or abandoned. Woodes Rogers claimed that African prisoners were 'troublesome Goods', though in preparation for conflict with the Spanish or French he promised to free thirty-five 'lusty fellows' if they fought with the English.[167] The position of women was more problematic. If retained by their captors, they were exposed to exploitation for sex or labour. As a potentially disruptive presence and an additional burden on the limited resources of the ship, however, it was in the interest of most captains to dispose of such captives as soon as possible.

The published account of Rogers' privateering voyage around the world sheds some light on the experiences of female victims at sea and on land. Rogers was concerned to present an authentic report, in contrast to the 'romantick Accounts … and … strange Stories' of the buccaneers.[168] One of his underlying themes was to demonstrate the civil and modest behaviour of his men, as distinct from the debauchery and cruelty of the buccaneers. To avoid the disorder of the buccaneers, who 'liv'd without Government', he drew up a code of regulations, or a constitution as he termed it, though this failed to prevent the periodic outbreak of mutinous behaviour among some members of the company.[169]

Outward bound, as the expedition took in provisions at Cork, Rogers recorded the brief liaisons between his men and local women, in what may

[166] TNA, HCA 24/129/14. For the unclear boundary between property and sex, see K. M. Brown, *Good Wives, Nasty Wenches, and Anxious Patriarchs: Gender, Race, and Power in Colonial Virginia* (Chapel Hill, 1996), pp. 207–11.

[167] Rogers, *A Cruising Voyage*, pp. 247–8. A group of slaves were 'seized and sold as the effects of pirates' in 1720 on Barbados; *CSPC, 1719–20*, pp. 356–7, 362. See also A. Bialuschewski, 'Black People Under the Black Flag: Piracy and the Slave Trade on the West Coast of Africa, 1718–1723', *Slavery and Abolition*, 29 (2008), pp. 461–76.

[168] Rogers, *A Cruising Voyage*, p. xvi.

[169] Ibid., pp. xvii, 338.

have been a popular seafaring custom at the start of long and dangerous voyages. 'Our Crew', he noted, 'were continually marrying whilst we staid at *Cork*, tho they expected to sail immediately.'[170] The function and fragility of these unions were acknowledged by both parties who 'drank their Cans of Flip till the last minute, concluded with a Health to our good Voyage, and their happy Meeting, and then parted unconcern'd'.[171] Following in the footsteps of the buccaneers, the expedition raided the port of Guayaquil along the coast of Peru. A group of women who had sought refuge up-river were plundered of their personal possessions, including gold chains and earrings. Although the women were subject to body searches, Rogers insisted that his men kept 'their Hands on the Out-side of the Lady's Apparel'.[172] Their civility, he claimed, was rewarded with the offer of food and a cask of wine. At sea a prize was taken with a family aboard. As noted above, the elderly Lieutenant Glendall was appointed to guard the mother and her daughter. Although the younger members of the privateering company had 'hitherto appear'd modest beyond Example', Rogers 'thought it improper to expose them to Temptations'.[173] Informed that the women had 'some conceal'd Treasure about them', he ordered a 'Female Negro ... who spoke *English*, to search them narrowly'.[174]

This was followed by the seizure of a vessel carrying twenty-four slaves, male and female. Despite Rogers' claims for the behaviour of his company, he recorded the death of a youth, John Edwards, from a 'Complication of Scurvy and the Pox, which he got from a loathsome Negro', who was later given away so that 'she might do no further Mischief on board'.[175] Another woman, described as the 'prettiest Female Negro' taken in the prize, was presented as a gift to a young priest for his assistance in getting provisions ashore.[176] In a deeply unsettling passage, betraying overt anti-Catholicism, Rogers claimed that the 'Padre parted with us extremely pleas'd, and leering under his Hood upon his black Female Angel, we doubt he will crack a Commandment with her, and wipe off the Sin with the Church's Indulgence'.[177] Later in the voyage one of the remaining women gave birth to a baby girl, with the assistance of the chief surgeon. The captain insisted that she had been with the English for less than six months, 'so that the Child

[170] Ibid., p. 6.
[171] Ibid.
[172] Ibid., p. 179.
[173] Ibid., p. 243.
[174] Ibid.
[175] Ibid., p. 253.
[176] Ibid., p. 256.
[177] Ibid.

could not belong to ... our Company. But to prevent the other she-Negro (call'd Daphne) from being debauch'd in our Ship, [Rogers] gave her a strict Charge to be modest, with Threats of severe Punishment, if she was found otherwise.'[178] One of her companions was whipped at the capstan for having 'transgressed this Way'.[179]

It is difficult to gauge the degree to which Rogers' narrative was influenced by self-censorship or embroidered and sanitized for publication. His report of the modest behaviour of the privateering company was designed to demonstrate a well-organized and legitimate voyage, but it was also part of the growing cultural demonization of the buccaneers and pirates, whose cruelty towards women was either implied or openly acknowledged. Edward Cooke, the second captain on the expedition, drew on stories of Morgan's activities to illuminate the contrast. In the hands of such predators, described as a hellish company of monsters, 'women found no Mercy, unless they submitted to their Lust'.[180] Yet these privateering authors ultimately seemed to be indifferent to the fate of the women they encountered, plundered or took captive. In Rogers' creative and titillating account, where thinly clad colonial women were closely searched by seafarers and captive African women were exposed to sexual abuse or rape, female indignity, pain and distress were silently suppressed.

The violence inflicted on women by pirates was noted by Johnson in his sprawling *History*, with its extravagant and entertaining portrait of an antisociety of hellhounds and devils. But his description of the sexual exploitation of women by Teach cannot be corroborated by other evidence, while his account of Avery clearly drew upon previous fictionalized accounts. His gallery of villains included others, whose casual brutality towards women was recorded with little or no explanation or moral condemnation. Captain Edward England and company 'liv'd ... very wantonly for several Weeks' at Whydah in West Africa, 'making free with Negroe Women, and committing such outrageous Acts, that they came to an open Rupture with the Natives'.[181] Repeating a report from *Mist's Weekly Journal* of January 1722, Johnson noted that the company of Thomas Anstis raped a female passenger taken in a ship off Martinique: 'twenty one of them forced the poor Creature successively, afterwards broke her Back and flung her into the

---

[178] Ibid., p. 279.

[179] Ibid.

[180] E. Cooke, *A Voyage to the South Seas, and Round the World*, 2 vols (London, 1712), I, p. 438. It has been argued that pirates usually treated women prisoners fairly well; Rankin, *Golden Age of Piracy*, pp. 35, 82 (for reference to pirates ravishing women on Providence).

[181] Johnson, *General History of the Pyrates*, p. 117

Sea'.[182] Another captain, Thomas Howard, retired ashore along the Malabar coast of India, marrying a 'Woman of the Country … [but] being a morose ill natur'd Fellow, and using her ill, he was murder'd by her Relations'.[183]

Although the main victims of pirate aggression continued to be men and boys, this catalogue of abuse demonstrates the growing victimization of women during the later seventeenth and early eighteenth centuries. It is impossible to estimate the scale or extent of the violence, though the capacity for cruelty appears to have varied in accordance with differences in the organization and structure of shipboard companies, as well as with the ethnicity of potential victims. Sea raiders, pirates and privateers formed companies of violent men who were increasingly habituated to a crude, transient and alienated lifestyle which inhibited close relationships with women. They included disordered individuals, maybe small in number, who were prepared to abuse women at any opportunity. George Shelvocke, commander of a privateering expedition sent out in 1719, subsequently complained bitterly of the conduct of some of his fellow officers, including captain Hatley who provoked concern among the company when he shot an albatross. At St Catherine's Island, off Brazil, Shelvocke heard 'daily complaints of his abusing women in the grossest manner; and further, that he, and a gang that used to go about with him to buy fresh provisions, had threatened to ravish old and young, and set their houses on fire'.[184]

There was one final danger to women, particularly facing the wives or partners of men who retired from a career of plunder at sea. While the psychological consequences of a life of piracy are irrecoverable, difficult problems faced alienated, violent and possibly traumatized men as they struggled to cope with life ashore. Johnson's brief report of the pirate captain who abused his wife, after settling ashore in India, indicates the inability of some men to break with their violent pasts. The risks for men and women in such circumstances may be illustrated by a case concerning Robert Hallam, who was accused of the murder of his pregnant wife at the Old Bailey in 1732. Hallam was a mariner, promoted to the position of mate, who evidently earned respect for his behaviour and conduct as an 'expert, knowing Sailor'.[185] He retired from seafaring life following his marriage in 1720 or 1721. He had sufficient resources to set himself up as a waterman on the river Thames, and to acquire an alehouse, which his

---

[182] Ibid., p. 289; *The Weekly Journal*, 13 January 1722, reprinted in Baer (ed.), *British Piracy*, I, p. 357; Snow, *Pirates and Buccaneers*, p. 123.

[183] Johnson, *General History of the Pyrates*, p. 494.

[184] Shelvocke, *A Voyage Round the World*, p. 23.

[185] www.oldbaileyonline.org (accessed 21 May 2009), OA 17320214.

wife, Jane, managed. In his defence Hallam claimed that she was a debauched drunk, who threw herself out of a window. However the court heard that she was held in good repute by the neighbourhood, while according to local talk he was chasing strange women.

During the course of Hallam's testimony it emerged that he had served aboard pirate ships, allegedly as a forced recruit. He recalled in some detail the first occasion of his recruitment into the company of captain Hinds. During a threatening encounter, Hinds

> called for a Quarto Bible, and laid it on a Table; then the Captain went down to the Cabbin, and brought up a drawn Sword and a cock'd Pistol; the Pistol he gave to a Black, and said to him, Whoever of these Men doth not what I command him, shoot him thro' the Head, which if you don't do, I'll stab you dead thro' the Body.[186]

Hallam and his companions all swore an oath of loyalty, holding their right hands over a corner of the Bible. Eleven days later, he and a fellow recruit escaped ashore at Martinique, where officials were prepared to hang them as pirates. They were saved by the evidence of their former captain. But Hallam was subsequently taken on three separate occasions by pirates, and forced to serve with them, until he had the good fortune to escape. His luck ran out in February 1732, when the court found him guilty of the murder of his wife and child.

In addition to the female victims of pirate violence, there were a number of women who were abducted by the Barbary corsairs, and held in captivity for prolonged periods. Their experiences in the hybrid borderland society that existed in Algiers and other North African ports were of a rather different order compared to those of the colonial or native women already discussed. Although the number was small compared with male captives, it was still significant, especially during the first half of the seventeenth century when exposed ports and harbours in south-west England and Ireland were subject to corsair raids. During raids in 1625 and 1640 about sixty men, women and children were carried off as captives from Mount's Bay in Cornwall. Across the Irish Sea many of the inhabitants of Baltimore, more than 100 in total, including eighty-nine women and children, were abducted during a raid of 1631. Female passengers aboard ships were also vulnerable to capture by the corsairs. In 1636 a group of fifty men and boys, and seven women, bound for Virginia, were taken and later sold as slaves in Salé. The following year captain William Rainsborough

---

[186] Ibid. For violence against women by demobilized sailors see M. Lincoln, *Naval Wives and Mistresses, 1750–1815* (London, 2007), pp. 136–7.

redeemed about 300 English captives held at Salé, which included twelve women.[187]

There is some evidence to indicate that the corsairs may have deliberately seized women, primarily for their economic value. John Dunton, a captive at Salé, claimed that his master, who had an interest in a corsair vessel, 'comaunded him to goe Pilott in her to come to the English Channell for the taking of English woemen being of more worth then other'.[188] European women seem to have commanded higher prices in the slave markets of Barbary, while the charge for their redemption was also greater. In 1646 Edmond Cason, who was dispatched by parliament to redeem English captives in Algiers, reported that 'they come to much more ... then I expected, the reason is, here be many women and children which cost 50l. *Per* head'.[189] By contrast, skilled seafarers were valued at £32. Cason redeemed 244 captives, including twenty-one women. At least one-third were originally from London; another third came from Youghal and Baltimore in Ireland; the remainder were from scattered backgrounds ranging from Edinburgh and Dundee to Plymouth and Falmouth. Two of the women, including Bridget Randall of London who was taken with her husband, John, were accompanied by children. According to Cason's report, the cost of redeeming the women, based on prices set by their owners, was usually significantly greater than that for men.[190]

Little evidence survives of the conditions under which English women were held captive in Barbary. Reports of horrific and slavish treatment, including the use of torture and forcible conversion, were part of a wider cultural perspective that was ideological in content and purpose. Unfortunately redeemed captives, such as Alice Wheeler who was taken with her family bound for New England, left no record of the ordeal they underwent. Their capture, which in Wheeler's case led to the loss of her husband and children, was shocking enough. While conditions in Barbary varied, the experience of captivity was difficult, disturbing and destabilizing. It involved such prolonged periods that captives were forced to face up to the

---

[187] TNA, SP 71/1/157; SP 71/13/29–31; Garcés, *Cervantes*, pp. 17, 148–52, discusses the 'borderline situations' of captives.

[188] TNA, SP 16/332/30, I.

[189] *A Relation of the Whole Proceedings Concerning the Redemption of the Captives in Argier and Tunis* (London, 1647), p. 12. Christian women were highly prized because of their household skills according to de Sosa; Garcés (ed.), *An Early Modern Dialogue*, p. 203.

[190] *A Relation*, pp. 17–24, for a list of the redeemed captives; Jamieson, *Lords of the Sea*, p. 102; Matar, *Britain and Barbary*, pp. 71–2; Playfair, *Scourge of Christendom*, pp. 63–71.

prospect of never returning home. The group of women redeemed by Cason in 1646 included Joan Bradbrook and Ellen Hawkins of Baltimore who had lived in captivity for nearly fifteen years. Yet it is possible that cultural and religious attitudes shielded women from the worst abuse. Many were probably employed as domestic servants, though others may have been absorbed into local economies of concubinage. Unusually during the 1670s and 1680s captivity provided an opportunity for two resourceful English women to enhance their status as the wives of local rulers in North Africa; for others, the silence of the evidence suggests lives of abandonment and sorrow.[191] Despite the indignity and humiliation, as well as the traumatic experiences of captivity and separation, it may well be that in some cases women suffered less at the hands of their Barbary captors than at those of the buccaneers and their successors.

*

The evidence assembled in this chapter underlines the permeable boundary between agency and victimhood, as it affected a growing number of women who were either the direct or indirect victims of maritime predators. The consequences for women varied over time and place. Violent behaviour by pirates grew more intense after the 1650s and, in the case of the English, was effectively exported to more distant regions such as the Caribbean. The emergence of long-distance piracy, accompanied by changes to its structure and character, appeared to lessen the restraint on the behaviour of sea rovers. Under certain conditions they were capable of the most shocking brutality. At the same time, and running throughout the period, though with declining force, the Barbary corsairs captured thousands of men, and a smaller number of women, from the British Isles. The results for many women were catastrophic; robbed of close relations, spouses or sons, many were reduced to poverty, though the agency and activism of a proportion were reflected in a campaign of petitioning that helped to keep alive the captive problem. But piracy operated within a wider, slow-moving social and cultural context which shaped responses to female victimization. As such, some women, the wives and mothers of captives for example, were identified as 'good' victims, who were worthy of

---

[191] Matar, *Britain and Barbary*, pp. 100–10; *Several Voyages to Barbary* (2nd edition, London, 1736), pp. 14–36, for an account of M. de Bourk, daughter of Count de Bourk, who was taken by Algerian corsairs before she was aged ten, and her ill-treatment and bondage. S. Dearden, *A Nest of Corsairs: The Fighting Karamanlis of Tripoli* (London, 1976), p. 21 (for concubinage). Earle, *Corsairs of Malta*, pp. 64–5, 78–9, argues for the well-treatment of women by the corsairs; Garcés, *Cervantes*, pp. 42–5, 141–5, and Clissold, *Barbary Slaves*, p. 4, liken the experience to the twentieth-century concentration camp.

sympathy and support. By contrast the experiences of others, who were violently or sexually abused by pirates, were uneasily, but quietly, ignored or presented in such a manner as to raise doubts about their status as real victims.

~ 5 ~

The Women Pirates
Fact or Fiction?

During the sixteenth and seventeenth centuries women played a varied and vital role ashore in maintaining piracy, yet very few were directly involved in roving at sea. Indeed the idea of women pirates seems unsettling, if not outlandish, challenging male expectations and fears regarding gender stereotypes. At least one modern study emphatically declares that, with the possible exception of the Chinese, 'no woman is known to have committed piracy at sea'.[1] Captain Johnson, whose rogues' gallery of sea rovers included Anne Bonny and Mary Read, two of the most notorious female pirates, disarmingly admitted that their lives were like a novel or romance. But he insisted that the 'odd Incidents of their rambling Lives ... [were] supported by many thousand Witnesses ... who were present at their Tryals, and heard the Story of their Lives, upon the first Discovery of their Sex'.[2] While defending the veracity of his account, Johnson laboured to include Bonny and Read within the ranks of Anglo-American pirate communities of the early eighteenth century. The 'Truth of it can be no more contested', he proclaimed, 'than that there were such Men in the World, as *Roberts* and *Black-beard*'.[3]

---

[1] J. Rogoziński, *Honour Among Thieves: Captain Kidd, Henry Every and the Story of Pirate Island* (London, 2000), p. 276 n41. But see J. Stanley (ed.), *Bold in Her Breeches: Women Pirates Across the Ages* (London, 1995). By contrast a fictional female hero, Fanny Campbell, has been misidentified as a real person; see K. Anderson, 'Female Pirates and Nationalism in Nineteenth-Century American Popular Fiction', in G. Moore (ed.), *Pirates and Mutineers of the Nineteenth Century: Swashbucklers and Swindlers* (Farnham, 2011), pp. 97–8. For the role of Chinese women aboard pirate ships see the account by a female captive, F. Loviot, *A Lady's Captivity*, introduction by M. Lincoln (London, 2008), p. 84.
[2] Johnson, *General History of the Pyrates*, p. 153. Women aboard ship, including prisoners, could be a source of discord; H. F. Rankin, *The Golden Age of Piracy* (Williamsburg, 1969), pp. 30–1, 36.
[3] Johnson, *General History of the Pyrates*, p. 153. Among the legends regarding Teach is one of a woman who guarded his treasure on the Isle of Shoals, where she died

Johnson's ambivalent history, and the tension between fact and fiction which it betrayed, was highlighted by his claim that Read abhorred piracy, turning to it only by compulsion. In doing so, both she and Bonny became more bold and resolute than their male companions, though they retained some degree of feminine modesty. His treatment of the lives of these two women, which included cross-dressing, love and rivalry at sea, their capture and subsequent trial on Jamaica, when they evaded execution on the grounds of being pregnant, was certainly entertaining. But it went beyond entertainment in its presentation of a strange, and inadvertently subversive, report of their exploits at sea with captain John Rackam and his company. Their pursuit of an independent life appeared to be a striking example of autonomy and agency that broke free from patriarchal constraint or control. At the same time Johnson laid the basis for the development of folk legend, elevating the pirate women to mythic status within popular culture and memory, while also serving as a salutary warning of the dangers of wayward women threatening male roles and masculinity. Its fascination continues to exert a powerful hold over modern interpretations and responses. The iconic realization of Bonny and Read as unlikely heroines was captured in a commemorative stamp issued by the post office on Jamaica in 1971, based on illustrations from the second edition of Johnson's *History*.[4]

There were other women who were involved in piracy and piratical venturing during this period. But they amounted to little more than a handful, unless there were others who successfully concealed their identities at sea. On balance this seems unlikely to have occurred on a significant scale. Female participation in piracy thus appears exiguous, episodic and eccentric, lacking coherence or structure. It varied in location and character, ranging from the coastal raiding and plunder undertaken by Grainne O'Malley in the west of Ireland to sporadic river piracy along the Thames, and including the activities of Read and Bonny in the Caribbean. It was undertaken, either willingly or otherwise, in association with men, although the actual role of women aboard pirate ships is difficult to recover. Nor is it easy to locate such apparently random and opportunistic enterprise within any tradition of female maritime venturing, though in literary terms as pirates they might be

awaiting his return; E. R. Snow, *Pirates and Buccaneers of the Atlantic Coast* (Boston, 1940), pp. 256–7.

[4] www.gleanerjm.com (accessed 26 May 2010); Johnson, *General History of the Pyrates*, pp. 153–65; U. Klausman, M. Meinzerin and G. Kuhn, *Women Pirates and the Politics of the Jolly Roger* (New York, 1997), pp. 191–210, argue that Rackam would never have become a pirate without Bonny. They also suggest that Bartholomew Roberts may have been a woman (p. 179). J. Dollimore, *Sexual Dissidence: Augustine to Wilde, Freud to Foucault* (Oxford, 1991), pp. 284–306, on male roles and masculinity.

confused with Amazonian warrior women, whose daring and courage played on male fears regarding power, authority and gender.[5]

The limited participation of women in piracy demonstrates its strikingly gendered nature as a crime. This remained a fundamental and unchanging characteristic, though it was inseparable from the wider context of maritime enterprise. In effect the custom of the sea, though by no means monolithic or impervious to change, restricted the opportunities for women as would-be seafarers, from among whom so many pirates were recruited.

Women at sea: custom and culture

Despite its modern association with romance and recreation, the sea was a dangerous place for all who sailed on it during this period. Real or imaginary dangers, including accident and injury, shipwreck and fire, disease and debilitation, as well as the horror of sea monsters, so vividly portrayed on maps and woodcuts, haunted the lives of seafarers. The risks were compounded with the threat posed by human predators, pirates, privateers and corsairs, who could turn the deck of any vessel into a bloody battle-ground. The problems increased dramatically on longer voyages, when scurvy or tropical disease, aided by poor diet and hygiene, spread like wild-fire among many ship's companies. Such conditions discouraged potential recruits. Many of those who served at sea were probably reluctant or unwilling members of a seafaring fraternity who were driven, rather than attracted, to an unusual work cycle with modest remuneration.

This environment held out little opportunity or appeal for women. They were out of place at sea, straying into a shifting frontier which was also a heavily gendered zone of labour, travel and trade, war and depredation. Neither an extension nor a mirror of the land, the seafaring world developed its own culture which denied or precluded a female presence, except under controlled conditions. Maritime folklore was also profoundly super-stitious regarding women aboard ship, seeing them as a potential source of malevolence or bad luck. An experienced and well-travelled seaman, Edward Barlow, blamed the loss of one of the king's ships, through fire at Chatham in 1669, on the temporary presence of the wife of the gunner.

---

[5] For images and the tradition see, for example, A. Fraser, *The Warrior Queens: Boadicea's Chariot* (London, 1988); S. Macdonald, P. Holden and S. Ardener (eds), *Images of Women in Peace and War: Cross-Cultural and Historical Perspectives* (London, 1987); G. Walker, *Crime, Gender and Social Order in Early Modern England* (Cambridge, 2003), pp. 86–95. During the 1650s Jacquotte Delahaye was the leader of a pirate gang in the Caribbean until she was killed in conflict with the Spanish; C. H. Parker, *Global Interactions in the Early Modern Age, 1400–1800* (Cambridge, 2010), p. 77.

During a cold winter's night the couple carelessly left a dish of burning coals, to provide them with some warmth, which set fire to the cabin and rapidly spread beyond. For Barlow the moral of the accident was self-evident. A good vessel was destroyed 'through the means of having women on board and to be pleased with what they want, they being such _____ evils, doing more harm than good wheresoever they come'.[6] Merely talking about women at sea could be risky. In 1684 a group of rovers, under the command of John Cook, noted that a great storm followed their conversation on 'the Intrigues of Women', on which they 'concluded [that] the discoursing of Women at Sea was very unlucky'.[7] The suspicion and superstition, though not amounting to a taboo as such, appear to have been widely shared among sailors, who sought to keep wives, partners and other women safely ashore.

There was no legal prohibition against women working at sea; nor in terms of physical or mental capability was seafaring beyond their capacity. Although women's position in the labour market ashore was weak, they engaged in varied forms of work including household and domestic service, the agricultural and textile trades, and a range of other crafts, some of which were physically demanding. But seafaring custom and culture, mutually reinforcing each other, prevented their employment aboard vessels. The prevailing assumption, demonstrated by surveys of the merchant marine for example, was that seafaring was a masculine activity undertaken by men with the assistance of boys. Thus the maintenance of the domestic economy of the ship, such as cooking and washing, work which would have been performed by women ashore, remained firmly in male hands. In these circumstances sailors acquired a strong self-identification with their work, sometimes in the face of hostile attitudes from landed society, which reinforced its gendered character.[8]

[6] B. Lubbock (ed.), *Barlow's Journal of His Life at Sea in King's Ships, East & West Indiamen & Other Merchantmen From 1659 to 1703*, 2 vols (London, 1934), I, p. 171. Women at sea were unusual or transgressive; see J. Mack, *The Sea: A Cultural History* (London, 2011), pp. 30, 161–2. For later practice see S. J. Stark, *Female Tars: Women Aboard Ship in the Age of Sail* (London, 1996); and M. S. Creighton and L. Norling (eds), *Iron Men, Wooden Women: Gender and Seafaring in the Atlantic World, 1700–1920* (Baltimore, 1996).
[7] 'Capt, Cowley's Voyage Round the Globe', in W. Hacke, *A Collection of Original Voyages* (London, 1699), pp. 6–7; O. H. K. Spate, *The Pacific Since Magellan, Volume II: Monopolists and Freebooters* (London, 1983), p. 145; B. Little, *The Buccaneer's Realm: Pirate Life on the Spanish Main, 1674–1688* (Washington, 2007), pp. 113–14.
[8] M. Rediker, *Villains of All Nations: Atlantic Pirates in the Golden Age* (London, 2004), pp. 110–11, argues that seafaring work for women was too strenuous and disturbing. For work more generally see A. Clark, *Working Life of Women in the Seventeenth Century*

Yet women had longstanding working associations with the sea and seafaring. These included shipping, the provisions and retailing trades, small, insecure businesses as fishwives and oyster-women, and part-time enterprises such as prostitution or receiving stolen plunder. As such they occupied a marginal or niche position. In some cases this was a physical reality, especially for women who worked the waterside, traversing the ill-defined space between land and sea, while operating under male regulation. In 1657, for example, the corporation of Plymouth ordered that no woman was to go trucking to vessels without permission. Presumably they were selling provisions and clothing to visiting sailors, though some may also have been engaged in prostitution. Those who ignored the order, including boatmen, faced a fine of five shillings, while the women were also 'to be set in the stool and haled up three times'.[9]

For women at sea the limitations on labour were accompanied by the constraints of culture. As a complex structure, the ship developed its own way of life and institutional infrastructure which created an insecure and impermanent environment. This was a social world with its own hierarchy and code of conduct based on gendered assumptions, underpinned by male comradeship and the exclusion of women. Although the community of the sea may often have been an ideal, disrupted by conflict and mutiny, the character and challenges of seafaring life promoted a feeling of brotherhood, which in some circumstances was strengthened by friendships and homosocial bonding. Community and culture were cultivated by shared labouring conditions in an unusual space that functioned as a place for work, habitation and recreation.

Although mariners were recruited from a wider pool that included landsmen, extended service at sea influenced behaviour and appearance. On land seamen were identified by their dress and personal possessions, a distinctive rolling gait and a pattern of speech that was inflected with the language of the sea. As a character, the mariner was known for his hardiness, unruly and sometimes violent behaviour, as well as his drinking and blasphemy. As Barlow complained, the sailor was often dismissed by

(London, 1919); and M. K. McIntosh, *Working Women in English Society, 1300–1620* (Cambridge, 2005). For the impact on women see P. Sharpe, 'Gender at Sea: Women and the East India Company in Seventeenth-Century London', in P. Lane, N. Raven and K. D. M. Snell (eds), *Women, Work and Wages in England, 1600–1850* (Woodbridge, 2004), pp. 53–9.
[9] R. N. Worth (ed.), *Calendar of Plymouth Municipal Records* (Plymouth, 1893), p. 64; A. Fraser, *The Weaker Vessel: Woman's Lot in Seventeenth-Century England* (London, 1984), p. 119; Clark, *Working Life*, pp. 36, 219–21.

landsmen as an 'old dog' or 'old rogue'.[10] In responding to hardship and hostility, seafarers celebrated their own culture in maxims such as 'A merry life and a short [one]', a theme echoed by pirates and other rovers.[11]

The way of life of seafarers shaped their wider relations ashore. While many were married with families, in general their relations with women were more fragile and vulnerable than those among the landed poor. Drawing on his own experience, Barlow noted that seamen's wives needed to be 'agreeable and industrious'; he might have added long-suffering and independent.[12] The life cycle of many mariners was usually inimical to the maintenance of close, loving relationships with spouses or partners, leaving many women to run households while taking on additional work to cover the absence of men. To some extent, for men, the emotional deficit was compensated by the care and camaraderie that prevailed among shipboard companies, though at the same time seamen were subject to cruel, some-times barbaric, punishment, which appears to have grown worse during the later seventeenth and early eighteenth centuries, as masters and officers tried to assert their authority and enforce discipline on longer and more hazardous voyages. Under these conditions, work and culture effectively defined the ship as a gendered site, characterized by masculine ideology and sustained by male associations. In effect men at sea formed a working community which was unable to include women within its ranks because of the disruptive threat they posed to the organization, as well as the coop-eration and mutuality, of shipboard society. Nor is there much evidence that women wished to challenge this closed structure, despite their commemoration or idealization in ships' names and figures.[13]

Of course women went to sea and in growing numbers during the seven-teenth century, but it was usually for the specific purpose of travel or migra-tion, and under supervision. They were rarely unaccompanied. Indentured servants and slaves, a special category, were usually transported in groups.

[10] Lubbock (ed.), *Barlow's Journal*, I, p. 160.

[11] Ibid., pp. 160–2.

[12] Ibid., II, p. 310.

[13] The ideology can be detected in phrases such as the 'manly resolution of seafaring men' in *The Lives, Apprehensions Arraignments, and Executions, of the 19 Late Pyrates* (London, [1609]), reprinted in Baer (ed.), *British Piracy*, II, p. 22. On authority and discipline see M. Rediker, *Between the Devil and the Deep Blue Sea: Merchant Seamen, Pirates, and the Anglo-American Maritime World, 1700–1750* (Cambridge, 1987), pp. 205–53. The ship was often seen as female; Mack, *The Sea*, pp. 137–8, 163. For images of the ship as woman see the examples in H. L. Smith and S. Cardinale (compilers), *Women and the Literature of the Seventeenth Century* (New York, 1990), pp. 188, 296. On shipboard relations see also L. Wallace, *Sexual Encounters: Pacific Texts, Modern Sexu-alities* (Ithaca, 2003), pp. 48–9.

The experiences of some women at sea, notably those of rank and status, could be adventurous, out of the ordinary, though sometimes dangerous. Travelling to Spain with her husband during the 1650s, Ann Fanshawe risked capture by a Turkish corsair during the voyage. Spurning the safety of her cabin, and against the advice of her spouse, she crept onto the deck, disguised in the clothing of one of the ship's boys, in order to witness negotiations between the rival captains. Admitting her lack of discretion, Fanshawe subsequently explained it as 'the effect of that passion ... [she] could never master'.[14]

A small number of women accompanied pirate captains at sea, but the practice was unusual. Its disruptive consequences were illustrated by the reaction of the company of captain Jennings to his behaviour, as reported in the published report of his trial in 1609. At Baltimore the pirate persuaded an Irish woman to accompany him aboard ship. The subsequent loss of ten or eleven members of the company during a violent encounter with a Spanish ship, in the wake of a narrow escape from a naval vessel, provoked an outburst of discontent and mutinous anger among the survivors. With the ship 'so out of order, it was a just judgement of God against them, in suffering their Captaine to bring his whore aboard ... to wallow in his luxurie'.[15] Jennings' associate at sea, captain Roope, stoked the mutiny, warning that 'successe in their condition was never found, when a woman was more Master of the Captaine, then the Captaine of his men, that in all the purchase (though unlikely yet) they should ever take, through the inticing flatteries, with which he seemed to be besotted and bewitched, the maine profit thereof should redownd to her'.[16] Thus inflamed, the mutineers broke into Jennings' cabin, where he was embracing his mistress, and reproved him for such loose conduct. After a violent affray, he was replaced as captain by Roope. Jennings was imprisoned in the gun room, but no further reference was made to the presence of the woman. The trial record was designed as a morality tale which culminated in the pirate's acknowl-

---

[14] Fraser, *Weaker Vessel*, p. 69. A small number of women went to sea as wives, mistresses or prostitutes; C. T. Fury, *Tides in the Affairs of Men: The Social History of Elizabethan Seamen, 1580–1603* (Westport, 2002), pp. 212–13; and on naval wives at sea, see M. Lincoln, *Naval Wives and Mistresses, 1750–1815* (London, 2007), pp. 37–8; N. A. M. Rodger, *The Wooden World: An Anatomy of the Georgian Navy* (London, 1986), pp. 76–9, 92.

[15] *The Lives, Apprehensions ... of the 19 Late Pyrates*, in Baer (ed.), *British Piracy*, II, p. 27.

[16] Ibid., pp. 1–3, 27. Roope survived to become an associate of Peter Easton; R. Dudley Edwards, 'Letter-Book of Sir Arthur Chichester 1612–1614, in the Library of Trinity College, Dublin', *Analecta Hibernica*, 8 (1938), p. 63.

edgement of guilt and his execution. But it exposed the disorderly and divisive impact of women aboard ship, reportedly perceived by a pirate company whose misogyny was barely concealed by the drama of the voyage.

For most women, especially those who were poor and dependent, the experience of the sea was more likely to be an ordeal. Living in cramped, unhygienic spaces, lacking privacy and suffering sickness, such women could face routine bullying and intimidation. They were, moreover, acutely vulnerable to physical and sexual abuse. During 1675 the High Court of Admiralty heard a harrowing case concerning the death of a maid servant, Anne Foster, at sea. After a prolonged period of taunting, apparently the result of her dishevelled appearance, a group of sailors stripped and scrubbed her in a barrel of water. She was washed with mops and beaten with a rope; according to one witness, her stomach and thighs were badly bruised. She died several days later. Conditions for slave women were worse. Subject to pornographic inspection by white sailors, some young women and girls were repeatedly molested and raped. The dangers increased with longer voyages. After prolonged discussion the East India Company allowed young women to travel east to provide spouses for its factors and agents. A 'Modish Garb and Mien is all that is expected from any Women that pass thither', one observer noted, but the voyage was difficult for women, 'considering the Hazard, as well as length of the Voyage, with some other Casualties that sometimes happen on Board'.[17]

Fear of women's power and reputed capacity for evil also had potentially dangerous consequences. On land witches were known to be able to raise storms and sink ships. At sea bad weather or unusual conditions could provoke accusations of witchcraft. The experience of the visionary and radical prophet Anna Trapnel demonstrates the hazardous presence of women at sea. After a disruptive visit to Cornwall in 1654, during which she was accused of being a witch, she was arrested and transported aboard ship to Portsmouth, to appear before the Council of State in London. At Dartmouth she was cursed following claims that she 'bewitched the winds, [so] that the ships could not go to sea'.[18] During the voyage she was forced to share a small cabin with a maid 'which lodge was very little, it being in the Masters Cabbin'.[19] Although she avoided the terrible seasickness that

---

[17] TNA, HCA 1/101, f. 144 (for Foster); HCA 24/129/14 (for the rape of the slave girl). On the East Indies see J. Ovington, *A Voyage to Surat in the Year 1689*, ed. H. G. Rawlinson (Oxford, 1929), pp. 88–9; Sharpe, 'Gender at Sea', pp. 64–5.

[18] A. Trapnel, *Report and Plea. Or, a Narrative of Her Journey From London into Cornwall* (London, 1654), pp. 21, 35; P. Mack, *Visionary Women: Ecstatic Prophecy in Seventeenth-Century England* (Berkeley, 1992), pp. 79–80, 94–8, 101–2.

[19] Trapnel, *Report and Plea*, p. 35.

afflicted her companion, Trapnel hurt her leg against the side of the vessel, leading her to question the motives and cruelty of men who 'never considered whether my nature could bear the Sea'.[20] At least she survived her ordeal. In the same year an elderly woman, Mary Lee, was accused of provoking storms at sea aboard a ship bound for Maryland. After days of tempestuous weather she was hanged by the ship's company as a witch and her body was cast overboard.[21]

Collectively these conditions explain why seafaring in general, as well as piracy, remained heavily gendered activities. Women pirates were highly unusual. It is therefore difficult to establish any kind of tradition of female enterprise from such discontinuous activity. The aberrant behaviour of women pirates, at times deliberately transgressive, was unprecedented. But it remained erratic in character, and linked with male piratical enterprise, while being scattered across diverse locations.

Coastal raiding and river piracy

Coastal piracy was a longstanding problem around the British Isles, though it assumed various forms ranging from opportunistic, haphazard robbery to entrepreneurial, planned plunder. The upsurge in such activity during the period from the 1560s to the 1580s was linked with the growth of longer-distance venturing. It was accompanied by the expansion of piracy and robbery along the river Thames, a crowded, lightly regulated, commercial highway that attracted organized criminal gangs. Localized enterprise of this nature depended on widespread support and connivance ashore. Acting independently or in association with others, women played an important, but often neglected role as maintainers and receivers, while providing a variety of services for visiting rovers. There was also scope for more direct participation, either coastal or offshore, as demonstrated by the activities of a number of women during the later sixteenth and early seventeenth centuries. Their exceptional experiences provide an unusual perspective on the expansion of small-scale organized piracy, as well as indicating its inherent diversity within changing contexts and environments.

Grainne O'Malley, the most prominent representative of these women, has acquired legendary status in Ireland. Described by an English official in 1577 as a 'most famous femynyne sea captain', her adventures at sea were

[20] Ibid., p. 36.
[21] A. Games, *Witchcraft in Early North America* (New York, 2010), pp. 43–4. Two other women appear to have suffered a similar fate in 1658 and 1659.

celebrated and elaborated in subsequent folklore.[22] At the same time she has been assimilated into a tradition of warrior women, a 'veritable Diana of the Atlantic', who at various times has served as a figurehead for Irish nationalism.[23] As Ireland's pirate queen, more recently she has been portrayed among a pantheon of 'wild Irish women', whose unconventional lives cut across social, political and religious structures.[24] The reality may have been less dramatic, but no less arresting, as O'Malley carved out a role as a political and seafaring leader, within an environment characterized by violence and alarming change.

It was a combination of context and personal agency which launched O'Malley on her maritime career. Within Gaelic society in the far west of Ireland, she was a woman of high status and position. As the daughter of Owen Dubhdara O'Malley, chief of the O'Malleys who had extensive lands and maritime rights, including a fleet of galleys, based in Clew Bay, she had the resources to secure her position within local society. They enabled her to marry the lord of the O'Flahertys of Connemara; and on his death she married Richard an Iarainn Burke, a leading member of the Burkes of Connacht. A widow by 1583, she retained her prominence, petitioning Queen Elizabeth and her chief minister, Lord Burghley, during the 1590s in an attempt to claim her rights according to English law and custom.[25]

Inhabiting a remote, frontier region bounded by bog and marsh, and bordering the Atlantic, the O'Malleys had a tradition of coastal seafaring, including piratical enterprise, which ranged from the west of Ireland to the isles of north-west Scotland. Local rivalries, which cut across family alliances, were increasingly overlaid by the threatening incursions of outsiders, including Scots mercenaries and English settlers and officials. The arrival of the English, though small in number, was followed by occasional naval patrols along the coast which had far-reaching implications for the maintenance of O'Malley sea power. Within Clew Bay this was

[22] M. O'Dowd, 'Grainne O'Malley', *Oxford Dictionary of National Biography* (Oxford, 2004), online edition, www.oxforddnb.com (accessed 12 September 2012); J. C. Appleby, 'Women and Piracy in Ireland: From Grainne O'Malley to Anne Bonny', in M. MacCurtain and M. O'Dowd (eds), *Women in Early Modern Ireland* (Edinburgh, 1991), pp. 56–9, reprinted in C. R. Pennell (ed.), *Bandits at Sea: A Pirates Reader* (New York, 2001).
[23] B. Fuller and R. Leslie-Melville, *Pirate Harbours and Their Secrets* (London, 1935), p. 189; A. Chambers, *Granuaile: Ireland's Pirate Queen c.1530–1603* (4th edition, Dublin, 2003), pp. 164–78.
[24] M. Broderick, *Wild Irish Women: Extraordinary Lives from History* (Dublin, 2001), pp. 280–7.
[25] O'Dowd, 'O'Malley'; idem, *A History of Women in Ireland, 1500–1800* (Harlow, 2005), pp. 22, 27, 31, 99.

represented by a network of coastal fortifications and a fleet of galleys and boats. In an exposed, marginal maritime region, dotted with hundreds of small islands, their seafaring ventures flourished, despite English efforts to exert authority over the area.

Although the size of the O'Malley fleet was rarely recorded, it varied in number and size of vessels. Most were small or modest in size, sometimes described as 'baggage boats', which combined oars with sail.[26] According to English report, some were capable of carrying up to three hundred men; however, their ordnance was small and of limited use against well-armed vessels. Such craft were ideally suited for coastal raiding and plunder, but they were vulnerable when faced with the challenge of a Tudor warship. During the summer of 1601 captain Charles Plessington, who was patrolling the coast of west Ulster and Connacht in one of the queen's ships to intercept Spanish vessels, encountered two galleys reportedly owned by O'Malley. They were under the command of her illegitimate son, and manned with followers from the O'Flahertys. After a brief skirmish with the ship's boat, which was ended by the English use of their great shot, Plessington forced one of the galleys, powered by thirty oars, ashore. The presence of a naval vessel, which the captain claimed was a 'great terror along the coast', threatened the O'Malleys' customary way of life, based on the exploitation of scant resources on land and at sea.[27]

Against this background, O'Malley's maritime activities remain shrouded in obscurity and ambiguity. Little evidence survives of her seafaring ventures, and much of it is from an English perspective that ranged from the inquisitive or interested to the hostile and condemnatory. Revealingly she is rarely mentioned in Gaelic sources. While this probably reflects an inherent gender bias regarding powerful female leaders, it may also have demonstrated her limited political significance within Gaelic Ireland. At the same time, English descriptions of her, including Sir Henry Sidney's account of 1577, following a meeting with O'Malley and her second husband, portraying her as 'well more than Mrs Mate with him', suggest that her notoriety was used by officials to deliberately feminize and emasculate Gaelic society.[28] Other reports that she 'thinketh herself to be no small Lady' indicate a degree of mockery and misogyny among the English that drew on a long tradition of hostile reportage.[29]

The O'Malleys used their vessels for a variety of purposes, ranging from

---

[26] *CSPI, 1588–92*, p. 333.

[27] *CSPI, 1600–1*, pp. 436–7; *CSPI, 1599–1600*, p. 335.

[28] O'Dowd, 'O'Malley'; idem, *History of Women in Ireland*, p. 253; Chambers, *Granuaile*, p. 57.

[29] *CSPI, 1574–85*, p. 407.

offshore plunder and coastal raiding to the transport of Scots mercenaries. Family members, including O'Malley herself, were usually employed as commanders. At her meeting with Sidney in 1577, at Galway, she offered him the use of a force of three galleys and 200 men. Although intended as a gesture of goodwill, the offer was not taken up. When, two years later, the president of Connacht complained that the west coast was infested with English pirates, O'Malley was a prisoner in Dublin, possibly because of her support for native resistance to the newcomers. Following her release, she was actively involved with her second husband in trying to halt the growing influence of English administrators in the lordship of the Burkes.[30]

After the death of her second husband, O'Malley made Carraighowley Castle, located within a secluded part of Clew Bay, her headquarters in a determined effort to 'maintain herself and her people by sea and land'.[31] At sea this meant the persistence of small-scale coastal and sea raiding, including the plunder of fishing vessels, often fuelled by resentment against the traders of Galway or rivalries with Gaelic clans in the west and north. In 1590 she raided the Isle of Aran with two or three vessels 'full of knaves'.[32] Recently granted to Sir Thomas le Strange, the island was claimed by the O'Flahertys. Among the victims were several of le Strange's men, spoiled of possessions worth about twenty marks. During the 1590s these raids ranged north as far as Lough Swilly and Sheep Haven in Ulster.

From an English perspective this predatory seafaring soon became dangerously entangled with rebellion. In 1593 Sir Richard Bingham, the president of Connacht, described O'Malley as a 'notable traiteress and nurse to all rebellions in the province' for the past forty years.[33] The accusation was overdrawn and coloured by Bingham's animosity to the Burkes, O'Flahertys and O'Malleys in general. Their hostility to the spread of English rule and administration, manifest in the Composition of Connacht implemented in 1585, was inflamed by Bingham's intemperate methods. English concern at the influence of the Scots, and alarm at the potential support by the Spanish for rebels in the west and north, aggravated an already volatile situation during the 1580s and 1590s. In order to deal with the maritime threat, Bingham had at least one galley constructed by an English shipbuilder, which he used in an attempt to clear the islands in Clew Bay. According to a report of 1599, the O'Malleys, who were

[30] O'Dowd, 'O'Malley'; Chambers, *Granuaile*, pp. 75–82; *CSPI, 1574–85*, p. 157; *CSPI, 1586–88*, p. 141.

[31] O'Dowd, 'O'Malley'.

[32] *CSPI, 1588–92*, pp. 226, 333. And for raids north see *CSPI, 1592–96*, p. 259; *CSPI, 1600–1*, pp. 436–7.

[33] *CSPI, 1592–96*, p. 141.

'much feared everywhere by sea', killed the shipbuilder and seized his vessel.[34]

Under these conditions O'Malley skirted a fine line between loyalty and disobedience. Accusations by Bingham of her support for rebel activity during the later 1580s were followed by her visits to London in 1593 and 1595, during which she skilfully exploited her status and gender to appeal to the monarchy for the release of family members under arrest, while claiming her own rights as a widow in Gaelic society. While O'Malley galleys seem to have aided English interests in Mayo, elsewhere they supported rebel activity. Reports that rebels used vessels provided by the O'Malleys and O'Flahertys were accompanied by alarming news that five or six of their galleys were blockading the river Shannon, and transporting rebel forces and munitions from Ulster into Munster.[35] Such activity strikingly demonstrated the potential development of Gaelic sea power as an auxiliary naval force that could be used either in the service of, or against, the English.

Yet O'Malley hung back from direct participation in the large-scale rebellion which engulfed much of Ireland during the 1590s. Under cover of war and insurrection, the closing years of her career appear to have been marked by an upsurge in the customary pursuit of coastal raiding and plunder. In 1600 the mayor of Galway complained of the seizure of vessels bound thence by the O'Malleys and O'Flahertys, who were also accused of the murder of local men. According to reports of the following year, the O'Malleys and other rebels lived by the plunder of fishermen and other small vessels sailing along the coast. In June 1602 Sir Oliver Lambert informed the Lord Deputy that the Gaelic predators spared no one; they 'continually make prize of all they take'.[36] Adopting Bingham's tactics, Lambert was in the process of acquiring a galley to clear the coasts of the menace.

O'Malley's death during the early seventeenth century failed to end this endemic problem of localized depredation. But it was overshadowed by the spread of piracy from England, and gradually curtailed by an increase in naval patrolling. Although O'Malley was periodically labelled a pirate and rebel by hostile English sources, such labels fail to do justice to her remarkable ability to survive in a changing and increasingly unfavourable environment. For her, piratical enterprise combined custom and tradition with policy, as Gaelic groups in the west struggled to adapt to the challenges of

[34] *CSPI, 1588–92*, p. 223; *CSPI, 1599–1600*, p. 335.
[35] O'Dowd, *History of Women in Ireland*, pp. 27, 99; *CSPI, 1592–96*, pp. 152, 315; *CSPI, 1588–92*, p. 397; *CSPI, 1599–1600*, pp. 153, 480.
[36] *CSPI, 1599–1600*, pp. 258–9, 421, 428, 446–7.

English rule. Within this context her seafaring activities represented an unprecedented case study in female agency.

Across the Irish Sea, in England and Wales, there was nothing to compare with O'Malley's career. Women's direct participation in piracy was highly unusual. It was scarcely registered, occurring in ambiguous, sometimes confusing circumstances. The closest equivalent to Grainne O'Malley, at least in terms of status and position, was Lady Elizabeth Killigrew of Arwenack in Cornwall, a region with a strong piratical tradition. The Killigrews were a powerful, well-connected family. Its head often served as one of the vice admirals of the county, as well as holding the post of governor of Pendennis Castle, overlooking Falmouth harbour. They were also at the heart of a far-reaching pirate network in south-west England that ranged across the Irish Sea. Based at Arwenack, which had secluded access to the sea, the Killigrews maintained close relations with the pirate fraternity, serving as receivers and suppliers, as well as providing entertainment ashore. Acting as brokers, they used their influence to harbour and protect visiting pirates, while being employed as officials to combat the problem. In June 1580, for example, the Privy Council instructed Sir John Killigrew to investigate complaints that a company of pirates were allowed to escape at Falmouth, 'by the negligence of the Vice admirall … or his Deputie'.[37]

Financial problems and an extravagant lifestyle appear to have made the Killigrews more incautious. In 1582 several Spanish merchants complained to the council of the seizure and plunder of a vessel in Falmouth haven by a group of local men who included the servants of Sir John. It was a 'foul crime', during which members of the ship's company were thrown overboard during the night.[38] The vessel was taken to Ireland, where it was reported to lie ruined and rotten. Killigrew and other Commissioners for Piracy in Cornwall were instructed to examine the case. Sir John was subsequently ordered to attend the council, to answer allegations against him. Although he went to London, he 'secretlie lurked in some place … [and] could not be founde'.[39]

One of the Spanish merchants also seemed to implicate Lady Elizabeth in the robbery. Her role may have been exaggerated by the circulation of local stories and rumour. In 1595 her son, John, who was accused of being in league with pirates, denied accusations that he used his influence at court to halt 'the course of justice against his mother for a most infamous murder

---

[37] *APC, 1581–82*, p. 110; D. Mathew, 'The Cornish and Welsh Pirates in the Reign of Elizabeth', *English Historical Review*, 39 (1924), pp. 339–41, 346–8.

[38] *CSPD, 1581–90*, pp. 42, 53; *CSPF, 1582*, pp. 282–3.

[39] *APC, 1581–82*, pp. 356–7; A. L. Rowse, *Tudor Cornwall: Portrait of a Society* (London, 1941), pp. 392, 412–13.

and robbery at Falmouth'.[40] She was, he insisted, innocent of such charges. Nonetheless according to later accounts, Lady Elizabeth led the assault on the Spanish ship; moreover, she was reportedly put on trial, and sentenced to death, but pardoned. As in the case of some other women of rank, such as the wife of Sir Edward Denny of Tralee, Lady Elizabeth was involved in maintaining piracy, but the case against her as a female pirate was weak. It appeared to be based on hearsay and rumour, which was embroidered by later legend.[41]

Stronger evidence survives for allegations against several women of London of being involved in the robbery of shipping along the Thames, in association with men, during the 1630s. River piracy was a long-running problem which became an acute issue during the later sixteenth and early seventeenth centuries. Fuelled by the rapid growth of trade and shipping, and facilitated by poor regulation and policing, gangs of river pirates preyed upon vulnerable vessels as they lay moored, often with only one caretaker aboard. Such activity varied from opportunistic, almost random theft by individuals or small groups to organized, structured robbery by larger bands of robbers. It included the seizure of selected parcels of commodities, such as provisions and items of cloth or clothing, and other disposable and more valuable goods, including belts embroidered with silver and gold, as well as ready money.[42] It was loosely linked with the larger criminal fraternity or underworld in London, and it was rooted in the marginal and poor communities of the rapidly growing seafaring parishes of the East End, with access to the city and beyond. These communities protected and provided support for such pirates and robbers, in which women were actively engaged, especially as the receivers of stolen booty. In these circumstances it was possible for some women to play a more direct role in the robbery of ships on the river.

During June 1634 Elizabeth Patrickson, her husband, William, and Thomas Joyner were arrested and imprisoned in Newgate on suspicion of piracy. Patrickson and Joyner were sailors who lived in communities close to the river: the former was from Wapping, the latter came from Milton in Kent. Both men were indicted for robbing a wherry on the Thames, carrying off one gammon of bacon, twelve ducks and a piece of lace. A

---

[40] Mathew, 'Cornish and Welsh Pirates', p. 340.

[41] P. Pringle, *Jolly Roger: The Story of the Great Age of Piracy* (London, 1953), pp. 28, 31–2; N. Williams, *The Sea Dogs: Privateers, Plunder and Piracy in the Elizabethan Age* (London, 1975), pp. 158–9. On Denny see *CSPI, 1588–92*, p. 192; Mathew, 'Cornish and Welsh Pirates', p. 341.

[42] TNA, HCA 1/7, ff. 8, 13, 87, 101–2. J. McCullan, *The Canting Crew: London's Criminal Underworld* (New Brunswick, 1984), pp. 17–19, 117–20, 155–8.

separate bill, which included Patrickson's wife, concerned the theft of two pieces of Holland cloth, two handkerchiefs and two sacks, which were taken out of a hoy. When the prisoners appeared at the admiralty sessions they included John Whinnett, alias Winniard. Elizabeth Patrickson and others were also accused of receiving stolen goods. According to the charges, the men, operating either as a pair or a gang of three, boarded several vessels on the river which were rifled of various goods, including 14 shillings from one and £5 4s from another.[43]

The booty was disposed among a network of receivers, most of whom were women and possibly close associates or neighbours. Patrickson's wife allegedly received four pairs of sheets and other goods, such as two pillow-bears and one hand towel. Mary Percevall, a spinster of West Smithfield, was accused of receiving a gown. Jane Francis, a resident of West Smith-field, whose husband was a coachman, was also suspected of receiving goods from the ships. Francis Stoddard, whose husband Thomas was a vict-ualler of St Salvatore's parish in Southwark, reportedly acquired a pair of green curtains and other commodities. In addition, Joan Harris and her spouse Edmund, a porter, also of St Salvatore's, allegedly received a suit of cloth and other apparel.[44]

The pirates made an unconvincing defence before the judge of the High Court of Admiralty. Patrickson denied any involvement in the robbery, but admitted that he had known Joyner for three or four years. When questioned about his wife's part in receiving goods out of the vessels, he replied that he had given her a gown, one pair of sheets and a pair of gloves, to sell for him. But he claimed that the goods came from Robert Greene, of whom he provided no further information. Patrickson was unable to say if they were stolen out of the ships, as alleged. Joyner and Whinnett both confessed that their previous examinations, read to them but not formally recorded, were accurate. Joyner also provided the court with an explanation for his attempt to evade arrest by a constable. Thus 'hee ran away thinking that hee had bin arrested for thirty pounds that hee owed to one John Lambert of Milton, not suspecting that hee had bin apprehended upon any suspicion of piracy or felony'.[45] Debt and other bonds of obligation may have been important motives for the involvement of men and women in the increase of river piracy during the early seventeenth century.

[43] E. Berckman, *Victims of Piracy: The Admiralty Court 1575–1678* (London, 1979), pp. 49–50; G. Walker, *Crime, Gender and Social Order in Early Modern England* (Cambridge, 2003), pp. 170–6, for criminal associations between women and men.
[44] TNA, HCA 1/60, ff. 125–8; HCA 1/101, f. 61.
[45] TNA, HCA 1/50, ff. 1–1v, 6v–7. Patrickson was also accused of piracy off the Isle of Wight.

Elizabeth Patrickson's case was followed by several others. In September 1638 Jane Randall and Margaret Pope were both charged with suspicion of piracy, for stealing various cottons, wool, goat's hair and other goods, valued at £40, out of a lighter on the Thames. Later in the year Jane Beckensfield was likewise charged with stealing cloth 'to a great vallue' out of another vessel.[46] All three women denied the charges, but in circumstances that left open the possibility that at least two of them were involved as receivers. Beckensfield admitted receiving a piece of cloth, fitting the description of that stolen, from Jane Crowder, which was 'in lewe of a debt'.[47] Margaret Pope, moreover, appeared to implicate her associate, Randall. Claiming that she recently entered Randall's house, by chance she saw both husband and wife packing up a parcel of cottons. Thereafter 'they were Cast out of a boate into' Pope's yard, and 'afterwards taken away againe by the said Randall'.[48]

Little further evidence survives for the resolution of these cases, though the indictment of Patrickson and others was certified as a true bill. At the least, as suggested by other cases heard by the High Court of Admiralty, they affirmed the active role played by women in supporting the growth of piracy along the Thames. Indeed, proceeding against Patrickson and other women was an overt acknowledgement by the court that piracy was defined across a continuum of criminality, composed of discrete, but interlaced activities, ranging from robbery to receiving. Such cases were partly initiated as a response to a growing problem. They also occurred at a time when the personal monarchy of Charles I vaunted its naval prowess, while seeking to assert its sovereignty at sea. The inability of the regime to prevent piracy along the Thames, an open gateway to the city and Westminster, was thus an embarrassment which called for effective action against the women as well as the men who were involved in it.

The actions of groups of women, cooperating with men, in the seizure of cargoes of grain aboard ships provide an illuminating counterpoint to the activities of these female river pirates or receivers. Occurring during periods of dearth and high prices, such seizures were in an entirely different category, and handled accordingly, compared to the cases discussed in this chapter. The forcible acquisition of grain at sea had a different meaning, structure and performance from that of piracy, which seems to have been recognized even by its victims. It involved communities of the poor, or their representatives, in direct physical action, which was in the strictest sense

---

[46] TNA, HCA 1/101, f. 85.

[47] Ibid.

[48] Ibid., f. 88.

robbery or a form of plunder, but which was often described as tumultuous, riotous behaviour. These food riots were played out before an audience of local officials, who were forcefully reminded of their responsibilities towards the poor. Their structure and performative features, such as the way in which the crowd was organized and operated from the shore, served to distinguish grain seizures from piracy. Even when the latter included gangs of poor men and women operating along the Thames, in search of food and clothing, the distinction was not merely one of degree; it was rooted in means and motive, and shaped by context and cultural response, including a shared awareness of the law.[49]

The role of women in such action was illustrated by a case from Southampton during 1608. Struggling to cope with the consequences of local dearth, which raised the price of wheat to at least six shillings a bushel, the corporation impounded a vessel in the harbour which was bound for London with a lading of fifty quarters of grain. Local officials were concerned that the 'common poore people of this Towne this day beinge readdie to rise in tumultuous manner' would take action themselves.[50] Later that day a group of women, assisted by men, boarded the vessel in an attempt to carry off its cargo. Several days later four women and their husbands were bound over to appear at the next quarter sessions for their part in the tumult. Officials blamed the disturbance on a group of men. John Hudson, the town crier, was the 'principayll of those that animated the woemen in there disorderlye risinge about the corne'.[51] He was accused of carrying some of the women on his shoulders out to a boat, from which they boarded the vessel. Although Hudson was dismissed, losing his badge and staff, within two days 'uppon his submission and promise of amendment he was restored to his office againe'.[52] The number of women who participated in the action in Southampton is unknown, but a similar grain riot of 1629, during which a Flemish ship was boarded in the port of Maldon in Essex, involved more than 100 women and children.[53] The size of the crowd, one of the largest in which women were involved during this

---

[49] C. Tilly, *Contentious Performances* (Cambridge, 2008), pp. 62–71.

[50] J. W. Horrocks (ed.), *The Assembly Books of Southampton*, 4 vols (Southampton Record Society, 1917–25), I, pp. 61–2; D. Underdown, *Revel, Riot, and Rebellion: Popular Politics and Culture in England 1603–1660* (Oxford, 1987), pp. 116–19; J. Walter, 'Grain Riots and Popular Attitudes to the Law: Maldon and the Crisis of 1629', in J. Brewer and J. Styles (eds), *An Ungovernable People: The English and Their Law in the Seventeenth and Eighteenth Centuries* (London, 1980), pp. 47–84.

[51] Horrocks (ed.), *Assembly Books*, I, p. 63.

[52] Ibid.

[53] Walter, 'Grain Riots', pp. 48, 52–3, 62–5.

period, was in part a reflection of the severity of the local crisis which was exacerbated by the ineffective response of local officials towards the export of grain.

The development of a specific structure for grain seizures rested on wider assumptions regarding economic fairness and social responsibility. Consequently it enabled officials to demonstrate compassion and sympathy for the plight of the poor, particularly during hard times. While it provided opportunities for women to play a prominent part in local riots or risings, in association with men, their actions were not identified as piracy, even by victimized traders and shipowners. Indeed the leniency with which such seizures were generally handled by local agencies suggests a shared understanding of the law which lent some degree of legitimacy to participants which was lacking in cases of piratical plunder.[54]

Although female involvement in coastal and river piracy was wide-ranging, the evidence indicates that it remained highly unusual and deeply ambiguous. Revealingly there may have been more scope for women to take part in grain riots, such as those in Southampton or Maldon, and less risk of punishment, than in the robbery of ships offshore. Piracy on the Thames may provide a possible exception to this pattern. Its growth depended on an unusually close relationship between robbery and receiving, in which women were well placed to act. But their role in this specialized form of plunder, including the selection of stolen booty, was closely linked with their position in the labour market and household which tended to set them apart from male associates or partners.

Piracy and plunder in colonial America

The transatlantic migration of English piracy and sea-roving revived a flagging form of enterprise, but within a context that influenced its development and direction, including the opportunities for female agency. It was initially concentrated within the Caribbean, a volatile and violent region, where it was possible for Europeans to flout convention, behaving in a manner that shocked metropolitan society. The availability of secure bases and the prospect of rich booty encouraged its rapid growth across the region and beyond, along the eastern seaboard of North America. For the English, who led the way in the expansion of piracy, Caribbean plunder was characterized by a deep-seated confusion between buccaneering, privateering and piratical activity. Against a background of endemic local-

---

[54] Ibid., pp. 62–82; A. Wood, *Riot, Rebellion and Popular Politics in Early Modern England* (Basingstoke, 2002), pp. 19–20, 40–8, 95–100.

ized conflict overlaid by intermittent international war, adventurers combined legitimate plunder with piracy often with the connivance of local officials.[55]

Although seaborne depredation continued to be predominantly a male activity, marked by an aggressively masculine code of conduct and behaviour, within a rapidly developing transatlantic community of seafarers, a small, but growing number of women began to appear on pirate ships. Either through compulsion or consent, they were present as prisoners and captives, servants or slaves, and even occasionally as wives or mistresses. Captain Bear of Jamaica, for example, cruised the waters around Cuba and neighbouring islands during the 1680s accompanied by his wife.[56] It was in such unsettling, unusual, though short-lived conditions, that the piratical careers of Mary Read and Anne Bonny unfolded.

The renown or notoriety of these two women pirates rested on the work of captain Charles Johnson. His *History* of 1724 effectively rescued them from potential oblivion. It has shaped all subsequent accounts. While Johnson's identity still remains a matter of debate and speculation, his text imaginatively mixed fact with fiction. Apart from a printed report of the pirates' trial on Jamaica, however, his description of their lives cannot be corroborated by other evidence. As a result of his account of their behaviour at sea, Bonny and Read have acquired legendary status as the women pirates, whose lives have been repeatedly represented and recycled with little regard for the limitations of Johnson's work.[57]

In an entertaining discussion, which drew on the emerging genre of criminal biography, Johnson portrayed the careers of Read and Bonny as a 'History full of surprising Turns and Adventures'.[58] But his limited knowledge of their lives at sea led him to create elaborate stories of their

---

[55] See, for example, *CSPC, 1689–92*, pp. 664–5, 739–40; *CSPC, 1693–96*, pp. 345, 398, 503–6, 630–1.

[56] Two corsair captains in the Mediterranean were accused of holding slave girls in their cabins to the 'great scandal of the crew'; P. Earle, *Corsairs of Malta and Barbary* (London, 1970), p. 189.

[57] For recent discussion see Rediker, *Villains of All Nations*, pp. 103–26; D. Cordingly, *Life Among the Pirates: The Romance and Reality* (London, 1995), pp. 73–82; idem, *Heroines and Harlots: Women at Sea in the Great Age of Sail* (London, 2001), pp. 89–98; J. Peakman, *Lascivious Bodies: A Sexual History of the Eighteenth Century* (London, 2004), pp. 224–30; D. Starkey, 'Voluntaries and Sea Robbers: A Review of the Academic Literature on Privateering, Corsairing, Buccaneering and Piracy', *Mariner's Mirror*, 97 (2011), pp. 145–6.

[58] Johnson, *General History of the Pyrates*, pp. 6, 153. For scepticism regarding their early lives see M. Campbell, 'Pirate Chic: Tracing the Aesthetics of Literary Piracy', in Moore (ed.), *Pirates and Mutineers*, pp. 17–18.

Figure 5 Portraits of the women pirates Mary Read and Anne Bonny dressed in seafaring slops and heavily armed with a variety of hand weapons. The illustration, from Johnson's history, illuminates the functional use of mariner's dress during their brief presence aboard the pirate ship of captain John Rackam off Jamaica. (Female pirates Anne Bonny and Mary Read, illustration from C. Johnson, *General History of the Pyrates* (London, 1724), copyright National Maritime Museum, Greenwich, London, catalogue number D7496-B).

origins and background, with such striking parallels that they would be barely credible, if they were not, at least in part, made up. Johnson's purpose was to provide context, coherence and validity for a startling, unprecedented episode in the history of English piracy that many readers might dismiss as fiction. In the interests of veracity, and in accordance with the genre, Johnson's text was supported by illustrations. The first edition included one of both women dressed as sailors. On the left Mary Read wields a cutlass and an axe in either hand. Facing away, Anne Bonny holds an axe, though it is dangerously pointed towards her. Both women carry a pair of pistols attached to their jackets. Pictured on land, three vessels lie in the background as a reference point for their maritime exploits. By contrast a Dutch translation of 1725, published in Amsterdam, presented them in more sexualized and dramatic poses, almost as bare-breasted Amazonian warriors.[59]

Johnson claimed that he was 'more particular' with their lives than those

[59] Rediker, *Villains of All Nations*, pp. 106–8; Stanley (ed.), *Bold in Her Breeches*, p. 182; M. Ogborn, *Global Lives: Britain and the World* (Cambridge, 2008), pp. 188–92. K. Grovier, *The Gaol: The Story of Newgate – London's Most Notorious Prison* (London, 2008), pp. 186–9, on illustrations.

Figure 6 A powerful portrait of Anne Bonny from the Dutch translation of Johnson's history which provides an interesting contrast to Figure 3. The bare-breasted, almost sensuous pose, while drawing on various traditions, including that of Amazonian warrior women, was designed to appeal to a male audience while capitalizing on the growing demand for stories of notorious criminals. (Anne Bonny, female pirate, illustration from Johnson, *Historie der Engelsche Zee-Rovers* (Amsterdam, 1725), copyright National Maritime Museum, Greenwich, London, catalogue number 7750).

Figure 7 A portrait of Mary Read which complements that of Anne Bonny in the Dutch edition of Johnson's history. According to a later edition of the work, the women pirates were greater names than Blackbeard, Avery or Bartholomew Roberts. (Copyright The British Library Board, C. Johnson, *A General History of the Pyrates* (London, 1725)).

of other pirates, insisting that it was 'incumbent, on us, as a faithful Historian, to begin with their Birth'.[60] His detailed account of their childhood was meant to be informative, though it bordered on sensationalism. Its narrative strength also suggested that their early lives prepared them for their subsequent roles as cross-dressing pirates. From an early age Mary Read, an illegitimate child, was dressed as a boy to conceal her identity. Her mother already had a son with her seafaring husband. His failure to return from a voyage left her in difficult circumstances as a lone parent. On the death of her son, therefore, she resorted to the masquerade of passing her daughter off as him, in order to deceive her wealthy and supportive mother-in-law into providing a weekly allowance for the child. The disguise continued after the death of the mother-in-law. According to Johnson, Read grew bold and strong, developing a 'roving Mind'.[61] By implication she acquired masculine characteristics, enabling her to join the company of a man-of-war, presumably dressed in male attire. Thereafter she travelled to Flanders, serving as a soldier, and earning the regard of her officers.

At this stage she fell in love with a comrade. Overwhelmed, she began to neglect her duties: '*Mars* and *Venus*', it seemed, 'could not be served at the same Time'.[62] On revealing her true identity, her lover thought he had acquired a mistress. But Read remained reserved and modest, insisting on a proper courtship and marriage. Once the military campaign was over, the couple married and established an inn, the Three Horse-Shoes, near Breda. Benefiting from the celebrity that came with the marriage of two troopers, the business flourished until the untimely death of Read's husband. Assuming a male appearance, she entered military service in Holland, before sailing for the West Indies.

Outward bound the vessel was taken by English pirates. Read was detained, though Johnson failed to provide any details of her role aboard the pirate ship. Taking advantage of a recent proclamation, with the offer of a pardon, the company gave up piracy in favour of lawful employment. Determined to 'make her Fortune one way or other', Read travelled to Providence in the Bahamas, 'to go upon the privateering Account' with other former pirates.[63] Once at sea, the recruits, including Read, mutinied and returned to their old trade. While in male disguise, as a member of the

[60] Johnson, *General History of the Pyrates*, p. 159. For the diffuse borders between forms of writing and literature see J. P. Hunter, *Before Novels: The Cultural Contexts of Eighteenth Century English Fiction* (New York, 1990).
[61] Johnson, *General History of the Pyrates*, p. 154.
[62] Ibid.
[63] Ibid., p. 156.

company led by captain John Rackam, she met Anne Bonny who took a 'particular Liking to her ... as a handsome young Fellow'.[64]

In broad outline the childhood of Anne Bonny, or Bonn, also included a similar experience of disguise and cross-dressing. She was an illegitimate child of a servant whose life, Johnson claimed, seemed to '*cross an old Proverb ... that Bastards have the best luck*'.[65] The servant's relationship with Bonny's father, a lawyer who lived near Cork, was discovered by his wife, in a convoluted episode that played inventively on the theme of disguise and mistaken identity. Suspicious, the wife spent a night in the servant's bed, which her husband duly visited. As a result both wife and mistress became pregnant. The child of the servant, a girl, was dressed and brought up as a boy. Her father claimed that she was a relation, who he was bringing up to be his clerk. Following a dispute with his wife, who uncovered the truth of the child's identity, the lawyer lived openly with the servant as his partner. When his business faltered, as a result of the scandal, he migrated to Carolina. He was accompanied by his mistress, now presented as his wife, and their child. As a successful lawyer and trader, he acquired the resources to purchase a large plantation. On the death of her mother, Anne kept house for her father, earning a reputation for a fierce temper. Reports that she killed a maid servant were dismissed as groundless by Johnson, though 'she was so robust, that once, when a young Fellow would have lain with her, against her Will, she beat him so, that he lay ill of it a considerable Time'.[66]

Spurning the prospect of a good match, she married a young, penniless sailor, with whom she moved to Providence in search of employment after being disowned by her father. Pursuing a libertine lifestyle, she was discovered in a hammock with another man. Shortly after, Rackam who was one of her lovers, agreed to purchase her from Bonny in a wife sale. Although the governor intervened to stop the transaction, the pirate persuaded her to elope, in favour of a life at sea as his lover, dressed as a man. When she became pregnant, Rackam put her ashore at a secluded location on Cuba, described by Johnson as a secure love nest to which he and other members of his company regularly returned to see 'their Dalilahs'.[67] Bonny returned to the sea after the birth of the child. As in several other cases, the pirates

---

[64] Ibid.; Stanley (ed.), *Bold in Her Breeches*, pp. 154–7, 176–85.

[65] Johnson, *General History of the Pyrates*, p. 159. Bonny was also known as Ann Fulford; Cordingly, *Life Among the Pirates*, p. 75.

[66] Johnson, *General History of the Pyrates*, p. 164.

[67] Ibid., pp. 149, 623–4. On wife sales see R. O'Day, *Women's Agency in Early Modern Britain and the American Colonies: Patriarchy, Partnership and Patronage* (Harlow, 2007), pp. 196–7.

surrendered on the promise of a royal pardon. While serving on a priva-teering expedition, however, Rackam returned to his old trade accompanied by his female partner.

At this stage the lives of Bonny and Read crossed. By coincidence, it seemed, there were two women masquerading as men among Rackam's company. Although Bonny's identity appeared to be more common knowl-edge, Read remained in disguise. Nor was she 'suspected by any Person on board till *Anne Bonny*, who was not altogether so reserved in Point of Chastity, took a particular Liking to her'.[68] The prospect of a liaison at sea was cut short by Read's admission of her sex. Unaware of the revelation, and inflamed by jealousy, Rackam was only prevented from cutting her throat by Bonny's disclosure of the secret. Rackam was enjoined to keep the infor-mation from the rest of the company. But the truth came out when Read fell passionately in love with a young fellow who was possibly a forced recruit. After exposing herself to him, she confessed her story. Their rela-tionship was sealed, in Johnson's words, by 'one of the most generous Actions that ever Love inspired'.[69] Quarrelling with another member of the company, Read's partner agreed to go ashore to resolve the matter by fighting. Anxious and aware that her lover would be derided as a coward if he failed to proceed, she intervened. Challenging the pirate to a duel with sword and pistol, she killed him two hours before the planned fight. There-after the lovers 'plighted their Troth to each other', living as husband and wife aboard ship.[70]

Johnson provided little information on the piratical careers of Bonny and Read. According to his account of Rackam, the pirates haunted the coasts of Cuba and Jamaica. They seized several prizes, disrupting the fishing and coastal trades. But rich booty eluded them. As 'they had but few Men', Johnson reported that 'they were obliged to run at low Game, till they could increase their Company'.[71] With a complement of less than a dozen in total, the shortage of recruits may explain why the pirates were willing to tolerate the presence of women aboard ship. Yet Johnson insisted that they secured their positions by their bravery and resolute conduct. Indeed, no one 'was more forward or couragious' than Bonny.[72]

---

[68] Johnson, *General History of the Pyrates*, p. 156.
[69] Ibid., p. 157. On the significance of such revelations of identity (usually baring breasts), see Anderson, 'Female Pirates and Nationalism' in Moore (ed.), *Pirates and Mutineers*, pp. 108–9. Peakman, *Lascivious Bodies*, pp. 220–4, notes the tolerance of British society towards cross-dressing, so long as sex was not involved.
[70] Johnson, *A General History of the Pyrates*, p. 158.
[71] Ibid., p. 150.
[72] Ibid., p. 165.

The history of Rackam's pirate company was brief. In September 1720 the pirates were caught off Negril Point, along the north-west coast of Jamaica, by captain Barnet in a well-manned sloop sent out by the governor of the island. Although they tried to escape, Barnet's vessel caught up with them. They were taken 'after a very small Dispute'.[73] True to their assumed characters, Bonny and Read, with one other pirate, were the only members of the company to put up any resistance, remaining on deck, defying their attackers, while the others hid below. Read called on them 'to come up and fight like Men'.[74] When no one stirred, she fired into the hold, killing one of her companions and wounding others.

The pirates were put on trial before a court of admiralty held at St Jago de la Vega in November 1720. Sir Nicholas Lawes, governor and vice admiral of Jamaica, presided with the assistance of councillors, officials and two naval captains. The guilty verdicts were scarcely in doubt, despite apparent sympathy for the circumstances of the women. According to Johnson, the case against Bonny was aggravated by the desertion of her lawful husband. The evidence against Read included a damning hearsay report of a conversation with Rackam, which appeared to contradict her claim that she detested piracy. Defiantly dismissing any fear of execution, she reportedly asserted that true pirates would expect no other punishment. Otherwise she scornfully suggested that cowardly rogues, who cheated widows and orphans or oppressed their poor neighbours ashore, would turn to robbery at sea, and the 'Ocean would be crowded ... so that the trade, in a little Time, would not be worth following'.[75]

Rackam and four members of his company were executed the day after the trial, at Gallows Point in Port Royal. Their bodies were left in chains at various places along the coast as an example and warning to others. Before the execution, Bonny was allowed to see her former lover, 'but all the Comfort she gave him, was, *that she was sorry to see him there, but if he had fought like a Man, he need not have been hang'd like a Dog*'.[76] Following their trial, both Bonny and Read successfully appealed to the court for a stay of execution on the grounds that they were pregnant. According to Johnson, the court was prepared to review Read's case, but she died of gaol fever. Bonny gave birth in custody, after which she was reprieved, but no evidence survives for her subsequent life.[77]

[73] Ibid., p. 150.

[74] Ibid., p. 156.

[75] Ibid., p. 159; *The Tryals of Captain John Rackam, and Other Pirates* (Jamaica, 1721), reprinted in Baer (ed.), *British Piracy*, III, pp. 7–66.

[76] Johnson, *General History of the Pyrates*, p. 165.

[77] According to later evidence Bonny was released from gaol, returned to Charleston

Such sensational stories, tantalizing and teasing readers, turned Johnson's *History* into an instant success. New editions and translations followed, while parts of the text were regularly recycled. But it was a deceptively hybrid work, crossing boundaries between history and reportage, and mingling fact with fiction. It included romance, entertainment and real life adventure. As such, it presented readers with an ambiguous, enigmatic text. Although it was based on a range of sources, and purported to be history, the author may not have been primarily concerned with accuracy. Johnson harvested his material to produce an entertaining collection of pirate biographies which was emblematic of growing concern about crime, gender roles and civility, and the relationship between criminality, identity and disguise. It also contained a thinly veiled ideological edge, sharpened by satire, which provided clarification or confusion for readers. Intriguingly a report in *The Weekly Journal* of August 1724 claimed that at least one reader had dismissed it as a 'shim-sham Story', and an 'impudent Libel upon great Men'.[78] Reporting at second hand, the *Journal's* correspondent tactfully refrained from identifying who Blackbeard was meant to represent. As 'for the two female Pyrates', however, 'it was so plain that you might as well have writ their Names and Titles at length ... adding very civilly, that any Fool might have found that out'.[79]

Yet the piratical careers of Bonny and Read cannot be dismissed as fiction. The report on the trial of the pirates, published in Jamaica during 1721, included details of their exploits at sea which may have inspired Johnson's account. Together they were accused of four cases of piracy against a variety of small vessels owned by English settlers. The plunder included fish and tackle, worth £10, taken out of seven fishing boats; two sloops valued at £1,000; a schooner with a value of £20; and a sloop worth £300. None of these vessels were laden with valuable cargo.[80] Without a larger company of recruits, they would have been of little value to the pirates, unless their owners were willing to redeem them.

This small-scale piratical activity was confirmed by several witnesses, who also provided information on the roles of Read and Bonny aboard Rackam's ship. Dorothy Thomas was in a canoe sailing along the north

and married a local man with whom she had eight children; see D. Cordingly, 'Anne Bonny', *Oxford Dictionary of National Biography* (Oxford, 2004), online edition, www.oxforddnb.com (accessed 12 December 2012). On the cultural legacy see Rediker, *Villains of All Nations*, pp. 118–26.

[78] *The Weekly Journal or Saturday's Post*, 29 August 1724, reprinted in Baer (ed.), *British Piracy*, I, pp. 361–2.

[79] Ibid., p. 362.

[80] *The Tryals of Captain John Rackam*, in Baer (ed.), *British Piracy*, III, pp. 25–7.

coast of Jamaica, which was plundered of most of its lading of stock and provisions. She identified the two women as members of the pirate company. They 'wore Mens Jackets, and long Trousers, and Handkerchiefs tied about their Heads'.[81] Armed with a pistol and machete, they cursed at their companions who seemed reluctant to kill Thomas, as they urged, in order to prevent her being a witness against them. Despite their masculine dress, she recognized they were women 'by the largeness of their Breasts'.[82] The swearing and profligate behaviour were noted by Thomas Dillon, the master of a sloop which was taken in Dry Harbour, Jamaica. More revealing evidence was provided by two French men who were seized off Hispaniola and forced to sail with the pirates. They declared that both women 'were very active on Board, and willing to do any Thing; That *Anne Bonny*, one of the Prisoners at the Bar, handed Gun-powder to the Men'.[83] Their cross-dressing, the subject of so much comment and speculation, was a functional, if nonetheless creative response to their circumstances. Thus when the pirates pursued or attacked another vessel, 'they wore Men's Cloaths; and at other Times, they wore Women's Cloaths'.[84] Crucially the French witnesses added that neither woman seemed to be detained by force aboard the pirate ship.

Reports of the trial reverberated around the north Atlantic world, channelled along well-established networks of commerce and communication. In February 1722 *The Boston Gazette* reported the arrival of captain Samuel Lancelott, commander of the *John*, from Jamaica, with news of the execution of Rackam and ten of his company, and of 'two Women … taken with them [who] were Condemned, but pleaded their Bellies'.[85] Undoubtedly the news was widely reported in London, providing Johnson with raw material for his *History*. As such, the published record of the trial, despite its own imperfections, is the only surviving evidence which includes eye-witness testimony of the brief piratical careers of Bonny and Read. It confirms their presence among Rackam's company and the use of masculine dress and behaviour. But it also indicates that the fluid presentation of identity was more a social necessity than an expression of cultural dissidence. The description of Bonny employed as a powder monkey, a position

[81] Ibid., p. 27.
[82] Ibid.; D. Cordingly, *Spanish Gold: Captain Woodes Rogers and the Pirates of the Caribbean* (London, 2011), pp. 189–90.
[83] *The Tryals of Captain John Rackam*, in Baer (ed.), *British Piracy*, III, p. 28
[84] Ibid. On the common practice of cross-dressing among women see M. R. Hunt, *Women in Eighteenth-Century Europe* (Harlow, 2010), p. 126.
[85] *The Boston Gazette*, 6–13 February 1722, reprinted in Baer (ed.), *British Piracy*, I, p. 320; Rediker, *Villains of All Nations*, pp. 67–8.

occupied by boys and occasionally women aboard naval vessels, also suggests that they may have served in an auxiliary role.[86] This still leaves a question mark hanging over their physical condition, particularly if Bonny was as heavily pregnant as to give birth in prison shortly after her capture and trial.

Although the way in which Bonny and Read were recruited into piracy is unknown, some women could be caught in ambiguous, almost accidental circumstances, as illustrated by a case heard before a court of admiralty held at Williamsburg, in Virginia, during August 1727. The court was presided over by Robert Carter, the president, with the assistance of councillors and officials. Four prisoners appeared before them. They included John Vidal, a 'man of desperate fortune' who was identified by several witnesses as the captain of the gang, Thomas Allen, Edward Coleman and Martha Farley, whose husband, Thomas, had escaped.[87] The men were accused of piracy against several small vessels off Ocracoke Inlet in North Carolina. Martha Farley was indicted as an accessory to piracy. If the court found her to be guilty, she would face the same penalty as the pirates.

A combination of misfortune and resentment, underpinned by the more alluring prospect of Caribbean plunder, seems to have led the group into small-scale coastal robbery. They appeared to be down-at-heel traders or planters, who were reduced to a life of vagrancy and begging. One witness claimed that they called themselves 'Gentlemen of Fortune'.[88] They intended sailing to St Thomas' Island or Curacao once they had acquired a suitable vessel for that purpose. Their mode of operation exposed the continuing vulnerability of coastal traffic to piratical attack, but it also revealed the weakness of such small, poorly armed groups in the face of determined resistance.

The group assembled either by accident or design during May. Michael Griffin, who had known Vidal for several years, met him at the town of Bath, and agreed to accompany him to Cape Fear with Allen and Coleman. Travelling down-river in a *piragua* or large canoe, they were joined by Farley, his wife and two children in a separate canoe. All the men, with the possible exception of Vidal, were armed. Reaching Ocracoke, they saw a schooner, part-owned by John Snoad, a resident of the colony, lying offshore. According to Griffin, who was now alarmed at the course of the voyage, on sighting the vessel Farley exclaimed that Snoad 'had Cheated

---

[86] On women serving in this way undisguised see D. Dugaw, 'Balladry's Female Warriors: Women, Warfare, and Disguise', *Eighteenth Century Life*, 9 (1985), pp. 8–9.
[87] *CSPC, 1726–27*, pp. 346–7; TNA, HCA 1/99/9, ff. 2–8v.
[88] TNA, HCA 1/99/9, f. 5v.

him and now he would be revenged of him, for if it Cost him his Life he would take the schooner'.[89] Unwilling to take part, Griffin feigned sickness, going ashore to seek assistance at an inn or ordinary run by Josias Whitehouse. His wife offered to lay a hot brick at Griffin's side, where he pretended to be in pain. Alert to the trick, Farley returned him to the canoe and compelled him to participate in the boarding of the schooner. Griffin did so, but he went unarmed. The pirate incredulously demanded 'how he dared to come aboard without his Arms', adding that he 'had a Good mind to blow his brains out for it'.[90]

Jonathan Howard, the master of the schooner, the *Anne and Francis*, which was ready to depart for Boston, described the seizure of the vessel. About midday he noticed a canoe approaching from the shore. Suspecting the intentions of those aboard, Howard walked the deck with a gun in his hand. When it failed to fire, he 'put a hat of one of his Men on a handspit to make the best show he could to frighten them'.[91] The ruse failed. Rowing alongside, Coleman pointed his pistol towards the master. With three others, including Griffin, he boarded the vessel. The master and his company of three men were bound and placed in the cabin. When Howard was brought back on deck, Vidal, now armed with a pistol, was in charge. He instructed the master and his men to take the schooner over the Bar and out to sea. Prevented by wind and tide, Vidal warned the master that 'he suspected Treachery, and if he discovered any he would murder him'.[92]

Later in the afternoon a small sloop was sighted which the pirate gang planned to take, with the apparent intention of returning the schooner to Howard. Sailing in the *piragua*, three of the pirates, with a forced recruit from Howard's company, boarded the sloop. They returned with the master, Roger Kenyon, and three other men, bound as prisoners. According to Kenyon's later testimony, he was well acquainted with Vidal, who stayed at his house when he traded in the country. On their meeting, however, Vidal threatened him with a pistol. Alarmingly the pirate 'swore he would blow his Braines out, for that he had arrested him for five pounds when he had nott Cloaths to his back, and that he had forced him upon that enterprise, meaning as he understood, the Piracy'.[93] In his defence, Kenyon blamed his wife, claiming that she had ordered the arrest without his consent. Aware that Kenyon was an experienced pilot, Vidal ordered him and the other prisoners to help get the ship out to sea. But after three

[89] Ibid., f. 7.
[90] Ibid., ff. 3, 7v.
[91] Ibid., f. 3.
[92] Ibid., f. 3v.
[93] Ibid., ff. 3v, 4v.

days of endeavour, struggling against adverse conditions, they had made little progress.

About this time a trading vessel returning from Barbados, under the command of John Porter, was wrecked on the nearby banks. Vidal and others, including several of the prisoners, went to investigate. Finding Porter 'crying that he was undone', the pirate captain declared that he would take nothing from the wreck, except some rum and provisions for his sea store, as well as weapons which he needed to defend himself.[94] Porter had already buried his personal possessions, including gold coins, rings and a watch, in the sand, but they were discovered by one of the pirates. Another also seized a pair of gold buttons from the master's coat sleeves. Vidal took charge of the booty, worth about £40, which he later showed to Kenyon, boasting 'by God Roger, this is better than begging, for I can't work'.[95] According to one of the witnesses, the pirate captain and Coleman quarrelled after a drinking bout ashore, possibly over the division of the plunder. Vidal took up a sword against his companion, who responded by threatening the captain with a gun. After being cut with the sword, Coleman ran away.

To celebrate their success Vidal and some of the pirate gang, with several prisoners in their custody, spent a night ashore drinking at Whitehouse's inn. Andrew Frasier, a young man returning to North Carolina from Virginia, was also there. Informed earlier of the seizure of the schooner, he expressed a willingness to sail out in a canoe to cut its cables, so that it would drift ashore. On being informed of this by Whitehouse's wife, Vidal angrily informed Frasier that he was now his prisoner and would be taken aboard the ship. Boldly the young man replied 'if he must, he must, but he would have a Trial about it', remonstrating with the other prisoners that 'it was a shame for such a Company of people to be drove by one pistol'.[96] The following morning, Frasier seized his opportunity. As the company launched the *piragua*, he struck Vidal across the head with a tiller. At the same time Howard seized his pistol, striking the pirate across the forehead with it. When they sought the assistance of Kenyon, however, he 'ran away crying what have you done? What have you done?'[97] But Vidal was in no condition to put up any resistance; submitting to his assailants, he begged for mercy.

Returning to the schooner, which the rest of the pirate gang deserted, Vidal was questioned by Frasier about several pieces of gold. Although he

[94] Ibid., ff. 3v, 4–4v.
[95] Ibid., f. 5.
[96] Ibid., ff. 5, 6v.
[97] Ibid., ff. 6v–7.

denied any knowledge thereof, when Frasier threatened 'to throw him overboard, he owned he had the money in the foot of his stocking and from thence it was taken'.[98] Thereafter Vidal was taken under guard to Bath, where he was handed over into the custody of the provost marshal. The rest of the gang, including Martha Farley, escaped in a rowing boat. As they were drinking in a house at Nuce, Griffin persuaded a boy, with a gift of five shillings, to inform local officers of the pirates' presence. Although they escaped, all but Farley's husband were soon captured and sent to Williamsburg for trial.

Martha Farley appeared to be a bystander throughout most of this short-lived episode. To some witnesses and officials she was almost an invisible presence. Reporting on the pirates' leader, Carter noted that 'before he had encreased his gang, he was sett upon by some of the country people and taken with two more of his first gang and one press't man', apparently forgetting or ignoring the arrest of the woman.[99] While the pirates were active off Ocracoke, she seems to have stayed ashore with her two children, possibly with the Whitehouses. Yet she may have been more than a passive spectator. Howard, the master of the schooner, declared that whenever he was in conversation with his mate 'in the Cabbin, he bid him take care for that the Prisoner, Martha Farley, told everything that was said to her husband'.[100] At the insistence of the latter, moreover, she received a pair of women's shoes which Howard brought from New England.

As legal proceedings came to a close during August 1727, the accused were offered the opportunity to speak in their defence. Farley blamed her husband, still at large, for her predicament. He 'brought her from her Friends in South Carolina and carried her about with two children begging'.[101] She followed him, 'not knowing his design, and thought that she was returning to her Friends'.[102] Lacking evidence, and with the future of two small children to consider, the court discharged her. For his part, Vidal claimed that until recently he 'lived with a good reputation, [and] that he came of a good Family, his Father being a merchant in Dublin'; moreover, until the present misfortune, he informed the court that 'he had never been accused of any ill action'.[103] With Coleman and Allen, who offered no defence, he was found guilty of piracy. Subject to royal approval, Vidal was subsequently reprieved by the governor of Virginia.

---

[98] Ibid., f. 7.
[99] *CSPC, 1726–27*, pp. 346–7.
[100] TNA, HCA 1/99/9, f. 4.
[101] Ibid., f. 8.
[102] Ibid., ff. 8–8v.
[103] Ibid., f. 8; *CSPC, 1726–27*, p. 353.

By an unusual coincidence another court of admiralty held at Williamsburg two years later, in August 1729, heard a similar, but even more desperate, case of piracy in which a woman was directly involved with a group of five men. The accused were identified as Edmond Williams, George Caves, Edward Edwards, Jeremiah Smith and George Cole alias Sanders, as well as Mary Critchett. Earlier in the year, in May, the gang seized a sloop, the *John and Elizabeth*, at the mouth of the Piankatank river which flowed into Chesapeake Bay in Virginia. As the master and his servant lay asleep aboard the moored vessel, about one o'clock in the morning, it was boarded by raiders. John Grymes, master and owner, informed the court that he was woken by voices, which included a command to 'get under sail'. Williams, the leader of the group, struck him on the shoulder, 'saying you son of a bitch, if you offer to make any resistance, you are a dead man'.[104] The master was held in the cabin, while the pirates unsuccessfully tried to persuade his servant, Alexander Abbott, to join them. According to Abbott's testimony, they were a group of former convicts, transported to the colony and sold, who had fled from their masters. When they boarded the sloop they called out to each other 'make ready your Cutlaces', to terrify its occupants, though no weapons were to be seen the next day.[105] They appeared to be an amateurish, unarmed band of reckless rogues, though Williams boasted 'that if they could get more hands, they would pursue the like piracys'.[106] Their recklessness was qualified by a degree of organization, but their evident lack of knowledge and experience of the sea seems to have led to their subsequent capture.

As dawn broke, the pirates tried to get out into the Bay. As a result of their inexperience and lack of familiarity with the channel, they ran the sloop aground on several occasions. They were thus compelled to use the master to pilot them down-river. Once in the Bay, however, with little or no wind, they were forced in the wrong direction, coming to anchor off Tangier Island. Two of the company went ashore for water, but they were questioned by the local inhabitants who 'threatned to take them up as Runaways'.[107] Alarmed that the islanders had gone in search of assistance, when the pirates sighted a boat off a neighbouring island, Williams cut up some oars to use as weapons to defend themselves. At the same time the master and his servant were returned to the cabin, while Mary Critchett sat on the hatch to keep it secure. The boat veered off, enabling the gang to sail

---

[104] TNA, HCA 1/99/8.
[105] Ibid.
[106] Ibid.
[107] Ibid.

down the Bay later in the night. Unable to make much progress because of contrary winds, after four days Grymes and Abbott were put ashore below York river. Before his release, the pirates robbed the master of his shoes, a silk handkerchief which he wore around his neck, a coat, shirt and jacket. They also took a new jacket from the back of the servant, though he was given an old coat in exchange. The pirates gave the master four hides, out of a lading of fifteen, 'to shelter him from the weather'.[108] Abbott recalled that at their departure, Critchett 'blamed the rest of the Crew for suffering them to goe ashore because, said she, these men will certainly betray us, and we shall be pursued and taken'.[109]

The pirates failed to make it out of the Bay. Although details of their capture are lacking, it is likely that they were unable to navigate the sloop safely to sea. They were all found guilty of piracy and sentenced to be hanged, 'within the ebbing and flowing of the sea', at a place to be decided by the president of the court.[110] If she was executed, Mary Critchett would be the only recorded case of the execution of a woman for piracy either in England or in the American colonies during the period covered by this study.[111]

*

The evidence presented in this chapter demonstrates that women's direct participation in piracy was an exceptional occurrence. There is no evidence that significant numbers of women sailed the seas aboard pirate ships, though small groups supported and operated alongside gangs of river pirates preying on shipping on the Thames. Few women were arraigned for piracy, and only one may have been executed for it. Their involvement in sea robbery was often ambiguous and in association with men. As no tradition of female piracy emerged, the legacy left by the few women pirates was uncertain. Johnson's skilful embroidery of the lives of Bonny and Read was applied by others, in different contexts, to the exploits of Grainne O'Malley and Elizabeth Killigrew. While the former became a powerful symbol for Irish patriots and nationalists, as part of a longer tradition of appealing heroines, the latter came to be portrayed as a Jezebel by some local historians and antiquarians. The reality was rather different. As long as the sea was a dangerous and uncontrolled place, both custom and culture accorded little room or role for women aboard sailing ships. Nor was there an overriding compulsion or motive for women to challenge these conven-

[108] Ibid.
[109] Ibid.
[110] Ibid.
[111] In November 1809 Edward Jordan, fisherman, and his wife were tried for piracy and murder at Halifax, Nova Scotia; Snow, *Pirates and Buccaneers*, pp. 319–25.

tions. Yet in the wake of the careers of Bonny and Read, a small, but growing number of women went to sea during the eighteenth century, ironically to serve with the royal navy and marines.[112]

---

[112] Mathew, 'Cornish and Welsh Pirates', p. 340 n6; Chambers, *Granuaile*, pp. 164–78. Popular tales of Bonny and Read provided the reading public with examples of female independence and bravery. On women in the navy see Peakman, *Lascivious Bodies*, pp. 229–30.

Epilogue

England played a leading role in promoting and maintaining seaborne plunder of varied forms from the 1540s to the 1720s. Building on medieval tradition, piracy and privateering flourished within the local waters of the British Isles. Its expansion overseas initiated a process of predatory globalization which led English adventurers to prey on shipping across the oceans and seas of the world. Adapting to local conditions it was grafted on to corsair enterprise in the Mediterranean and merged with buccaneering in the Caribbean. It was a remarkably dynamic, but also fragmented, development. At times of intense activity thousands of male recruits were attracted into piracy. At least 1,000 rovers were operating during the later sixteenth and early seventeenth centuries. During the period from 1716 to 1726 between 1,000 and 2,000 pirates were active at any particular time; collectively as many as 5,000 were at sea across these years.[1] After decades of cultural adaptation and improvisation, pirate groups had acquired a defiant, unrepentant lifestyle, appearing as a kind of social banditry. Their conduct, contradictory and chaotic, violent and abusive, cannot be easily explained by economics alone. Though driven by the quest for booty, pirate recruits also appeared to be in search of a lost world of reciprocity and mutuality at sea, which saw some groups masquerading as 'Robbin Hoods Men' during the 1720s.[2] The retribution and punishment inflicted on some ship-masters was a direct result of changing maritime conditions and labour relations, as owners and merchants tried to raise productivity levels among the merchant marine. Such conditions were dramatized by shipboard politics, providing a breeding ground for discontent and mutinous behaviour which was increasingly linked with piracy.

That this was an activity dominated by men, habituated to transient lives and characterized by unpredictability and irregularity, seems to be self-

---

[1] M. Rediker, *Between the Devil and the Deep Blue Sea: Merchant Seamen, Pirates, and the Anglo-American Maritime World* (Cambridge, 1987), p. 256.
[2] Ibid., pp. 267–9; J. F. Jameson (ed.), *Privateering and Piracy in the Colonial Period: Illustrative Documents* (New York, 1923), p. 304. P. Leeson, *The Invisible Hook: The Hidden Economics of Pirates* (Princeton, 2009), vigorously argues in favour of an overriding economic interpretation of piracy.

evident. Since the publication of Johnson's entertaining and influential collection of pirate biographies, histories of piracy have repeatedly emphasized the male and masculine aspects of seaborne predation, effectively denying or limiting the possibility of female agency. According to this view, maritime robbery and plunder involved groups of aggressive and disorderly men sailing the seas in search of booty with little apparent concern for the need for bases or markets. The result is an imbalance in the study of piracy which favours the seaborne activities of rovers, to the neglect of its wider dimensions, including the community of interest that existed between sea and land. Yet as this study shows, piracy was more than the robbery of ships at sea: it was a commercial or business enterprise based on far-reaching relations, ranging across a wider web of irregular commerce, exchange and gift-giving. As Johnson acknowledged, moreover, there were land pirates who were prepared to relieve their maritime counterparts of the plunder they brought ashore.[3] They were part of a larger infrastructure that maintained piracy. It included networks of supporters, a miscellaneous section of local communities, whose assistance was motivated by varied aims and ambitions, though it was often concealed by ambiguity. From the 1540s onwards, when the monarchy threatened receivers with the same punishment as pirates, officials struggled to deal with the problem.[4] Their mixed success demonstrated the way in which piracy was embedded within widely scattered coastal regions and communities, ranging from south-west England, Wales and Ireland to Jamaica, Bermuda or Rhode Island in colonial America. This characteristic of piracy, the result of economic and social necessity, created opportunities for extensive and varied interactions between pirates and women, as documented by this study.

The role of women as supporters of piracy and other forms of maritime plunder demonstrates the multi-faceted nature of female agency, especially within seafaring and shore-line communities. This varied over time and according to context. Around the British Isles, from the 1540s to the 1630s, women of varied backgrounds, including wives and widows, as well as mothers and other kin, maintained a range of contacts and relations with pirates and sea rovers. They included small numbers of women of rank, including Lady Howard, whose servants dealt with visiting pirates at Lulworth on her behalf, and Lady Denny, who was directly involved in receiving booty, sometimes in association with her husband, in the west of Ireland. More typically poorer women of humble backgrounds were closely

---

[3] Johnson, *General History of the Pyrates*, pp. 56–7; C. M. Senior, *A Nation of Pirates: English Piracy in its Heyday* (Newton Abbot, 1976), pp. 124–44.

[4] R. W. Heinze, *The Proclamations of the Tudor Kings* (Cambridge, 1976), p. 221.

involved in dealing with visiting rovers in many parts of south-west England. Most of these contacts may have been irregular and opportunistic, but some, such as the relationship between Anne Piers and her son, John, in Padstow during the 1580s, amounted to partnerships in the disposal and dispersal of pirate plunder. While women profited from occasional, often small-scale transactions with rovers, they provided provisions and hospitality in exchange. Such relationships were vital to the persistence of organized piracy around the British Isles.

The structure of piratical enterprise, especially its dependence on markets ashore, thus illuminates patterns of female criminality within urban and rural communities.[5] Although the inherent ambiguity of receiving plunder from the sea may have limited prosecutions before the High Court of Admiralty, women engaged in close and collaborative relations with pirates. Whether driven by need and necessity, or opportunity and calculation, their actions were related to local conditions, including a common experience of uncertain employment and remuneration, which in London encouraged their participation in river piracy and theft. But the support that women showed for pirates was also motivated by family bonds and loyalties. At some risk to themselves, mothers and wives harboured and protected men accused of piracy, while occasionally resorting to intimidation and physical violence to frustrate the implementation of the law.

This pattern of activity followed in the wake of the expansion of piracy, and the use of overseas bases, but it was modified by different contexts and conditions. Across the Atlantic it was loosely linked with informal colonial settlement, though the persistent link between piracy and overseas expansion after the 1620s awaits further investigation. The spread of large-scale piracy to south-west Ireland during the early stage of this process was accompanied by the emergence of a lawless sea-shore society, which created the conditions for a flourishing business between pirates and settlers. It included an organized traffic in sex. The symbiotic relationship between prostitution and piracy, evident along the coast of Munster, also emerged within the Caribbean, notably at Port Royal on Jamaica. The development of a wider structure of exchange, informed by past practice, supported the growth of buccaneering, piracy and privateering in the region. But the growth of long-distance piracy effectively marginalized the economic func-

---

[5] On female criminality, in addition to work by G. Walker, *Crime, Gender and Social Order in Early Modern England* (Cambridge, 2003), see A. Capern, *The Historical Study of Women: England: 1500–1700* (Basingstoke, 2008), pp. 132–5; J. M. Beattie, *Policing and Punishment in London 1660–1750: Urban Crime and the Limits of Terror* (Oxford, 2001), pp. 28–9, 37–8, 53–4, 63–71: R. Shoemaker, *Gender in English Society 1650–1850: The Emergence of Separate Spheres?* (Harlow, 1998), pp. 296–302.

tion of women as receivers, undoubtedly as a result of conditions in overseas bases and ports such as Port Royal, New York and Madagascar. At the same time it strained relationships between pirates and wives, though the number of married men recruited into piracy seems to have been in decline. While some men struggled to retain contact with spouses in England, others, including single male recruits, pursued a libertine lifestyle of short-term casual sex and contacts. In these circumstances they formed cross-cultural liaisons with women of varied ethnicity in parts of the Caribbean, West Africa and the Indian Ocean. Most of these relationships were fleeting or short-lived, though potentially of far-reaching consequence. Occasionally they paved the way for longer-term unions. An English visitor reported meeting a retired pirate, captain Kennedy, at Malacca in 1694, who married a native woman of 'great repute for her skilful use of love philtres and poisons'.[6]

The interdependency between pirate groups and female supporters or associates thus furnishes striking evidence for women's agency. But it was twinned with victimhood. While some women benefited from their contacts with sea rovers, others, possibly a larger number, suffered. Piracy could have catastrophic consequences for the lives of many women. During 1588, for example, Margaret Johnson petitioned the Privy Council for assistance in facilitating a suit in the High Court of Admiralty for the recovery of a vessel taken by pirates who had murdered her husband.[7] Arbitrary and unpredictable in impact, the hardship piracy inflicted on women suggests a gendered dimension to poverty that was most acutely felt in seafaring communities. It was recognized in legislation of the reign of Charles II, providing for a levy on shipowners which was to be distributed among the defenders of vessels attacked by pirates, 'having special regard unto the Widows and Children of such as have been slain in that Service'.[8] A large number of women, especially in London and the south west, were also affected by the capture and captivity of men and boys by the Barbary corsairs. Their varied responses to such traumatic experiences effectively used petitioning and propaganda to keep the issue in the public sphere. It also enabled some women to present themselves as innocent casualties who were entitled to assistance in the recovery of captives from North Africa. At the same time, however, women were increasingly the direct victims of pirate violence. Against a wider background of aggressive interpersonal

---

[6] S. C. Hill, *Notes on Piracy in Eastern Waters* (Bombay, 1923), pp. 97, 140–1.

[7] *CSPD, 1581–90*, p. 481.

[8] *A Discourse of the Laws Relating to Pirates and Piracies* (London, 1726), reprinted in Baer (ed.), *British Piracy*, III, pp. 303, 305.

relations, influenced by culture and environment, some rovers were capable of inflicting brutal punishment on women, especially in the Caribbean and Indian Ocean. Though influenced by international conflict and rivalries, the rape, abuse and humiliation of women may also have been the result of the peculiar lifestyle of pirates at sea, especially as they ranged far beyond the British Isles in search of new hunting grounds.

The dual nature of female agency mirrored the broader roles and experiences of women in society which shaped their relations with pirates. Yet some women went beyond this, inadvertently challenging or aggressively invading male-dominated institutions and spheres of influence. Most notably, the petitioning campaigns of poor and humble wives during the 1620s and 1630s involved groups of angry women side-stepping or breaking with protocol to present their grievances to the monarchy and Privy Council. Their behaviour exposed fissures within patriarchal authority, as it struggled to deal effectively with a novel and protracted social problem. Difficult as it is, given the inherent bias in the written evidence, the experiences of the silent victims of piracy, such as the slaves taken by a 'parcell of Pyrates' in the West Indies who were smuggled into Rhode Island during 1721, must also be recognized and set against this more active approach of appealing for assistance.[9] They formed part of a broader range of contact between pirates and native peoples that deserves more attention than it has so far received.

Either as agents or victims, the evidence regarding women's role in the business of piracy indicates an interrelationship with men, neither subordinate nor equal, which is still rarely acknowledged. Yet female agency provides an unusual perspective on the broader nature of piracy as it developed from the 1540s to the 1720s. It also suggests areas for future work on the subject, including the emergence and development of pirate culture, and its representation through sexuality and violence, particularly as it developed alongside the growth of long-distance piratical enterprise. Above all, it draws attention to the lack of detailed work on the structure and organization of piracy as a local and transatlantic type of enterprise, including the functioning of markets and fairs, as well as the disposal of booty through trade, exchange and gift-giving. While women were involved in all these areas, it is their role as partners in a longstanding and

[9] D. S. Towle (ed.), *Records of the Vice-Admiralty Court of Rhode Island 1716–1752* (American Historical Association, American Legal Records, Volume 3, Washington, 1936), pp. 110–11. In France women's petitioning undermined the patriarchal foundations of society according to G. Weiss, 'Humble Petitioners and Able Contractors: French Women as Intermediaries in the Redemption of Captives', in W. Kaiser (ed.), *Le Commerce des Captifs* (Rome, 2008), pp. 333, 342–3.

dynamic form of maritime criminality which seems most arresting. Yet the involvement of female associates briefly featured in one of the best books ever published on pirates. It may come as a surprise to some that Long John Silver, the villainous old buccaneer who stalks the pages of *Treasure Island*, by Robert Louis Stevenson, was married. Like the pirate captain Tibault Saxbridge whose wife and daughter ran an inn in Dublin during the early seventeenth century, Silver's spouse was left to manage a similar establishment when he returned to the sea on a dramatic expedition in search of buried treasure. Indeed Squire Trelawney speculates that it was the wife who 'sends him back to roving'.[10] At the end of the voyage, as young Jim Hawkins makes his literary *envoi*, he reports Silver's disappearance. Although the 'formidable seafaring man with one leg has at last gone clean out of my life', he expresses a hope that 'he met his old negress, and perhaps still lives in comfort with her'.[11] There is little evidence to suggest that the real Silvers managed to achieve this. But the recovery of the lives and experiences of the women who supported and maintained pirates, or who were abandoned and abused by them, is surely long overdue.

[10] R. L. Stevenson, *Treasure Island*, ed. J. Seelye (London, 1999), p. 39.
[11] Ibid., p. 190.

BIBLIOGRAPHY

Manuscript Sources

British Library, London
Additional MS 12430
Additional MS 12505
Cotton MS Nero B III
Cotton MS Otho E VIII, IX
Lansdowne MS 26, 33, 142, 162
Sloane MS 49

Devon Record Office, Exeter
Q/S 128/1–147 (Quarter Sessions, petitions)
1180/PW1(V) (East Budleigh, register book)

London Guildhall Library, London
Broadside 12.12 (petition to parliament)

London Metropolitan Archives, London
CLC/526/MS 30045/1 and 2 (Trinity House of Deptford, transactions)
MISC MS/156/9 (a brief for captives, 1691)
P 92/SAV/1915, 1918–22 (briefs for captives, 1620)

The National Archives, London
CO various (Colonial Office, miscellaneous papers)
HCA 1/ (High Court of Admiralty, oyer and terminer records)
HCA 13/ (High Court of Admiralty, examinations)
HCA 14/ (High Court of Admiralty, exemplifications)
HCA 24/ (High Court of Admiralty, libels and sentences)
PC 2/ (Privy Council, registers)
SP 12/ (State Papers, Elizabeth I)
SP 16/ (State Papers, Charles I)
SP 29/ (State Papers, Charles II)
SP 63/ (State Papers, Ireland)

Printed Sources

A Full and Exact Account of the Tryal Of All the Pyrates Lately Taken by Captain Ogle (London, 1723)

A New Generall Collection of Voyages and Travels, 4 vols (London, 1747–7)

A Relation of the Whole Proceedings Concerning the Redemption of the Captives in Argier and Tunis (London, 1647)

A True Relation of the Lives and Deaths of the two most Famous Pyrats, Purser and Clinton (London, 1639, repr. Amsterdam, 1971)

Acts of the Privy Council of England, 1542–1631, 46 vols, ed. J. R. Dasent *et al.* (London, 1890–1964)

Acts of the Privy Council of England, Colonial Series, 1613–1745, 3 vols, ed. W. L. Grant *et al.* (London, 1908–10)

C. H. Adams (ed.), *The Narrative of Robert Adams, a Barbary Captive: A Critical Edition* (Cambridge, 2005)

K. R. Andrews (ed.), *English Privateering Voyages to the West Indies 1588–1595* (Hakluyt Society, Second Series, 111, 1959)

—— *The Last Voyage of Drake & Hawkins* (Hakluyt Society, Second Series, 142, 1972)

J. C. Appleby (ed.), *A Calendar of Material Relating to Ireland from the High Court of Admiralty Examinations 1536–1641* (Irish Manuscripts Commission, Dublin, 1992)

J. H. Baer (ed.), *British Piracy in the Golden Age: History and Interpretation, 1660–1730*, 4 vols (London, 2007)

R. Blome, *The Present State of His Majesties Isles and Territories in America* (London, 1687)

J. S. Brewer *et al.* (eds), *Calendar of the Carew Manuscripts 1515–1603*, 4 vols (London, 1867–70)

D. Buisseret (ed.), *Jamaica in 1687: The Taylor Manuscript at the National Library of Jamaica* (Kingston, 2008)

Calendar of Patent Rolls Preserved in the Public Record Office 1461–1582, 24 vols (London, 1897–1986)

Calendar of State Papers, Colonial Series, 1547–1660, ed. W. N. Sainsbury (London, 1860)

Calendar of State Papers, Colonial Series, America and West Indies, 1661–1730, 37 vols, ed. W. N. Sainsbury *et al.* (London, 1880–1937)

Calendar of State Papers, Domestic Series, of the Reigns of Edward VI, Mary, Elizabeth, 1547–1603, 7 vols, ed. R. Lemon (London, 1856–70)

Calendar of State Papers, Domestic Series, of the Reign of Edward VI, 1547–1553, ed. C. S. Knighton (London, 1992)

Calendar of State Papers, Domestic Series, of the Reign of Mary I, 1553–1558, ed. C. S. Knighton (London, 1998)

Calendar of State Papers, Domestic Series, of the Reign of James I, 1603–25, 4 vols, ed. M. A. E. Green (London, 1856–9)

Calendar of State Papers, Domestic Series, of the Reign of Charles I, 1625–1649, 21 vols, ed. J. Bruce *et al.* (London, 1858–93)

Calendar of State Papers, Domestic Series, 1649–1660, 13 vols, ed. M. A. E. Green (London, 1875–86)

Calendar of State Papers, Domestic Series, of the Reign of Charles II, 1660–1685, 28 vols, ed. M. A. E. Green *et al.* (London, 1860–93)

Calendar of State Papers, Domestic Series, James II, 1685–1689, 3 vols (London, 1960–72)

Calendar of State Papers, Domestic Series, of the Reign of William and Mary, 1689–1702, 11 vols, ed. W. J. Hardy *et al.* (London, 1895–1937)

Calendar of State Papers, Domestic Series, of the Reign of Anne, 1702–1706, 4 vols (in progress), ed. R. P. Mahaffy *et al.* (London, 1916–2006)

Calendar of Letters and State Papers Relating to English Affairs, Preserved Principally in the Archives of Simancas, 1558–1603, 4 vols, ed. M. A. S. Hume (London, 1892–9)

Calendar of State Papers and Manuscripts, Relating to English Affairs, Existing in the Archives and Collections of Venice, 1558–1639, 24 vols, ed. R. Brown *et al.* (London, 1890–1923)

Calendar of State Papers, Foreign Series, of the Reign of Edward VI, 1547–1553, ed. W. B. Turnbull (London, 1861)

Calendar of State Papers, Foreign Series, of the Reign of Mary, 1553–1558, ed. W. B. Turnbull (London, 1861)

Calendar of State Papers, Foreign Series, of the Reign of Elizabeth, 1558–1589, 23 vols, ed. J. Stevenson *et al.* (London, 1863–1950)

Calendar of State Papers, Ireland, Henry VIII, Edward VI, Mary, and Elizabeth, 1509–1603, 11 vols, ed. H. C. Hamilton *et al.* (London, 1860–1912)

Calendar of State Papers, Ireland, Tudor Period, 1571–1575, ed. M. O'Dowd (London and Dublin, 2000)

Calendar of State Papers, Relating to Ireland, of the Reign of James I, 1603–1625, 5 vols, ed. C. W. Russell *et al.* (London, 1872–80)

Calendar of State Papers, Relating to Ireland, of the Reign of Charles I, 1625–1647, 2 vols, ed. R. P. Mahaffy (London, 1900–1)

Calendar of State Papers, Relating to Ireland, 1647–1670, 5 vols, ed. R. P. Mahaffy (London, 1903–10)

R. Caulfield (ed.), *The Council Book of the Corporation of Youghal* (Guildford, 1878)

M. C. Clayton (ed.), *The Council Book for the Province of Munster c.1599–1649* (Irish Manuscripts Commission, Dublin, 2008)

E. Cooke, *A Voyage to the South Sea, and Round the World, Perform'd in the Years 1708, 1709, 1710, and 1711*, 2 vols (London, 1712)

J. S. Corbett (ed.), *Papers Relating to the Navy during the Spanish War 1585–1587* (Navy Records Society, 11, 1898)

W. Dampier, *Voyages and Discoveries*, C. Wilkinson (London, 1931, repr. Amsterdam, 1971)

—— *A New Voyage Round the World*, ed. N. M. Penzer (London, 1937)

P. Dan, *Histoire de Barbarie, et de ses Corsaires* (2nd edition, Paris, 1649)

H. de Castries *et al.* (eds), *Les Sources Inédites de L'Histoire du Maroc: Archives et Bibliotheque d'Angleterre*, 3 vols (Paris, 1918–35)

R. de Lussan, *A Journal of a Voyage Made into the South Sea, by the Bucaniers or Freebooters of America; From the Year 1684 to 1689* (London, 1698)

A. de Morga, *Sucesos de las Islas Filipinas*, translated and edited by J. S. Cummins (Hakluyt Society, Second Series, 140, 1971)

D. Defoe, *A Review of the British Nation, Volume 4: 1707–8*, 2 vols, ed. J. McVeagh (London, 2006)

—— *The Life, Adventures, and Pyracies, of the Famous Captain Singleton (1720)*, ed. P. N. Furbank (London, 2008)

—— *A General History of the Pyrates*, ed. M. Schonhorn (London, 1972)

E. S. Donno (ed.), *An Elizabethan in 1581: The Diary of Richard Madox, Fellow of All Souls* (Hakluyt Society, Second Series, 147, 1976)

C. Downing, *A Compendious History of the Indian Wars; With an Account of the Rise, Progress, Strength, and Forces of Angria the Pyrate* (London, 1737)

R. Dudley Edwards, 'Letter-Book of Sir Arthur Chichester 1612–1614 in the Library of Trinity College, Dublin', *Analecta Hibernica*, 8 (1938), pp. 3–177

J. Esquemeling, *The Buccaneers of America*, ed. W. S. Stallybrass (London, 1924)

C. H. Firth and R. S. Rait (eds), *Acts and Ordinances of the Interregnum, 1642–1660*, 3 vols (London, 1911)

M. A. Garcés (ed.), *An Early Modern Dialogue with Islam: Antonio de Sosa's Topography of Algiers (1612)*, translated by D. de Armas Wilson (Notre Dame, 2011)

W. Hacke, *A Collection of Original Voyages* (London, 1699)

R. Hakluyt, *The Principal Navigations Voyages Traffiques & Discoveries of the English Nation*, 12 vols (3rd edition, Glasgow, 1903–5, repr. New York, 1969)

—— *Discourse of Western Planting*, ed. D. B. and A. M. Quinn (Hakluyt Society, Extra Series, 45, 1993)

F. E. Halliday (ed.), *Richard Carew of Antony: The Survey of Cornwall* (London, 1953)

G. G. Harris (ed.), *Trinity House of Deptford Transactions, 1609–35* (London Record Society, 19, 1983)

HMC, *Calendar of the Manuscripts of the Marquis of Salisbury*, 24 vols (London, 1883–1976)

HMC, *Twelfth Report, The Manuscripts of the Earl Cowper*, 3 vols (London, 1888–9)

P. L. Hughes and J. F. Larkin (eds), *Tudor Royal Proclamations*, 3 vols (New Haven, 1964–9)

R. D. Hunt (ed.), 'Henry Townshend's "Notes of the Office of a Justice of Peace", 1661–3' (Worcestershire Historical Society, Miscellany II, New Series, vol. 5, 1967), pp. 68–137

J. F. Jameson (ed.), *Privateering and Piracy in the Colonial Period: Illustrative Documents* (New York, 1923)

C. Johnson, *A General History of the Pyrates* (London, 1725)

—— *A General History of the Lives and Adventures of the Most Famous Highwaymen, Murderers, Street-Robbers, &c. To Which is Added, a Genuine Account of the Voyages and Plunders of the Most Notorious Pyrates* (London, 1734)

L. E. Elliott Joyce (ed.), *A New Voyage and Description of the Isthmus of America by Lionel Wafer* (Hakluyt Society, Third Series, 73, 1934)

M. F. Keeler (ed.), *Sir Francis Drake's West Indian Voyage 1585–1586* (Hakluyt Society, Second Series, 148, 1981)

E. Kellet, *A Return from Argier. A Sermon Preached at Minhead ... 1627 at the Re-admission of a Relapsed Christian into Our Church* (London, 1628)

V. von Klarwill (ed.), *The Fugger News-Letters 1568–1605* (London, 1926)

List and Analysis of State Papers, Foreign Series, Elizabeth I, 1589–1596, 7 vols, ed. R. W. Wernham (London, 1964–2000)

F. Loviot, *A Lady's Captivity among Chinese Pirates in the Chinese Seas*, introduction by M. Lincoln (London, 2008)

J. Maclean (ed.), *Letters from George Lord Carew to Sir Thomas Roe, 1615–1617* (Camden Society, First Series, 76, 1860)

G. E. Manwaring and W. G. Perrin (eds), *The Life and Works of Sir Henry Mainwaring*, 2 vols (Navy Records Society, 54 & 56, 1920–2)

R. G. Marsden (ed.), *Select Pleas in the Court of Admiralty*, 2 vols (Selden Society, 6 & 11, 1894–7)

—— 'Voyage of the Barbara to Brazil, A.D. 1540', *Naval Miscellany II* (Navy Records Society, 40, 1912), pp. 3–66

—— *Documents Relating to the Law and Custom of the Sea*, 2 vols (Navy Records Society, 49 & 50, 1915–16)

J. H. Matthews (ed.), *Cardiff Records*, 6 vols (Cardiff, 1898–1911)

N. E. McClure (ed.), *The Letters of John Chamberlain*, 2 vols (Philadelphia, 1939)

A. L. Merson (ed.), *The Third Book of Remembrance of Southampton 1514–1602*, 3 vols (Southampton Record Series, 2, 3 & 8, n.s., 1952–65)

J. Morgan, *A Complete History of Algiers* (London, 1731, repr. Westport, Conn., 1970)

E. Murphy (ed.), *A Calendar of Material Relating to Ireland from the High Court of Admiralty 1641–1660* (Irish Manuscripts Commission, Dublin, 2011)

J. G. Nichols (ed.), *The Diary of Henry Machyn, Citizen and Merchant-Taylor of London* (Camden Society, First Series, 42, 1848)

W. Notestein (ed.), *The Journal of Sir Simonds D'Ewes from the Beginning of the Long Parliament to the Opening of the Trial of the Earl of Strafford* (New Haven, 1923)

P. Oliver (ed.), *Madagascar; Or, Robert Drury's Journal, During Fifteen Years' Captivity on that Island* (London, 1890)

M. Oppenheim (ed.), *The Naval Tracts of Sir William Monson*, 5 vols (Navy Records Society, 22–23, 43, 45 & 47, 1902–14)

[P. Osborne], *Reasons for Reducing the Pyrates at Madagascar* (London, 1707)

J. Ovington, *A Voyage to Surat in the Year 1689*, ed. H. G. Rawlinson (Oxford, 1929)

C. R. Pennell (ed.), *Piracy and Diplomacy in Seventeenth-Century North Africa: The Journal of Thomas Baker, English Consul in Tripoli* (London and Cranbury, 1989)

M. J. Prichard and D. E. C. Yale (eds), *Hale and Fleetwood on Admiralty Jurisdiction* (Selden Society, 108, 1992)

Privy Council Registers Preserved in the Public Record Office, Reproduced in Facsimile, 1637–1645, 12 vols (London, 1967–8)

D. B. Quinn (ed.), *The Voyages and Colonising Enterprises of Sir Humphrey Gilbert*, 2 vols (Hakluyt Society, Second Series, 83 & 84, 1938–9)

—— *The Roanoke Voyages 1584–1590*, 2 vols (Hakluyt Society, Second Series, 104 & 105, 1955)

—— *New American World: A Documentary History of North America to 1612*, 5 vols (London, 1979)

W. Rogers, *A Cruising Voyage Round the World: First to the South-Seas, Thence to the East-Indies, and Homewards by the Cape of Good Hope* (London, 1712)

G. Shelvocke, *A Voyage Round the World by the Way of the Great South Sea* (London, 1726)

A. Hassell Smith *et al.* (eds), *The Papers of Nathaniel Bacon of Stiffkey* (Norwich, 1979)

W. Snelgrave, *A New Account of Some Parts of Guinea, and the Slave Trade* (London, 1734)

The Arraignment, Tryal, and Condemnation of Capt. John Quelch and Others of His Company &c (London, 1704)

The Grand Pyrate: Or, the Life and Death of Capt. George Cusack the Great Sea-Robber (London, 1676)

The King of Pirates: Being an Account of the Famous Enterprises of Captain Avery (London, 1720)

The Life and Adventures of Capt. John Avery (London, 1709)

The Present State of Jamaica (London, 1683)

The Tryals of Joseph Dawson [et al.] (London, 1696)

The Tryals of Major Stede Bonnet and Other Pirates (London, 1719)

J. Todd and E. Spearing (eds), *Counterfeit Ladies: The Life and Death of Mal Cutpurse, The Case of Mary Carleton* (London, 1994)

A. Trapnel, *Report and Plea. Or a Narrative Of Her Journey From London into Cornwall* (London, 1654)

D. J. Vitkus (ed.), *Piracy, Slavery, and Redemption: Barbary Captivity Narratives from Early Modern England* (New York, 2001)

R. N. Worth (ed.), *Calendar of the Tavistock Parish Records* (Plymouth, 1887)

—— *Calendar of the Plymouth Municipal Records* (Plymouth, 1893)

I. A. Wright (ed.), *Spanish Documents Concerning English Voyages to the Caribbean 1527–1568* (Hakluyt Society, Second Series, 57, 1929)

—— *Documents Concerning English Voyages to the Spanish Main 1569–80* (Hakluyt Society, Second Series, 71, 1932)

—— *Further English Voyages to Spanish America 1583–1594* (Hakluyt Society, Second Series, 94, 1951)

Secondary Works

S. Agha and E. Kolsky (eds), *Fringes of Empire: Peoples, Places, and Spaces in Colonial India* (New Delhi, 2009)

S. D. Amussen, *Caribbean Exchanges: Slavery and the Transformation of English Society, 1640–1700* (Chapel Hill, 2007)

K. R. Andrews, *Elizabethan Privateering: English Privateering During the Spanish War 1585–1603* (Cambridge, 1966)

—— *Drake's Voyages: A Re-Assessment of their Place in Elizabethan Maritime Expansion* (London, 1967)

—— *The Spanish Caribbean: Trade and Plunder 1530–1630* (New Haven, 1978)

—— 'The Elizabethan Seaman', *Mariner's Mirror*, 68 (1982), pp. 245–62

—— *Trade, Plunder and Settlement: Maritime Enterprise and the Genesis of the British Empire, 1480–1630* (Cambridge, 1984)

—— *Ships, Money and Politics: Seafaring and Naval Enterprise in the Reign of Charles I* (Cambridge, 1991)

J. C. Appleby, *Under the Bloody Flag: Pirates of the Tudor Age* (Stroud, 2009)

J. Baer, '"Captain John Avery" and the Anatomy of a Mutiny', *Eighteenth Century Life*, 18 (1994), pp. 1–26

—— *Pirates of the British Isles* (Stroud, 2005)

G. Bak, *Barbary Pirate: The Life and Crimes of John Ward, The Most Infamous Privateer of his Time* (Stroud, 2006)

V. Barbour, 'Privateers and Pirates of the West Indies', *American Historical Review*, 16 (1910–11), pp. 529–66

M. Baumber, *General-At-Sea: Robert Blake and the Seventeenth-Century Revolution in Naval Warfare* (London, 1989)

S. Bawlf, *The Secret Voyage of Sir Francis Drake 1577–1580* (New York, 2003)

C. Beal, *Quelch's Gold: Piracy, Greed, and Betrayal in Colonial New England* (Washington, DC, 2010)

T. Beattie, '"Entirely the Most Absurd and False Narrative that was ever Deliver'd to the Publick": An Inquiry into What Really Happened on George Shelvocke's Privateering Voyage', *Mariner's Mirror*, 97 (2011), pp. 163–76

I. A. Bell, *Literature and Crime in Augustan England* (London, 1991)

L. Benton, *Law and Colonial Cultures: Legal Regimes in World History, 1400–1900* (Cambridge, 2002)

—— *A Search for Sovereignty: Law and Geography in European Empires, 1400–1900* (Cambridge, 2010)

A. Bialuschewski, 'Between Newfoundland and the Malacca Strait: A Survey of the Golden Age of Piracy', *Mariner's Mirror*, 90 (2004), pp. 167–86

—— 'Pirates, Slavers, and the Indigenous Population in Madagascar, c. 1690–1715', *International Journal of African Historical Studies*, 38 (2005), pp. 401–26

—— 'Black People under the Black Flag: Piracy and the Slave Trade on the West Coast of Africa, 1718–1723', *Slavery and Abolition*, 24 (2008), pp. 461–75

C. V. Black, *Pirates of the West Indies* (Cambridge, 1989)

R. H. Bloch, *Gender and Morality in Anglo-American Culture, 1650–1800* (Berkeley, 2003)

W. J. Bolster, *Black Jacks: African American Seamen in the Age of Sail* (Cambridge, Mass., 1997)

J. Boulton, *Neighbourhood and Society: A London Suburb in the Seventeenth Century* (Cambridge, 1987)

H. V. Bowen, E. Mancke and J. Reid (eds), *Britain's Oceanic Empire: Atlantic and Indian Ocean Worlds, c. 1550–1850* (Cambridge, 2012)

P. Bradley, *The Lure of Peru: Maritime Intrusion into the South Sea, 1598–1701* (London, 1989)

C. Brant and D. Purkiss (eds), *Women, Texts and Histories 1575–1760* (London, 1992)

F. Braudel, *The Mediterranean and the Mediterranean World in the Age of Philip II* (2nd edition, London, 1972)

A. Bray, *Homosexuality in Renaissance England* (London, 1982, revised edition, New York, 1995)

R. Brenner, *Merchants and Revolution: Commercial Change, Political Conflict, and London's Overseas Traders, 1550–1653* (Cambridge, 1993)

K. M. Brown, *Good Wives, Nasty Wenches, and Anxious Patriarchs: Gender, Race, and Power in Colonial Virginia* (Chapel Hill, 1996)

R. O. Bucholz and J. P. Ward, *London: A Social and Cultural History, 1550–1750* (Cambridge, 2012)

B. R. Burg, *Sodomy and the Perception of Evil: English Sea Rovers in the Seventeenth-Century Caribbean* (New York, 1983)

A. Burl, *Black Barty: Bartholomew Roberts and his Pirate Crew 1718–1723* (Stroud, 2006)

T. Burnard, *Mastery, Tyranny, and Desire: Thomas Thistlewood and His Slaves in the Anglo-American World* (Chapel Hill, 2004)

N. Canny, *Making Ireland British 1580–1650* (Oxford, 2001)

A. Capern, *The Historical Study of Women: England, 1500–1700* (Basingstoke, 2008)

B. Capp, *Cromwell's Navy: The Fleet and the English Revolution 1648–1660* (Oxford, 1989)

G. T. Cell, *English Enterprise in Newfoundland 1577–1660* (Toronto, 1969)

A. Chambers, *Granuaile: The Life and Times of Grace O'Malley c. 1530–1603* (Dublin, 1979)

K. N. Chaudhuri, *Trade and Civilisation in the Indian Ocean: An Economic History from the Rise of Islam to 1750* (Cambridge, 1985)

M. Chaytor, 'Husband(ry): Narratives of Rape in the Seventeenth Century', *Gender & History*, 7 (1995), pp. 378–407

E. P. Cheyney, *A History of England from the Defeat of the Armada to the Death of Elizabeth*, 2 vols (London, 1914, repr. New York, 1948)

A. Clark, *Working Life of Women in the Seventeenth Century* (London, 1919, repr. 1982)

S. Clissold, *The Barbary Slaves* (London, 1977)

M. Cohen, *The Novel and the Sea* (Princeton, 2010)

L. Colley, *Captives: Britain, Empire and the World, 1600–1850* (London, 2002)

—— *The Ordeal of Elizabeth Marsh* (London, 2007)

G. Connell-Smith, *Forerunners of Drake: A Study of English Trade with Spain in the Early Tudor Period* (London, 1954, repr. Westport, Conn., 1975)

J. Corbett, *Drake and the Tudor Navy*, 2 vols (London, 1898, repr. Aldershot, 1988)

—— *The Successors of Drake* (London, 1900)

D. Cordingly, *Life among the Pirates: The Romance and the Reality* (London, 1995)

—— *Heroines and Harlots: Women at Sea in the Great Age of Sail* (London, 2001)

—— *Spanish Gold: Captain Woodes Rogers and the Pirates of the Caribbean* (London, 2011)

M. S. Creighton and L. Norling (eds), *Iron Men, Wooden Women: Gender and Seafaring in the Atlantic World, 1700–1920* (Baltimore and London, 1996)

R. Davis, *The Rise of the Atlantic Economies* (London, 1973)

R. C. Davis, *Christian Muslims, Muslim Masters: White Slavery in the Mediterranean, the Barbary Coast, and Italy, 1500–1800* (Basingstoke, 2003)

S. Dearden, *A Nest of Corsairs: The Fighting Karamanlis of Tripoli* (London, 1976)

S. Dickie, *Cruelty and Laughter: Forgotten Comic Literature and the Unsentimental Eighteenth Century* (Chicago and London, 2011)

G. F. Dow and J. H. Edmonds, *The Pirates of the New England Coast, 1630–1730* (Salem, 1923)

M. Duffy *et al.* (eds), *The New Maritime History of Devon*, 2 vols (Exeter, 1992–4)

D. Dugaw, 'Balladry's Female Warriors: Women, Warfare, and Disguise in the Eighteenth Century', *Eighteenth Century Life*, 9 (1985), pp. 1–20

R. S. Dunn, *Sugar and Slaves: The Rise of the Planter Class in the English West Indies, 1624–1713* (2nd edition, New York, 1999)

J. Druett, *Hen Frigates: Wives of Merchant Captains under Sail* (London, 1998)

P. Earle, *Corsairs of Malta and Barbary* (London, 1970)

—— *The Sack of Panama: Captain Morgan and the Battle for the Caribbean* (London, 1981)

—— *The Last Fight of the Revenge* (London, 1992)

—— *Sailors: English Merchant Seamen 1650–1775* (London, 1998)

—— *The Pirate Wars* (London, 2003)

D. Ekin, *The Stolen Village: Baltimore and the Barbary Pirates* (Dublin, 2006)

J. H. Elliott, *Imperial Spain 1469–1716* (London, 1963)

—— *Empires of the Atlantic World: Britain and Spain in America 1492–1830* (New Haven, 2006)

S. Ellis, 'Tom and Toakafo: The Betsimisaraka Kingdom and State Formation in Madagascar, 1715–1750', *Journal of African History*, 48 (2007), pp. 439–55

C. L'Estrange Ewen, *Captain John Ward, 'Arch-Pirate'* (Paignton, 1939)

—— *The Golden Chalice: A Documented Narrative of an Elizabethan Pirate* (Paignton, 1939)

—— 'Organized Piracy Round Britain in the Sixteenth Century', *Mariner's Mirror*, 35 (1949), pp. 29–42

—— 'The Pirates of Purbeck', *Proceedings of the Dorset Natural History & Archaeological Society*, 71 (1949), pp. 88–109

L. Faller, *Turned to Account: The Forms and Functions of Criminal Biography in Late Sevententh- and Early Eighteenth-Century England* (Cambridge, 1987)

Sir G. Fisher, *Barbary Legend: War, Trade and Piracy in North Africa 1415–1830* (Oxford, 1957)

A. Fletcher, *Gender, Sex and Subordination in England 1500–1800* (New Haven, 1995)

Sir W. Foster, *England's Quest of Eastern Trade* (London, 1933)

R. Fowke, *The Real Ancient Mariner: Pirates and Poesy on the South Sea* (Bishop's Castle, Salop, 2010)

E. T. Fox, *King of the Pirates: The Swashbuckling Life of Henry Every* (Stroud, 2008)

A. Fraser, *The Weaker Vessel: Women's Lot in Seventeenth-Century England* (London, 1984)

A. Froide, *Never Married: Singlewomen in Early Modern England* (Oxford, 2005)

B. Fuchs, *Mimesis and Empire: The New World, Islam, and European Identities* (Cambridge, 2001)

C. A. Fury, *Tides in the Affairs of Men: The Social History of Elizabethan Seamen, 1580–1603* (Westport, Conn., 2002)

—— (ed.), *The Social History of English Seamen, 1485–1649* (Woodbridge, 2012)

N. Gerassi-Navarro, *Pirate Novels: Fictions of Nation Building in Spanish America* (Durham, NC, 1999)

P. Gerhard, *Pirates of the Pacific, 1575–1742* (Lincoln, Nebr., 1960)

J. Glete, *Warfare at Sea, 1500–1650: Maritime Conflicts and the Transformation of Europe* (London, 2000)

P. J. P. Goldberg, *Women, Work, and Life Cycle in a Medieval Economy: Women in York and Yorkshire c.1300–1520* (Oxford, 1992)

P. Gosse, *The History of Piracy* (London, 1932)

E. Graham, *Seawolves: Pirates and the Scots* (Edinburgh, 2005)

P. Griffiths, *Lost Londons: Change, Crime and Control in the Capital City, 1550–1660* (Cambridge, 2008)

J. F. Guilmartin, *Gunpowder and Galleys: Changing Technology and Mediterranean Warfare at Sea in the 16th Century* (Cambridge, 1974)

J. Guy, *Tudor England* (Oxford, 1988)

R. Harding, *The Evolution of the Sailing Navy, 1509–1815* (Basingstoke, 1995)

C. H. Haring, *The Buccaneers in the West Indies in the XVII Century* (London, 1910)

G. G. Harris, *The Trinity House of Deptford 1514–1660* (London, 1969)

D. D. Hebb, *Piracy and the English Government, 1616–1642* (Aldershot, 1994)

J. Heers, *The Barbary Corsairs: Warfare in the Mediterranean, 1480–1580* (London, 2003)

P. Higgins, 'The Reactions of Women, with Special Reference to Women Petitioners', in B. Manning (ed.), *Politics, Religion and the English Civil War* (London, 1973), pp. 179–222

S. C. Hill, *Notes on Piracy in Eastern Waters* (Bombay, 1923)

T. Hitchcock and R. Shoemaker, *Tales from the Hanging Court* (London, 2006)

O. Hufton, *The Prospect Before Her: A History of Women in Western Europe. Volume One 1500–1800* (London, 1995)

A. Hughes, *Gender and the English Revolution* (Abingdon, 2012)

C. E. Hughes, 'Wales and Piracy: A Study in Tudor Administration 1500–1640' (University of Wales, MA thesis, 1937)

M. R. Hunt, *Women in Eighteenth-Century Europe* (Harlow, 2010)

D. G. E. Hurd, 'Some Aspects of the Attempts of the Government to Suppress Piracy during the Reign of Elizabeth I' (University of London, MA thesis, 1961)

A. G. Jamieson (ed.), *A People of the Sea: The Maritime History of the Channel Islands* (London, 1986)

—— *Lords of the Sea: A History of the Barbary Corsairs* (London, 2012)

M. Jarvis, *In the Eye of All Trade: Bermuda, Bermudians, and the Maritime Atlantic World, 1680–1783* (Chapel Hill, 2010)

C. Jowitt (ed.), *Pirates? The Politics of Plunder, 1550–1650* (Basingstoke, 2001)

—— *The Culture of Piracy, 1580–1630: English Literature and Seaborne Crime* (Farnham, 2010)

J. Judd, 'Frederick Philipse and the Madagascar Trade', *New York Historical Society Quarterly*, 55 (1971), pp. 354–74

W. Kaiser (ed.), *Le Commerce des Captifs: Les Intermediaires dans L'Echange et Le Rachat des Prisonniers en Méditerranée, XVe–XVIIIe Siècle* (Rome, 2008)

H. Kamen, *Spain's Road to Empire: The Making of a World Power, 1492–1763* (London, 2003)

H. Kelsey, *Sir Francis Drake: The Queen's Pirate* (New Haven, 1998)

—— *Sir John Hawkins: Queen Elizabeth's Slave Trader* (New Haven, 2003)

P. Kemp and C. Lloyd, *The Brethren of the Coast: The British and French Buccaneers in the South Seas* (London, 1960)

U. Klausman, M. Meinzerin and G. Kuhn, *Women Pirates and the Politics of the Jolly Roger* (New York, 1997)

A. Konstam, *Blackbeard: America's Most Notorious Pirate* (Hoboken, 2006)

—— *Scourge of the Seas: Buccaneers, Pirates and Privateers* (Oxford, 2007)

G. Kuhn, *Life under the Jolly Roger: Reflections on Golden Age Piracy* (Oakland, 2010)

A. P. Kup, *A History of Sierra Leone 1400–1787* (Cambridge, 1961)

K. Kupperman, *Providence Island, 1630–1641: The Other Puritan Colony* (Cambridge, 1993)

K. E. Lane, *Pillaging the Empire: Piracy in the Americas 1500–1750* (Armonk, 1998)

P. Lane, N. Raven and K. D. M. Snell (eds), *Women, Work and Wages in England, 1600–1850* (Woodbridge, 2004)

J. Latimer, *Buccaneers of the Caribbean: How Piracy Forged an Empire 1607–1697* (London, 2009)

A. Laurence, *Women in England 1500–1760: A Social History* (London, 1994)

R. Lee, *Blackbeard: The Story of Edward Teach, the Real Pirate of the Caribbean* (Stroud, 2008)

P. Leeson, *The Invisible Hook: The Hidden Economics of Pirates* (Princeton, 2009)

M. Lincoln, *Naval Wives and Mistresses, 1750–1815* (London, 2007)

P. Linebaugh and M. Rediker, *The Many-Headed Hydra: The Hidden History of the Revolutionary Atlantic* (London, 2000)

J. Linnekin, *Sacred Queens and Women of Consequence: Rank, Gender, and Colonialism in the Hawaiian Islands* (Ann Arbor, 1990)

B. Little, *The Buccaneer's Realm: Pirate Life on the Spanish Main, 1674–1688* (Washington, DC, 2009)

—— 'Eyewitness Images of Buccaneers and Their Vessels', *Mariner's Mirror*, 98 (2012), pp. 313–26

C. Lloyd, 'Bartholomew Sharp, Buccaneer', *Mariner's Mirror*, 42 (1956), pp. 291–301

—— *The British Seaman 1200–1860: A Social Survey* (London, 1968)

—— *English Corsairs on the Barbary Coast* (London, 1981)

H. A. Lloyd, *The Gentry of South-West Wales, 1540–1640* (Cardiff, 1968)

D. Loades, *The Tudor Navy: An Administrative, Political and Military History* (Aldershot, 1992)

—— *England's Maritime Empire: Seapower, Commerce and Policy, 1490–1690* (Harlow, 2000)

A. K. Longfield, *Anglo-Irish Trade in the Sixteenth Century* (London, 1929)

V. W. Lunsford, *Piracy and Privateering in the Golden Age Netherlands* (New York, 2005)

M. MacCarthy-Morrogh, *The Munster Plantation: English Migration to Southern Ireland 1583–1641* (Oxford, 1986)

J. Mack, *The Sea: A Cultural History* (London, 2011)

G. Maclean and N. Matar, *Britain and the Islamic World, 1558–1713* (Oxford, 2011)

R. G. Marsden, 'The Early Career of Sir Martin Frobisher', *English Historical Review*, 21 (1906), pp. 538–44

J. Marx, *Pirates and Privateers of the Caribbean* (Malabar, 1992)

N. Matar, 'Wives, Captive Husbands and Turks: The First Women Petitioners in Caroline England', *Explorations in Renaissance Culture*, 23 (1997), pp. 3–29

—— *Turks, Moors, and Englishmen in the Age of Discovery* (New York, 1999)

—— *Islam in Britain, 1558–1685* (Cambridge, 1998)

—— *Britain and Barbary, 1589–1689* (Gainesville, 2005)

D. Mathew, *The Celtic Peoples and Renaissance Europe* (London, 1933)

C. Matson, *Merchants and Empire: Trading in Colonial New York* (Baltimore, 1998)

E. A. McArthur, 'Women Petitioners and the Long Parliament', *English Historical Review*, 24 (1909), pp. 698–709

J. McDermott, *Martin Frobisher: Elizabethan Privateer* (New Haven, 2001)

—— *England and the Spanish Armada: The Necessary Quarrel* (New Haven, 2005)

C. I. Mcgrath and C. Fawke (eds), *Money, Power, and Print: Interdisciplinary Studies in the Financial Revolution in the British Isles* (Cranbury, 2010)

M. K. McIntosh, *Working Women in English Society 1300–1620*

(Cambridge, 2005)

J. L. McMullan, *The Canting Crew: London's Criminal Underworld 1550–1700* (New Brunswick, 1984)

S. Mendelson and P. Crawford, *Women in Early Modern England 1550–1720* (Oxford, 1998)

M. Mollat (ed.), *Course et Piraterie*, 2 vols (Paris, 1975)

G. Moore (ed.), *Pirates and Mutineers of the Nineteenth Century: Swash-bucklers and Swindlers* (Farnham, 2011)

A. Neill, *British Discovery Literature and the Rise of Global Commerce* (Basingstoke, 2002)

A. P. Newton, *The Colonising Activities of the English Puritans: The Last Phase of the Elizabethan Struggle with Spain* (New Haven, 1914, repr. Port Washington, NY, 1966)

—— *The European Nations in the West Indies 1493–1688* (London, 1933, repr. 1966)

M. B. Norton, *Founding Mothers and Fathers: Gendered Power and the Forming of American Society* (New York, 1996)

—— *Separated by Their Sex: Women in Public and Private in the Colonial Atlantic World* (Ithaca, 2011)

P. B. Nutting, 'The Madagascar Connection: Parliament and Piracy, 1690–1701', *American Journal of Legal History*, 22 (1978), pp. 202–15

K. O'Brien, *Women and Enlightment in Eighteenth-Century Britain* (Cambridge, 2009)

R. O'Day, *Women's Agency in Early Modern Britain and the American Colonies: Patriarchy, Partnership and Patronage* (Harlow, 2007)

M. Ogborn, *Global Lives: Britain and the World* (Cambridge, 2008)

G. O'Hara, *Britain and the Sea since 1600* (Basingstoke, 2010)

M. Oppenheim, *A History of the Administration of the Royal Navy and of Merchant Shipping in Relation to the Navy from 1509 to 1660* (London, 1896, repr. Aldershot, 1988)

—— *The Maritime History of Devon* (Exeter, 1968)

L. C. Orlin (ed.), *Material London, ca. 1600* (Philadelphia, 2000)

G. D. Owen, *Elizabethan Wales: The Social Scene* (Cardiff, 1964)

C. H. Parker, *Global Interactions in the Early Modern Age, 1400–1800* (Cambridge, 2010)

M. Parker, *The Sugar Barons: Family, Corruption, Empire and War* (London, 2011)

D. Parry, *Blackbeard: The Real Pirate of the Caribbean* (London, 2006)

J. H. Parry, *The Spanish Seaborne Empire* (London, 1966)

D. Pawson and D. Buisseret, *Port Royal, Jamaica* (Oxford, 1975)

J. Peakman, *Lascivious Bodies: A Sexual History of the Eighteenth Century*

(London, 2004)

W. Pencak and C. E. Wright (eds), *Authority and Resistance in Early New York* (New York, 1988)

C. R. Pennell (ed.), *Bandits at Sea: A Pirates Reader* (New York, 2001)

C. Peters, *Women in Early Modern Britain, 1450–1640* (Basingstoke, 2004)

R. Phillips, *Untying the Knot: A Short History of Divorce* (Cambridge, 1991)

R. L. Playfair, *The Scourge of Christendom: Annals of British Relations with Algiers Prior to the French Conquest* (London, 1884, repr. Freeport, NY, 1972)

D. Pope, *Harry Morgan's Way: The Biography of Sir Henry Morgan 1635–1684* (London, 1977)

J. Prebble, *The Darien Disaster* (London, 1968)

P. Pringle, *Jolly Roger: The Story of the Great Age of Piracy* (London, 1953)

M. Prior (ed.), *Women in English Society 1500–1800* (London, 1985)

D. B. Quinn, *Ralegh and the British Empire* (London, 1947)

—— *Explorers and Colonies: America, 1500–1625* (London, 1990)

—— *England and the Discovery of America, 1481–1620* (London, 1994)

D. B. Quinn and A. N. Ryan, *England's Sea Empire, 1550–1642* (London, 1983)

S. Randrianja and S. Ellis, *Madagascar: A Short History* (London, 2009)

M. Rediker, *Between the Devil and the Deep Blue Sea: Merchant Seamen, Pirates, and the Anglo-American Maritime World, 1700–1750* (Cambridge, 1987)

—— *Villains of All Nations: Atlantic Pirates in the Golden Age* (London, 2004)

R. C. Ritchie, *Captain Kidd and the War Against the Pirates* (Cambridge, Mass., 1986)

N. A. M. Rodger, 'A Pirate's Log', *Mariner's Mirror*, 67 (1981), pp. 201–4

—— *The Wooden World: An Anatomy of the Georgian Navy* (London, 1986)

—— *The Safeguard of the Sea: A Naval History of Britain 660–1649* (London, 1997)

—— *The Command of the Ocean: A Naval History of Britain 1649–1815* (London, 2004)

—— 'Queen Elizabeth and the Myth of Sea-Power in English History', *Transactions of the Royal Historical Society*, Sixth Series, 14 (2004), pp. 153–74

J. Rogoziński, *Honour among Thieves: Captain Kidd, Henry Every, and the Story of Pirate Island* (London, 2000)

S. Ronald, *The Pirate Queen: Queen Elizabeth I, Her Pirate Adventurers, and the Dawn of Empire* (Stroud, 2007)

S. Rose, *The Medieval Sea* (London, 2007)

A. L. Rowse, *Sir Richard Grenville of the 'Revenge'* (London, 1937)

—— *Tudor Cornwall: Portrait of a Society* (London, 1941)

R. Saunders, *If a Pirate I Must Be ... The True Story of Bartholomew Roberts, King of the Caribbean* (London, 2007)

G. V. Scammell, 'War at Sea under the Early Tudors: Some Newcastle upon Tyne Evidence', *Archaelogia Aeliana*, Fourth Series, 38 (1960), pp. 73–97 and 39 (1961), pp. 179–205

—— *The World Encompassed: The First European Maritime Empires, c. 800–1650* (London, 1981)

—— *The First Imperial Age: European Overseas Expansion c. 1400–1715* (London, 1989)

—— *Ships, Oceans and Empire: Studies in European Maritime and Colonial History, 1400–1750* (Aldershot, 1995)

J. Scott, *When the Waves Ruled Britannia: Geography and Political Identities, 1500–1800* (Cambridge, 2011)

C. M. Senior, *A Nation of Pirates: English Piracy in its Heyday* (Newton Abbot, 1976)

F. Sherry, *Raiders and Rebels: A History of the Golden Age of Piracy* (New York, 1986)

R. B. Shoemaker, *Gender in English Society, 1650–1850: The Emergence of Separate Spheres?* (Harlow, 1998)

R. K. Skowronek and C. R. Ewen (eds), *X Marks the Spot: The Archaeology of Piracy* (Gainesville, 2006)

D. Souhami, *Selkirk's Island* (London, 2001)

O. H. K. Spate, *The Pacific since Magellan, Volume II: Monopolists and Freebooters* (London and Canberra, 1983)

J. Stanley, *Bold in Her Breeches: Women Pirates Across the Ages* (London, 1995)

S. J. Stark, *Female Tars: Women Aboard Ship in the Age of Sail* (London, 1998)

D. Starkey, *British Privateering Enterprise in the Eighteenth Century* (Exeter, 1990)

—— 'Voluntaries and Sea Robbers: A Review of the Academic Literature on Privateering, Corsairing, Buccaneering and Piracy', *Mariner's Mirror*, 97 (2011), pp. 127–47

J. P. Stern, 'Politics and Ideology in the Early East India Company-State: The Case of St Helena, 1673–1709', *Journal of Imperial and Commonwealth History*, 35 (2007), pp. 1–23

A. Taylor, *American Colonies: The Settlement of North America to 1800* (London, 2001)

A. Tenenti, *Piracy and the Decline of Venice 1580–1615* (London, 1967)

G. A. Thomas, *Pirate Hunter: The Life of Captain Woodes Rogers* (Barnsley, 2008)

N. Thomas, *Islanders: The Pacific in the Age of Empire* (New Haven, 2010)

R. Thompson, *Women in Stuart England and America: A Comparative Study* (London, 1974)

J. E. Thomson, *Mercenaries, Pirates and Sovereigns: State-Building and Extraterritorial Violence in Early Modern Europe* (Princeton, 1994)

A. P. Thornton, *West-India Policy under the Restoration* (Oxford, 1956)

R. Thrower, *The Pirate Picture* (London, 1980)

C. Tilly, *Contentious Performances* (Cambridge, 2008)

A. Tinniswood, *Pirates of Barbary: Corsairs, Conquests and Captivity in the Seventeenth-Century Mediterranean* (London, 2010)

T. Travers, *Pirates: A History* (Stroud, 2007)

R. M. S. Tugwood, 'Piracy and Privateering from Dartmouth and Kingswear, 1540–1558' (University of London, MA thesis, 1953)

H. Turley, *Rum, Sodomy, and the Lash: Piracy, Sexuality, and Masculine Identity* (New York, 1999)

L. T. Ulrich, *Good Wives: Image and Reality in the Lives of Women in Northern New England 1650–1750* (New York, 1991)

D. Valenze, *The First Industrial Woman* (Oxford, 1995)

D. Vickers with V. Walsh, *Young Men and the Sea: Yankee Seafarers in the Age of Sail* (New Haven, 2005)

L. Voight, *Writing Captivity in the Early Modern Atlantic: Circulations of Knowledge and Authority in the Iberian and English Imperial Worlds* (Chapel Hill, 2009)

G. Walker, 'Rereading Rape and Sexual Violence in Early Modern England', *Gender & History*, 10 (1998), pp. 1–25

—— *Crime, Gender and Social Order in Early Modern England* (Cambridge, 2003)

L. Wallace, *Sexual Encounters: Pacific Texts, Modern Sexualities* (Ithaca, 2003)

J. Warner, 'Marital Violence in a Martial Town: Husbands and Wives in Early Modern Portsmouth, 1653–1781', *Journal of Family History*, 28 (2003), pp. 258–76

G. Weiss, *Captives and Corsairs: France and Slavery in the Early Modern Mediterranean* (Stanford, 2011)

A. Whiting, '"Some Women Can Shift it Well Enough": A Legal Context for Understanding the Women Petitioners of the Seventeenth-Century English Revolution', *Australian Feminist Law Journal*, 21 (2004), pp. 77–100

M. E. Wiesner-Hanks, *Women and Gender in Early Modern Europe* (3rd edition, Cambridge, 2008)

D. E. Williams, 'Puritans and Pirates: A Confrontation between Cotton

Mather and William Fly in 1726', *Early American Literature*, 22 (1987), pp. 233–51

G. Williams, *The Great South Sea: English Voyages and Encounters 1570–1750* (New Haven, 1997)

—— *The Prize of All the Oceans: The Dramatic True Story of Commodore Anson's Voyage Round the World and How He Seized the Spanish Treasure Galleon* (London, 1999)

—— *Buccaneers, Explorers and Settlers: British Enterprise and Encounters in the Pacific, 1670–1800* (Aldershot, 2005)

N. Williams, *The Sea Dogs: Privateers, Plunder and Piracy in the Elizabethan Age* (London, 1975)

P. Williams, *The Tudor Regime* (Oxford, 1979)

—— *The Later Tudors: England 1547–1603* (Oxford, 1995)

S. Willis, *The Admiral Benbow: The Life and Times of a Naval Legend* (London, 2010)

P. L. Wilson, *Pirate Utopias: Moorish Corsairs and European Renegadoes* (New York, 1995)

J. Wolf, *The Barbary Coast: Algiers under the Turks 1500–1830* (New York, 1979)

A. Wood, *Riot, Rebellion and Popular Politics in Early Modern England* (Basingstoke, 2002)

G. Wycherley, *Buccaneers of the Pacific* (Indianapolis, 1928)

R. Zacks, *The Pirate Hunter: The True Story of Captain Kidd* (New York, 2002)

D. Zaret, *Origins of Democratic Culture: Printing, Petitions, and the Public Sphere in Early-Modern England* (Princeton, 2000)

Websites

www.oldbaileyonline.org
www.oxforddnb.com

Index